The Gift of Teenagers

The Gift of Teenagers

Connect More, Worry Less

Rachel Kelly

First published in Great Britain in 2025 by Short Books,
an imprint of Octopus Publishing Group Ltd
Carmelite House
50 Victoria Embankment
London EC4Y 0DZ
www.octopusbooks.co.uk
www.octopusbooksusa.com

An Hachette UK Company
www.hachette.co.uk

The authorized representative in the EEA is Hachette Ireland, 8 Castlecourt Centre,
Dublin 15, D15 XTP3, Ireland (email: info@hbgi.ie)

Distributed in the US by Hachette Book Group, 1290 Avenue of the Americas,
4th and 5th Floors, New York, NY 10104

Distributed in Canada by Canadian Manda Group, 664 Annette Street,
Toronto, Ontario, Canada M6S 2C8

ISBN 9781804193167

A CIP catalogue record for this book is available from the British Library.

Typeset in 11/15pt Sabon LT Pro by Jouve (UK), Milton Keynes.

Printed and bound in Great Britain.

1 3 5 7 9 10 8 6 4 2

Publisher: Jo Morrell
Commissioning Editor: Katie Forsythe
Creative Director: Mel Four
Senior Editor: Leanne Bryan
Copy Editor: Joanna Smith
Illustrator: Jonathan Pugh
Production Controller: Sarah Parry

This FSC® label means that materials used for the product have been responsibly sourced.

Publisher's note
This book is not intended as a substitute for the advice of a healthcare professional, medication,
or other strategies. Although the publisher and author have made every effort to ensure that the
information in this book was correct at the time of going to press, and while this publication is
designed to provide accurate information in regard to the subject matter covered, mistakes do
happen and we would welcome the chance to correct any outstanding errors. Please get in touch
with the author via https://rachel-kelly.net/ for updates for future editions.

For Charlotte

*

'Only connect . . . Live in fragments no longer.'

E.M. Forster, *Howards End*

CONTENTS

Introduction 1

PART ONE: Connecting with Yourself

1. Your relationship with yourself and your partner or co-parent 11
2. Your relationship with your own parents 23
3. Your brain and its glitches 35
4. Adopting supportive and kindly viewpoints 51
5. Coping with challenging emotions 67
6. Looking after your physical health 81

PART TWO: Connecting with Your Teenager

7. The teenage brain and supporting its development 93
8. Staying connected and letting go 109
9. Encouraging independence 121
10. Communication 131
11. Arguments and lying 145

PART THREE: Your Teenager's Connection with Themself

12. Their appearance 159
13. Their sexuality 171
14. Their gender identity 197

PART FOUR: Your Teenager's Connection with Others

15. Their siblings 219
16. Creating a village 229

CONTENTS

17. Bullying   249
18. Endings   263

PART FIVE: Your Teenager's Connection to the Wider World

19. An academically pressurized and unsafe world   275
20. The digital world   289
21. Drugs and drinking   299

PART SIX: Connecting with Help

22. Understanding and identifying a mental health condition   317
23. Helping a teenager with a mental health condition   331

Epilogue   349
Further resources for teenagers and parents   353
Glossary of mental health conditions   357
Endnotes   375
Acknowledgements   395
Index   397
About the author   405

FINDING PEACE WITH YOUR PARENTS

INTRODUCTION

We live in a time of huge worry about our teenagers and their mental health – from fears of a phone-obsessed adolescence to concerns about an offline world of bullying and drugs. But what if we parents don't need to be so fearful? What if our teenagers are a gift we can all learn from?

You may be reading this and thinking, She's mad! Teenagers a gift? More like a nightmare! Moody. Snappy. Communicating via the occasional WhatsApp from a darkened room. Indeed when I told a friend about the putative title of this book, he joked that it must be a slim volume.

It's true that in general the lot of the teenage parent is a sorry one: right now parents are generally less happy than non-parents, something known as the 'parental unhappiness gap'. In this, Britain comes a close second to the USA.[1] More colloquially, there's talk of the 'motherhood penalty', and even the view that parental stress is a public health issue.[2] Society has made parenting harder by forcing people to work longer hours for shrinking pay and raising the costs of getting any help. And grandparents are often too frail to help by the time their children become parents. It's tough out there. I get it.

But stay with me. I really believe that raising my own five children in an anxious age has led to several gifts, the first being some psychological growth of my own (and I hope that doesn't sound smug: I've plenty more to learn and there are plenty of other ways to learn apart from being a parent of teenagers). And maybe parenting *your* teenagers can contribute to your growth, too.

Raising resilient teenagers begins with becoming a more resilient – and better informed – parent and person, someone who has learned to manage their own emotions and thinking patterns, become aware of their parenting style, and understood the world teenagers are growing up in. Counterintuitively, the fact that this period can be so painful – and shepherding my own five children through adolescence has been among the most agonizing things I've done – is exactly why we are forced to grow in new and deep ways.

If we nurture our own psychological health, we can be examples to our teenagers, who can learn from us. Calm parents; calmer teenagers. (And when I say parents, my thoughts are also addressed to grandparents, step-parents, godparents, teachers and healthcare professionals: anyone who wants to help young people.) Thus armed, we can engage with our adolescents better and discover how their brains work (short answer: not always like ours!).

Which brings me to the second gift that teenagers can deliver to us parents: the chance to connect with them as burgeoning adults. We can establish a new relationship with them, a blessing that can last a lifetime.

In my own life, raising teenagers taught me to accept a different role for myself as a mother. I realized that my children no longer needed me in the same way as when they were small – to make them their favourite spaghetti Bolognese (not so secret ingredient: a splosh of red wine) or drop them off at school. More independence for children (a good thing) can make us parents feel redundant (not such a good thing).

I found peace in thinking about these changes as a chance to develop a fresh bond. As our children become young adults, the space for a new kind of relationship with them emerges. It is based on love for, and connection with, them as individuals with their own lives. The people who they truly are rather than the people we want them to be. The relationship might not have the same dependency as a parent has with young children, who are continually under their wing, but that does not mean the relationship must be less intimate.

The Lebanese-American poet Khalil Gibran put it thus in his poem *On Children*:

> *Your children are not your children.*
> *They are the sons and daughters of Life's longing for itself.*
> *They come through you but not from you,*
> *And though they are with you yet they belong not to you.*
> *You may give them your love but not your thoughts,*
> *For they have their own thoughts.*[3]

No one was more surprised than me that raising teenagers could lead to this new and fulfilling relationship. I began my time as a parent of adolescents consumed by worry. For a start, the world in which teenagers find their identity has always been different from the world in which their parents grew up, but those differences are stark right now. Anyone over fifty has lived at least half their life without the internet, and particularly without social media or streaming services: a different experience from that of our teenagers. Even teenagers' understanding and means of coping with mental health problems may be different. We may feel in touch with them, but our outlook is from a different era – the Cretaceous, or possibly the Jurassic. The generations don't see eye to eye on sexuality, gender, class, climate change or race. The attitudes that informed so much of our own upbringing are gone. We need to move on, and I worried I might not be able to do so.

I also had personal reasons to be especially concerned that any teenager of mine might succumb to mental health problems as it was something I had experienced myself, albeit as a young adult. I had been a highly anxious teenager and succumbed to two serious depressive episodes as a young mother.

There were so many worries, both in the world and inside my head, that at first I found it tricky to stop being the 'anxious mother' looking at my offspring with pitying eyes. Would something awful happen to one of my teenagers, especially as I had an unusually large family of five, upping my chances that at least one of them would fall into difficulties? Might they become excessively anxious themselves?

Indeed, in some ways it's easier to be someone who worries. There's a widespread view that worrying about our children's welfare is a good thing, and the more we worry, the better parents we must be. At least if we're worrying, we're doing something. I know I've done this countless times myself, bonding with other parents about quite how concerned I am about my child and the difficulties young people today face (like the horrors of social media, or the turbulent world in which they are growing up). And the thing is, all these concerns are valid. Plenty of teenagers do find life challenging, social media is concerning, and there's succour to be had swapping notes with other parents.

But I can't be the only parent who knows that sometimes a kind of competitive, performative worrying creeps in. *The Anxious Generation*, which is the title of Jonathan Haidt's recent book on adolescent mental health, is arguably as much a description of us parents as our offspring. There is a risk, as parents, of over-projecting our worries and, in doing so, losing a sense of perspective.

I knew I had to stop being so stressed. Worrying about my teenagers wasn't good for me, and certainly stopped me being able to appreciate the good times. Nor, crucially, was it good for them. When we are concerned about someone, the underlying assumption is that there is something wrong with that person. We are saying, without perhaps realizing it, 'You are vulnerable and unable to look after yourself on your own.' Moreover, we're saying that we, the caring, loving parent, are going to fix it. We are indirectly taking responsibility for someone else's behaviour and trying to control it. But no-one likes to be thought a victim. And no-one likes to be controlled by someone else. Instead of trying to control or fix our teenagers, we can stand alongside them as they work out who they want to be, and indeed as we do the same for ourselves. The more we are able to show up honestly as we are, the more they are able to be who they are.

And the calmer we are, I've found, the more we have to offer to others, our teenagers included. If we worry, they will worry in turn. Instead, we can model what a more accepting and compassionate person looks like and share ways we have found to be less stressed. This approach invites teenagers in turn to find their own contentment.

Here at least I have some advantage. I'm interested in mental health, and consider myself an ambassador into that world, someone who has written a book or two on the subject and has links with charities, academics and experts in the field, and a person who can report on sensible ways to worry less about teenagers, and connect with them more. I feel I can share useful strategies I've learned with my adolescents and perhaps help others do the same.

This book reflects my recent finds. I've spent the best part of five years visiting schools, talking to adolescents, their teachers and parents, and to lots of experts ending with 'ist' – psychologists, therapists, neuroscientists and psychiatrists. I have three boys and two girls. Our eldest son is now 30; our second son is 28; our elder daughter is 25; and the youngest two are twins, a boy and a girl, now 21. However, this book was largely written when they were younger and I was in the thick of raising adolescents. It's important to acknowledge that my experience will be different from yours: there are millions of teenagers and parents out there, navigating complicated lives in their own brave and brilliant ways.

I've concentrated on the phase experts called 'middle adolescence' – between the ages of 14 and 18. Of course this is a rough guide as children develop at different rates. This is the time when most dramas arise, when teenagers are struggling to find their own identity, when problems such as bullying, relationship and friendship traumas, drug-taking and exam pressure are at their height, and it can be challenging to see them as positive years. Yes, there are thousands of smaller hills to climb, which are stressful and demanding at other times, but the giant peaks, as it were, mostly happen in this middle period rather than in early adolescence (between 9 and 13) or in later adolescence (between 19 and 25). I've concentrated mainly on what Freud called 'ordinary human unhappiness' rather than mental health problems.

The need for us parents to be calm through this bumpy period explains much of the structure of this book. If our teenagers are to be a gift to us, then we need to dial down the worry and instead increase our ability to be close to them and understand their lives and the different challenges they are facing. Which is why so much of this book is about connection – connecting to ourselves, connecting to our teenagers, and connecting to their world.

In Part One, I look at how our own relationships with ourselves and others may affect our parenting, as well as how our brains work and the stresses in our lives. This is about self-care and self-reflection. I hope this may help you work through some of your own emotional blocks and childhood problems to avoid unintentionally passing down less helpful relationship patterns. This section is about realizing too that no child needs an ideal parent. They just need someone who is decent, willing to accept that they sometimes get things wrong, usually well-intentioned, sometimes grumpy but basically reasonable – a good enough father or mother.

In Part Two I turn to how we relate to our teenagers. Part of worrying less and enjoying a deeper connection with adolescents is to understand and know more about what's happening to them in greater depth – how their brains work and develop; how things shift over the course of their adolescence; the different preoccupations that come at different ages and how we may support them through all these changes and teach them to stand firm, to deal with their own feelings and develop their own resilience; and how we can let go ourselves.

To understand their reality still further, Part Three is about a teenager's relationship with themselves and their body: how they may feel about their appearance, gender and sexuality, all of which can be subject to dramatic change through adolescence.

I then turn to their outer world in Part Four, their significant relationships with others, including their siblings, friends and other adults. I cover some of the challenges they may face in such relationships, whether that's dealing with bullies or facing loss and break-ups.

And in Part Five, I turn to the environment in which they are growing up, one that can feel pressurized, unsafe and full of challenges, from the digital world to the appeal of drink and drugs and a widespread view that why bother when the world is on fire? All these were new areas of experience and understanding for me that came with being a mother of teenagers, something for which I became grateful as my horizons widened.

Finally, in Part Six, I move my focus from everyday problems we can face as parents to what our relationship with mental health professionals might be if expert help is sought. When a child faces a mental health problem, it can be difficult to imagine that anything good can come of this painful experience. But even in the darkest of times, our teenagers can be our teachers and guides to our own journey of self-discovery and self-reflection. There can be rubies among the rubble.

Throughout the book, I offer ideas on how we, as parents, might support our offspring in all these spheres of their lives. Support is the key word here. We might imagine that they are pieces of clay we can mould through hard work and put ourselves in a position in which we are deciding what is right and wrong for another individual. A power struggle is almost inevitable and is something we'd do better to avoid. The more we try to force someone to do something they don't want to do, the more likely they are to resist and for tempers to flare. We as parents are likely to come out of an argument more bruised, as we are older, more tired, and generally have less energy. Even if we temporarily win a power struggle, we will never be able to impose our will indefinitely. It's about collaboration and support rather than always asserting our authority, about respecting their reality rather than imagining that we know what they feel and must fix all their problems. Our reward will be a relationship in which we can both be ourselves.

No parent can ever not worry at all, and I've had plenty of heart-stopping moments myself on what has been inevitably a choppy ride. But my aim – through the building of increased understanding, closer connections and better relationships – is to help you bring your parental anxiety levels down from, say, an eight or nine out of ten to a more manageable three or four, and take your enjoyment levels up to an eight or nine, to the point where you can see this period as one that contains blessings as well as bruisings. Ultimately, my aim is to help you appreciate your children's teenage years, the people they are becoming, the life lessons they teach you, and yes, on occasion to tell them what's what as the adult in the room.

I like to think of this period as a rich tapestry with dark and light threads interwoven. Yes, there are fears, sometimes huge ones, and it won't always be fun. But even on the darkest days there are flashes of light, just as our most joyful experiences have moments of sadness. There's laughter as addictive as the finest dark chocolate, and all-you-can-eat hugs as well as heartbreak. We can find beauty, warmth, love and learning through the difficulties, and grow as a result – both as individuals, and as those who enjoy new and nourishing relationships with our soon-to-be adults. Gifts indeed.

Blink, and this phase of your life is over. One minute they're all pigtails and muddy knees, the next they're using your razor in the shower and telling you about things of which you know nothing but find riveting. By some mysterious alchemy, they are no longer children but companions. Here's to enjoying all that they give us.

FIGURING OUT THE TEENAGE BRAIN

PART ONE

CONNECTING WITH YOURSELF

1

YOUR RELATIONSHIP WITH YOURSELF AND YOUR PARTNER OR CO-PARENT

Before we begin to think about your relationship with your teenager, let's start with you. You might find this a bit bewildering. Why doesn't this book jump straight into the topic of teenagers themselves? Most parents are just muddling through, dealing with crises as they arise, chatting with friends if trouble crops up, and making it up as they go along. And I was like that too. But because of my own history of mental health problems, I became more introspective, considering my own psychological wellbeing as well as that of my children.

And I came to this conclusion: for all of us, our main relationship is with ourselves. We spend more time with our own thoughts, feelings and choices than with anyone else's. We are capable of self-criticism, self-destruction and self-contempt. We're also the person we've had the longest relationship with – 59 years in my case. It follows that in our efforts to enjoy and connect with our teenagers, we need first to enjoy and connect with ourselves.

I've been interested in mental health ever since I experienced severe depression in my thirties when my oldest children were still toddlers. However, my interest was turbocharged when I became a mother of teenagers. I was hungry for new ways of learning to get along with – and, indeed, liking – myself, so I could stay steady in the face of the inevitable dramas and criticism I would face bringing up adolescents. This was my teenagers' gift to me: they made it essential that I did some work on myself as the best way to enjoy the roller-coaster years of their adolescence. But this work was for their sake too. One of the biggest predictors of good outcomes for teenagers is their parents' wellbeing, studies show. And these links run in

11

both directions – parents are more likely to see their mental health deteriorate when they have a child with an emotional disorder.[1]

Well, you might be thinking, all well for you, but who has time to care for themselves and make themselves strong in preparation for understanding and being there for their teenagers? I hope that I can persuade you that it will be time well spent, for both of you.

It's amazing how much time it took me to realize that my own mental health was worthy of attention. Now, finally, I can say I have needs of my own. Even now I find it hard to write that sentence. Try saying it out loud. See if it is difficult for you to do so, too. The reason is not just that it sounds like a unappetizing catchphrase from a therapist's couch, but because it comes across as selfish. A good parent is often seen as one who is endlessly self-sacrificing. I beg to disagree.

We all have needs. Looking after yourself without being annihilated by the demands of your children is a starting point for being an effective parent (though of course not the only one). Parenting can at times feel like a long and gruelling grind. To give just one example, the average parent spends 52 hours a month driving their teenager around, according to a 2023 survey of 1,700 British parents.[2] If we are to stay the course, everyone benefits if we are as strong and balanced as possible.

Try to see the challenging period of being a parent of teenagers as the reason to prioritize this work. This is hard to do, as our culture makes us believe that if we aren't punishing ourselves for something, we risk being egotistic. The word self-care has a negative charge, with its whiff of all those other bad 'self' terms, like self-pity, self-serving, self-indulgent and selfish. Perhaps think instead of self-respect. We wouldn't deny that to anyone else. Nor would most of us deny that we are better able to look after others if we care for ourselves. Self-care, I've learned, is childcare and is not a selfish but a selfless act.

You might even find you enjoy being curious about the relationship you have with yourself. Where does it come from? How were you yourself brought up? Rethinking some of your assumptions and imagining how you might view things in a different way sounds as if it might be a struggle, and in some ways it is. But it also might be exciting to feel you can change your story; that you have agency over who you are – and the kind of parent you want to be.

I understand. For years I didn't find the time for myself, and ill health was the result. I'm urging you to find the time for yourself, somehow. Here's why.

COMING FIRST

The first reason why self-care is important is that our health may suffer if we fail to prioritize ourselves. We need not feel guilty about taking time away from our teenagers – by looking after ourselves and taking responsibility for ourselves we are being good role models for them.

I am an example of what can happen if we fail to look after ourselves. I crashed and burned, trying to be all things to all people, but was not there for myself when I became depressed in my thirties. At the time, I was juggling motherhood with my work in the newsroom at *The Times*, trying to keep all the balls in the air while at the same time feeling anxious that I couldn't, that I was failing at everything. The last person I was looking out for was me. In the end my body took over. I fell prey to debilitating anxiety-driven depression, and two severe depressive episodes followed.

For several years I was no good to anyone: we cannot pour from an empty cup. Sacrificing ourselves on the altar of parenthood in the end can prove self-defeating. We can't look after anyone else if the stuffing is knocked out of us.

Your teenager is going to be okay without you for a bit. The idea of 'parenting' as an active verb means that practically all of us feel guilty for not spending enough time with our adolescents, especially if we are single parents. But our teenagers can enjoy relationships with other adults, something we can encourage and a topic I will look at in more detail later. We are not necessarily better parents for spending more time with our adolescents. They may well not want to spend that much time with us anyway! The quality of our interactions with our children at this stage matters more than the quantity.

While it can be hard to imagine ourselves as examples for our teenagers, especially if we ourselves suffer from low self-esteem at times, we can teach them more by how we behave than by what we say. For years I didn't feel that I was any kind of example to follow, given my own mental health problems. But even if we find life difficult, we can be influential mentors by showing our teenagers the importance of getting help. They know that it is okay not to be okay at times.

Teenagers may also benefit from seeing that we believe it is important to have time for ourselves. They too need to learn to prioritize their psychological wellbeing. By taking care of our own needs – by exercising, seeing a counsellor, making space for a friend, or whatever keeps us steady – we are setting an example for them. In my own case, it was a big first step when I took up boxing at the weekend, about five years ago. At first that felt outrageous! Surely weekends are for family time? To be there for my teenagers? But the Sundays I put on my gloves were the days I felt my best. I would return from a class in the park with a different kind of energy. I felt physically stronger, and psychologically different too. What had been difficult exchanges with my teenagers before I went out now seemed more effortless. Tricky topics lost their charge. I was sending two messages: first, that they too could have time out for themselves, and second, they might feel more balanced if they did so.

None of us is the perfect example of a supportive, mentally well-adjusted person. Who can say they always manage their own emotions, deal with their negative thoughts, bounce back from setbacks, remain present and focused when engaging with their children, and always take exercise and eat healthily? But our children can learn from that as well. It might sound counterintuitive but the only way to help our teenagers feel a sense of unconditional confidence is to accept that it is alright to make mistakes. We are not aiming to show them our perfect selves.

Instead, we can be examples of human plasticity – we are still learning and growing. Our children can watch us changing the relationship we have with ourselves, becoming kinder or less judgemental, and learning to cope with our own complicated feelings. The late psychologist Julius Segal coined the term 'charismatic adult' for someone from whom a child or adolescent gathers strength.[3] That adult can be you. You can still be charismatic while at times feeling anything but charming, which is a useful lesson for your teenagers.

I hope I have persuaded you of the need to look after yourself and your own mental health, and don't worry – later I have some ideas about how to do so. Think of this as relationship No.1. A second important relationship you need to look after is with your teenager's other parent (assuming someone, or more than one other person, is also involved, which of course is not always the case).

YOUR RELATIONSHIP WITH
YOUR TEENAGER'S OTHER PARENT

While there are multiple combinations and ways of being a parent, easy relations with the others involved, and not tradition, is our aim.[4] My own model of parenting has been conventional. I'm married and my husband and I have raised our family together. We've had to discover how to co-parent in positive and peaceful ways. Other parents have different challenges, whether they are single parents or some other parenting combination.

None of this has been easy and has required lots of, at times difficult, conversations and indeed conflicts. If we do argue, we also try to repair those arguments and ideally apologize in front of our children, so that our teenagers aren't frightened of conflict. But we have found ways to work together more.

All this matters, both for your teenagers and you. If you are in a couple, ideally both parents need to be involved in parenting, unless your child is at risk in some way. Evidence suggests the absence of fathers is a factor in behavioural difficulties in boys, including struggling at school, addiction and getting involved in crime.[5] For your teenagers, your relationship with your partner, as my friend the therapist Tara Saglio puts it, is 'the amniotic fluid that a child grows up in. Children internalize the relationship and it forms the building blocks for their own relationships.'[6]

Children put a strain on relationships. Differing ideas on raising children have always provoked arguments among couples, alongside conflicts over work, in-laws, bothersome friends and sex. But studies have found that couples argue more when bringing up teenage children than at any other stage.[7] Marital happiness drops sharply as soon as the first-born child goes through puberty. Divorce also peaks in the mid- to late forties, coinciding with the age when many couples' children reach adolescence. While there are multiple reasons for this – women arriving at menopause and reassessing their lives, for example – one undoubted factor is parents at war over how to bring up their teenagers.

Here are two thoughts that have helped me have a smoother emotional relationship with my children's father, which has benefited my own relationship with him, and my ability to connect with my teenagers. The first is that it can be hard to hand over responsibility to the other parent. You may see their involvement as a threat to your own intimacy with your teenagers, and as challenging your views. But although you may see things differently, you can nonetheless behave as a united front, and this is good for you and your teenagers. And the second thought is that the relationships between you, your partner and your teenager can get caught up in messy triangles, which are best avoided.

TEAMWORK

The first requirement for peaceful co-parenting is for parents to work together – obvious, you might think, but not always easy. Some parents long for more help and support from their other half (if they exist), but there may not be much we can do about lacklustre spouses or partners who imagine they deserve a medal for sorting the occasional packed lunch. We can, though, do something about ourselves, if we are the ones who find it hard to share parenting. This is known as 'gatekeeping', whereby one parent tries to keep the other parent out. This is common with mothers in particular, though fathers can do this too. We don't talk about 'our children', but 'my children'.

There are plenty of reasons we may do this. If we act alone, we are in charge and can do things our way. There is no need for a united front, just our own view. Our partner's parenting blueprint may not fit with ours. It's easier for them not to be involved.

We may also want to be judged as good parents. With women, this status may mean more in a world of working women. This is about being someone nurturing; the stereotypical female is a caregiving, hands-on person who is judged by time spent with her children. Absence is synonymous with neglectful mothering. For allegedly liberated, working women, there's a tension. Giving up waiting at the school gates in favour of others is giving up being perceived by society as a hands-on proper mother. There's a fear of being shunned for not being constantly involved. 'How funny. We all know your son from seeing him with his dad at the park, but we don't even seem to have met you before.'

This need to fulfil the stereotype of being a capable mum can mean some mothers don't let their partners pull their parenting weight. Perhaps the partner can't meet their standards (or, just as frighteningly, if the partner is marvellously competent, they might feel redundant). It is all too easy to decide that others – usually fathers – are more trouble than they are worth. A father may hurry to help, but in the mother's view he does it all wrong. This view is embedded in our culture where father figures in cartoons are often comically inept, and even more so in many advertisements. A 2020 study of American sitcoms analysed scenes of TV dads from 1980 to 2017 and discovered that dads appear less frequently than mums in key parenting scenes, and when they are shown, the study describes their parenting as 'humorously foolish'.[8] There is of course an understanding among dads that if you do something badly enough you won't be asked to do it again, a sort of weaponized incompetence which means some men avoid domestic tasks.

This is eased by the fact that, traditionally, society has favoured mothers being in charge, right from birth. There may not always be enough space or facilities for fathers to stay in maternity or neonatal wards (which focus on maternal milk production), and baby-changing facilities are often to be found in women's toilets. Doctors and schools frequently call the mother, rather than the father. Even though many fathers want to do an equal shift, and it has been legal for a decade for dads to share parental leave, only a minority feel able to do so.

Ideally we want to encourage fathers to be involved. Self-evidently, they can bring imagination, energy, insight and tenderness to the job, and many do. We can abandon the double standards whereby men and women are judged differently when it comes to being parents: no man is a hero just because he prepares the occasional lunch box, and no mother needs to continually demonstrate quite how capable she is.

Time is on our side. Societal norms are softening. The old stereotype that men went out to work, and women were left with a part-time job and the children is just that – an old stereotype. Office of National Statistics data show that, in 2023, one in nine stay-at-home parents are now fathers, up from one in fourteen in 2019.[9] The number of dads who left the workforce to look after their family rose by 34 per cent over the same period – 141,000, up from 105,000.[10] As gay couples choose to have families through surrogacy or adoption, there are now teenagers whose only caregivers are male.

The more I learned about a father's role in teenage development, especially their role in fostering confidence and self-respect in boys, the more I was grateful for my husband's involvement and sympathetic to parents without partners, or with partners who are unable to help. How they might manage and engage others in the care of their teenagers is the topic of Chapter 16.

Yes, others may see things differently from you – which you might say is self-evident. What wasn't so obvious to me is that it is a good thing for your teenagers. You will probably be different kinds of parents – authoritarian versus liberal, for example. It is impossible for two parents (let alone more) to share all the same views on child-rearing, or indeed any other topic – and wouldn't life be boring if we agreed about everything? But instead of seeing this as a threat, we can reframe difference as something we can respect and work with; we can complement the other parent's style. A breakthrough for me was not labelling an approach 'right' or 'wrong' but just different. We each bring something to the table, and between us can agree a joint approach that takes something from each of our parenting styles.

Take the topic of how we view missing school in my household. My view is that I am usually pleased to have my teenagers at home. If they don't want to go to school, perhaps there is a reason for it, and by staying home we can figure it out. This view probably reflects my own teenage experience of being allowed to stay at home.

My husband's view is that missing school is less of an option. A teenager who wants to stay home is being a bit wilful. Letting them miss school may give them an unrealistic view of the way the world works. It is not a good preparation for life.

Both views have their merits, but I used to struggle to see his point of view. Differences between us felt personal. This might sound self-centred, but in the past I would take it as a criticism if my husband disagreed with me. I didn't like feeling wrong: who doesn't prefer to be right? Now I realize that seeing things differently does not mean I am to blame, or wrong. It is not about me at all. It is just that each of us views the world through our own individual lens.

Fathers and mothers bring different parenting skills to bear, right from the start. In a 2012 Israeli study, scientists compared 15 couples of parents of babies aged four to six months. The parents' brain activity was assessed by brain scanners while they watched videos of their children playing. Both mothers and fathers showed activity in the areas of the brain linked to empathy and understanding others' feelings, equally demonstrating the strong attachment they felt to their child. But in other areas of the brain, there was a distinct difference. In mothers, the evolutionally ancient limbic system, which governs affection and nurturing of others, was the most active part of the brain. In contrast, in fathers, the relatively young neocortex, which is associated with 'social cognition' or the way we process and use information in social contexts, was set alight, reflecting a father's role in teaching and encouraging his children to strive towards independence.[11] This helps explain a familiar sight in playgrounds around the world: dads reading happily on a bench, while mums are hovering by the climbing frame.

Understanding these evolutionary differences has helped me be more appreciative of my husband's different approach, rather than thinking that I know best. I have become much more curious about his ideas and am embarrassed that I sometimes used to dismiss them. We don't know best, only what we know. Often our views follow patterns that became engrained into us as children when we began to interpret the world in a certain way, according to our unique experiences. It took many years for me to learn that how I see things is just how I see things.

Notwithstanding that we see things differently, and that different views have merit in a complex world, parents still need a united front and clarity on any given topic, according to psychologists. Otherwise children will divide and conquer. Hard as it can be, we've both strived for consistency: agreeing on rules and boundaries is fundamental to avoiding conflict, both between us, and with our teenagers, who find it confusing to be confronted by different parenting styles. For us, the decision on the topic of staying home from school reflected both our views: I compromised by agreeing that unless obviously unwell, our children should go to school. My husband compromised in agreeing that we should also try to find out more about what was going on.

Whatever kind of partnership we are in, it's good to avoid power struggles. Divorced parents I spoke to told me that one way to stay calm in the face of provocation from a former spouse is to hold in mind the image of their teenager in the future – what will their memories be? Another told me that any opportunity to show that you and your former partner can discuss and cooperate – choosing a joint birthday present for example – are to be grabbed. Teenage children of divorced parents said what they hungered for was clarity and structure from both parents, and what they most disliked was bad-mouthing of either parent of the other.

Every parenting alliance is different, and of course there are many parents who are not in a partnership. At first sight, thoughts on cooperating with a co-parent might not seem relevant. But nearly all teenagers benefit from others being involved in their upbringing, which can help dilute the impact of only one caregiver on the child. We may just have to accept at least some areas of disagreement with others involved in raising our children, be they grandparents who don't know about gluten-free food, or godparents who get in a muddle with preferred pronouns.

TRIANGLES

Being aware of my own parenting lens has smoothed relations with others involved. So too has becoming more aware of what I think of as 'triangular traps'. Here are two of the most obvious kinds. In the first triangle, I intrude into my husband's relationship with one of our children. In the second kind, during an argument or issue between me and my husband, we use one of the children as a focus or substitute for what is happening between us as a couple.

Let's take an example of the first type of triangle, intervening in my husband's relationship with our children. I used to imagine he would be a similar kind of parent to me. And if he wasn't, or behaved in a way I didn't like to one of the children, then I felt I should jump in and tell him so. (Ironic, you may say, considering I've just told you I didn't like him disagreeing with me!) Perhaps I felt that mothers knew best, and that I was more central to my children's welfare than their father, despite his involvement.

Sometimes I jumped in because I felt protective of the children, thinking that they couldn't handle their own relationship with their father. On one occasion on holiday with some friends, my husband felt one of our teenagers had been rude to a fellow guest about their cooking, and told him so in no uncertain terms after the meal.

I saw the altercation differently: I thought my son hadn't been offensive but had been trying to be amusing. The boy was upset by his father's ticking off. I stepped in, told my husband he was being unfair, and tried to comfort our son. These days, I would keep out of the triangle. My teenager later told me my involvement had made things worse. He wanted his own relationship with his dad; and actually, he felt he had been flippant and, arguably, rude to the guest, albeit while trying to be funny. He welcomed his father setting some boundaries about his behaviour and teaching him to be wary of the fine line between humour and rudeness. Equally, my husband was understandably annoyed that I had challenged his own parenting style, pots and kettles coming to mind.

The second type of triangular trap is when some tension in your relationship with your co-parent spills into an issue with one of the children. For example, if you feel that your partner doesn't listen to you, you might be sensitive to your child experiencing the same. Or if you feel sensitive that your partner is bossing you about, you might overreact if he tells one of the children what to do.

Co-parents may need time away from their teenagers to find ways to talk about their own problems as a couple. 'Relationship care' is as important as self-care. Studies show that homes full of conflict in turn make it harder for teenagers to regulate their own feelings.[12] Avoid scrapping with your partner if you can.

An ease in our relationship with our partner or co-parent makes dealing with our teenagers easier in turn. We may need time to sit down together, away from the scrum of family life, to concentrate on each other and our relationship. This can include reflections on how each of us has been brought up, and our own expectations of parenting.

Life became easier between my husband, myself and our teenagers when we both acknowledged and tried to step out of these kinds of triangles. Indeed, I've taken to walking away altogether to disentangle myself, muttering 'Step out of the triangle, step out of the triangle' as I do. As far as possible I try to let my husband interact with our children as he sees fit. They have their own relationship.

By realizing how different my partner and I are, by believing that that is a good thing and we can still create a united front which is the stronger for both our views, and by stepping out of triangles, I now have a smoother relationship with my husband when it comes to looking after our teenagers.

*

To sum up, building good relationships, both with yourself and with your co-parent, is the first step to putting yourself in a good place to relate to your teenagers. You could see the start of their adolescence as the spur you need to spend some time nourishing and understanding both relationships, as some bumpy times will inevitably lie ahead. This kind of self-reflection will help you better support your child, like a healthy bamboo cane which supports a growing sweet pea plant. It will help you protect and support them, rather than impede and control, and provide a stable framework.

Given my own circumstances, I have shared more thoughts for those who are in a stable relationship, than those who have to negotiate with, say, an ex-partner or their new spouse, and struggle to get any help. But whatever kind of relationship you are in, you can imagine being a parent as being a bit like playing a game of cards. We are all dealt different cards, be they aces, number cards or jokers. So far I have discussed two cards we each hold: our own psychological health, and the role of others involved in our parenting. Sometimes we hold good cards – a supportive partner, or good psychological health ourselves. Sometimes the cards are less good – perhaps we have had our own emotional troubles or are struggling with a partner. Whatever hand we hold, it makes sense to identify what those cards feel like and how they affect us, and how we might understand, reflect on and play those cards to the best of our ability. The next card we hold as parents concerns another important relationship: the one we have with our own parents.

2

YOUR RELATIONSHIP WITH YOUR OWN PARENTS

What kind of relationship did you have with your own parents? How were you parented? And how is that influencing your own parenting now? Our own memories of childhood and being a teenager may lie dormant until we have children of our own, but then they can burst into dramatic life. Our teenagers are liable to remind us of ourselves at a similar age, and the emotions we went through, and how our own parents responded at that time. For some of us, this can be an opportunity, gifted by the arrival of our children's adolescence, to address some long-buried problems about how we were brought up.

We can live in the story of our past and with the parenting blueprint we inherited. Or we can become more aware of our interpretations and our past experiences, and decide they don't need to control everything about our future behaviour. Many of us realize that how we choose to parent does not need to echo how we ourselves were parented. The challenge is that it's tricky. How do we keep in a metaphorical sieve those aspects of our upbringing that were helpful, and let go of those which were less so? The relationships and the patterns of behaviour involved are complex, often buried in our subconscious, and times change dramatically between the generations, as we've seen. This makes the question even trickier. However, we do have some agency, which is the subject of this chapter.

'ATTACHMENT' STYLES

The first step to moving on from mimicking the parenting we received is to become more attuned to how we were brought up. We need to consider how we adapted to our own parents and family members to get love and attention and our needs met, something psychologists sometimes describe as our 'attachment' style. This may in turn affect our parenting style. Attachment is a complex area dealing with how young children develop a relationship with their main caregiver, about which thousands of social science papers have been written. It is impossible to summarize easily, but to simplify, researchers believe that people emerge from babyhood with an attachment style that carries on in adulthood. The idea of attachment theory was developed in 1969 by the psychologist and psychiatrist John Bowlby. Bowlby divided people into three main camps: those who were anxiously attached, those who were securely attached and those with an 'avoidant' attachment style. (Another category was added later on – disorganized attachment, for children who fear their parent or carer.) Anxious children need lots of reassurance and fear being abandoned. Secure children enjoy closeness without becoming overly dependent. Avoidants shun intimacy and closeness because they want to remain independent or because they feel safer below the parapet.[1]

Broadly speaking, we are 'securely' or 'insecurely' attached. However, within these wide categories are nuances, described as 'attachment tendencies'. A person may tend towards being both anxiously and avoidantly attached. Sometimes they cling a bit more; at other times they push away. Even those with what psychologists call a 'secure-secure' pattern will still have moments when they seek space.

The bit that is relevant to us as parents is that our own attachment tendencies may affect our parenting style. But we must be careful: it's easy to oversimplify and reduce an entire relationship to a tick-box exercise appearing to measure the quality of parenting we received. In my case, to say I was at times 'insecurely' attached doesn't begin to describe all the richness and variety of my upbringing. But it has helped, in a limited way, to explain one aspect of how I am as a mother, namely that I am sometimes fearful of rejection and need to be liked. And, as you may have gathered, find it hard to set rules for my teenagers.

This kind of awareness may make us less likely to be at the mercy of seemingly irrational emotions. Instead, we can spot the aspects of our upbringing that cause us to behave in certain habitual ways and hold what psychologists call certain 'core beliefs'. These are deeply held and rigid assumptions which we have about ourselves and the world around us. They usually stem from childhood. When we recognize these, we can begin to change our inherited ways of thinking and behaving: there are detailed suggestions for how we might do so in the next chapter.

This may be a painful if not impossible process, especially if our parents behaved in a cruel fashion and we suffered deep childhood trauma. We may need to ask for professional help to process such difficult experiences and heal from them. Ideally we want to get to the point where we are less interested in blaming our parents, which is disempowering. We may not have been loved in the way we craved, but that's not to say most parents weren't trying their best to love us in the ways they could. Instead, it's more useful for us to be curious about any positive traits of theirs we want to emulate, and negative ones we would like to shed.

We can reflect that perhaps our parents may have been reflecting the parenting they themselves received, and the times in which they were brought up. While the poet Philip Larkin famously wrote, 'They fuck you up, your mum and dad', the next line of his poem went on to say, 'They may not mean to . . .' For those of my generation – I'm in my late fifties – some of our parents' responses and behaviour might seem harsh to younger parents better schooled in listening to their children's feelings. Theirs was the post-war generation who rarely talked about their emotions or interrogated them, mirroring their own parents who had been through the war.

However, we can do things differently. We can start asking questions about our upbringing and how it influenced our development as a person. Question one is how our parents' behaviour influenced our own tastes and the sort of people we have become. Question two is how that in turn has influenced us as parents. The two are clearly connected. The aim is to arm ourselves with a new awareness and understanding of our own behaviour and character. Then, ideally, we can progress to letting go of the less helpful patterns and keeping the helpful ones.

PARENTAL INFLUENCE

Let's begin by thinking about how your personality was influenced by your parents. A tall order, clearly. The topic is difficult and wide-ranging. Difficult because it is hard to make a direct link between how you were brought up and your character. Your disposition may have equally been influenced by genetics or other aspects of your environment, and – more importantly – by the way you chose to interpret your parents' behaviour, which may or may not have reflected their intentions. Wide-ranging because it includes subjects such as your emotional reactions, your prejudices and snobberies, your likes and dislikes, the words you say. Nonetheless, you can begin to observe your own behaviour and emotional reality, and the patterns in the way you think and feel that may have been influenced by the way your parents brought you up. This matters, because it in turn affects your behaviour as a parent.

Here's how I've tried to do this. If I am overcome by a powerful feeling, I pause and try to figure out if my response might be linked to my childhood. Typically, what can happen is that a strong story I wrote in my head as a child, and the emotions that accompanied that interpretation of events, will bubble up and colour my interactions now, even though I am no longer a child. In my case, when I feel left out, or when I feel frightened, I can quickly regress to feeling like a vulnerable kid.

Take this memory from my childhood (amid many happy ones) about feeling left out. I was hiding in a bedroom at my grandparents' house aged about six, sobbing. I wanted to be found and comforted by my mother. Eventually she did come. She was a devoted parent, but she was uneasy talking about emotions – arguably more common then than it is now. The comment I remember was, 'Don't be such a dying duck.' I also remember feeling that being whiny and tearful was not an entirely loveable thing to be. It was easy to create a narrative that I was being rejected, even though I know now how much my mother loved me.

There is an inevitable link between some of these dormant insecurities from childhood and how I relate to my children. Seemingly small interactions can trigger a strong reaction in me if I'm not careful. If a daughter tells me she doesn't want to chat right now, or my son walks into school without saying goodbye when I drop him off, I can feel that old painful feeling of rejection bubbling up inside me.

Instead of thinking, no big deal, they just don't want to connect or communicate with me right now, that's okay, I imagine the same kind of rejection I experienced at times when I was younger.

Being aware of how the past is playing out in the present can help us change these patterns. If I experience childhood memories of feeling left out, I tell myself that's not the same as being rejected now, and more than that, maybe that was just a story I wrote at the time which may or may not have been true. My children just want to hang out with their friends. I have plenty of friends of my own. I can also respond in a way that may now be more appropriate to the person I have become – I'm 59, not 6! As a result, I began slowly changing my behaviour. I learned not to bombard them with calls and texts, hoping for a call back. I now resist the need when I say, 'Love you', for them to say, 'Love you' back.

Or take my dislike of conflict. I can remind myself that the pattern in my upbringing was that we rarely got into arguments. If my older sister and I squabbled as children, my mother would call upstairs and tell us to stop behaving like a 'bunch of fishwives'. She also never seemed to fight with my father. If there was an argument, it felt frightening, because it happened so rarely.

Again, this has naturally influenced the adult and the parent I have become (though I'm changing!). Hitherto I have avoided arguments. I have been frightened by conflict, and by feeling angry myself. Instead, I have tended to be a people-pleaser and sometimes have avoided saying what I really think, especially if I have feared it might lead to a quarrel. While this can make sense, there can also be a cost to limiting my own self-expression and not speaking my own truth. Arguments, I now realize, can have advantages. And that includes arguments with your adolescents. It's okay for our teenagers not to always like us. We are not their friends. Just because avoiding disputes was how I was brought up doesn't mean it always makes sense.

Now I am no longer so frightened of being angry. It's okay to be cross and for others to be cross with me. Good even. Therapy taught me that one explanation of depression is that it is anger turned inwards: we repress our feelings of anger to the point that eventually they find their expression in a mental health condition. Later in life I have become more in touch and aware of when I'm angry, but for many years I found it hard not to panic if I had an argument with one of my children, and hated it if they didn't like me.

Let's say a teenager borrows my house key without telling me, leaving me locked out: a minor infraction, but then most arguments normally involve something seemingly trivial. One part of me is cross. My day is derailed. And I share these angry thoughts with my teenager by text. It is not just about the key, I say. It is about thinking of others, being respectful, sharing space. All reasonable, you might think. But then the other part of me, the five-year-old part that is frightened of conflict, undermines my straight talking. Quickly I find myself back into wanting-to-please mode. When my texts are not returned, I can panic. Before I know it, it is me apologizing to my teenager. 'Silly me for lending you the key!' Only now, with more awareness, I see this pattern from my own childhood and realize it is not a helpful one.

Our emotional reality is not necessarily fixed. We can, luckily, find ways to change some of these early governing patterns that created our personalities, especially if we find compassion for the little left-out children we once were, or imagined ourselves to be. Instead, we can discover who we really are and what we really want now. We can then ask, How do I want to be with my own children? What example do I want to create for them? While our responses might have been understandable and appropriate as a child, do we need to be defined by them as adults? We can make new choices.

MUDDYING THE WATERS

We can also resolve to become more aware of how we project our own damaging thoughts onto our children – conflating our own experience with theirs.

Much heartache can be saved if we stop confusing how we feel with how they feel: psychologists talk of the need for maintaining boundaries, and the importance of avoiding 'enmeshment' when boundaries blur. Sometimes we may even confuse our child's success with our own, living vicariously through our children's achievements. I'll never forget one mother shouting at the school gates that she herself had passed the entrance exam for a particularly prestigious school.

Let's return to my long-standing fear of rejection. I imagined that because this is my emotional reality, it must be the same for my teenager. I was projecting my own hurt onto my teenagers. Just because I minded desperately about not being included doesn't mean they necessarily did. Our children are different from us.

Or maybe you worry that your teenager seems to have few friends. If you have lots of friends, and that's important to you, you might assume it is important for them. But maybe they are less social. They don't need to be asked to parties to feel okay about themselves. Maybe they would rather stay at home or watch a football match. We, their parents, feel deeply on their behalf, but what if this is a waste of our emotional energy? More than that, few people like others feeling sorry for them, especially when have had their feelings misjudged in the first place.

This matters, as the less we project ourselves onto our teenagers, the more we can respond to the people they really are and become attuned to their reality and the emotions they are having, rather than being caught up in our own. Otherwise we are more likely to acknowledge only our own feelings, and parent ourselves rather than them.

COPYCAT

So far in this chapter, I've discussed how our relationship with our parents (among many other factors) may have influenced our personalities, in my case being fearful of rejection and disliking scenes; and how this in turn has affected our roles as parents. I've also talked about the need to separate our resulting emotional reality from our children's. Now I want to focus on the parenting style we witnessed growing up and how we may be following family 'scripts', sometimes without realizing it.

The idea of family scripts was developed by the child and family psychiatrist John Byng-Hall.[2] There are three kinds. First, replicative scripts, whereby (unsurprisingly) we replicate the parenting that we received, positive and negative. This can be as specific as a preferred way to load the dishwasher, or much more general, as in how to express intimacy. In my own case, my mother was tolerant of mess, so I replicated that 'script' and found it hard to tell my teenagers to pick up their clothes. She always signed her cards to us 'All love M' and so do I. Second are corrective scripts, which are a conscious decision to parent differently, and indeed to be different. People run away from their inherited scripts in different ways, sometimes moving abroad, changing religion or even changing their name, which was the case for a cousin of mine who moved to Canada. Less dramatically, in my case, whereas my parents rarely talked about their emotions, I often do, and try to validate rather than dismiss my children's feelings. My mother was physically a little distant, but I try to hug my children. Such corrective scripts can be risky: if our parents were harsh disciplinarians, for example, the danger can be that we overcompensate for our past hurts by indulging our children.

Third are improvised scripts, which combine what we value from our upbringing with what we have learned from relationships and experience as we have matured. These are thought to be the most resilient and healthy scripts, not least because if two adults are parenting teenagers, they each bring their own scripts to the process. An improvised script allows for a degree of blending of approaches and behaviours from both parties. In forging something new, we walk away from the past. Instead of reacting without thought, perhaps instinctively we can strive to widen our horizons and the choice of behaviours we can enjoy.

Most often, we follow replicative scripts and tend to parent as we were parented, which as I have said may not necessarily be a bad thing, depending on the parenting we received. We often imitate our parents, having similar attitudes and behaving in similar ways, because this feels familiar and safe. When we were children ourselves, disagreeing with a parent could make us vulnerable. They held power over us, and our strongest instinct was to please them. Even though we are now adults, and our parents have no more power over us, we may have internalized their points of view or created a similar family environment for ourselves. It can feel as if we are being loyal to our parents by behaving like them.

This imitation of our own backgrounds can extend to our choice of partner. We may choose a partner who replicates a dynamic from our past. They have a familiarity to which we may be unconsciously drawn. This can make it harder to break the mould and offer our children something different because in such a case, not just us, but our partner also, mimics the behaviour of our own parents.

It can also influence our attitude to sensitive topics. Take our approach to money, for example. If our parents worried about money when we were little and have been careful with it since, we may well have a similar outlook. If we think our teenager is being careless with money, the fear from the past may bleed into our fear today. Or perhaps we went without as children. We may overcompensate now because to imagine disappointing teenagers with a scaled-down Christmas is to feel the pain of our childhood disappointment. Perceived penny-pinching strikes a nerve. We may spend money on them in an attempt to buy their love or to connect with them. Ideally we should want to give them a sense that while money is important, it's not everything, and that monetary and emotional value are separate things. One has nothing to do with the other.

Imitation can be dangerous if we mirror less helpful behaviour or language that we ourselves experienced as teenagers – in my case, parroting the phrase 'Don't be such a dying duck!' We unwittingly recreate the atmosphere of our own childhood, which is unlikely to be appropriate in an entirely new context.

This may be most likely to occur in stressful situations. Naturally, the emotional stakes are high when things have gone wrong, and it is easy to unthinkingly repeat the way our own parents disciplined us. We can lose it in the same way our parent might have got angry with us. Instead, we would be better adopting a new, improvised script.

TWEAKMENTS

Pause for a moment and acknowledge the positives your parents gave you: it is easy (and perhaps fashionable) to accentuate the negatives, but sometimes our parents got it right and imitating their behaviour may not be a bad thing at all (though with the proviso that your children aren't you and might need different treatment). Being fucked up by our parents (to borrow again from Larkin) is not mandatory.

Then see if you can tweak the less positive aspects of how you were brought up, in small and large ways. In my case, I valued my parents' love of ideas and intellectual rather than practical pursuits – gardening was viewed as outdoor housework. But I have tried to celebrate lots of less scholarly enthusiasms in myself and my children: there's nothing I love more than potting up some geraniums. To take another example, my mother was loving in a practical way, making trips to the library on my behalf, or picking me up from school. But she found it hard to ever say she loved me, something I would try to do with my own teenagers.

In another bit of improvisation, I have tried to widen the range of emotions that are acceptable in family life. We are more at ease with having arguments and accepting of anger than I experienced when I was growing up (although when I checked this point with my own children, they told me I am still argument-averse, and they find it hard to be angry: we are always a work in progress).

Writing our own new, improvised script can be a challenge: we are taking on the weight not just of our parents, but of the generations before them. We can be sympathetic to ourselves if we are trying to do things differently – or be 'cycle-breakers' – and there are bound to be bumps with our partners in the process. We also may have to be careful. We may inadvertently go overboard in our desire to change family patterns, in our passionate hope to be better parents than our own. A desire for emotional intimacy, for example, might be experienced as being overbearing by our teenagers, who may need more privacy than we did. While we worry that they may feel neglected, it's possible they may feel intruded upon. Be mindful that when we swing too far the other way, we are still distorting our behaviour based on our history. Rather than deciding on the qualities that matter to us, we are still mimicking our parents as we are still placing them centre stage in our own responses, rather than choosing ways of relating and connecting that acknowledge the positives while disregarding the negatives.

While it's difficult to write an improvised script, it's not impossible. Three things have helped me. The first is to give it time. We might imagine that replicating our parents' parenting, or reacting against it, would be easy to identify. But it can be harder than it seems because there are ways that our upbringing can influence us subconsciously. It takes a while to realize that what feels like instinct is often an inheritance. A second approach is to be aware of language, especially the common phrases and aphorisms that echoed during our upbringing: these can be clues as to the kind of parenting approaches and values our own parents espoused. Finally, jotting down what's working well about our own improvised script in a notebook is an encouraging reminder that change is possible – and indeed will keep happening down the generations.

*

Ultimately, we can have a better chance of growing into the supportive, connected parents that we want to be if we learn to step back and realize that our reactions are mostly about us, as well as the parenting we received, good and bad. We can become aware of our attachment styles and core beliefs, even though this is a complex topic; and we can become aware of how we were influenced by our parents – another big topic! Then we can begin to become more aware of how our emotional past plays out in the present as a first step to changing these patterns. We may be able to free ourselves from some of these early ways of responding, especially if we do so with compassion.

Part of this awareness is being sensitive to how we can conflate our experience with our children's. But our teenagers are different from us. Just because we feel something deeply doesn't mean that they will. We have our hang-ups; they have theirs. Equally, we may be echoing our parents without realizing: beware being a copycat. While it's hard to change, especially if we suffered deep childhood trauma, we can learn to pause in terms of our reactivity. Strike when the iron is cold. Remember, our main relationship is with ourselves. Knowing ourselves and making sense of our experiences helps us shed the destructive layers from our past that limit us now. Having teenagers can prompt us to venture into our own childhood and upbringing, and the thoughts and feelings we have regarding that time, and to do so with strength, curiosity and compassion. And we can move on. As the therapist and writer Julia Bueno shared with me, 'I am no longer a child of my parents, but the universe.'

3

YOUR BRAIN AND ITS GLITCHES

et's continue with the idea that we are all holding a set of cards as parents – one card being the relationship we have with ourselves, another how we get along with our co-parents, and a third being our own upbringing and how we feel about our parents, as we discussed in the last chapter. Another card we might examine, and usefully add to our pack if it is something we are ignorant about, is an understanding of the workings of the human brain. If we want to be more relaxed parents, able to enjoy our adolescents a bit more, we may need a greater understanding of how our brains work, and how this affects our behaviour, our relationships and the ways we think. If someone experiences anxiety about flying, just understanding the mechanics of flying can make them more relaxed about their flight, and this same idea applies to understanding our brains.

Despite the tremendous research that has been done, in some ways our knowledge of the brain and the nervous system – the brain's communication network to the body – remains slight. Here's an example. Researchers have spent years making a detailed, synapse-level map of the neural connections in the brain of a maggot, the larva of the common fly.[1] Imagine the level of research needed to even begin to map the neural connections of a human.

What we do know is that while our brains are of astonishing brilliance, they are full of glitches, glitches that particularly affect worried parents. The glitches arise because different parts of the brain evolved at different times. The modern human brain combines both older and newer structures. In some ways it is well designed, but in other ways the design works less than perfectly. Imagine it a bit like an old house that has had different bits added over time, and the plumbing and central heating don't work efficiently between the different sections of the building.

These structural quirks in our brains manifest themselves in some problematic patterns of behaving and feeling in today's world. Under stress we can feel highly anxious, uncomfortable or at times furious – even like our existence is in danger. At these moments, it is all too easy to blame either the trying world in which we live, or those around us, including our teenagers whom we imagine to be wrong in some way. Our brains are actually designed to find blame: if we find something or someone to blame, there's something to fix, and that can make us feel safe again. Finding blame is most people's go-to, number-one 'get safe' strategy.

More helpful, I've found, is to be aware of my brain's quirks. When things are difficult at home, and I've shouted up the stairs once too often, I often mumble to myself, 'Oh, there goes my wonky brain.' Later in the book I will share more detailed strategies that can help with these behaviours and feelings, but for now, it is enough to set out the 'brain cards' with which we are dealing.

There are a couple of brain gremlins that I have found especially helpful to know about in my life as a parent of teenagers. The first is that our brains can easily mistake everyday challenges for life-threatening disasters. And the second is that we are all continually interpreting the world around us according to our previous experience, confirming in our minds the stories we habitually tell ourselves.

WONKY BRAINS

Let's take the first oddity. We don't live in a world of sabre-toothed tigers anymore, but we are still running the same 'fight, flight, freeze or fawn' software (the 'fawn' response is when we try to please someone to avoid conflict). Our brains were built for survival, not happiness. These reactions are thanks to our sometimes faulty stress response and our core-held belief that we live in an unsafe world, even though this is not actually true. However, given that most parents are highly anxious about their children's safety, it's worth dwelling on how our brains respond to threat.

When we feel threatened, the brain's fight or flight centres switch on automatically and instantly. These parts of our brains, especially a bit called the amygdala, react without the need for conscious thought, because this automatic response to danger gives us a survival advantage. If we see a sabre-toothed tiger, we haven't got time to think anything through, or stand around and chat. We have a split second to run. We are all descended from those who escaped.

Now take the case of a modern-day threat: a teenager who is late coming home one evening and doesn't answer the phone – one of my own personal nightmares. I would panic. My brain would imagine a life-threatening disaster, fuelled by a news schedule full of horrors. My child's survival might be at stake. Mad as it sounds, I might ask myself, has my child been abducted? Attacked on their way home from school?

A threat combines the actual event – an unanswered call – and the 'what if' scenarios based on minimal information that we quickly tell ourselves relating to that event. In the story we tell ourselves, we are often responding not just to the new situation (of an unanswered call) but also to all the times in our lives when we have previously felt strong emotions related to that threat.

It is hard to distinguish between the child who has been abducted and the one who is temporarily not picking up her phone because she is with her friends. Our responses are out of proportion. Abductions and attacks are unusual: a less dramatic explanation is more likely. However, we can feel threatened, even when we don't need to feel in danger. And these feelings of danger can lead to over-reacting.

In such situations, remind yourself of how our brains developed as we evolved. Be especially aware of situations that routinely make you panic, those to which your brain has learned to react with especial speed and drama. Give yourself time for your automatic fear response to calm down, perhaps with some breathing exercises to soothe your nervous system. One helpful idea I've found is the need to return to one's 'window of tolerance'. This concept was originally developed to describe the optimal zone of arousal for a person to function in everyday life.[2] When a person is operating within this window, they can cope with their emotions effectively. In this calmer window, we can realize that a less dramatic explanation is almost certainly the case. (We can also formulate a rule with our teenager to avoid the same drama happening again: in this case, a no-turning-off-phone rule.)

MISINTERPRETING THE WORLD

A second common brain glitch that affects us as parents is the way our brains often interpret the world in accordance with the beliefs, views and values that we already hold. Again, there are understandable evolutionary reasons why our brains work like this. The world is too complex to let in all the external information that is jostling for our attention. If we did, our senses would become overwhelmed. So our brains have a gatekeeper centred on something called the thalamus, which is in charge of whether we let information into our conscious awareness or not. Our words, and the stories we tell ourselves repeatedly, affect our behaviour rather than the real information around us. And those behaviours start to become automatic and turn into instinctive habits.

This would be fine if our stories and behaviour patterns were positive and the world was full of good news about adolescents. But unfortunately, our brains naturally seek out the negative, and there are plenty of negatives to choose from when it comes to bringing up teenagers at the moment, from fears that they will become mentally unwell, to a future in which they are unable to get jobs. As one psychologist puts it, our brains are 'Teflon for positive' stories and 'Velcro for negative' ones.[3] Danger, illness or bad weather could affect the survival of our ancestors, so it was important to spot these things early and think about countering them. Our brains have not evolved beyond this. Scientists call this the negativity bias. When something bad happens, our brains buzz with more electricity than when something good happens.

If we are in the habit of telling ourselves more negative stories about young people, and interpreting the world as a frightening place, then our gatekeepers will keep preferentially letting in information that confirms the existence of danger and problems, which in turn fuels a cycle of negative thoughts.

What does this mean for us as parents? It means that if, for example, we believe that our teenagers are part of an anxious generation who will have mental health problems, then we will keep finding evidence that supports that interpretation of the facts. Likewise, if we believe our teenagers will never get work, we are drawn to bad economic news about the future.

ALL IS NOT LOST

What, then, can we do about these two brain glitches that tend to make life much gloomier for us parents of teenagers? The first step is to find compassion for ourselves when our minds spiral, because the negative thoughts won't stop completely. They are part of being human. Second, we should find reassurance in the fact that we can change our thoughts. Our brains are continually changing. The science of neuroplasticity – how brains change in response to learning – suggests that learning can take place at any age. We can discard unhelpful ways of thinking. Every time we learn new ways of thinking, our brains form, strengthen and connect neural pathways. We only need to find a process by which we can control our thoughts.

Here's what helped me – a lightbulb moment, as it were. A therapist told me that the key point is to remember that negative thoughts reside in my interior world. We each have an interior and an exterior world. The exterior contains everything in the physical world, everything we experience with our five basic senses. The interior world is the world of our thoughts, emotions and imagination. It is in this inner world that stressful and anxious thoughts reside. This inner world is where we can mistake everyday challenges for life-threatening disasters; where we compare and despair; and where we are all continually interpreting the world around us according to our previous experience, confirming in our minds the stories we habitually tell ourselves.

Many of us make the mistake of trying to change our thoughts by changing the external world around us. But fearful and anxious thoughts are only partly caused by external circumstances. They are mostly caused by our perception of, and our response to, those circumstances. Different people react differently to external things; for example, many people think that spiders are extremely creepy, whereas others keep tarantulas as cuddly pets. Trying to change the outer world to change your thoughts (by eliminating all spiders, say) is inefficient. The good news, however, is that there are effective ways to control our inner worlds.

CHICKEN AND EGG

The first step is to become more aware of our thoughts – not always easy as they can become tangled up with feelings, but a skill worth acquiring because on the whole it is our thoughts and beliefs about an event that significantly influence our emotions and actions. Here's an example. Suppose your teenager introduces you to a friend of theirs, let's call her Amanda, who's come round to the house for a cuppa. As you talk to her you notice that she doesn't seem to be listening, and often looks around the room. Gosh, you might think, this girl is so rude! She won't even look at me while I'm talking with her! How do you feel? Angry most likely.

But what if instead you thought, Amanda must think I'm really boring – just an uninteresting middle-aged mum? You might feel sad. And finally, what if you were to think, Amanda's probably got something on her mind, maybe she's getting a bit anxious? You'd feel concerned about her. You may have felt three different emotions because of those three different thoughts. Often, we're not aware of our thoughts and beliefs because they are so automatic. But they are there, and they affect the way we feel.

We have no way of knowing exactly what was happening to poor old Amanda: we are not privy to the inner workings of her soul. But we can become aware of our own thoughts, and renaming them as 'stories' can help. It instantly suggests that however convincing they can seem, thoughts are not true. They are just the stories we tell ourselves, as if they were true. This is a huge idea to grasp and one I took ages to understand.

They may not just be stories we are writing in our heads: they may sound like a dialogue, as if someone else is talking to us inside our minds. Or, indeed, as if someone is giving a running commentary on us. Often that commentary feels negative. But remember, it is just a commentary, not reality.

Take another example: my teenager does not respond to my text messages to come down and join me for a cup of tea when they are in their room (yes, all parents sometimes communicate like that, including to each other). My thoughts might have been that they don't want to spend time with me: remember, I'm on the lookout for signs of rejection! Perhaps when I criticized them earlier that day for having a messy room, they felt upset and they haven't forgiven me. Perhaps they do not like me. I am no good at being a mother. All these thoughts lead to a feeling of sadness.

Once again, I have no idea why my teenager has not responded to my text. I've written a story. A different thought could be that they are tired or maybe even need to catch up with some homework. But I have manufactured plenty of interpretations, or stories, in my head.

Their constant presence in our lives means that thoughts are powerful, especially if we keep having the same ones. They build up over years of thinking the same things repeatedly. Over time, we build neural pathways, or routes in our brains, which lead us back to these familiar thoughts. And unfortunately the brain glitches we've discussed mean that we often mistake everyday challenges for life-threatening disasters, and that we also tend to be continually interpreting the world around us according to our previous experience, confirming in our minds the stories we habitually tell ourselves.

Anything can trigger these kinds of well-worn neural loops that encourage us to return to our deeply embedded core pattern of thinking. It becomes almost automatic – so automatic that we often don't even question our thoughts.

IDENTIFYING THINKING TRAPS

But we can fight back! We can say no to automatic thoughts, and yes to questioning them, a process that begins by identifying a dozen common 'cognitive distortions'. The following thinking traps (highlighted in bold below) are taken from a partial list in Leahy, Holland and McGinn's *Treatment Plans and Interventions for Depression and Anxiety Disorders*[4] and are widely used in cognitive behavioural therapy (CBT). Some of them flow naturally from my two earlier brain glitches; others are fresh ways of distorted thinking.

The first over-arching source of negative thinking – as we've seen – is the belief that we live in an unsafe world full of threats. Quite a few common cognitive distortions huddle together, as it were, under this umbrella. Here are four to watch. The first is **fortune-telling**, where we predict the future, and usually negatively – things will get worse, or there is danger ahead. We can do this both about ourselves ('I'll never be able to provide for my teenagers') but also about our teenagers ('She will fail that exam' or 'He will never get a job').

A second common cognitive distortion that stems from the feeling that the world is a scary place is **catastrophizing**: we believe that what has happened or will happen will be so awful and unbearable that we won't be able to stand it. 'It would be terrible if my teenager fell seriously ill with a mental health problem. I would never be able to cope.' We might also think that our teenagers will be unable to survive getting poor grades in their A-levels. 'They would be shattered.'

A third is **negative filtering**. We focus almost exclusively on the negatives and seldom notice the positives: 'Look at all the times I've argued with my teenager' rather than all the times you've got along; or 'Look at all the times he has come home late' rather than the fact that he did the washing up without being asked. We also focus on all the negative news about teenage mental health problems and reports of an anxious generation, rather than more positive research, which does also exist.

A fourth and related distortion is **discounting positives**. We claim that the positive things we or others do are trivial. 'That's what parents are supposed to do, so it doesn't count when I drive him back from a party' or 'It's no big deal that his teacher is nice about him: she's nice about everyone.'

When it comes to the second over-arching source of negative thinking – that our brains keep finding evidence for the beliefs we already have – once again quite a few common cognitive distortions tend to cluster under this hat. One is our **inability to disconfirm**. We reject any evidence or arguments that might contradict our negative thoughts. For example, if we believe our teenager is irresponsible and doesn't help, we ignore the fact they took their granny shopping or helped their younger sibling with their homework. Or if we imagine all teenagers are always anxious, we reject as irrelevant any evidence that they can sometimes be quite jolly. This makes it practically impossible for us to be swayed from our strongly held thoughts.

We may also tend to **mind-read**. We assume that we know what people think without having sufficient evidence of their thoughts. 'My child thinks I'm a loser' or 'She doesn't like me.' **Over-generalizing** is another common thinking trap linked to the way our brains keep finding evidence for the beliefs we already have. We perceive a global pattern of negatives based on a single incident: 'This generally happens to me. I seem to fail at a lot of things' or 'I always get it wrong with my teenage daughter' or 'She never wants to talk to me.'

Finally, **dichotomous thinking** means we tend to view events or people in black and white terms: 'I get criticized by everyone' or 'It was a complete waste of time.' If it's about our teenagers: 'They always slam the door on me; they will never treat me with respect' or 'There's no hope for any of them. Their generation is lost.'

There are a few other faulty ways of thinking that are also worth noting, though they have played less of a role in my own life as a parent.

Labelling: We assign global negative traits to ourselves and others: 'I'm undesirable' or 'He's so lazy.'

Blaming: We focus on the other person as the source of our negative feelings and refuse to take responsibility for changing ourselves: 'She's to blame for the way I feel now' or 'My parents caused all my problems.'

What if? We keep asking a series of questions about what if something happens, and we fail to be satisfied with any of the answers. 'Yeah, but what if I get anxious?' or 'What if I can't catch my breath?' If it's about our teenager, what ifs are often about their health and safety ('What if they get mugged coming home from a party?') or their futures ('What if they fail their exams/don't go to university/never get a job?').

Emotional reasoning: We let our feelings guide our interpretation of reality. 'I feel depressed, therefore my marriage is not working out' or 'I feel like a lousy mother, therefore my children will be failures.'

ESCAPING THINKING TRAPS

Knowing about all these faulty ways of thinking makes it easier to spot when we are losing the parental plot. I've found that calling out the thinking by name, be it catastrophizing, dichotomous thinking or over-generalizing, begins to lessen its grip. 'Name it to tame it,' as professor of psychiatry Dan Siegel puts it.[5]

Here's how it might work. One of my own favourite negative thought patterns is to assume the worse if I reach out to one of my teenagers with a plan and I hear nothing back. I must have offended them! I So I can name our old friend catastrophizing. Despite often having enjoyed fun trips or coffees together, I also slip into mind-reading and assume I know for sure they don't want to come. So now my reaction might be, Oh, here is the 'I've got it wrong' story again: I've been mind-reading with a spot of catastrophizing thrown in.

In this situation, we need to describe the facts and consider an alternative interpretation. It can be fun to think of the wildest, most opposite thought possible. This might even make us smile. It will remind us that thoughts are simply thoughts and do not have to be believed. Maybe a new wildly opposite thought, in this example, could be: 'My teenager thinks I'm the best mum that ever lived in the entire history of mums. She loves hanging out with me! She's just got her phone off.'

Or are there other ways the situation can be viewed? Be curious. What would someone else say? Your sister? 'You always imagine the worst! I know your ways!' Or what about your best friend? Is there another way of looking at things? You could talk, in the third person, as if you were that friend; you could even make the dialogue imaginative – what would someone from a different culture say?

Perhaps imagine catching your thoughts, almost as if they were balls in the air. As thoughts come thick and fast, this image acknowledges how difficult the process can be. At this point, you are not trying to adjust or challenge your thoughts. All you are trying to do is to be aware of them.

Stop seeing your thoughts as instructions or truth. Remind yourself that we humans live with a running commentary in our heads. Thoughts are simply bits of language – mental events, if you will – that move through the mind like the weather passes through the sky, or like a train that comes into a station and then leaves again. You could also imagine watching your thoughts as if they were a film: as a piece of fiction rather than as fact. This will influence whether your thoughts have a chance to affect your feelings and behaviours. Remember the mantra 'Thoughts are NOT facts' and repeat ten times.

You might like to imagine a thought as like catching an old boot rather than a fish – you can throw it back into the river because it doesn't mean anything. It's unsupported by evidence. This will also help you to consider the possibility of other options.

Or you could use a simple, 'Maybe you've just made up that interpretation.' I like the word 'maybe' as it gently introduces doubt about negative thinking. It invites the possibility of a different interpretation. Throw in a 'What else is possible?' too.

Then choose an interpretation of events more in line with those facts – probably in my case, my teenager does like my company, but she loves her friends too. My behaviour follows the new interpretation rather than the previous thought. I have a nice cup of tea rather than desperately wondering whether to chase up my teenager.

The more we tell ourselves a different story, the more we will come to believe a more balanced alternative. Over time this becomes a new way of thinking. This isn't easy and doesn't happen quickly, especially if we have held the same negative thoughts for a long time. But, little by little, we can nurture these new thoughts as if they were tender plants, moving from 'maybe' to 'actually'. We can affirm them by using positive statements – in my own case, when it comes to thoughts about being rejected, I might say, 'Actually, I'm an okay mum', then 'I'm quite a good mum', then 'My teenagers do like hanging out with me on occasion!' to finally, 'Sometimes they actively seek out my company!' We need to keep reminding ourselves of all the evidence against the unhelpful way of thinking.

In time, this process becomes just as automatic as our negative stories were. When people master their thoughts in this way, many of them become less depressed, anxious and angry – and become calmer, less fearful parents. Gradually you will become more and more conscious of these different kinds of thinking traps – in how you view yourself and the world and how you think about your teenagers. My experience is that using these different perspectives to be more flexible in my thinking and to entertain other possibilities has made me a less frantic person and – yes, you've got the gist – parent. Most of the time.

ADDING IN THE MAGIC RETHINKING INGREDIENT – GENTLENESS

We can gently remind ourselves that it is completely normal to create these kinds of painful stories that influence our feelings and lead us to behaviours that do not serve us. 'Oh hello, I recognize this old story' we might say in a soothing way.

We need to just keep deploying that gentle voice: we are not going into battle with the mind and its muddles here. Negative thoughts are simply our human brains doing what they do best and what evolution has designed them to do – remembering, imagining, looking for danger and analysing it.

We might notice how easy it is to catastrophize, to imagine the worst, and to think we cannot cope. These are all to be expected from a brain designed to look for danger in order to avoid it.

My friend Jimi Slattery used to run a wonderful charity called Compassion Matters, which taught compassion in schools and worked with parents and pupils. He reminds me of the need for embracing complexity and ambiguity in the way we (and indeed teenagers) talk to ourselves. 'I see so much polarity in the language parents use,' Jimi says. 'Things are good or bad, harmful or helpful. I recommend parents try to use more ambiguous and gentler language.' We need to be gently training our minds into new neural pathways that will serve us better. At a biological level, when we adopt a soothing voice and a relaxed, knowing smile, our brains release soothing chemicals which bring feelings of calm and comfort. If we talk to ourselves in this way, there will be more chance of forming a new neural pathway that is more psychologically flexible.

This approach has become commonplace and is one psychologists regularly use. A good starting point could be to ask, 'Is this a kind way of thinking about myself? Am I being compassionate to myself when I think like this?' This approach reflects the work of a hero of mine, Professor Paul Gilbert, who has contributed to the government's National Institute for Health and Care Excellence (NICE) guidelines for depression, and has published over a hundred academic papers. He pioneered Compassion Focused Therapy and developed the three systems model of how we manage emotions: the threat, drive and soothing system[6] (see page 75). I try to channel my inner Prof Gilbert, questioning my thoughts but with gentleness, instead of criticizing myself or comparing myself with others who manage not to think like that.

Self-compassion is a theme to which I will return more than once. Because sometimes, kindness is our best bet when, actually, dark thoughts make sense and are inevitable. If one of your teenagers is self-harming, or you yourself get some bad news at work, painful thoughts are a logical response to challenging circumstances. All we can do is find compassion for ourselves in these moments of sadness. While it can be possible to challenge negative thoughts to some extent, it is an obvious and important point that sometimes negative thoughts make sense and are inevitable.

A DIFFERENT ANSWER: CHANGING YOUR FOCUS

If we can't question or re-imagine our thoughts – and sometimes we just can't if they are actually appropriate for the circumstances – we might aim instead to stop the thoughts through distraction, or by thinking about something else entirely. We might say to ourselves, 'Stop! Enough of that. These thoughts are not helping me.' Psychologists, unsurprisingly, call this 'thought stopping'. Even done in a kind and warm way, the cue 'Stop!' is effective because it distracts us and is recognized by the brain as a ticking off and a 'punishment-orientated command', just as we might stay 'Stop' to a small child who is doing something wrong. When we find unhelpful thought patterns or loops taking over, saying 'Stop' in this way weakens the habit. The more frequently we do this, the more effective the cue.

(Just to complicate matters, some therapists believe that thought-stopping actually makes things worse and causes negative thoughts to dig in more – what we resist, persists. Saying no could feel as if we are punishing ourselves with a command, which might actually fire up our threat system. If saying no doesn't work for you, return to being kind and compassionate to yourself. I find sometimes it works for me, sometimes not, and the same will probably be true for you.)

I find consciously focusing on all five senses another good distraction – I ask myself, what am I seeing, hearing, smelling, tasting and touching right now? Doing this wrenches our brains away from experiencing difficult thoughts, giving us a space to feel grounded in the present moment. (This is one aspect of a wider approach known as mindfulness, which also encompasses meditation techniques to focus awareness on what we are doing right here, right now.) It acts as a reminder to our bodies that we are safe, rooted in the present, rather than in the grip of challenging thoughts (often regretting the past, or worrying about the future) that we cannot control. Shifting focus in this way onto our senses also provides us with a more everyday adventure: a contrast and distraction from the drama of dreadful thoughts.

In addition, we might even – odd as it sounds – experience a sense of fun, if for example, we go to the window and notice the birds outside or the colour of some flowers or observe some neighbours chatting. Indoors, we might notice the colour of the bedroom walls without having thought about it for ages. Don't be surprised if you notice some irritating things too, perhaps the smell of drains or the noise of traffic. Noticing the whole of the moment you are in can be grounding and soothing if you pay attention without creating too much of a story. Try just seeing the moment as containing both pleasant and less enjoyable parts.

By doing so, you can escape from your whirling mind for a moment and come back into your body for just long enough to make it impossible to return to the exact place you left off, thus breaking the cycle. The previous thought pattern will not have the same hold on you second time round.

If distraction isn't working, think of something else entirely – something positive, perhaps the times your teenager appreciates you. Decide what you are going to think about. Is it the fury you feel when your teenager leaves their plate in the sink and doesn't do the washing up? Will you let your thoughts jump to all the other times they left the kitchen in a mess? And their bedroom too? And failed to thank you?

Or might you think of the delight you felt when they told you how grateful they were that you remembered their favourite cereal? Or that time when they did the shopping and added in some nice bubble bath for you? Even better, they did so without being asked. Or the time they made you a birthday card?

What we choose to focus on stimulates those neural pathways in our brains. The more we focus on the positive moments for which we can be grateful, the more those neural pathways grow and develop. We can decide on what we will focus on and change our brain's make-up.

I love this technique as a tool to cope with distorted thinking. In each situation, I focus on the positive and what there is to be grateful about. Without sounding too smug, there is almost always something to cherish. The more we think in this way, the more we can counteract wonky thinking and our maddening brains and their habits. Instead of feeling unappreciated (no-one has noticed that the fridge has been filled yet again, for example), we can focus instead on when they recognized our efforts (the handwritten message in the birthday card saying how much we matter to them).

*

While we still have much to learn about how our minds work, we know that our brains are full of glitches, an understanding that has made me gentler on myself when I lose it with my teenagers and start blaming them for everything, including the weather. I have become conscious of quite how wonky our brains are; that they make us quick to catastrophize and to look for evidence for the beliefs that we already hold. But there are also ways to stop us falling into these thinking traps and to outwit many negative thought patterns. Yes, it takes time to tell ourselves different stories. But naming our thoughts, challenging them, using positive statements, and doing all of the above with gentleness, really has made me a less panicky parent. So too has changing my focus if I find I'm losing the parental plot, especially my newfound ability to concentrate on the positive in any situation (well, most of the time).

These new ways of challenging our thoughts can be helpful not just in our lives as parents, but more generally. One of the blessings I have found in being a parent of adolescents is that learning more about the brain has affected all areas of my life, not just my dealings with my children. Once again our teenagers can be a gift. Even better, I've adopted two positive perspectives on parenting that counteract negative thinking: that I am a good enough mother, and that I believe in being gentle with myself when I make mistakes. How we can incorporate these supportive and kindly viewpoints into our inner worlds is the subject of the next chapter.

4

ADOPTING SUPPORTIVE
AND KINDLY VIEWPOINTS

All parents of teenagers experience challenging times, when we feel hopeless and think we are failures who get everything wrong with our offspring. Such thoughts are especially prevalent right now, a time of high parental anxiety, given the relentless headlines that we are facing an adolescent mental health crisis. We can feel hopeless even if we aren't coping with the kind of mega-disasters some people have to deal with: this doesn't mean our problems are not challenging and we don't feel wretched about our inability to deal with them.

I have found it useful to adopt some positive stories about myself, as well as challenging the way I habitually think. Two in particular have proved helpful to me as a parent in these turbulent times, and indeed more broadly in my life – I am good enough, and mistakes are okay. Many of us need ways to dial down the critical voices. I've yet to meet a parent who isn't trying their best and could do with being a bit gentler on themselves. Do so, and you can demonstrate a more relaxed approach to your teenagers, who if anything are even harder on themselves than we parents are.

SAYING NO TO PERFECTIONISM

I blame the rise of perfectionism. It's a dangerous idea that has been gaining traction for several decades now. I know I have often compared myself to other parents and felt like I did not measure up. In a rushed attempt to improve my efforts, I once foolishly bought myself a parental self-help book, titled something along the lines of *How to Be a Brilliant Mum*. Far from helping, it made me feel even worse. I felt that I was not brilliant, and I needed to change.

Or another occasion I was applauded by one of my editors for writing an article well. Rather than delighting in her praise, I felt vulnerable. Maybe I was only liked when I excelled. It is all too easy for our brains to warp success into a condition of love. Perfectionism is damaging for both our teenagers and ourselves.[1] Not only does it engender this miserable feeling of being unworthy, it can also hold us back. Neither we, nor our teenagers, take risks, for fear of exacerbating those unpleasant feelings of failure even more.

This drive for perfectionism was identified by the British psychoanalyst Donald Winnicott as early as the 1950s.[2] He specialized in relationships between parents and children. In his clinical practice, he often met parents who felt like failures: parental shortcomings came with shame and fear of social judgement. Psychologists developed a model for measuring perfectionism in 1991,[3,4] and gradually as a society we have gravitated further and further towards an ideal of flawlessness, even as the challenges we are facing as parents have become more complex.

One reason may be society's fixation on economic growth. In our capitalist system, companies and marketeers encourage us to be dissatisfied with how we are, in the quest for greater sales. A second reason may be the rise of social media and its images of perfect individuals and idealized family life, which have exacerbated our tendency to compare ourselves to others. The mythical perfect parent is alive and well on Instagram. In insidious ways, social media chips away at the feeling that we are fine. (It chips away at many other aspects of our wellbeing too, a topic I look at in more detail in Part Five.) We see other people who seem to be having more fun at family meals than our own dismal affairs, who are more accomplished, richer and more glamorous parents than we are. Whereas once we might have compared ourselves to our neighbours or friends, now we can compare our family life and ourselves to the world's most successful and powerful people.

Not only are we not as impressive as those we see on our screens, we also don't have as many followers, likes or retweets as them. We don't matter on social media in the way they do. Again, naturally, we feel we don't match up. We are not good enough. And we are most certainly not perfect.

This tendency to compare ourselves and our children with others is known rather obviously by psychologists as 'social comparison'. It is not our fault: again, thousands of years of evolution are at work. It turns out that all animals compare themselves, and we too have inherited brains that create this impulse because our survival depended on it.

The difference now is that the digital world offers us far more information about the achievements of others, from another child's exam grades to knowing who has passed their driving test first. These relentless comparisons can cause us heartache. If our child messes up – and whose child doesn't? – we can start to compare ourselves to others who seem to be handling things so much better than us. This is worse for parents whose feelings are enmeshed with their children's and have loose boundaries. A teenager's failure feels like theirs.

A third reason for the ever-expanding trap of perfectionism is our competitive culture. As the Texan academic Kristin Neff has argued, 'Our culture has become so competitive we need to feel special and above average just to feel okay about ourselves . . . [We create] what psychologists call a "self-enhancement bias": puffing ourselves up and putting others down.'[5] Part of this competitive need to feel special came with the rise of the self-esteem movement in the 1980s. If we felt high levels of self-worth – 'You're special!' – then in turn we experienced less depression and anxiety, the argument went. Yet the problem is that this kind of egoistic self-esteem tends to be based on needing to be better than others. Take feeling good about how we dress – it turns out I will not enjoy self-esteem by having an okay wardrobe: to feel good, I need to be thought stylish and fashionable. And crucially, more stylish and fashionable than other mothers.

Relying on self-esteem in this way provides little psychological shelter in a storm. We cannot all be special, and belief in the benefits of the self-esteem movement has largely died out in the psychological science literature. But it remains alive in popular culture. I was struck when reading Hadley Freeman's account of her anorexia that she was tipped into the disease by a friend's comment that she wished 'to be normal like you'.[6] But Hadley didn't want to be normal; she wanted to be special.

While telling ourselves that we are terrific is not the same as telling ourselves we need to be perfect, the two are dangerously close. To flatter our own sense of self, we have to believe that we are amazing people achieving great things, but in order to do that we may start setting unrealistic goals, feats that are beyond us. Indeed, we may start striving for perfection.

How then can we dial down this drive to be the best? Not just in general, but when it comes to being parents? And most importantly, how can we reduce some of the shame and disappointment in ourselves for not managing this? How can we instead believe we are good enough? And make this attitude an essential part of our parental thinking? Four strategies have helped me: believing in the virtues of imperfection, adopting a less goal-oriented approach, focusing on my inner worth, and becoming less judgemental of myself and others.

Why messing up makes sense

To strategy one. Let's return to Winnicott. He coined the phrase 'the good enough mother' in his 1971 book *Playing and Reality*, a collection of papers published during his career. He acknowledged the inevitability of imperfect parenting, believing that the good enough mother starts with an 'almost complete adaption to her infant's needs'. But over time she allows the baby to experience small moments of frustration. She is not perfect, but 'good enough'.

It is not just that we don't need to be perfect, but that we should avoid it for the sake of our children. We need to fail our children on a regular basis so they can learn to live in an imperfect world. There is no such thing as mistakes, only chances to learn. We flourish as a consequence of self-repair and so do our teenagers.

There are many advantages of being imperfect parents for our adolescents. When we admit to our own vulnerabilities, and the muddles we have made, our children realize that it's okay; all of us get stuff wrong from time to time. If our relationships and work lives always run smoothly, and we endlessly meet our objectives and never seem to mess up, the more pressure we put on our children to be the same. By aiming for good enough we allow them to do the same.

Furthermore, witnessing failure and messiness and muddle in us parents can help challenge our teenagers. Teenagers need struggles to grow: the challenge of having imperfect parents can help them do so. If we have failed in our working life, and recovered, we give our children the example that no experience is without value. In my case, having serious depression meant I left my job as a newspaper reporter. It seemed a terrible setback at the time but led to a new life writing about mental health. My teenagers have seen that stumbling blocks can become stepping stones.

The pressure of perfection can further backfire on your children: you will have exhausted yourself by trying to be perfect. I did just this when two of my teenagers were facing exams. I tried to be the perfect 'exam mum': sending good luck cards, buying them wall charts on which to fill out their exam schedules, popping up to their rooms for supportive chats, telling them that it was all going to be fine. One teenager turned to me from their desk and told me that I was actually interrupting them. What they needed was some time to themselves to do some work! It was a relief to stop trying to be the perfect mum. And not being the perfect mum allowed the possibility that my teenagers need not be perfect students either.

A more relaxed approach, Winnicott argues, is to aim for being good enough; and that comes with the acknowledgement that you will not always feel even that. Calmer parenting comes from accepting imperfections, especially when we feel flat. People who are at least risk of serious mental health problems or relationship difficulties are those who can be kind to themselves when they do not feel great.[7] They believe in themselves and feel okay about themselves even on their worst days when they feel they have failed most. They understand that we do not have to be perfect to be loveable.

This kind of psychological flexibility and self-compassion gives people the best launching pad for feeling a steady sense of positive self-worth. It is not influenced by the fluctuations of their achievements, nor by how people around them are doing or how others view them. It is a less tiring way to be a parent: they do not have to convince themselves that they are reaching the heights of perfection that they have targeted to be worthy of their own praise.

The trick is to avoid the extremes of feeling perfect or feeling worthless. On the one hand, perfection is impossible and only sets us up for failure. On the other, if we already believe we are worthless, there is a strong temptation to give up. It is easier to adjust our behaviour and thoughts if we believe we are a unique mixture of everything – from occasionally near-perfect to now and then completely flawed. Realizing we are capable of both good and bad allows us to accept that we will spend most of our time somewhere in the middle – being good enough.

Processes rather than goals

The second way to feel good enough is to look at activities, and our approach to them, as either 'telic' or 'atelic' pursuits. Telic activities – from the Greek *telos*, meaning goal or purpose – dominate our lives. Give the presentation, pass the exam, write the book. The value of each is perceived in terms of the completion of the goal. The more goals we complete, the closer we edge to feeling perfect.

The immediate problem with telic activities, of course, is that finishing the task throws up a new dilemma: if the purpose was to finish the task, what is the purpose now the project is completed? What next? The answer is often to take on another project. Life, and our children, are then in danger of being seen as a series of projects – both personal in the case of parenting, and professional. Our sense of fulfilment is only temporary, during the brief window when a project is completed. The pressure is then on to complete the next project.

Contrast this with atelic (non-goal-based) activities. The value of these pursuits does not lie solely in their completion. To find such activities, ask yourself why you are doing something. Is it for the result? Or because you find it fulfilling? It might be walking for walking's sake, especially circular trips rather than A-to-B walks. Baking for baking's sake, and not necessarily to produce a cake for someone's birthday. Reading a book not because it will deepen your knowledge, but because the subject just interests you.

It is particularly beneficial to partake in an activity at which we are unlikely to excel. If we know from the outset that we are only beginners, just as we are beginner parents, we may be less judgemental and lose our fear of looking silly. Looking silly is good! This is a gentle, practical way of stepping off the perfectionist treadmill. When we know that we are novices, our expectations of ourselves will be low and our self-criticism less vocal.

I remember a climbing trip, finding myself wearing a safety harness attached to a rope. It was terrifying. But good fun too. It was impossible to have any thoughts of perfectionism. The same with a recent game of bridge where the other players were all semi-professionals. They did not voice their bids aloud with 'ums' and 'ahs' as I was used to in my knockabout games, but silently placed bidding cards on the green baize. At the end of the game, they discussed the hand among themselves, in terms I couldn't follow. As it was obvious I couldn't compete from the start, the only thing for it was to forget trying to win and simply live in the moment and enjoy the process.

Enjoying the process in this way need not involve our own action. Sometimes, just reading stories or accounts of different places or times or people in different worlds provides a way of engaging in the lives of those who adopt a less task-focused, approval-seeking mentality.

Adopting a more atelic approach to life means we can escape from focusing only on achieving goals. This is particularly important because our goals are often based on what the world thinks of as achievements. Society is designed to direct us towards outward goals from an early age – getting into a good school, decent exam results, attending a highly rated university, landing an impressive job. But we may be prioritizing other people's view of what makes for achievement over the health of our own emotional lives. Given society's focus on results, it is unsurprising that many parents can also become focused on recognizable measures of success in their children. Get them out of nappies! Tick. Teach them how to read! Tick. Get them to pass their exams! Tick. Teach them how to drive! Tick.

Yet ironically, racing around all day ticking things off lists may make us (and our teenagers) less creative. The comedian John Cleese, in his book on creativity, emphasizes the importance of play, and playing around with ideas.[8] The psychologist Guy Claxton argues that our assumption that the quick-thinking 'hare' brain will outsmart the slower intuition of the 'tortoise' mind is misguided – the more playful, contemplative and less result-driven tortoise often achieves greater rewards and creative outcomes than the hare.[9]

While the atelic approach is hard to adopt, it can bring benefits in defeating perfectionism. To embrace it we need to cultivate a relationship with our own values and beliefs, rather than what the world perceives as important goals.

You're okay anyway

This brings me to my third strategy for feeling good enough: focusing on inner worth. Our inner calm comes from feeling connected with ourselves.

True confidence comes from focusing on our innate qualities as a human being: the gifts with which we were born. These qualities stand, whatever else we do and whatever boxes we tick that are recognized as valuable by others.

To be confident, we must avoid linking our worth as humans to the tasks we take on or the goals we may achieve. We need to approach our existing activities with a new attitude: without dumping all our goals, we must try not to be so goal-fixated. Taking this step is closely linked to ceasing to need outward approval for those same achievements. When we are goal-driven we tend to be drawn not just to the achievements themselves but also to how others will evaluate us as a result. We wish not only to achieve our goals, but for others to recognize them and tell us how well we have done.

We want medals, rewards and praise – what psychologists call 'external reinforcers'. We seek out others to congratulate us on our achievements, and only feel valid if this happens. This of course immediately makes us vulnerable: we cannot control whether anyone pats us on the back or not. However, we can control what we think about ourselves: whether we approve of, or even like, ourselves. In short, whether we believe we are valid. And we are valid because of every miraculous breath we take.

If we can naturally feel okay about ourselves, we can be more motivated by activities chosen for our own enjoyment and fulfilment, rather than those designed to please others. This can make life much less stressful. For many years, I looked for outward approval – or was 'looking for myself where I was not' in the words of one therapist. I only felt good when someone else affirmed my value. I was only okay as a teenager if someone included me in their party, or a teacher praised my work, or the school newspaper published an article I had written. As I became an adult, this habit continued: I only felt good enough when someone else affirmed me. What I had done, or written, or indeed was, was not good enough without external approval.

But given that I didn't feel good enough within myself, no amount of outside affirmation was ever going to fill the void. So I redoubled my efforts. Only now have I begun to feel that I'm okay anyway and am less needy of others telling me so. The less I seek outside validation and the more I realize I don't need it, the more it seems to come to me. Which is unsurprising when you think about it – how do we expect anyone else to approve of or like us if we don't approve of or like ourselves?

It is such a relief. I find myself no longer relying on other people's approval, but instead focusing on my own validation. It is as if a weight has been lifted from my shoulders. I feel a whoosh of freedom. I am no longer like a small child who needs someone else to pat them on the head to feel alright about themselves. I feel good enough.

Becoming less judgemental

Finally, strategy four. We've discussed deploying a gentle voice when challenging our negative thoughts, and this is particularly helpful when we find ourselves being judgemental. Doing stuff without judging how good we are at doing it, or what others might think of us doing it in the first place, is my final way of defeating the curse of perfectionism. If we can accept ourselves and our own perceived failings, we can accept other people's. This is important. For example, we may feel we are somehow superior when we hear that someone's child has dropped back a year at school. Our own insecurity as parents means we may delight in such news: we cannot be such bad parents ourselves, as someone else is worse.

However, the more we judge others, the more we judge ourselves. It is counterproductive: it puts us back on the validation treadmill. By not judging others, we allow ourselves a more open and curious approach, outside the dynamic of winning or losing, of being right or wrong.

Just as painful is the feeling that other parents are judging our parenting. I remember hearing via the grapevine that another parent thought one of my teenagers was spoilt. One answer is to accept that we can't control whether anyone will judge us. It's likely that some will. We must be aware that criticism is likely to affect us only if we agree with it on some level. So, the best way to become more immune to judgement is to stop judging ourselves.

We must allow ourselves to be aware that judgement directed towards us is usually less about us, and more about the judge (though of course there are times when we do muck up, and we do need a ticking off, albeit kindly delivered). But in general, if someone is judging you, make a point of noticing what sort of mood that person is in. Compassion Focused Therapy believes in asking ourselves what someone else is motivated by. Are they feeling threatened? Probably. Or driven to get something done?

Maybe. Or wishing to soothe you? Unlikely. Chances are that if someone is being judgmental, they are not coming from a happy place, and if we make that connection, we can notice in turn what motivates us in response. Rather than feel threatened, we can choose not to take the judgement of others personally.

This is true even in the case of self-judgement. If you are judging yourself, you may be looking at yourself through someone else's eyes. You have probably been practising self-judgement or caring about the opinions of others for quite a while, and it may take some effort to break the habit. Be patient with yourself and give yourself credit for knowing how to go about it. While these concepts are simple, they're not always easy to apply. Start by asking some questions: how can you rethink these thoughts so that they are less critical and more understanding?

Despite all our efforts to be less critical, such thoughts have a way of popping up because it is so much part of our society to judge and rate the behaviour of others. It is also part of how our brains are made: we are looking for safety, and safety comes from being accepted by the group, rather than being criticized as not okay. But while we cannot always control judgemental thoughts, we can become aware of the extent to which they are prevalent. You might hear yourself talking about another parent, 'She's much too bossy. She always tried to get her child to finish her food. That's why her daughter has eating problems now!' If you do, pause. You could label the pattern with a general statement such as 'Judging thoughts have arrived', or 'My critical voice is coming up again'.

You might wonder if you are constructing a narrative about a dynamic that you don't fully understand or know. We rarely know what someone is going through. Other parents are likely to be the experts on their own teenagers. No matter how much we disagree with someone's parenting style, or indeed anything else about them, it is not our place to judge if we can possibly help it. Instead, we can try to acknowledge the inevitable complexity of the situation rather than thinking in black and white, bad and good terms.

If nothing else works, you might try connecting with your body with a generous movement, like wrapping your arms around your torso with a hug. Or give yourself a smile. Even a generous stretch of your arms up to the sky could make you feel more open and a bit freer from the curse of making comparisons and judgements in a fruitless bid to be perfect.

ADOPTING A 'GOOD ENOUGH' APPROACH WITH YOUR TEENAGERS

The less we try to be perfect parents ourselves, the less we are likely to impose perfectionism on our children. Believing in the virtues of imperfection, adopting a less goal-oriented approach, focusing on their inner worth, and becoming less judgemental are all good approaches to engaging with our teenagers. In my day-to-day family interactions, enjoying the process of any of their endeavours or pursuits, rather than concentrating on a results-based performance approach, has proved the most helpful way to become a calmer parent. This is about being with our children in everyday moments, rather than focusing on the results of our parenting.

Take helping your teenager with their homework. Rather than worrying if their essay will get a top mark, a happier collaboration might involve discussing sentences, the creative process and how to structure arguments. Yes, your child might want that top mark too, but it is not something they or you can control. What they can control, and maybe enjoy, is the actual writing. They can get 'in the flow', into the moment when their competence matches the challenge at hand. The subsequent absorption in the process of writing helps them avoid the judgemental narrative in their own head. They too can adopt more flexible thinking, becoming less goal-focused and believing more in their inner worth, avoiding being judgemental of themselves and others.

We could reinforce these ideas about how to defeat thoughts of parental perfectionism in our inner worlds by using affirmations, simple supportive statements like 'I do not need to try to be a perfect parent' or 'It is okay to not feel okay sometimes about being a mother' or 'Children accept that parents make mistakes!' We can stick them on a mirror – somewhere they will be seen easily and influence our thinking every day and become more automatic. We are innately imperfect; that is a good thing, and once we realize this we can settle instead for something achievable.

REDEFINING MISTAKES

Let's assume we're cracking the 'good enough' game. What about redefining what we imagine are mistakes? It's a closely related topic, but one deserving of its own section as it's proved such a liberation to change my thinking on this. The point is, as parents we will mess up. We will not always manage to be the parents we would want to be. Our children's adolescence is a time of such change that there are endless opportunities to make what seem like mistakes. No other animal has such an intense period of development as human adolescence, when so much is happening to our offspring. Given the pace of new experiences we are encountering, it is hardly surprising that we parents can lack confidence and feel as if we are tripping up. All the time!

The challenge is to allow ourselves to view experiences that we might previously have thought of as failures as chances to learn. Mistakes are okay. In the words attributed to the inventor Thomas Edison – familiar to every entrepreneur, motivational speaker and sports coach – 'I have not failed. I've just found 10,000 ways that won't work.' That is not to say these learning opportunities won't be painful and difficult. But the more we see that what society commonly thinks of as setbacks are in fact opportunities to learn, then the more our confidence will be boosted and may become (almost) unshakeable. The glory of this period of steep learning and intense experiences for us as parents is that it is impossible not to emerge wiser. Just as the destructive volcanic ash creates the most fertile soil, so do our most intense and difficult times often lead to the most growth.

LEARNING FROM FAILURE –
IN THE LEAST PAINFUL WAYS POSSIBLE

The road to calmer parenting is paved with many bumps and potholes. They are agonizing at the time, but are there to teach us something new.

I have been something of a late developer as a parent. I remember, to take just one example of many supposed failures, a fairly recent setback when I decided to leave one of my older children in charge of a younger child's teenage party. With no adults present, chaos ensued. So did a major row between the two siblings: one guest was so drunk that the older child asked them to leave, while the younger teenager (whose party it was) wanted them to stay. There was a lot for me to learn about boundaries, rules and sibling relationships.

Now instead of allowing these kinds of supposed setbacks to knock my confidence as a parent, I try to be grateful for them. My route to becoming a confident parent is not to imagine I will do everything right, but to be gentler with myself when, inevitably, things don't go according to plan. In these moments we can congratulate ourselves on our good intentions and our willingness to learn.

I might be giving the impression that this is easy. In fact, I have needed many years of trial and error to embed this view in my psyche. And there have been painful times en route. Part of this willingness to rethink supposed failures is to remind ourselves that life is in constant flux, that our learning is continuous, and that this is an endlessly fascinating journey.

I am reassured by the idea that parenting is a constant and unfolding process. However much we develop as parents, there is always more to understand about our teenagers and indeed ourselves. I was not the same parent when I was a younger mother as I am now, and I will keep changing as the years go by.

New lessons must be learned throughout the teenage years and beyond. Relationships are always evolving and need constant reinvention if we wish them to grow with us. No matter how straight and true the road we drive, we must always make course corrections. Even on a straight road, we continually turn the wheel and make frequent tiny adjustments.

Affirmations can once again help us to adopt this growth mindset. Two that I like particularly are 'I am changing as a parent and will love myself in each precious moment' and 'I am capable of growing as a parent in incredible and unpredicted directions'.

And if rethinking supposed failures remains elusive, remember other ways to challenge negative thoughts: deploying a gentle voice, naming thoughts to tame them, coming up with alternative thoughts in a playful way, stopping seeing thoughts as instructions, treating yourself gently, and changing your focus – all ways to shift stubborn thinking styles discussed in the previous chapter.

THE MORE THE MERRIER

Counterintuitively, the more we make mistakes, the less fearful of making them we become. By embracing new challenges as a parent, by trying stuff out and getting it wrong, a new perspective can creep up on us: that the world is full of infinite variety. We cannot fail at something; instead we can be curious about trying something new and seeing if it suits us and enjoying the possibility of change. Indeed, the same approach can help our teenagers. One of my favourite phrases for any teenager facing a drama is 'What else is possible?' Nothing is fixed. Not their grades, their appearance or their personality. There can be a terror in thinking all these things are decided, but they are not.

The changes we make do not have to be big; they can involve small ways of embracing different approaches to a task. Allow the fact that we parents are often put in a double bind by our teenagers. Whatever we do will not be right. They tell us not to call them. So we don't. Then we are blamed for not being in touch. In the past, I might have said sorry, or spent time working out where the supposed mistake was. Now I would be curious about our different perspectives, and not blame myself in the same way.

Let them come home on their own from a party, even if a bit of you is screaming, 'I'm making a terrible error,' and they might have to walk home because they miss the night bus. And trust in yourself that if you do make a mistake, it is at least one step on the path to feeling less daunted and trying new ways of doing things in the future.

*

Let's end this chapter on a note of realism. Yes, learning to feel good enough and to reframe mistakes have been wonderful additions to my ways of thinking since I became a mother to teenagers – and I remain grateful to them for prompting me to adopt these new approaches. However, we can all still find ourselves racked with parental guilt as things will inevitably go wrong. Reassure yourself that despite blips, you can always make amends so that disagreements don't feel scary or permanent for either you or your children. I've found the best way to do this is to contextualize what happened. If you have screamed at your teenager for not clearing up the kitchen because you were shattered by a long day at work, later that night you can always go upstairs and say, 'I was tired and I took it out on you. I was being human.' 'Rupture and repair' is the psychological term for this: there is disconnect, and then, through acknowledgement, reconnection. Even then, we won't always remember to 'repair'. Emotions can run high, both for us and our teenagers. But even this is okay. There are ways of managing our feelings, so at a deep level our teenagers feel secure. This is the subject of the next chapter.

5

COPING WITH
CHALLENGING EMOTIONS

In the last two chapters, we've discussed new perspectives on thinking traps and embraced the concepts of being good enough parents and believing that mistakes are okay. Thinking in these ways can help us feel more positive, so it has been worth spending time considering how we might adjust our thoughts. Changing how we think can change how we feel.

But sometimes feelings can overwhelm us. These feelings may well be natural and understandable reactions to the roller-coaster ride that comes with bringing up teenagers. They may be feelings that, as we have seen, have been deeply buried in our subconscious from our own childhoods, which only now bubble up. Parenting a teenager can open up a dark side of ourselves. One friend told me that adolescence isn't difficult for teenagers, but for their parents.

I know I felt a new depth and intensity of feeling as the mother of adolescents, one I hadn't known before, and certainly hadn't experienced when the children were younger. Who isn't going to feel desperate if a teenager is suicidal? Or mad with a murderous rage if they've trashed the kitchen and the bin is full of empty vodka bottles – yet again? Or threatened by a shaking fear if we can't get hold of them? Sometimes in these states I would observe smiley young mothers walking their charges to school and think, if they only knew what dramas lay ahead.

These are understandable responses, provoked by life with adolescents, and our first instinct may be to wish we didn't have to experience such painful and powerful sensations. Equally, we worry that our own strong feelings may impact our teenagers. I regret the times I have shouted at my adolescents, unable to contain my fury.

But what if these powerful feelings are actually a blessing? Our culture tends to value our cognitive thinking brains over our emotional minds, so it's easy to become numb to our feelings. But emotions can give us insights. They can tell us more about what we are drawn to, and what we want to avoid, as well as what others are feeling – as long as they are not out of control. I have been particularly drawn to the work of the renowned parenting author Steve Biddulph, whose latest book, *Wild Creature Mind*, is about how we've lost touch with the 'animal' or feeling parts of our minds. Biddulph says we need to trust our gut feelings, and I agree.[1]

The trick is not to be frightened of our feelings, and to learn how to regulate them. Thanks to our teenagers' provocations, we can be emboldened to find compassionate new ways to deal with, and benefit from, such strong passions. In turn we can be good models for our teenagers of how to do this, given that they too are often coping with overwhelming emotions, and help them to talk openly too. Studies have found that the ability to express negative feelings protects against future depression.[2] The more we embrace feelings ourselves, the more our teenagers are likely to express their own feelings without fear or shame of being judged. We want to give them the message that emotions are okay, and nothing they can't handle. That it's okay to cry if they are a boy, or to be angry if they are a girl.

WHAT EXACTLY IS AN EMOTION?

In 1890, the pioneering psychologist William James defined four basic emotions – fear, grief, rage and love.[3] More recently, the psychologist Carroll Izard took it up to ten – fear, anger, shame, contempt, disgust, guilt, distress, interest, surprise and joy. Any other emotions, such as love and envy, are just combinations of these ten.[4]

All these emotions express themselves physically in some way, particularly in our facial expressions. The face has more than forty muscles, many of them around the mouth and eyes. Fear may feel like a knot in the stomach or tightness in the throat; embarrassment may cause us to blush; anxiety may come with a churning stomach or dry mouth, sweating and shortness of breath. Sadness may bring a feeling of heaviness and fatigue. Joy may be accompanied by a feeling of lightness in the body and a warm heart.

We have numerous sayings referring to this mind-body connection. We describe an angry person as 'hot-headed', someone who is doubtful as having 'cold feet', someone 'being paralysed with fear' if frightened, or having 'nerves of steel' if they are calm. Some psychologists also point out that emotions have different physical energies. Positive emotions such as excitement, delight and astonishment make us feel more energetic; depressed or bored emotions can make us feel lethargic.

Psychologists believe that certain emotional responses are basic and automatic, while others can be learned (or conditioned) through repeated experiences. For example, our initial reaction to seeing a dog may be to smile and laugh. But after being bitten by a dog, we may learn the emotional response of fear. This is called classical conditioning.

There are moments when we have little control over our feelings. Many of us find it hard to stay rational when we feel bursts of fury or waves of sadness. This is unsurprising given the often unpleasant bodily sensations that accompany these strong emotions. This is especially true if our emotions are triggered by traumatic events from the past. Some people are born more sensitive to these moments of reawakened trauma than others, while some – for example, those with post-traumatic stress disorder – can become more sensitive. In this case, our feelings can overwhelm us. Psychologists call this 'emotional dysregulation'.

If we wish to be more measured, authoritative but empathetic parents, we need to find ways to deal with moments when we might be overwhelmed by our emotions, especially when we feel anger and fear and we can't think our way out of trouble. While we cannot stop emotions, we can learn some ways to manage or modulate them with compassion, to put them into context and be less reactive.

PLAYING DETECTIVE

Managing feelings is a process psychologists call 'emotional regulation'. It begins with becoming more attuned to what exactly we are feeling, just as we are learning to figure out our thinking styles. Often we are not sure, especially in complex situations. Moreover, there may be a need that underlies our feelings, of which we may be even less aware.

I like a technique developed by the clinical psychologist Marshall Rosenberg,[5] who was best known for his ideas about Non-Violent Communication (NVC). Rosenberg developed two lists of basic human feelings. The first list has about a hundred feelings we can experience when our needs are being met – feelings like being calm, confident and mellow. The second list is another hundred or so feelings we can experience when our needs are not fulfilled – like being distressed, hurt or sad. The idea is for us to identify our feelings, as opposed to our thoughts or interpretations. In NVC these processes are referred to as 'evaluations'.

The mindfulness teacher Mary Louise Morris introduced me to this approach. 'I've noticed that just being able to identify their feelings, without being asked to explain them, can bring relief to adults, as well as teenagers,' she says. You could ask a teenager to describe the feeling in their body. Is it a lump, or a tightness, or a churning? Perhaps it has a colour? Doing so creates a slight sense of objectivity and spaciousness. And often, when you describe the feeling, it begins to change. I have done this myself in therapy. I will describe a tension in my chest if I'm angry, for example, but as I do so, the feeling begins to move, and sometimes melts altogether. I've paid the feeling the attention it needed. On other occasions, I need a second step: to identify the need underlying the feeling, and clarify it into some kind of resolution of what to do. The basic idea is that frustration, anger, sadness or other challenging feelings are the result of unmet needs.

It might be a need for autonomy, a need for connection or a need for some kind of physical nurturing. Once we have identified what needs underpin our strong feeling, we can plot how to meet them. NVC resources online provide lists of feelings and needs which can be printed out, and apps such as iGrok ('Grok' meaning to understand and empathize, coined in a sci-fi novel by Robert A Heinlein) also have lists which can be easily referred to when you are out and about.[6] I often use this approach with my teenagers. What need is underneath that feeling? What might they do to fulfil it? If encouraged to find their own answers, they take responsibility for sorting themselves out and feel better as a result.

I'm a fan of this approach of taking responsibility for our own feelings. The truth is, they are largely ours. While other people can affect our feelings, it does not necessarily help us to put too much blame on them. Then there's nothing we can do, as we can't change other people. But we can change ourselves and our reactions to others, and this is empowering.

When I first had therapy, I spent much of my sessions accusing others of making me feel bad. The therapist I was working with, Kristen Gygi,[7] introduced what at first felt like a radical idea. What if I was talking less about all these other difficult people and more about myself? Yes, others impact us, but we have agency in how we choose to respond. What if I could do something about how I felt about myself, rather than playing the blame game?

The only person we can truly change is ourselves, as we've seen. So play detective. Ask yourself, what has made you feel so strongly about something? Could it be the aforementioned longing for something? An unmet need? Where did that feeling come from?

Let's say I feel furious about my teenager's unmade bed and bowl of congealing cereal on the bedside table, or a floordrobe of dirty laundry (which I often am). Might it have something to do with how I am feeling in the present? Did I arrive home from work tense? Did I have a tough chat with someone earlier? Is that resentment spilling out onto a child now?

Or am I reacting to something I felt about myself in my past? As we have seen, this can continually play out in the present.

My mother rarely asked us to tidy our rooms, which means I find it hard to tell my own children in a straightforward way that I need them to keep their rooms clean. Is my real frustration more about my own inability to set guidelines, or express myself honestly – which perhaps I copied from my own mother, who rarely corrected us when I was growing up, perhaps from a fear of being disliked herself? Keep on bringing to mind the way in which you were parented. Remind yourself that you don't want to re-enact old scripts.

All of this playing detective has helped me process my own feelings, and become better at regulating them. But sometimes I just want them to make their bed.

ACCEPTANCE

Regulating our feelings is not just about identifying them and taking responsibility for them. It is also about accepting that these difficult moments are going to happen, but they are not all of us, just a small part of us that needs our attention. While anger and fear might not seem in any way useful, and they are deeply unpleasant to experience, they evolved to help us survive and avoid danger. You might try the metaphor of a sailing boat to accept such difficult feelings and improve your ability to stay emotionally regulated.

Imagine a small boat with canvas sails. Now think of all the different features it needs to cruise along, such as the dimensions of its sails, the amount of wind needed to fill them, and how tightly or loosely they are attached to the mast. Remind yourself that a boat stays upright because equal and opposite forces keep the craft steady and moving. A boat sailing properly copes with a great deal of push and pull.

Apply this image to your own life. We sometimes have the impression that our human lives should – almost literally – be plain sailing. We may imagine that to be happy and balanced we should be free from fear and anger and even free from challenging life events. But imagine instead that you are like a sailing boat: once you do, you can see that a mixed picture is more realistic.

Imagine what would happen if conditions were too easy on our boat? Imagine the boat leaning to one side and tipping, going nowhere because the wind is not strong enough. Some gusts of wind are needed for the sails to fill and for the boat to right itself, and for the sail to become upright and tense again. Now imagine if that tension becomes too much: the grip needs to be loosened to let the sail billow out. Joy needs to be reintroduced to ease the boat back on its way.

Becoming more aware of the inevitability and, indeed, the necessity of all types of different feelings can help us to accept them as part of the messy business of being human. We can lean into them. Letting them be there gives them acknowledgement, and sometimes permission to disappear. And crucially, we will be less likely to act on them.

THE POSITIVES – SEEING
THE GOOD SIDE OF EMOTIONS

Embracing our feelings can be made easier by realizing that these moments of emotional overwhelm are not entirely negative. They can lead to intimacy, provide us with psychological insights about ourselves, and lead to change. First, let's consider the issue of intimacy. Sharing intensely emotional moments can make us feel close to one another. There is huge warmth to be gained when we feel desperate, and someone gives us a hug. Trying to talk us out of our sadness has no place in that moment of emotional connection. There is a universal desire in human beings to have our feelings understood and acknowledged.

Without showing our feelings, how can anyone ever know us? The American academic and wonderful storyteller Brené Brown puts this well: if we can't show vulnerability, she reasons, if we can't take risks, then nothing good can happen – no love, no intimacy, no trust, no creativity, no real joy.[8]

We may resist sharing our vulnerabilities for fear that others might reject us: our ancestors relied on being accepted in the group for survival. When someone asks how you are, it is easy to say, 'I'm fine', whatever your emotional state. This is particularly true for some fathers, who can struggle with showing their vulnerability. Some men still feel there is only one narrow way of being a father, largely based on traditional ideas of masculinity, which are about strength. In turn, some mothers often find it difficult to own their feelings of extreme anger. Women are raised to be people who care and nurture for others, and a furious woman is not someone society welcomes.

Yet hiding our vulnerabilities means we may miss out on the prize of intimacy which meets so many human needs – the desire to belong, the wish to trust and connect with others, to be open and express ourselves freely, and know that we will not be judged. I remember, aged around 14, finding my mother sobbing in the kitchen. I had been especially grumpy on the way home from school – nominally about the click of the indicator in her new car, but actually about not being included in a trip with some girls in my class. She told me how upsetting she found my rudeness and how rejected she felt – when all she had done had been to come and collect me! I was amazed to discover her vulnerability, which she normally kept hidden. As a result I felt much closer to her, and more aware of the consequences of my behaviour, indeed that what I did affected her at all.

There's clearly a balance here: sharing our vulnerability with our teenagers (as opposed to the adults in our lives) needs to be handled carefully. No teenager wants an overly vulnerable parent. Geraldine Thomas, a psychotherapist who works with families, uses doll figures to represent family members.[9] When a parent doll falls over, children always rush to pick them up. Teenagers are often coping with their own overwhelming feelings; they can't routinely cope with ours too. But I've found there's much to be said for on occasion letting your teenager know that you too bleed.

The second advantage of being open about what we are feeling is that these feelings provide us with psychological insights about ourselves. Emotions convey information, as long as they are not out of control. Clearly, if we feel warm and loving towards someone, then we want to spend time with them. If our feeling is one of contempt, then we wish to avoid someone. Recognizing this is what psychologists call 'emotional awareness'. Being aware of what a feeling is, giving it a name and exploring the truth of what is really happening emotionally can lead us to accept the feeling and use it as a guidance system. Language can help here. When our teenager has taken our credit card and bike key, instead of saying to ourselves, 'I am angry,' we could try saying, 'This is anger.' By doing this, we are quietly acknowledging to ourselves the presence of emotions, while allowing detachment. We could add 'right now' to remind ourselves that all feelings pass. We are accepting their existence in the moment.

By contrast, if we refuse to experience our negative feelings – by ignoring them, suppressing them, or distracting ourselves – they can often intensify, leading to higher levels of distress and unresolved problems, and sometimes even to physical expression such as headaches, tension or illness. To work on our feelings, we must unpack them, be curious about them, face up to them, and at times sit with unpleasant sensations.

The more we learn to explore emotions – not just difficult ones but happier ones too – the more we see them as something that can contribute to our own psychological growth. These ways of thinking about emotions differently may make it easier for us to accept difficult feelings when they arise, as they will, especially when confronted by strong emotions in our teenagers. Such understanding may make us less reactive if a teenager swears at us, or bursts into hysterical tears. But there are also practical things we can do to cope better when we are experiencing strong emotions.

GETTING PRACTICAL

We have established that our brains were developed to be highly sensitive to threat, which is why we're so good at negative thinking. Luckily we also have a 'soothing system', which we can use when we want to cope with tough feelings. This soothing system is known as the parasympathetic nervous system. It helps us rest, digest and calm down. (We also have a 'drive' system, which helps us achieve goals, according to the three-system model developed by my friend the psychologist Professor Paul Gilbert, whom we met in an earlier chapter when talking about developing a kindly voice.[10]) We can activate the soothing system by physically relaxing. The more time we spend using the soothing part of our nervous system, the more we can reappraise and reduce the power of our threat system and the strong feelings of fear or anger that arise from it, when they do not serve us.

Moving on from feeling threatened will allow more reasoned conversations with our teenagers about their behaviour, rather than confronting them when we are still seething with emotion. This avoids our teenager 'catching' our own feelings – or us catching theirs! Threat leads to threat. Instead we want to de-escalate, and calmly problem-solve together.

Before we do this, we need a pause from the immediate heat of the moment. Becoming aware of our breathing and slowing it down, even for as little as 90 seconds, gives us the space to cope with our feelings and those of a distressed teenager. **Concentrating on breathing** helps us in three ways: first, because it acts as a new physical anchor. Instead of paying attention to all the unpleasant physical sensations that come with strong emotions, we focus on the more pleasant sensation of breathing. Second, mindful breathing shifts our focus to the present moment, away from whatever has caused the emotional storm. This can simplify things when we are overwhelmed. And third, mindful breathing tricks the brain into thinking that our emotional state is different from what it actually is. Focussing on our breathing reassures our body that we are safe after all. When we are happy, our breathing is regular and steady. Regular, mindful breathing reduces the stress hormone cortisol by activating the parasympathetic (relaxing) nervous system.

There are other advantages to using breathing techniques to cope with strong feelings. The act of breathing is our own: it is a technique we can use at any time and in any place, and one that forms part of many approaches, from yoga to meditation. Quite simply, it is something to which we can always turn.

Once we feel a bit calmer, there's another basic mindful **breath awareness exercise** we can use if we have more time and are not in the throes of an emotional drama with a teenager. I like it because it's so simple: after all, when we are het up, anything complex may be beyond us. We are not trying to slow or change our breathing, but to become more mindful and aware of it. Note each breath – this breath in, this breath out. Or count your breaths.

Close your eyes if that feels comfortable. Feel your breath. Notice the air moving through your nose or mouth. Notice the rising and falling of your belly. Notice the rising and falling of your chest. If it feels right for you, you may want to try to let go of tension in the belly region and make sure the breath has a chance to go all the way down. Keep paying attention to the physical feeling of your breathing.

Notice when your mind wanders from your breathing. Gently return your attention to the breath. Don't worry if you find your mind fretting or the dangerous feelings remaining – come back again to the next breath.

Observe your feelings. Just sit and pay attention. As hard as it is, observe them with an open, non-judgemental curiosity. Sometimes labelling them can help. And then gently let them go, like leaves floating down a stream. Come back to your breath repeatedly, without judgement or any expectations. When you're ready, gently open your eyes.

My next idea might not sound so appealing, but bear with me. Welcome to the vagus nerve, the longest cranial nerve in the body, made up of thousands of fibres divided into two bundles. It connects the brain with multiple organs ('vagus' meaning 'wandering' in Latin). The vagus is the main nerve in the parasympathetic nervous system. When the nerve is stimulated, it increases what is known as vagal tone, slowing the heart rate and breathing. In the early 2000s, researchers showed that **stimulating the vagus nerve** with electrical devices could help some patients who were severely depressed.

There are ways to improve vagal tone at home, though we need more research on the efficacy of different approaches. I've found the easiest method is to give myself a cold shock – whether that's splashing my face with cold water, taking a cold shower, sticking my feet into a bowl of iced water, wrapping an ice pack in cloth and placing it on my chest, or going outside with minimal clothing (the quickest and easiest method of all).

A final option is to **consciously relax the body**. This isn't about denying our feelings, rather about allowing us to experience them in full, but in a more comfortable way. Nor is it about pressurizing ourselves to get results, which as we've seen is generally a bad idea. Go gently with yourself, and don't expect relaxation exercises to work every time – half the time is fine. You can use the following relaxation technique even in the rush of a busy day of looking after children and going to work, perhaps as you sit in the car waiting for your teenager to emerge from the station, or as you stand by the front door, waiting for them to decide what they are going to wear before you drive them to a gig.

The technique involves gradually relaxing all your muscles in turn. Practise this ahead of when you might need it, then you can call on this technique easily and quickly when you are overwhelmed by difficult feelings. Lie down on a rug or the floor and close your eyes (having first given your teenager advance notice, so they don't think you're even more bonkers than they already imagine you are). Begin by breathing in through your nose. Hold your breath for a few seconds, then breathe out. Take another deep breath through your nose. Imagine your tummy is a balloon filling with air and then, as you breathe out, imagine all the air escaping.

Stretch out your legs in front of you, pointing your toes. Stretch out your arms either side of you, stretching all the way through to your fingertips. Now start to tense all the muscles in your body. Begin with your toes. Curl them over so they are clenched. Then think about tensing the muscles all the way up your legs and through your tummy. Imagine something is about to step on your tummy, then tense it into a hard wall. Tense your arms as well, so your arms are by your sides and even your fists are clenched. Bring your shoulders up around your ears. Last of all, scrunch up your face. Push your lips together and frown down into your face so your forehead is all crinkled. Now make your arms and legs go limp again. Relax your shoulders by bringing them down. Imagine yourself as a floppy rag doll. Take a deep breath in through your nose and breathe out again. Notice how relaxed and calm you feel.

A final way to cope with strong feelings is to **write things down**. The act of putting pen to paper, or finger to keyboard, takes time. It can give you space to let strong feelings subside before you engage your thinking brain in order to decide what best to do next. Jot down, 'How am I feeling right here, right now?' Studies suggest that this kind of expressive writing can help us process our feelings.[11]

Try 'free expressive writing' if you have more time (not during a drama). Just freely write down all your feelings each night, focusing on the most troublesome ones, with no other rules. If you feel embarrassed, you can get rid of your scribbles after you have finished. The expression of these feelings is the most important part. Remind yourself that this is about emotions, not thoughts. Keep making that distinction. You may want to draw or illustrate your writing too. You might try writing a list of your fears, and then replace 'I'm afraid of . . .' with 'Just allow yourself to feel frightened of . . .' The allowing diminishes the feeling and can be healing to the mind, and even the body, when they're besieged by strong emotions. A recent study showed that patients who were asked to write about their feelings before surgery healed more quickly than those who didn't.[12]

Alternatively, another literary opener might be to wonder, 'What if I could find compassion for my fearful self?' Perhaps imagine yourself as a small child. Picture your adult self taking that small child under their wing and giving them a hug. Be curious to see how these different approaches feel to you. Curiosity is better than fear, and I have found it a useful tool for emotional regulation and exploration. It's a bit like being my own detective, investigating what is really happening in my emotional life with the help of a notepad. I am not trying to think in a different way, but acknowledging and exploring my feelings with compassion.

*

To conclude, feelings are important, and one of the ways our teenagers can be a blessing is by forcing us to feel deeply and powerfully in ways we have not previously experienced as parents. They can also force us to find ways of managing our feelings. Allowing those feelings is about being intimate with ourselves, and knowing that even difficult feelings are not all bad. Sadness can be a sign that we might need to do something active or creative. Fear can lead to us finding our courage. Guilt can motivate us to reach out to others. Anger expressed safely can be harnessed in a good way as energy for causes about which we care: what we do with our anger is what matters.

We can't avoid emotions. But that does not mean that we should lose ourselves to them or let them overpower us. If anger, or any other emotion, feels overwhelming or has built up for some reason, take it somewhere safe and let it out, using some of the strategies in this chapter. Let people know you need some time to work out how you feel. Take that time, sense your way into that emotion and get to the bottom of it. Then come back to the topic – and anyone else involved – when you are more grounded and clearer. It's possible to feel strongly about something and remain cool, calm and collected. And we can all learn to do it.

6

LOOKING AFTER YOUR
PHYSICAL HEALTH

Regulating our emotions will alter our interactions with our teenagers, as well as our relationships with others and indeed ourselves. We may become calmer and more relaxed if we understand our own feelings. Our physical wellbeing, and whether we nurture our bodies, will also change our relationships with our adolescents: we are much better placed to cope if we are in good health. Ironically, the pressure that teenagers can put us under as parents can be the spur we need to finally exercise and eat well. In my case, I found that looking after my physical health became essential once I was the parent of adolescents, because of the physical and emotional demands involved, such as late-night taxi driving, or the strain of being concerned about their wellbeing. We will also create a healthy mirror for our teenagers, many of whom exercise less[1] and are more at war with their bodies than ever before.

While physical health might seem separate from emotional welfare, the two are intimately connected. When we are distracted or overwhelmed by our negative thoughts or emotions, we're less likely to choose to eat healthily or take exercise. By looking after our emotional wellbeing we are better able to look after our physical wellbeing. And vice versa. If we cherish and nurture our bodies, we cherish and nurture our minds: the links between gut health and mental health, for example, are now widely recognized (and I wrote a book about them – *The Happy Kitchen!*[2]).

That's all well and good; we all know the importance of moving more, eating healthily and sleeping well. But our good intentions may crumble under the pressures of too little time and too much stress. We may have to find different ways to think about food and exercise through this phase of our lives.

THE SECRET TO GETTING FITTER

What if we became more sympathetic to our resistance to what we think of as exercise? By which I mean going to the gym and standing on a treadmill. The fact is, we never evolved to take exercise for the sake of exercise in this way. Far from it. We evolved to avoid needless exertion. The reason is that physical activity costs calories that, until recently, were always in short supply (and still are for many people). When food is limited, every calorie spent on physical activity is a calorie not spent on other critical functions, such as maintaining our bodies, storing energy and reproducing.

However, we did evolve to be active in two ways, ways that might suit us as parents who haven't always got the time or inclination to go to the gym. First, we moved because we had no choice. We either moved to get food or to gather wood, and sometimes we moved in a frantic rush to escape predators. Secondly, we moved because it was fun and what we wanted to do – mainly playing games or dancing. Let's look at both of these.

There are everyday ways we can replicate a short, sharp shock of movement, the kind of movement our ancestors engaged in if they were being chased by a lion. (I'm assuming you don't need help with pottering, the other kind of movement our ancestors practised.) It might mean deliberately finding a way of cycling uphill on the way home from work. Or sprinting to tell your teenager it is supper time. How much of this kind of intense cardiovascular exercise do we need? I am wary of recommending a specific amount or type of exercise, as many such prescriptions are arbitrary. How much anyone needs to exercise depends on dozens of factors, such as their fitness, age, injury history and health concerns. Maybe it's more helpful to think about why we might exercise instead.

Research suggests that getting our heart rate up is one of the quickest and most effective ways to improve our mood, and staying emotionally steady ourselves is important when dealing with unsteady adolescents.[3] One reason is that cardiovascular exercise causes a chemical change in the brain. Even running upstairs can give us a brief 'runner's high', the kind of endorphin rush that follows high-intensity exercise. Getting our heart rate up also raises blood pressure, which in turn helps us become more alert.

A second approach to moving more is if we abandon the idea that it is about getting fit or losing weight, and instead think of it as something we might enjoy, just as our ancestors did, and just as small children do. When we are young, we do not have to think about taking exercise at all. Small children naturally delight in their physicality: they adore jumping and skipping and their general flexibility. Sadly, as we grow up we lose this instinctive enjoyment in our bodies' ability to move. How then to re-awaken this sense of fun?

The first step to enjoying exercise in this way is to dismantle many of the rules and judgements about how and when we should move. There are so many exhortations – we should or should not exercise in certain ways, in certain clothes and in certain places – that many of us feel guilty and, our old friend, not good enough. Exercise can become a form of punishment. The word is often associated with the hard work, sweat and goal-setting that often accompanies trips to the gym. It also seems to be associated with the weight-loss industry and with body image. The result is that some people find exercising makes them feel judged, or that they are failing to get results.

Maybe if we think of exercise as fun, we might find it easier to get fit. Instead of listening to others, we can ask our bodies what exercise feels good? Bodies like to move! If we can exercise outside, this will amplify the effect: we know that many people cheer up when exposed to natural light because of the mood-boosting impact of vitamin D. What we consider fun will look different for all of us, but for many it involves other people. You might consider moving with other parents who are similarly reluctant to exercise (or even with your teenagers, though don't expect them to say yes). If you agree to meet friends, you'll be obliged to show up, you'll enjoy feeling socially connected and you'll keep each other going. Like our ancestors, we are more likely to be active in groups. Find a class that involves movement (a better word than exercise) and that is friendly. Give it a try and commit to going a few times. At the least, you'll be a good example to your children.

In my exercise-as-pleasure category comes stretching. It is just such a delicious feeling to experience your limbs lengthening, and is something most of us naturally do on waking or if we feel tense. When we don't stretch, our muscles become shorter and tighter, which reduces our range of motion. Research suggests activities such as stretching and yoga benefit flexibility and help us become more attuned to our emotions: remember we are trying to be detectives.[4] These exercises help to open out muscle groups that may have become tight or restricted when we were feeling stressed, thereby reducing the symptoms of anxiety. Such stretching exercises can also reduce anxiety by encouraging us to focus on the present moment, concentrating on one aspect of our bodies in a non-judgemental way. I like the idea that being more physically flexible can make us feel more mentally flexible, which is useful when confronted with the kind of new scenarios that inevitably happen when coping with teenagers.

NOURISHMENT

I've had to adopt some mental flexibility around the topic of food too. It is particularly easy for parents to feel like failures at the first hurdle when it comes to what we ourselves eat, not to mention what we feed our offspring. Who hasn't ordered a takeaway, exhausted at the end of the day, all thoughts of cooking a distant dream? And felt terrible as a result.

We are 'good' parents if we eat healthily ourselves and rustle up a home-cooked meal; 'bad' parents if we put a frozen fish pie in the microwave and finish off the shop-bought apple crumble ourselves. We might even feel bad about eating our child's chocolate birthday cake – guilty as charged, M'Lud. We are only good when we make good food choices for ourselves and our children. How then can we establish a healthy relationship with food ourselves? We need to do this, both for our own wellbeing, and for our ability to parent our teenagers.

My answer has been to notice how judgemental I was around food – and then quit being so. Food is food – it's not good or bad. If we judge food, we start to judge ourselves, according to what we eat, and it's an exhausting way to live and a bad example to our children. See if you can adopt a gentler voice in your head, similar to the one you might adopt when assailed by negative thoughts. Instead of feeling guilty and that you have failed because you ate something 'bad', separate food from any manufactured judgemental diktats. Only then will it become easier to enjoy food, and stop beating ourselves up about our choices.

Listen to what your body is asking for. Healthy choices are having the food you need, responding to what your body instinctively wants in a flexible way. Part of this is about ditching rules around food, instructions such as 'no snacks'. Snack if you feel the need. If you want some chocolate ice cream, have some. See if you can connect to when you've had enough.

Ideally we also want to take pleasure in what we eat. This kind of approach involves taking that bit more time to savour and enjoy our food and eat with focus, rather than with the fridge door gaping while we're multitasking. Chew more, and slowly, and be more attuned to the taste and smell of the food. We should be responding to what our bodies want, and when they want it. Our bodies can guide us if we really listen to them. I found the more in tune I was with my body, the more I was able to decide if I had had enough, and the more I was able to say no if that was the case. Equally, we should allow ourselves more if we are still hungry. This is about listening to ourselves, rather than being made to feel more and more guilty by all the nutritional advice out there.

We should try to decouple the link between food and difficult feelings. If we are feeling sad, for example, there may be other ways to comfort ourselves other than with the biscuit tin. Food should be enjoyed, rather than providing an answer to emotional problems. There are lots of other strategies for handling our feelings, as we've seen, including breathing exercises, relaxation techniques or free expressive writing. If we can adopt some of them, then food is less likely to be a crutch, or become a source of emotional problems in itself.

BALM OF HURT MINDS AND HOW TO ACHIEVE IT

Lack of sleep has been one of the biggest causes of my own emotional dramas, and was how my depressive episodes started. Shakespeare was spot on when he described slumber as 'Balm of hurt minds, great nature's second course / Chief nourisher in life's feast'. Sleep affects all aspects of our effective functioning as parents, from how we feel to our energy levels, to our ability to think straight, to what we choose to eat. Poor sleep tends to lead to poor eating choices, as we are drawn to sugar to keep going.

Yet the day we become parents is the day we say goodbye to uninterrupted sleep, from when our children are young and they wake in the night, to when they are teenagers and we lie awake awaiting their return from a night out. What parent hasn't tossed and turned, alert to the click of the front door as their teenager finally gets home? Or been abruptly woken up by the sound of teenagers using the bathroom in the middle of the night after an evening out? We become so used to interrupted sleep that we no longer know how to sleep soundly, even if we are not being interrupted.

Older mothers may also face the extra obstacles that come with the menopause, which often coincides with their children reaching adolescence. The body's thermostat goes slightly haywire during the perimenopause, menopause and post-menopause, thanks to fluctuating hormones. Previously, oestrogen worked to keep the body's heat on an even keel, but now, with lower oestrogen levels, the body cools itself down by releasing heat via a hot flush, or night sweats.

So, how to cope with the disrupted sleep of the parent? Given my dislike of rules and diktats around food and exercise, you may be unsurprised to hear that my own answer has been to abandon all the many strategies and solutions usually offered as answers to insomnia, from establishing a routine at night to turning to a bath before bed.

Perversely, I started sleeping better when I stopped trying to improve my sleep problems! Focussing on all the strategies meant I was paying attention to the problem. It became bigger and bigger in my mind. The more I read books on the nature of sleep, and how much it matters to our wellbeing and all the steps I needed to take to sleep better, the more I panicked. It consolidated the idea that I had a problem that needed fixing.

The answer has been to reframe the issue. While the lack of sleep isn't ideal (we can still function on little sleep, though we may not be top of our game), what matters more is worrying about the lack of sleep. This was the insight that a psychiatrist shared with me when I was still recovering from serious depression and suffered from this kind of insomnia. We identify ourselves as insomniacs. We write a story that says we have a problem.

The key is not to define yourself as someone who has trouble sleeping. You are just someone who is having trouble sleeping well, right now. Just because this is affecting you today, it doesn't have to affect you tomorrow. It is possible to change things.

Instead of fixating on being an insomniac, gently shift your thoughts to a different topic. I love reciting a poem. Or you might revisit the ideas for changing your thoughts that we looked at earlier (see page 43), whether that is feeling grateful, adjusting your focus, or concentrating on the five senses in turn, all of which are relevant to the parent lying awake at night. Try allowing and accepting your feelings with kindness.

Having adjusted your thoughts and feelings, you may also need to adjust your body. If you are physically relaxed, your worrying mind will struggle to take over, as the more relaxed your body is, the more your brain gets the message 'I am safe' and starts to think accordingly. You can either use deep-breathing techniques or guided muscle relaxation.

Remind yourself of the guided muscle-relaxation techniques discussed in the previous chapter (see page 77), in which you tense all your muscles and relax them in turn as a way of coping with challenging feelings. Try to do this in a light-hearted way, which allows for the fact this may not work. If you feel you absolutely must relax, the stressful pressure will make it impossible.

When I first used these muscle-relaxing techniques, I would listen to someone's soothing voice instructing me to relax my muscle groups in turn: 'Now relax your toes, your ankles, your calves, your thighs . . .' Over the years I have internalized that soothing voice and can call on it at will. It works as a form of self-hypnosis: hypnotherapy has been shown to work in several medical situations, but self-hypnosis can be just as effective. The bit I particularly remember from the coach is his repeated phrase 'So slow, so heavy, so relaxed'. I now say it to myself, using it as a form of sleep script. You need to talk to yourself slowly, with lots of pauses, to slow you right down, to make you more receptive and give your brain time to absorb the messages.

Don't forget that feeling hungry can contribute to insomnia. Protein takes longer to digest than carbohydrates, so it keeps us feeling full. Fats do too; they are the slowest to digest of all the food groups. Some foods can even contribute to us feeling calm at night if they help us produce melatonin. Our melatonin levels naturally increase as we edge towards bedtime, as darkness is a trigger for its production. Few foods contain melatonin – goji berries may do – but we can aim for foods rich in tryptophan, which is involved in the synthesis of melatonin. These include bananas, potatoes, almonds, seeds and wholegrain oats. If my teenagers tell me they can't sleep, they know to pop down to the kitchen.

*

This first section of the book has been about you: your sleep, your nutrition, your feelings, your thoughts, your relationship with your own parents and with any co-parents, and how becoming the parent of an adolescent impacts them all. I myself had to grow and develop fast to be able to cope. Although it wasn't always an easy journey, I feel enriched by the experience. I wouldn't have had to develop as a person in these ways if it hadn't been for the arrival of my teenagers, which forced me to rummage deep into my psyche and nurture myself in new ways. I've shared ideas which I hope will help you to nourish your own connection and relationship with yourself as you too adapt to this new period in your life.

You might wonder how relevant all this is to your own role as a parent of teenagers. My view is that, firstly, caring and nurturing ourselves gives us the resources and energy to enjoy our children: in short, put your own oxygen mask on before you attend to your children. Secondly, we are acting as examples to them to care for their own physical and psychological selves. To sum up, a parent taking care of their emotional health is a parent taking care of their teenagers. Thus armed, it's time to think about your relationship with your not so little darlings.

(OR NOT)

PART TWO

CONNECTING WITH YOUR TEENAGER

7

THE TEENAGE BRAIN AND
SUPPORTING ITS DEVELOPMENT

Understanding ourselves as people and as parents may enable us to be calmer when we interact with our teenagers. Similarly, worrying less about our children starts with understanding more about them. We can thus feel more connected to them and enjoy them for the gift they are.

Our teenagers are different from us. They are different in multiple ways, regarding their physical needs, their emotions and their relationships. This second part of the book is about understanding our teenagers' brains and biology, the broad sweep of their adolescent development, and how these factors affect their behaviour. It's also about our relationship with them, so in this section I've tended to share examples from my own interactions with my children.

As our most complex organ, the brain is still developing into our twenties. The idea that adolescence is a time of distinct developmental change is relatively new. Up until about 15 years ago, there was a general agreement in neuroscience that most of our brain development happens in the first few years of life. But more recently, magnetic resonance imaging (MRI) studies have shown this to be incorrect: teenagers undergo a period of change a bit like the early growth spurt that affects a toddler's brain.[1] This period starts at around age 11 and lasts until about the mid-twenties.

Prior to adolescence, a child's brain grows connections between brain cells in excess of its needs. But at about age 11 or 12, the brain prunes back a significant proportion of these connections. This process is influenced by what our teenagers are exposed to through adolescence. Brain structures and pathways that are used are kept, and those that are not used are pruned away, rather like a gardener tending a rose, cutting back certain branches and allowing others to flourish. The way teenagers develop in this sensitive period is fundamentally shaped by their environment – an environment that was especially challenging for millions of young people during the Covid pandemic.

In general, adolescent girls' brains develop faster than boys. When scientists measure brain development, they find that in boys, connections to the prefrontal lobe – the bit of the brain associated with logical reasoning and regulating impulses – are on average (and there will be plenty of exceptions) about two years behind that of girls.

How exactly all these changes happen is highly complex and we still have much to learn. To simplify, humans do not fully develop their prefrontal lobes until around their mid-twenties. Without a fully functioning prefrontal lobe, the adolescent capacity to exercise restraint, to assess risk or weigh consequences is impaired. This makes teenagers vulnerable to online scams, easily influenced by fads, and fickle. This is a time when dying your hair blue, smoking weed, or ordering an ear-piercing kit on the internet feel sensible. It's not their fault; and there's no need to blame them or stigmatize them for characteristics such as poor impulse control.

But there are plenty of more positive changes happening to the adolescent brain through this period, and we do well not to buy into too many negative stereotypes about hopeless teenagers. It is a time of heightened empathy, intense feelings and an openness to new experiences. Our role is to try to create the healthiest environment in which their brains can develop. We have the chance to support their educational and social development as their brains are highly malleable and changeable through this period.

FOUR BIG CHANGES HAPPENING TO YOUR TEENAGER'S BRAIN

There's so much happening to the adolescent brain that it might seem silly to concentrate on just four aspects of development. But these are the changes that made most sense to me – I could link them almost directly to how my teenagers behaved every day. Let's begin with the teenage love of risk-taking, which is now often less of the sex, drugs and rock 'n' roll variety (all of which are on the decline among teenagers) but more about risks taken online and in the world of social media. Their executive decision-making function is still developing through this period, as we've seen. The still-maturing 'brake' circuitry in the front part of the brain may be particularly overwhelmed by the 'accelerator' region, compromising their ability to make thoughtful decisions. This is why young men are prepared to sign up as soldiers, a commitment that becomes less likely as people become more risk-averse as their brains mature. Neuroscientists have found that risk-taking peaks when teenagers are 14.[2]

Research suggests adolescent risk-taking is more subtle than stereotypes suggest. Risky behaviour is in fact often premeditated and calculated. Teenagers balance 'social risk' – whether they will be thrown out of their peer group – against the consequence of doing something we might think dumb. The cost of being excluded by their friends can outweigh any concerns, making risky behaviour a rational choice.[3] Brain imagery shows that for teenagers, physical danger is less frightening than the fear of losing face or the respect of their peers.[4] This means teenagers take more chances, and seek out pleasure and excitement in front of their friends.[5] Risk-taking doubles for boys when their friends are around but reduces if they are with their girlfriends.[6]

Risky behaviour varies according to gender: boys are more likely to fight and skip school, while girls are slightly more likely to smoke.[7] Overall, boys take more risks[8] and there may be an evolutionary explanation for this.[9] In our distant past, boys hunted and defended the village, both of which could be dangerous. Rash conduct is also more likely when teenagers are in a good mood: they may feel less inhibited and more likely to take risks to help sustain the high, overlooking outward signs that suggest that gains are unlikely or that there are dangers in this heightened 'happiness overdrive' mode.[10]

The second key development in the teenage brain is a more positive one: this is a time when teenagers are open to new experiences and learning new things – a need that was hard to meet during Covid.

The third aspect of these rapid brain changes is that the social part of the brain comes to dominate during adolescence, which explains the importance and impact of peer pressure. Even teenage mice experience peer pressure! Adolescent mice drink more alcohol if surrounded by other adolescent mice, which isn't true for adult mice, who drink the same no matter who they are with.[11] The stereotype is that peer pressure is nothing but a problem. But again, the reality is more subtle. It turns out that teenagers are more likely to be influenced by others to change for the better than adults[12], engaging in a generous act for example if others are doing the same. It is also a time when the part of the brain that allows us to take on other people's perspectives is still developing. Teenagers are highly sensitive, especially to what other people think about them. The gradual maturation of the prefrontal cortex allows teenagers to think more abstractly: to look at themselves in the way they imagine other people are considering them. Some researchers say that this new-found ability leads to heightened empathy and self-regulation.[13] But it may also make teenagers more self-consciousness.

A fourth key aspect of this period of brain development is that adolescents are often at the mercy of strong emotions. The emotional centres of their brains take in information rapidly and react equally fast. During stressful times, these emotional centres may dominate over their rational centres, which may prevent adolescents from being able to problem-solve. They experience greater emotional intensity than adults[14] [15], with adolescent girls experiencing even more intense feelings than adolescent boys.[16] Girls also experience greater emotional instability than do adolescent boys.[17]

It turns out that adolescents tend to experience many emotions at the same time. In a recent study from Harvard and the University of Washington, researchers tried to map the development of something called emotion differentiation, which is the ability to label distinct emotions in yourself.[18] This may be a sign of good mental health, as those with high emotion differentiation tend to use effective coping strategies in difficult situations instead of turning to options like alcohol or aggression.[19] Ultimately, the researchers found that while adolescents tended to experience many emotions simultaneously, they differentiated them poorly. In other words, a teenager might consistently feel angry and sad together, indicating that it is difficult for them to distinguish between the two.

Teenagers tend to overreact, even more than adults, not only to threats but also to positive emotions. They are experiencing emotions in Technicolor compared to our black and white. There are good sides to this sensitivity and impressionability. As parents, we might rejoice in our children's openness to joy through this period, an openness that becomes duller as we become older and more cynical. One 2010 study from Pennsylvania and Stanford Universities analyzed 12 million blogs for words associated with happiness.[20] Younger bloggers tended to use adjectives like 'excited', 'ecstatic' or 'elated'. Older writers tended to use words such as 'peaceful', 'relaxed', 'calm' or 'relieved'. A second study found that teenagers are also more easily inspired to do good than adults. Researchers asked groups of people how likely they are to do a generous act. They were then shown a fictitious statistic, showing that others in their age group had been more generous, and asked if they wanted to change their answer. Teens do so more readily than adults.[21]

But there is also a downside to this sensitivity. Teenagers can often be on an emotional roller-coaster and suffer meltdowns. Experiences really are more vivid and so, potentially, painful. This is exacerbated by the fact that so much is new. Teenagers might feel rational, but they may be driven by their emotions, even when the emotion is positive, such as (for example) the experience of falling in love. Falling 'head over heels' may mean just that: their passion has thrown them seriously off balance and they need to proceed with caution when making commitments because of the fervency of their feelings. They may only be able to see deeper character traits in their beloved when the chemical reaction has died down, and the part of the brain that does the rational thinking has had a chance to develop.

As if all that were not enough, these four big changes are happening at the same time as a flood of new hormones, or chemical messages. A section of the brain called the hypothalamus is responsible for triggering the pituitary gland. The hormones from the pituitary gland kick-start the production of specific male and female sex hormones.

These changes to their brains and all these new hormones result in all sorts of emotional and behavioural changes. Teenagers generally are at the mercy of brains that lead them to be risk-takers, open to new experiences, highly social, as well as highly emotional and sensitive. Let's look at how we as parents can help support their adolescent brain development by being aware of what's happening and going with the grain of the changes through this period. We can begin with some general thoughts on how to create an environment that in practical and emotional ways supports healthy brain development.

SLEEP AND FOOD

Most of this brain development happens at night. Sleep-deprived teenagers are less healthy, make worse decisions and are at greater risks of drink or drugs.[22] But most of us probably knew that. I didn't know, however, that adolescents release the sleep hormone melatonin later in the day than when they were younger, which means that adolescents naturally stay up later and get up later than adults, a phenomenum known as 'phase delay'. This is thought to be for evolutionary purposes, so that teenagers could develop independence without threat or interruption. Research suggests that whatever your natural body clock, you need to align with it.[23] Night owls should not defy their body clocks and wake up early. So the message to parents is: let your children lie in and allow them to match up with their natural sleep patterns as much as you can, at least in the holidays.

And be sympathetic to the nightmare that is the timing of the school day for most teenagers. Plenty of sleep scientists believe schools should start later to accommodate teenage sleep patterns, and a few pioneering schools have adjusted their start times. Adjusting to conform with adolescent sleep patterns in this way improves their school attendance and academic performance.

On the topic of getting enough sleep, get them an alarm clock so they don't need their phones in their rooms at night, and keep their phones on chargers downstairs: most teenagers are too lazy to venture from under their duvets once they're snug in bed. Research has found that late-night phone-use makes it harder to fall asleep, and the quality of sleep is poorer because the screen's blue light disrupts levels of melatonin.[24] 'How can I even try taking away their phone at night?!', I hear you say. A better bet may be to at least discuss the effects of phone use with your teenagers; they get to choose, but at least you've shared your desire for them to sleep well.

Knowing their sleep patterns has a nice extra bonus: it can help you plot when is a good time to chat. Peak wakefulness for teenagers tends to be

HOW TO SLEEP WELL

around 9pm. As long as you're not too tired yourself, this can be a good moment to get them to open up.

If they complain about insomnia, bear in mind that it is as true for them as it is for us that the more any of us tries to sleep, the more we are likely to remain awake. You inadvertently activate a fundamental threat system in the brain, telling you that something essential for life is unavailable to you. Instead, remind your children that their bodies are cleverer than them: if they stop worrying and trying to control their sleep patterns, their bodies will, when ready, take over, and sleep will become inevitable. You cannot force yourself to be sleepy any more than you can force yourself to be hungry. Instead, they can try meditation, writing in a journal, or reading something soothing until their eyes begin to close. Or suggest they adopt the strategies that we discussed in Chapter 6 about dealing with parental insomnia (see page 85). In particular, don't get cross at night-time snacking but actively encourage it, given how irregular teenage mealtimes can be and that feeling hungry can stop them getting to sleep, just as it keeps us awake too.

FOOD

Most, if not all, teenagers really are permanently hungry – not surprising, now you know how busy their brains are, and also given that they don't always eat what is nourishing. Social pressures mean that they go out with their friends to a movie, then eat popcorn and crisps. The odds are stacked against them: there are chicken shops just yards from playgrounds, while school canteens turn out mini pizzas at morning break, and adverts pop up in the middle of a game or on TikTok promoting junk food. Our species evolved in a world where calories were hard to come by and is predisposed to pounce on anything high in fat and sugar. These foods also tend to be cheaper: highly processed foods are on average three times cheaper for the consumer per calorie than healthier foods[25] and 68 per cent of the food consumed by the UK's 12–19-year-olds is ultra-processed.[26]

All of which means that it's tough to encourage our teenagers to eat healthily. Parents are tired. Teenagers like junk food, which hijacks their taste buds, and they often feed themselves, out of our sight. What's the answer? Not to beat ourselves up about our limited ability to influence them through this period. We are no longer deciding what food they eat in the way we once did. We can reassure ourselves that this is a time of change, and their eating habits will change too. Our best bet through this period is to be an example of someone who tries to eat healthily themselves and avoids judging their food choices.

Just as we are trying to avoid value judgements around food choices for ourselves, we want to avoid judging our teenagers' bodies and what they eat. Bodies are all different and all worthy of being respected. Trust adolescents to choose what they want to eat, to have their own likes and dislikes, and choose when they have had enough, so that they get to know themselves and their own bodies. It follows that we want to be wary about promoting any new popular diets around the kitchen table, especially those with lots of do's and don'ts, or that involve cutting out a food group, or 'clean eating' (which recommends choosing organic foods in their less processed states but which can be taken to an extreme whereby advocates aim to avoid all traces of any artificial colours or added sugar). Overly demonizing ultra-processed foods only makes them more enticing.

Given the world in which we live, it's inevitable that they will sometimes eat junk food (as will we). If we disparage unhealthy foods, they will either rebel and eat more of them, or become anxious around them. This can lead to eating disorders, which are on the rise in teenage girls. A study published in 2023 found that since March 2020, the number of teenage girls with eating disorders was 42 per cent higher than would be expected before the pandemic in those aged 13–16, and 32 per cent higher in those aged 17–19.[27]

Instead of berating them, and ourselves, for lapsing when we hungrily fall on a pizza, focus on the 80 per cent rule. Try to provide healthy food 80 per cent of the time. Share with them the joy of a ripe tomato exploding on their palate. Encourage them to enjoy mood-boosting and brain-building fishcakes, sardines, salmon, mackerel, maybe some fish oil supplements, as well as nuts, seeds and live yogurt. Put vegetables on the table first when teenagers are hungriest. Given the popularity of plant-based diets among teenagers, aim for a vegan base of beans or vegetables, then people can add eggs, meat or fish as they wish.

Zinc is important to teenage brain development: nutritionists recommend shellfish, avocado, lentils, oats and leafy greens. So are magnesium-rich foods: whole grains, milk, bananas, kiwis, cherries, fibre-rich vegetables and beans. If they have a smoothie for breakfast, you could add peanut butter for calcium, and oats for protein. One governor of a secondary school in a deprived area told me that nutritionists had recommended a wholemeal bagel with cream cheese for pupils who traditionally skipped breakfast. It's a good idea if your teenager is rushing out the door and hasn't eaten, not least as it's easy to prepare the night before and for them to carry. The cream cheese is a good source of calcium, high in protein, and contains vitamin A, while the bagel provides slow-release energy.

Our best bet for creating a positive food environment is to link food to fun and connecting with others. There are physical benefits to sharing meals: teens who eat regular family meals enjoy lower rates of obesity, eating disorders and substance abuse, as well as better cardiovascular health.[28] It follows that you should try to eat together with your teenagers, something most parents already know but find hard in practice, given conflicting schedules and the lure of phones. My own early efforts failed. I felt pressurized to cook perfect family meals, knowing their importance. I would take trouble cooking what I thought my children would like and would make a fuss about us all sitting down together, repeatedly shouting up the stairs for the children to come to meals. I was not the best company: I was resentful about all the effort I had made and the fact that no-one came when asked or seemed appreciative.

It was time for a different approach. I decided to cook what I wanted (it just wasn't realistic to expect them to cook), texted on the family WhatsApp rather than shouted when it was ready, and began eating with a magazine for company, even if the children hadn't come downstairs. Though my desire was that we would eat together, I was no longer trying to force anyone to join me. The less I tried to force the outcome, the less there was for my teenagers to push back against, and the more readily they joined family meals.

Shared mealtimes were not always sunshine and roses, but thanks to my own better mood and more relaxed approach, sometimes they became times when we discovered more about those around the table, learned how to deflect conflict and how to tell stories in an enjoyable way.

If conversation dried up, my failsafe answer was to ask what people had appreciated during their day.

Avoiding coffee at the end of the meal may be obvious, given how sensitive teens are to caffeine, which impedes sleep. Every 10mg of caffeine a young person consumes reduces their chance of getting eight and a half hours' sleep by 12 per cent. A Caffè Vanilla Frappuccino contains 95mg. Perhaps less obvious is how much caffeine lurks in other drinks. There is 80mg of caffeine in a 250ml can of Red Bull: there is no age limit in the UK for buying these energy drinks, unlike in some other countries.

ENCOURAGING SELF-CARE AND EXPLAINING THE 'SOOTHING SYSTEM'

Our last contribution as parents to creating an environment for healthy brain development is to help teenagers find good coping mechanisms to manage their difficult thoughts and feelings – as we know how sensitive they are. This is a time of high emotional drama, as we've seen. You may find it helpful to share ways you have learned to stay calm yourself(!), whether that's by using breathing exercises, by consciously relaxing, or by challenging your negative thoughts with cognitive behavioural therapy. The problem is that the teenage attention span may be too short for your pearls of wisdom. I was taken with the ideas of Dr Hester Riviere, an educational psychologist who works with vulnerable young people and their families in Oxfordshire.[29] She recommends telling teenagers about their 'soothing system' and how to activate it. This accessible and understandable approach incorporates many of the ideas I've previously shared but in an abbreviated way: a motorway approach, as it were, rather than a scenic route to moderating stressful thoughts and feelings.

Just as we adults can cope with difficult emotions by activating our soothing systems, so too can our teenagers. We can explain the aforementioned Paul Gilbert's three systems model (the threat, soothe and drive systems) with particular reference to how it might play out in their lives.

External threats for our youngsters are different from those affecting adults. They might include violent attackers in the playground, but also looming deadlines for schoolwork, or the prospect of an exam, or a forthcoming school report. Internal threats are more about the negative ways teenagers can think or talk to themselves – 'I'm such a loser!' or 'I always get things wrong!' (Sounds familiar? Well, teenagers are more like us than perhaps we care to realize.) When teenagers, and indeed anyone, is threatened, typically they go into the 'fight, flight, freeze or submit' response and produce lots of adrenaline and cortisol. Their brains have the same glitches that our parental brains do, which we discussed in Part One (see page 36). Just as we have a tendency to panic and jump to negative thoughts, so do they.

The drive system, meanwhile, is about pursuing and achieving stuff. It's accompanied by the pleasurable brain chemical dopamine. Teenagers will experience a flood of dopamine whenever they get something done, or achieve success – that might be passing exams or getting into the school football team.

Finally, the soothing system is when they feel calm, safe and relaxed. There are no threats to defend against and no goals that must be pursued. This system produces feel-good chemicals such as oxytocin and endorphins.

All systems are valid and important, and ideally we would circle easily between all three. But many of us – and especially teenagers – end up ping-ponging between the threat and drive systems, and not spending enough time in the soothing one.

We can get stuck in our threat system for two main reasons. The first is that evolution has designed us like this, as we've seen: the threat system saves us from being eaten by a lion. The second reason is because, again as we have seen, negative information captures our attention, thinking and memory more powerfully than positive information (this is referred to by researchers as a 'negativity bias'). For instance, we feel the sting of being reprimanded more powerfully than we feel the joy of praise.

Given how unpleasant it is to feel threatened, the obvious answer is to escape by switching to the drive system for a pleasant whoosh of dopamine. Teenagers thus oscillate between the torment of threat, and the temporary relief provided by the drive system. In the short term, this can be rewarding. After all, like us, youngsters are pain-averse, pleasure-seeking creatures.

However, this cycle can become exhausting in the long term because it leaves no space for failure – which is an inevitable part of the relentless pursuit of achievement to be found in many schools. Not all our teenagers' endeavours will work. Do more, be more, have more – these ambitions are all very well, until the moment you fail and trigger the threat system again. Many teenagers are therefore in a vicious cycle with no space for peace and contentment with what 'is'.

What Dr Riviere told me is that this is a pattern many adolescents easily recognize in themselves (as indeed many adults do too), especially because we expect adolescents to achieve so many goals – even more than we put pressure on ourselves to achieve. Pass more exams! Get into more teams! In other words, we want them to be busy in their drive system.

The answer is for our anxious children to understand that switching between the two systems is unhelpful, even though temporarily they might be distracted and get a hit of dopamine. Instead, they need to become better at accessing their soothing systems. The more they are able to support, nurture and soothe themselves, the more they are capable of being there for themselves if they fail (and they will eventually fail or make mistakes, because nobody is perfect all the time). This means they will be able to handle disappointment without spiralling into self-criticism, as well as avoiding the dreaded threat/drive ping-pong.

Teenagers can turn to the same approaches as us adults to feel soothed, including our trusted ally – slow, rhythmic breathing – which can make us all feel calmer and less stressed. Many studies have found that slow, rhythmic breathing can make us all feel calmer and less stressed.[30] A second approach is for teenagers to become more attuned to the presence of soothing emotions in their own lives. The more they become aware, the easier they'll find it to engage with them. One good question they might ask themselves is, 'At the times I feel calm and relaxed, what is going on?' They could keep a notebook, and jot down what's helpful. One daughter's list read 'Walk / hot bath / watching rom-coms I've seen before / dark chocolate' when she was 16. Once they know what kinds of things prompt soothing feelings for them, they can deliberately start stimulating them.

They might indulge in a smell that leaves them feeling comforted and calmed. As they inhale, ask them to savour the scent and notice the way their body feels as they do this. Or, suggest they wrap themselves in a thick duvet, and feel its warmth and the sensations of being held. Or encourage them to put on some music that makes them feel at ease, experiment with some gentle touch, like a hand massage, or go for a walk anywhere green.

While we can all benefit from sitting with difficult feelings, this is especially true for our teenagers. As Dr Riviere told me, 'Young people talk about anxiety as if it's on a chair, breathing fire at them.' A culture of 'everyone must have prizes' has meant that many young people find feelings of failure or sadness hard to bear. Our first instinct may be to step in and rescue them, as we cannot tolerate seeing them sad. Instead, we can gently challenge this panic in the face of their emotions and share some ideas of how they can become more at ease with strong feelings. I remember one occasion when one of our teenage daughters, then aged 15, was mortified that the chicken I was serving to one of their friends was undercooked. But no-one was going to die! My role was to help her be comfortable with the difficult feeling, not to tell her to snap out of it. We can help them identify and manage their emotions, share with them the image of a small boat (see page 72), and introduce them to the same relaxation techniques that (hopefully!) we ourselves are using.

They're sleeping well, eating healthily, and coping with their strong feelings (we hope). Now the question is whether we can give more specific help with any other aspects of their brain development. We've talked about their sensitivity and strong feelings, and how to help. Is there anything else we can do? Well, we can be cunning – we may be able to lean into other developmental changes, rather than fight them.

GOING WITH THE GRAIN OF ADOLESCENT BRAIN DEVELOPMENT – THE NEED FOR NOVELTY, RISK TAKING AND PEER PRESSURE

It can feel nerve-wracking as a parent to know that the teenage brain is drawn to thrilling new experiences and is less good at executive decision-making. We naturally worry that they will turn to drink or drugs. But seeking out new sensations promotes learning. By doing new things, our teenagers are expanding their knowledge and becoming more mature.

The answer therefore is to help guide our teenagers towards thrills that will help them grow, and away from those that may harm them, especially in their early teens (as already mentioned, neuroscientists have found that risk-taking peaks when teenagers are 14). This could mean encouraging them to join a boxing club, audition for a school play, or run a marathon.

Perhaps they could dive from the top diving board or try out rock-climbing. It could even mean supporting them to write a film script or take part in a poetry slam; experiment with some charity shop buys and a sewing machine. All these new experiences will fulfil their neurobiological development, and mean they are less likely to seek thrills elsewhere.

One of my own sons took up indoor rock-climbing at 18. He would return from his sessions in a sunnier and more philosophical mood, much chattier than when he left and reflective about the risks involved and how he enjoyed dealing with them in a safe way on the climbing wall.

By the same token, we can be alert to risk-taking. When my teenager got in a car with a friend who had been drinking, for example, I could see this as a case when their judgement was impaired, and they were drawn to risk. I needed to help them think through situations much more carefully, especially those in which their peers were involved. I tried to get to know their friends and their friends' parents to try to set common rules around risky behaviour. And to talk to them ahead about risky situations, helping them to rehearse ahead ways of ducking out of tricky situations – 'My mother is a harridan!' – and emphasizing my trust in them. By treating them more like adults, they became likely to act in kind, and plenty of studies attest to the strong links between parental expectations and risk-taking.[31]

Along with risk-taking and a thirst for novelty, we've seen that this is a time when teenagers care more about their friends than almost anything else. We parents can help by supporting healthy peer relationships – a huge topic given how many young people currently feel lonely (the focus of a chapter later in the book; see page 263). Ideally, we want to steer them towards their better adolescent selves, the social bit of them that wants to help others, and be vigilant if our teenager is in a peer group that puts them at risk.

*

Scary stuff, I agree, but I hope knowing a bit more about teenage brain development can make you feel more relaxed, because you at least know what's going on. It means you can take their behaviour less personally and less seriously – which also means you can have more fun with your adolescents and, yes, enjoy the gift that they are. Loosen up! The adolescent brain is still under construction. So when the door slams or one of your teenagers rolls their eyes, you can tell yourself biology is at work here. It's not about you! It's all about them. You don't need to intervene or panic; their emotions and brains are unfolding just as they should. For the time being, they are just different from us adults. They will not always feel this deeply or suffer so much.

Moreover, there's more good news. The development of the prefrontal cortex means this is also a time when teenagers can develop new aspects of cognitive thinking and wisdom. Their brains will become more adept at impulse control, problem-solving, decision-making and behaviour management over the years. Our role is to support our teenager's developing brain as much as possible. We can provide a healthy environment for its development, create opportunities for safe exploration, encourage healthy friendships, stay calm ourselves and communicate in a way they are more likely to be able to hear. Above all, we need to stay connected to them through this period – the subject of the next chapter.

8

STAYING CONNECTED
AND LETTING GO

Given the immaturity and volatility of their brains, teenagers need a high level of adult guidance to make positive and sensible choices, and we parents need to stay confident that we are the primary people to help them do so. This sentence might in the past have been redundant, but many parents have told me that they have felt undermined recently about the way that teachers in particular are stepping on their toes.

Here I have been struck by the work of Joanna Williams, a former teacher and author who has argued in a recent report that parents need to be left to do the parenting, teachers the teaching.[1] In many spheres, schools have taken on responsibilities once left to families, such as lessons about values, relationships or even deciding what goes into lunchboxes.

Yet it is our role to nurture and stay close to our teenagers through this period, a closeness and support that will greatly assist in the development of the prefrontal cortex. Because their brains are still developing at this stage of life, things can feel confusing and overwhelming at times for our teenagers. They are not quite at the stage of maturity where they should be expected to deal with all of life's complications and decisions without our support. It can be hard for them always to know what risks are reasonable for them to take, and how to keep themselves safe. We, their parents, can guide them by letting them know that we are there for them, providing them with emotional security through this period. They need to know that they can trust us, until they are ready to move on and we need to let them go.

Of course the reality is messy. We may want to stay connected, but our teenagers may beg to disagree. Or perhaps we may be unavailable when our teenagers need us. This is a confusing push-and-pull period for our relationship. One minute teenagers are independent, pushing us away, the next vulnerable, pulling us close. Nonetheless, we can at least attempt to be the kinds of parents who foster connection and in due course independence, and try to have established the first before we encourage the second.

This process of 'individuation' – a word first coined by Carl Jung, meaning taking on the responsibilities of adulthood – in general now seems to be happening later. Jean Twenge, a Professor of Psychology at San Diego State University, has found that teenagers are taking longer to grow up, adopting a 'slow life strategy'.[2] They are now less likely to work (part-time), drive, drink alcohol, take drugs, have sex or date than their counterparts 10 or 20 years ago. Dr Twenge argues this is because families have fewer children and spend more time cultivating each child's development. By contrast, a 'fast life' strategy was more common when there were fewer labour-saving devices and the average woman had bigger families. The result was that teens fended for themselves sooner.

This slower journey towards finding themselves has some advantages: it's good news that fewer teens are having sex or drinking, and Dr Twenge argues that it's likely to be beneficial that teens are spending more time developing socially and emotionally before they become grown up. However, a slower pace also means that teenagers may need more guidance as they transition into adulthood.

I have welcomed this gentler pace. Our continuing relevance as parents was reassuring to me, given that I was absent for periods of time when my children were little, either juggling office life or because of my depression. I worried they might, like me, be 'anxiously' attached – and I felt guilty. There were indeed challenges from their childhood. But whatever the past, we parents can still try to do our best now by making our teenagers feel as secure as possible. Even if we feel we were not always available when our children were tiny, all is not lost. New patterns can be created.

We want them to feel we value our relationship with them and are attuned to their needs and moods. We can try to be adults who respond to our adolescents in ways that make them feel seen, heard, understood, accepted and celebrated: in short, loved. The problem is that the adolescent brain's social development and the importance of peer pressure mean that teenagers often try to rely on other teenagers for these needs.

Teenagers are clearly no longer children, but nor are they yet mature adults. Adolescent development takes time – more than in the past, we now realize – and through this entire developmental period, we need to stay close to them. Competing links with peers can create instability, confuse teenagers' emotional systems, cause a lack of motivation, and impair decision-making abilities through this delicate stage.

In due course, our teenagers can come to rely more on their friends. Until then, immature teenagers can be fickle in their relationships with their contemporaries. They can lack much sense of responsibility to temper their own moods or commit to one another's wellbeing. At this early stage, we parents can offer unconditional acceptance instead of the unpredictability of some peer-to-peer relationships. Only when teenagers are old enough to feel these firm foundations and are independently able to appraise themselves, rather than needing the affirmation and approval of their peers, are their own relationships with their contemporaries more likely to be nurturing and nourishing. This chapter is about how we, their parents, can remain close and connected to our adolescents until they are ready to fly the nest.

INDIVIDUATION MAKES THEM MORE FOCUSED ON THEIR FRIENDS THAN YOU

When our children are little, staying close to them is relatively easy. We, their parents or carers, are the centre of their world. We are the people to whom they are closest. The people they trust the most. They search for us continually, even if we just pop out for a few minutes. We are the individuals who brighten their day simply by walking into the room.

Even negligent or inattentive parents are the objects of adoration at this stage. Children are designed to love their primary carers, as without them they would not survive. Attachment is a biological need. Hundreds of thousands of years of evolution inform this attachment. It really is a matter of life or death for a small child to win their parents' affection.

Then, sometimes quite suddenly, at around the age of 12, things begin to change. Adolescent development differs between individuals, but roughly speaking, between 12 and 14, teenagers begin to assert their independence from their parents. Socialization with their peers becomes important. School trips, for example, are especially important as teenagers forge an identity away from their parents and discover new passions. Many of these processes intensify between the ages of 15 and 16.

As a result, we parents cease to be such god-like figures when our children reach the age of 12 or so. They begin to argue with us, finding fault in how we dress to how we sip our coffee (I slurped, it turned out), and let's not get started on our taste in music. We can be embarrassing. Our rules seem old fashioned and silly. And as for our politics! In truth, during this phase many young people are not even sure they like their parents anymore, nor do they want to spend much time with them. These negative feelings can leave both us and our teenagers unsettled, as if something is wrong with us. Such emotions can make teenagers feel guilty too. Their rational minds know that their parents have not changed. But somehow their parents are rarely their favourite people anymore.

An influential psychologist called Erik Erikson, writing in the 1960s, argued that teenagers are creating their own sense of self, so much so that they may reject almost everything with which they have hitherto been comfortable.[3] This takes place between the ages of 12 and 18, the crucial time for the development of a person's identity, for both their 'belongingness' (the groups they identify with) and their personal identity (how they establish themselves to be unique outside their chosen groups).

A teenager's sense of identity is therefore created largely through their social interaction with peers, and increasingly through how they present themselves online to others. Socializing, going to parties and hanging out with friends all help define them. This explains why more sociable teenagers tend to develop their sense of who they are more quickly. And why our teenagers are so frantic to see their mates.

Individuation can be painful for adolescents, especially so for twins, who are not just separating from us, their parents, but also from their twin. They are leaving the safety of their home camp and existing tribe but may not yet have found a new one. They are somewhat in limbo. There's plenty of conflict with their parents – Erikson even argued that this time is one of crisis.

But the good news is that out of this conflict can emerge a unique human being, one with whom you can have a new relationship, and one with ideas of his or her own, who is forging their own identity through all the different interactions they are experiencing. This is about who a teenager is becoming, and what they want to create for their lives. If this individuation process did not happen, young people would find it hard to separate successfully from their home life and would never venture out into the world with confidence to make their own futures. It would be impossible for our teenagers to become their true selves if their parents continued to be the centre of their world.

STAYING CLOSE MATTERS, AS PEERS CAN BE UNRELIABLE

The challenge for us parents is to remain relevant through this gradual shift to independence, as it doesn't happen in a smooth line but in fits and starts. Though it may not always be obvious, teenagers still want connection with us, just as much as we want connection with them. In the face of seeming rejection, and closed bedroom doors, I continually reminded myself of this truth. Their natural development away from us and towards their peers doesn't mean that we are redundant. Ironically, the more secure and attached to us they feel, the more they are able to move on with ease in time.

This is a view espoused by Gordon Neufeld and Gabor Maté, who are the authors of *Hold On to Your Kids: Why Parents Need to Matter More Than Peers*.[4] They argue that, traditionally, peer relationships took a secondary place to those with adults until a teenager became fully adult themselves. Adolescence is an in-between stage. Abandoning adolescents too soon to their friends can lead to trouble. Maté cautions that encouraging teenagers to become independent should happen only when they are ready to take on the responsibilities of adulthood: you can't have independence without maturity and a sense of who you are, and this happens in the context of strong ongoing attached relationships with nurturing adults.

Parents need to appreciate, say Neufeld and Maté, that a teenager's instinctive, subconscious need for a guide is strong. 'Children cannot endure the lack of such a figure in their lives; they become disoriented.' That's not to say, though, that our child will always automatically see their parent as their mentor, especially if we seem bored by them. When a child believes their parent is not interested in them, they may, at a subconscious level, transfer their attachment from their parent to their peers, or others seemingly offering to play that role. Worse, to become accepted by their peers, they must become 'cool'. Cool, by definition, often involves the absence of warmth.

Maté argues that there are dangers to peer attachment happening before a teenager is ready. 'Kids were never meant to nurture one another or to be role models for one another,' Neufeld says. 'They are not up to the task. It's the immature leading the undeveloped. What's absolutely missing in peer relationships is unconditional love and acceptance, the desire to nurture, the ability to extend oneself for the sake of the other, the willingness to support the growth and development of the other.' We're the ones to offer that.

You might be reading this and thinking, Help! I've already lost my teenager to their friends! They don't want to spend time with me! You may also be thinking that you haven't got the time for this regular family time to connect with your teenagers, especially if you are juggling multiple children and a job too. I understand. I have felt thinly stretched myself as a parent of five – and guilty too. One study found that all parents, regardless of socio-economic background, feel that they should aspire to more intensive parenting.[5] Today this culture of the involved parent is pervasive. More educated parents spend roughly twice as much time with our children as parents did four decades ago, yet most of us worry we aren't doing enough.[6] We may find ourselves trapped between an excessive work culture and the crisis in social care, which means that, as well as looking after our teenagers, we may also be responsible for elderly parents as it becomes harder to access help elsewhere, whether that's from the state or our extended family in a world where few of us live close to our relations.

At the same time, the pressure to be successful at work is higher than ever. Many parents feel they are getting left behind economically. Teenagers are expensive: it is no longer enough just to clothe and feed them. We feel we must provide them with the latest phones, computers and fashions. The knock-on effect is that we must work harder in order for our teenagers to keep up with their friends. Then there's the cost of university. All this hard work takes us away from an intimate relationship with our teenagers.

But Neufeld and Maté argue that we must try to stay close. How on earth. are we going to do so, given the pressure on our time, and recalcitrant teenagers who don't want to hang out with us? It is possible, and here follow some practical ways and habits to strengthen their sense of connectedness to you.

HOW TO KEEP CONNECTED

Faced with a child's hostility or rejection, we parents should try not to see it as a problem about their behaviour, or to take the negativity personally. There's nothing wrong with your adolescent: it's the relationship that needs attention and the teenager's behaviour is just a function of that. You could go so far as to think that problematic behaviour is simply a teenager's solution.

This is not about trying to control or tell them off if they are behaving badly: instead, focus on improving your relationship and spending time as a family together as best you can. They may not admit it, but there will be times when they will be grateful that family culture offsets the adolescent landscape they are navigating and provides a welcome relief from the peer pressure they are under. At least when they are with you, they needn't worry about looking the part.

There is a strong argument that it is the quality of our interactions that matters, rather than their frequency; this is especially true as children mature. We can increase our presence not by increasing the time spent with our child, but by giving them greater focus and making time to listen. It is easy to be physically present but switched off, especially if we are tired. In fact, quality moments – that is, focused and meaningful engagement – don't only involve scheduled face-to-face teenager-centric exchanges. Quality time can be found in everyday activities that families are doing already – especially mealtimes or car journeys.

Playing a practical role in our teenagers' lives, helping with day-to-day stuff, might not seem particularly intimate or a way to foster connection. It's easy to feel no more than a personal-assistant-cum-taxi-driver, but I found that while these roles might seem demeaning they could be ways to have pockets of time together and to stay close. One of the most intimate moments of my week could be a trip to the supermarket with one of my teenagers. Connection can be easier to foster walking down the aisle chatting about the virtues of one shampoo over another than it is at home.

Surprise your child with invitations to interact, almost as if you were asking them on a date. We can be spending all day, every day with our child and yet not convey the message that we enjoy them. That's why invitations to some special one-to-one time with you are wonderfully powerful. There are hundreds of ways to connect, and if one doesn't work, no big deal, try another. 'Let's join a charity run and chat while we train.' 'Let's go on a road trip – and come home if we don't like it!' Even, 'Let's cook supper together!' The invitation doesn't have to be fancy. The point is you have deliberately reached out, showing your teenager that you want to be with them, and to get to know them.

There's nothing more flattering than really being interested in someone else. Make sure they know you are excited about such times together – either by expressing how much you're looking forward to them, or by often referring back to them later. Choose something your son or daughter really enjoys; don't let your teenager feel like they're just an add-on to one of your tasks or outings. And agree that you will both leave your devices behind when you go out together.

Consider the SLANT method as you interact: Sit up, Lean forward, Ask questions, Nod your head, Track the speaker. Your small gestures can speak volumes to your teenager about their worth in your eyes. Be known for welcoming their interruptions. Make a point of putting your phone aside, closing your laptop or pausing the TV show when your teenager is trying to engage you; let your face show you are listening. One of my teenagers, then aged 16, said, 'There's literally nothing I appreciate more than when you switch off your phone to talk to me.' Indeed the topic is so important, there are more ideas on how to listen and communicate in the next chapter.

Reconnect after separation, whether that's after school, after a sleepover, after a Saturday apart, even after a night's sleep. Take time to warmly re-establish your relationship before you start trying to hurry them through your parenting agenda, especially first thing in the morning when few of us are at our best. Do the same after any kind of emotional separation, too – after an argument or misunderstanding, or when you've had to discipline them. It's almost always the parent's responsibility to restore the relationship: we can't expect teenagers to do it – they are not mature enough to understand the need for repairing and reconnecting.

Build rituals into your day or week that help reunite you: Gabor Maté calls these 'collecting rituals'. I used to sometimes bring my teenagers something small in my bag at school pick-ups, maybe a little tube of lip balm, or a snack they particularly liked, which made the point that I had been thinking about them during my day. Teenagers can still enjoy a bedtime routine – they might dismiss such an idea, but the virtue of rituals, especially longstanding ones, is they have always happened and are reassuring to your teenagers in their familiarity. Nine times out of ten they may not elicit anything intimate, but sometimes they do in part because the context is less charged. Taking a dog out together has proved a good ritual for us. There's the element of routine, as the dog (in our case a shaggy golden wheaten terrier called Sammy) has to go out whatever, which takes the pressure off the trip being anything special or intense. You can avoid focusing on the teenager at all, so there's less pressure. I'm still grateful to have had all those evening walks with my own children and the dog, though many of them were spent in companionable silence.

Creating rituals is what Gabor Maté did with his own daughter when she was 15. He recalls in an interview, 'I decided, "I'm just going to reclaim her,"' he says. Can a relationship really be forged so unilaterally? 'Well, she wasn't that concerned about spending time with me in general,' Maté admits. But he wanted to be with her, and she liked the idea of eating out, so once a week they went out for dinner. For years, they kept their date. Sometimes the dinners went badly, but the next week they'd be back again, Maté says. Those evenings became a sacred space. It took a long time for his daughter to turn to him for advice, 'which would have been the natural thing for her to do all along,' he says. 'But it happened.'

Any physical activity that gets you both exercising hard together is powerful for building connection, so consider a high-energy session, if you can persuade your teenager to join you. (Unlikely, I know.) You'll notice that a fun, intense workout may bring intense experiences and emotions to the surface for your teenager, and they may want to talk these over with you – a sign your reconnection time is working well. Boxing worked for me and my teenage girls.

I have shared some ways to stay connected until our teenagers are ready for independence. All these approaches can contribute to what the American physician and researcher Martha Welch calls 'emotional co-regulation'.[7] When two people trust each other, they may just be walking the dog, but their bodies communicate and calm each other. They co-modulate each other's heart rates to produce 'cardiac calming', and produce what Welch calls 'higher vagal tone', when the body feels secure (and perhaps remind yourself of my earlier thoughts on the importance of the vagus nerve on page 76).

So let's assume you have nourished your relationship, and feel close and connected to your teenager. How are you going to stay calm when, as is inevitable, they want to move on? As indeed is right and proper.

REDEFINING YOUR RELATIONSHIP

It's painful. We may not be adapting as quickly as our children. Just as we have risen to one challenge, another appears. What worked well with our teenagers six months ago may now irritate them.

The speed of change can feel frightening because most of us are resistant to change in general, wherever it occurs in our lives. What we know feels reassuring. In contrast, when things change, we feel as if we are losing something. No wonder we may feel as if parenthood is one long goodbye.

But what if this change and this letting go need not be such a hurtful process? What if there is no need to grieve? What if we ceased to be resistant to change?

The truth is we are not losing our children. We are just letting go of one relationship and saying hello to another. We can still feel closely connected. I do so by pausing, closing my eyes and quieting my mind. I imagine a child next to me and feel into their presence. This has been my own answer to seeing less of my teenagers – to bring them and all the wonderful aspects of their character to mind, enjoy the deep love and connection I feel for them and know exists on a spiritual and energetic level even if I don't see them. I can accept the present lack of communication or contact between us in a peaceful way. It's true, they no longer need me. But we can replace need with love.

In fact, they don't need us much at all, which can feel difficult for us as parents. If we are not needed, we feel threatened on some level. But we need not feel so concerned. We can learn to be friends instead – adult to adult. Our relationship can level out, without the hierarchy of parent dominating child. We will need to work around our children's new emotional need for space. Our relationship will inevitably be different. We can like them and admire them as people. We can even laugh and have fun. And in doing so, we can be more relaxed about letting go. Like the seasons passing, we may have to wait until they wish to reconnect with us.

This is the new future relationship we need to bear in mind as our teenagers grow away from us. Don't take rejections personally. Be patient. Hang in there. You are wooing the teenager back into the relationship. Yes, there can be painful interludes, but they will pass. See this as a stage. As Mark Twain said, 'When I was a boy of 14, my father was so ignorant I could hardly stand to have the old man around. But when I got to be 21, I was astonished at how much the old man had learned in seven years.'

The more I have seen my children as individuals with their own destinies, rather than just as my children, the more our relationship has improved as they have grown older. I have a personality and so do they. We can learn to detach ourselves, rather than thinking we are responsible for all their needs and have to be intimately involved in their lives. One mantra I like to use is 'I am not my child'.

Be honest if you are imposing your own wishes on them. The sports-mad father who expects his son to make him proud on the playing fields, or the chic mother who demands that a tomboy daughter should follow her stylish example. Recognize that these are our desires, not theirs.

Furthermore we need to be able to see our desires for what they are: habit, or tradition, or social vanity – the idea that it is a child's duty to be a credit to us – and let our teenagers go. They have their own dreams, inclinations, feelings and thoughts. They have their own souls, and are set to live in a future where we will not even be present. To borrow again from Khalil Gibran:

> *They are the sons and daughters of Life's longing for itself.*
> *They come through you but not from you,*
> *And though they are with you yet they belong not to you.*[8]

It follows that we do well to focus less on the teenager that they currently are, and more on the person they are becoming. We might as well surrender to this forward-looking approach – it is our only option, really, since the process is inevitable. And – just maybe – we can enjoy it.

*

This chapter has been about navigating our ever-changing relationships with our teenagers, from ways to stay close and connected when they still need us, to staying calm about the need to let them go. In general, teenagers are taking on the responsibilities of adulthood at a slower pace, and us parents are remaining involved in their lives for longer than in the past. Inevitably, though, their focus shifts through this period from us to their friends. But we still matter, as their peers can be feckless. I've shared some ways we can stay close through these changes, by staying focused and being present, helping in practical ways, and building rituals into our day and week which reunite us after the inevitable separations. This requires constant adjustments on our part as parents. The aim is to replace our need to be needed with a new bond based on the connections that exist between us.

While change can feel daunting, we need not feel we are losing our children – we are saying hello to a new relationship and accepting the new people they are becoming, with their own destinies and dreams. We are not our children, and they are not us. Here too, our teenagers can be our teachers. They can show us that the more we allow them to be the people they are destined to be, separate from us, the more we too can be the people we are, not just narrowly boxed into our role as parents. They give us permission to flourish in newly independent ways, just as they too are seeking independence, which is the subject of my next chapter.

9

ENCOURAGING INDEPENDENCE

In the previous chapter, we looked at the relationship between parent and teenager, and the delicate art of staying connected, albeit in new ways as our teenagers seek independence. We discussed the idea that we could reframe this shift as being about letting go of one relationship and welcoming in a new one, and that this may naturally be a time of conflict.

Now I want to focus on a teenager's emotional development through this period, and how we can step back a little from the relationship between us. This is less about how we are getting along through this bumpy period, and how we are connecting, but about them as individuals. A well-adjusted, resilient teenager is one who is beginning to take responsibility for their feelings as a first step to independence, who is responsible for household chores, and who is allowed to roam free and make mistakes. How can we help them become this person?

TRUSTING THEIR FEELINGS

We want them to believe that most of the time they know best. They have their own intuition, and they can build their own emotional awareness. One of the greatest gifts we can give them is the confidence to believe in their own voice, and their own solutions to their own psychological problems. Encouraging them in turn will be a reminder that the same is true for us: as parents and people we should learn to trust our own guidance systems. By teaching them, we teach ourselves too.

Part of this is learning that we are all responsible for our own feelings – an idea I first touched on when discussing our own emotional regulation as parents (see page 69). It's easy to blame others if we are miserable – especially our own parents (not something, clearly, that we want to encourage!) – and it's true that of course others do affect how we feel. But as much as we want to deliver calm and contentment to them, this is not in our gift. As obvious as it sounds, we are not in control of what happens to them. I have five children, and it is impossible for them all to be content all the time. Of course I desire their wellbeing, and I ache when one of them is sad. However it's not for us to deliver happiness: we may at best be responsible for only moments of joy – the time we remember their laptop when they set off without it, or remember the right brand of trainers.

This might at first seem like a ghastly truth but the sooner our children realize that their own power is in fact something liberating, the better. Indeed, they may find that taking responsibility for their feelings gives them a powerful sense of agency and control. They might begin to find ways to cope with their difficult thoughts, to make things better for themselves, to handle their own meltdowns.

GETTING OUT OF THE WAY

Hmm, you might be thinking. You've just told me, in the last chapter, that I need to stay close to my teenagers. Now you're telling me to step back and let them take responsibility for their feelings. I agree, it's tricky, especially as witnessing emotional distress of any sort is painful. Our instinct is to jump in and help resolve their unhappiness, or to take away their anger, to return to a more idyllic and less complicated time when they were younger. Back then we really could put things right, whether that was assuaging their hunger with a boiled egg or soothing the pain of a scraped knee with a hug and a plaster.

But both can be true. We want to be alongside them – all the stuff about staying connected in my last chapter remains relevant – but also accept that there are times when we need to step back and leave them to it. Think of it as a dance in which we sit out some rounds. Boring as it may be, we need a balance. Only by getting out of the way ourselves on occasion can they learn about the emotional heavy lifting that life demands. Only by facing their feelings themselves can our children build the coping skills they will need down the road.

They need to learn how to judge risks for themselves, and to practise dealing with stress and frustration when life does not go according to plan. Unless our children experience the pride and gain the confidence that comes when they push through an obstacle and emerge stronger on the other side, they won't be ready for adulthood. The best way to deal with a brick wall is to find ways to scale it, rather than expecting someone else to take it away.

Perhaps the feeling we most often hope to turn around is that of sadness. It is instinctive to want our children to be happy, particularly if we fall into the trap of feeling responsible for their feelings. I know I find it difficult hearing that my children are miserable. My first instinct is denial: 'Don't be silly, you are fine. There's nothing to be sad about.' My second instinct is to try to fix whatever is causing the upset.

A child's unhappiness can make a parent feel like a failure. Since we do not want to feel like we are at fault, parents can find themselves arguing with their children, telling them that they cannot possibly feel what they self-evidently are feeling and pointing out all the positives and things they have to be grateful for. Instead of chatting more deeply and exploring the teenager's feelings, we want to close them down instead and trivialize their concerns. We perhaps cannot, or do not wish, to acknowledge that all of us from time to time feel desperate and sad.

Like us, our teenagers must develop their own skills of emotional regulation. Our role is to be confident that they can handle their own emotions, including failing. We need to allow our children to experience all their emotions in a safe way. They need to acknowledge that feeling sad sometimes is normal. Good psychological health, I feel, is about having emotions that make sense in their context, good or bad – and then managing them. It's about sadness, not depression; nervousness, not anxiety; painful experiences, not trauma. Distress is part of life. But so too is feeling joyful. Our job is to allow them to become familiar with a whole spectrum of feelings, some of them novel, and to be alongside them, letting them know that it is okay, whatever they feel.

The alternative is that they may become overly dependent on our views. Our advice may stop them finding answers for themselves. We do not want to find ourselves in a position in which they are ringing us three or four times a day, as I used to do with my own mother, unable to take any decision without checking with us first. Over time they will lose the ability to trust their own feelings, the surest guide to what is best for them. Inadvertently we are sending them the message that they are incapable. We are, unwittingly and with the best intentions, subtly undermining them. This ultimately will reduce their confidence. The more we rescue someone, the more we suggest they are broken and need fixing, and that only we know best.

Farbod Akhlaghi, a philosopher at Christ's College, Cambridge, adds a moral dimension to this argument.[1] He says everyone has the right to self-authorship and must make decisions about transformative experiences for themselves. This kind of autonomy is abused by well-meaning parents, who don't know any more than teenagers necessarily do about what is the best decision. None of us knows if a decision is right until afterwards. The person who is affected is not the person giving the advice, but the person receiving it. It is all too easy for us parents to slip into coercing or forcing them into a particular choice. Rather, it is for teenagers to make their own decisions and for us only to share our thoughts if asked: advice never works unless specifically requested.

Stepping back can feel painful. One of my children decided to take an A-level in a subject to which I didn't think he was suited. He failed to get the grade he needed in due course, which led to many repercussions, most of them challenging at the time. But I tried not to berate myself for not getting involved. I had played that game before with a different child. Disagreeing with their academic choice had only made them more determined. I held back second time around, and in the long run, the teenager learned a huge amount by making the mistake himself.

Always giving our teenagers what we think to be the answers to their emotional and practical challenges may seem to have the advantage of building an intimate bond with them. But even that may not prove to be true over the longer term. As our teenagers become adults, and finally begin to listen more to their own voice and feelings, they may even turn on us, their parents, for mollycoddling them during their younger years. They may be angry that we encouraged their dependence and didn't encourage them to make decisions of their own accord.

I was very dependent on my mother when growing up, always asking her opinion. Although at the time it felt supportive and loving of my mother, in retrospect I might have grown up more confident and less anxious if she had not always had an answer to my problems. I struggle to recall her saying, 'What do you think would be a good plan?' or 'What do you feel about it?' As a result, I became more and more reliant on her. I lost much of my ability to trust my own feelings. I found it hard to work out what or who I really liked.

When I was much older, in my late thirties or early forties, when I finally began to listen more to my own voice and to trust my own feelings, I turned on her. I was angry that I had overly relied on her and had not made decisions of my own, but only ones she had sanctioned or suggested. We had a painful few years, and only more recently reached a much calmer phase in our relationship. I realized that I had to take responsibility for my own decisions. Poor woman! It wasn't her fault. Sorting me out was done with good intentions, as is so often the case.

So yes, it is difficult to keep quiet, and step back, as my mother's experience shows. It is true that sometimes we are wiser and more experienced than our children. But whenever the opportunity arises, see if you can stop yourself from jumping in with the answer, at least initially. We can say a lot by saying nothing at all. We may communicate our support more effectively by holding them or stroking their arm. We can see ourselves more as a sounding board. My default answer to any dilemma they are facing is to ask what they are feeling, and where they think the answer might lie.

The key is to show empathy for their predicament and learn to listen. For example, we could say, 'You seem to be really bothered by this' and then help them work out what they might feel. It's about them, not us. Sometimes sitting with them, asking them to close their eyes and try out different statements can help. What feels true, to them?

VALIDATING THEIR FEELINGS

I have found the work of the relationship coach Matthew Fray helpful when it comes to validating teenagers' emotions.[2] He analyses common ways of invalidating other people, and while he writes about romantic relationships, his insights are useful for teaching teenagers too.

The first way of invalidating someone else's experience is to dispute the event itself. Let's say you team up with another mother and take your teenage daughters out for a coffee as a foursome in a bid to encourage their friendship, which is something I did. You think all went well. But your daughter has a different view. Afterwards she tells you, of the other girl, 'She spent the whole time checking her phone. She's not interested in hanging out with me.' And you reply, 'I didn't notice that! She seemed really interested in you. Of course she wants to be friends.' In short, you are disputing the other person's recollection of events. You reason with them and question their version of what happened – and so their problem is supposedly solved.

The second way is to assert that their feelings are wrong. In this case, the dialogue might go like this. Your daughter says, 'I didn't enjoy meeting up with your friend and her daughter at all. In fact, I actually felt sad that she ignored me. I'm not great at making new friends.' And you say, 'Don't be silly. It was fun to go out! There's no reason to feel bad. She liked you. Of course you are good at making new friends.' We decide the other person's feelings are mistaken. That their response is not fair or appropriate; that their response is the wrong reaction to what has occurred. What we are actually saying is, 'You need to recalibrate your feelings not to imagine rejection when it doesn't exist. Then you will not feel so bad anymore.' We are implicitly saying that they should try to feel differently because our emotions are better and healthier than theirs.

Instead, we can believe in the incident that has upset them and help them work out what they are feeling. This can be a simple acknowledgment, like, 'You're upset because you wanted to make a new friend but it didn't feel as though the other girl was interested in you' Mirroring and matching them, using the same language to show you understand, is the opposite of dismissing their feelings. Among the most helpful phrases is a simple, 'I'm hearing you' or asking, 'Let me get this right. You are saying X makes you feel Y? Is that right?' This is about them feeling heard, and having their feelings validated – what the psychiatrist Dan Siegel calls 'feeling felt'. It is about opening a conversation, rather than shutting things down or coming up with solutions. Doing so allows our teenagers to process their feelings. It does not help to be dismissive – 'There's no point worrying about that.' Nor to over-normalize – 'Oh, that happens to everyone.' You could try instead something like, 'I think that happens quite often, but it sounds really difficult.'

We want to help them be able to acknowledge difficult feelings, to sit with and allow them, and pass on our own skills of emotional regulation. Which naturally involves us staying calm. Strong reactions – and raised voices – to whatever they say can be like kryptonite to teenagers, given the sensitivity of their developing brains.

DOING LESS – HOUSEHOLD CHORES

Just as validating their feelings can be helpful in this process of encouraging their independence, so too can doing less, so they build their own competence. This is about teaching your teenagers how to look after themselves properly. However, many parents – myself included – enjoy looking after our offspring and try to do so for much longer than our own parents did.

It may be partly because we can cook, do the laundry and make their appointments more quickly and efficiently than them. There can be something pleasing about showing our competence. Sometimes we do more for our children as we are under pressure ourselves; it is quicker to do so. Or sometimes we keep helping them out as a way of showing our love.

But if you can, resist the temptation to do all their chores at home, or at the least do some chores together so that they pick up some basic household skills such as grocery shopping or doing the laundry before they leave home, for their safety apart from anything else. One teenager, on arriving at university, put her jumper in the oven to warm it up before she put it on. Another put her knickers in the microwave, thinking it was a washing machine, and they burst into flames.

But how do we actually get our teenagers to do such things as remembering to buy loo roll, familiarizing themselves with car insurance, removing a build-up of lint from the filter of the washing machine, or cleaning the toilet?

We get more of the behaviour we take notice of. If we regularly complain about freshly laundered clothes on the floor which our teenager hasn't put away, or crusted cereal bowls under the bed, then counterintuitively we are likely to get more of the same. A teenager is getting the message that they've done wrong and are bad and lazy. They will internalize this message and will have less incentive to change. By contrast, if we notice examples of helpful behaviour – 'I really appreciate you taking the rubbish out' or 'I noticed you tidied up the kitchen and emptied the dishwasher' – teenagers will be more likely to help. The trick is to be specific about exactly what they've done, rather than any generalities about being helpful, which are vague and could be annoying.

You could also be specific about sharing with your teenagers the true effort that goes into household chores. I remember writing a list of what exactly goes into making a meal, from its real start to its real finish. This means meal planning, writing down the ingredients on a shopping list, doing the grocery shop, cleaning the kitchen in preparation for cooking (this may include unloading the dishwasher or clearing the draining board), cooking the meal, setting the table, serving the meal, fetching all the things you forgot to put on the table, clearing the table, cleaning, scrubbing, rinsing, sweeping and wiping until all evidence of the meal that was cooked and eaten has disappeared. It was the level of detail that struck them, a level that in turn made them more willing to help, as they knew how much work others were doing on their behalf.

We want them to learn that cleaning up after themselves is part of being a functioning adult, and that housework and chores can and must be part of ordinary life. The more we give them responsibility for such goals, without overly supervising them beyond a broad framework like 'Can you sort this by Monday?', the more they are likely to respond.

We can present household chores as times when teenagers are allowed and able to zone out and inhabit a different state, away from the usual pressures of friends and homework. Suggest they let their thoughts and moods calm down when they hoover or walk the dog. Household duties give them a break while nurturing new skills. There's an easy satisfaction to sweeping the back patio or folding laundry, which can be pleasing antidotes to a challenging piece of coursework.

One shift in mindset that helped me is to 'treat them more like a lodger'. If you wouldn't routinely do it for a lodger, don't do it for them. Don't infantilize them by always cleaning their football boots, or doing their washing and ironing, or repeatedly taking their dirty mugs downstairs. Here's a simple way to put this approach into practice: every time they ask you to do something for them, see if you can be happy with them doing the task on their own.

ROAMING FREE

Independence starts at home, as teenagers learn to cope with their emotions and doing chores. But it also is about discovering the big bad world, which as we will see in a future chapter, is on the whole safer than we risk-averse parents imagine it. Perhaps they can walk the neighbours' dog, or offer to babysit the neighbours' children.

Remind yourself of your own childhood. Maybe you didn't grow up playing independently on bombsites like some of our grandparents did, but the chances are you had a less supervised and structured childhood than your offspring. The likelihood is you were not under adult supervision all the time, or even most of the time, and nor were you constantly being ferried to activities.

That doesn't mean it's easy. Letting teenagers roam free goes against the understandable desire to insulate our children from literal knocks and scrapes. One answer is to turn around the 'What ifs' when you're wracked by fear of what might happen if your teenager is let loose in the local shopping centre. Instead of 'What if she gets mugged?' or 'What if she doesn't get home?', try 'What if her journey goes to plan and she gains in confidence?'

Hold your nerve. Some psychologists have suggested that mental health problems have risen among this generation of teenagers as we are overprotective and have with good intentions made teenagers fragile.

Peter Gray, a professor at Boston College in Massachusetts in the US, argues that the primary cause of the recent rise in mental health problems is a 'decline over decades in opportunities for children and teenagers to play, roam and engage in other activities independent of direct oversight and control by adults'.[3] College students whose parents were most overprotective or controlling in their day-to-day lives reported higher levels of anxiety and depression.[4]

Yet taking risks, and stretching limits, yields benefits. If you shield muscles too much they atrophy; if you protect bones, and don't use them, you are vulnerable to osteoporosis. A similar approach applies to our teenagers: we must not treat them as Ming vases.

FINANCIAL INDEPENDENCE

Independence also means financial independence. We can have strong emotions around the topic of money. How we use and spend our money can be indicative of how we want to see ourselves – the provider or the protector – and what we value: security or status. It's also influenced by our childhood experience, as we have seen. In general, giving teenagers responsibility with some money of their own makes sense. An allowance can be a way of learning about budgeting. If you give them a little less than they want, they will learn about saving, and indeed running out of funds. You can teach them the difference between 'wanting' something – a phone upgrade, say, which they must fund themselves – and 'needing' something, be that food or electricity, which on the whole you will provide. A part-time job gives a sense of how hard it is to earn their own money for any extras they want.

*

Encouraging independence in our children can be challenging, because as their parents we would prefer them not to suffer. It involves them managing their own feelings, making mistakes, and us not rescuing them when things go wrong. It means letting them discover the world. While it seems that we are doing our best by protecting our children from setbacks and mistakes, by shielding them from difficulties when they are adolescents, we parents, with the best intentions, may be depriving them of the skills needed to deal with difficulties as adults.

Like a seedling that has only ever been on a sunny windowsill and handled with great love and care, they will be cut down by the first real frost. They may have a false sense of security, believing that nothing can ever hurt them and that, if it does, you will always come to the rescue. I know I had this kind of relationship with my own mother. I have tried – not always successfully! – to raise our own children differently. In doing so, I have had to question my own pattern of wanting to be rescued, and relying on the idea that help is always coming, rather than believing I could work things out myself. In encouraging my teenagers to find their independence, I have found more of my own too.

10

COMMUNICATION

In the last two chapters, we've looked at how to stay connected to our teenagers, a delicate dance between supporting them on the one hand, while encouraging their independence on the other. Our ability to do so effectively depends largely on how well we communicate with them, a thread that has run through everything I've already shared so far.

But communication is such an important skill, and such a challenging one to master in the digital age which has upended so many conversational conventions. Because of this, I'm devoting this entire chapter to the topic, adding some more helpful ideas to those I've already suggested (remember the SLANT method, for example? Sit up, Lean forward, and all that? If not, turn to page 116).

Our words need to match an ever-changing biological and technological reality. According to one study, children start tuning out their mother's voice as they enter adolescence because they no longer find it uniquely rewarding.[1] The researchers used MRI scans to reveal that teenagers did not neurobiologically register their mother's voice in the way they did as younger children – which is why they ignore your plea to tidy their rooms. Instead, the reward circuits in the teenage brain, beginning around the age of 13, prioritize unfamiliar voices. While this shift in favour of new voices is a sign of a healthy brain, it makes communication harder.

Another major modern derailer of our conversations is the ubiquitous mobile phone, which adds an extra person to every interaction and monopolizes our attention. Conversation became even harder in our house when my teenagers starting sporting little white cordless earbuds, or wearing flamboyant, outsized headphones which meant they could be easily mistaken for a 1970s radio DJ. Wireless and Bluetooth connection funnels sound into their ears and cuts out the voices of those around them. They are choosing to be in a world of their own.

Technological challenges combine with the bewildering speed at which teenagers are changing. As we've seen, one minute they are all puppy fat, the next they are towering over you with a six-pack. We ourselves can be confused by their physical appearance. Are we dealing with a child, or an adult? What parent has not walked back downstairs, reeling from a teenager's slammed door, when what had previously been a good topic now turns out to be off limits? Our relationship with them can change, fast. One minute a teenage daughter may be happy to talk about her body shape. The next, mentioning a swimsuit can lead to floods of tears. We need to be alive to these shifts, and agile about trying out new ways of chatting that also respect our teenagers' need for privacy. We will no longer know them in the way we once knew them as small children, when we understood what every laugh or tear truly meant. The aim now is to adopt a curious, open attitude, acknowledging that our teenagers are different from us, with a unique way of looking at the world and with their individual imperfections as well as strengths.

Biology, technology and the speed of change are against us. Which makes, er, 'affectionate communication' – the self-explanatory term psychologists use for any behaviour that conveys appreciation, fondness or love – all the more important. How can we talk about an array of problems with nothing taboo? Be able to express divergent opinions and manage conflict well? And provide emotional support for one another, even if that's just listening?

My ideal of good communication starts with a desire to know who my teenager really is, and setting aside my own agenda. There's something special for all of us about the idea that we are known and accepted for who we are. The geneticist and psychiatrist Danielle Dick[2] argues that parents need to have a sense of their teenager's personality traits. Are they extrovert? Conscientious? Neurotic? Dick doesn't believe in a 'right' way to parent. Rather, we should be aware of our own personality traits, and those of our teenagers, and how they combine. A neurotic teenager, for example, will be vulnerable to criticism, and parents need to adapt accordingly when we interact: perhaps encouraging a more timid teenager to try new things, or an extrovert one to have some quiet time.

Yet instead of being curious, we sometimes create stories of who we imagine our children to be, which are often linked to us and our own concerns. Only when we see them for who they are can we properly communicate with them. Indeed the irony of parenting is that children turn our moulds upside down. They come out in ways we never anticipated. It is not our job to change them, but to get to know and respect them. This chapter is full of ideas of how we might do so. Oh, and then there's the small matter of how they might get to know us in turn, and respect who we are too!

DEFEATING THE LURE OF PHONES

Getting to know our teenagers begins with how to compete with their phones – a topic so huge that it gets its own chapter later on in the book (see page 289) and I only touch on the topic here. Over the course of bringing up my own teenagers, phones became more and more ubiquitous. The older ones, who were less influenced by social media, tended to be chattier than the younger ones, who spent more time online. One of my younger teenagers, for example, made it clear he was not offering long conversations. After a few minutes, he would say, 'Thanks, Mum,' and close the door to return to his screen.

One approach is to lean into their interests, especially their digital life. We can be curious about the games they are playing, the music they are listening to, the videos and reels they watch, the YouTube influencers they admire or the podcasts they are enjoying. These are the building blocks of shared connections which foster intimacy. You may learn much en route, too. My life has been enriched by knowing a bit more about my own children's interests. From watching films about why a meat-free life may be healthier, to understanding TikTok; teenagers are impressive and have much to teach us.

You could, counterintuitively, ask their advice or help. The Franklin effect, named after the former US statesman, is when people like someone more after doing a favour for them. Your adolescents may feel more connected to you if they show you how to download an app which will help plan your business trip. Indeed, talking about your work may also be fruitful; it reminds them that you too have a life outside the family, just as they do.

GETTING TO KNOW THEM:
DIFFERENCES BETWEEN THE SEXES

Communication also needs to acknowledge that there are especial challenges when talking to teenage boys. Girls in general are more open about what is happening to them, be that their relationships or friendship circles. With boys it can feel more like they are behaving as permanently startled deer, who will bound away the minute you talk to them. If you do manage to engage them in conversation, it is likely to be factual, rather than about their emotional reality. I have often had to rely on finding out about my boys from their sisters, rather than them. It is a matter of comment at the school gate that parents of boys are often in the dark about their sons. Parents might be unaware of important topics such as their sons' fears about their reputations, if for example a boy is rumoured to have behaved badly to a girl. Fathers are often equally out of the loop.

How then is the best way to engage? Acknowledge that boys and girls communicate differently and lean into the difference. Boys often prefer more direct conversations and enjoy discussing plans and technical details rather than their feelings, so follow their lead. If we parents can engage in conversations of this sort, our teenage boys are then likely to be more forthcoming than if we jump in and immediately ask them about their emotional wellbeing.

We might also try side-by-side conversations, for example sitting in the car or on a walk, rather than talking face to face: teenagers (especially boys) may find it hard to look people in the eye when chatting. Scientists have found that, in conversation, adolescents spend 12 per cent less time looking at the other person's face compared with young adults.[3] This may not necessarily be rude or disrespectful; they may be trying their best to pay attention. However, teenagers find it harder to manage the demands of conversation, including memory, attention and processing content, because of the rapid changes to their thinking brains, as we saw earlier. They may look away, focusing on a plain wall for example, because this reduces the amount of complex visual information they need to take in while following the conversation. It is actually harder for them to listen to what we are saying while looking at us.

We can accept how brief some chats are with sons, and that's okay. The digital age has meant an abundance of information, which has narrowed the attention span in teenagers and adults alike.[4] In addition, messaging and communicating by emojis means that they are more used to shorter interactions.

This does not mean that short communications cannot be meaningful. One approach we might try is the five-minute chat. Naming and labelling the interaction in this way formalizes it and can make it feel more special. Say hello to your teenage boy, and ask if they have time for 'a five-minute chat'. Begin with something that happened to you today to get things started. Then ask them how their day was or something about school. Then put on the big ears.

LISTENING, TIMING AND TONE

A few more thoughts on how to listen well, something I touched on in Chapter 8 on staying connected.

When talking to someone we often think we are listening when in fact we're just waiting for an opportunity to speak, even when it's our own children talking. We are often busy composing our reply in our heads. But engaged listening means, instead, really trying to understand what the other person is trying to get across. Practise leaving space for them to talk and concentrate more on observing and listening, rather than thinking about what your response will be.

I will never forget one conversation with an 18-year-old girl, about whether to tell her best friend that she was going out with the girl's brother. On the one hand, she felt uncomfortable not being straight with her friend, and that by hiding the relationship she was being misleading. On the other hand, she was worried that there might be a confrontation between her and her friend if she fessed up. She imagined her best friend would be cross or would feel betrayed.

I asked her if she wanted advice, or for me to listen. The challenge was for her, not me, to realize what she really felt about the situation. She had to first calm down: she closed her eyes and became less agitated thanks to some breathing exercises. Gradually she disentangled her thoughts and feelings and found some answers – crucially, answers that were hers, not mine. She realized that while she did want to confide the truth at some point to her friend, now was not the right time for her. She had the answers. All I had needed to do was sit quietly.

Just as there's an art to listening, there's an art to recognizing when to talk. You could use the mantra 'Timing, tone and turf' – it's about when you chat, the tone you adopt and where you do it. Anthony Seldon, a writer and headmaster, believes that walking uphill is a great time to tackle a tricky topic. 'When you're all puffed out, the defences come down.' Conversations about guidelines on behaviour, or the time they come back at night, for example, are unlikely to be productive first thing in the morning.

In terms of tone, remember how sensitive teenagers can be and don't forget those developing teenage brains. When they tell us that somebody who isn't cool wore the same outfit as them to school, their brain is reacting as ours might when we've read about a terrible natural disaster with thousands dead and missing. This is why we might want to avoid saying, 'That's ridiculous!' Even non-verbal communication is powerful through this period. A tut-tut from a parent, or raised eyebrow from a friend or teacher, might not seem much. But it can make a teenager feel horribly criticized and attacked, as they respond in an intense way to this kind of communication. Imagine your teenager as a highly sensitive pet, who needs gentle stroking.

Gentle questioning can set the tone rather than giving our own answers. We want our teenagers to find their own responses, remember. 'What are you feeling? What are you going to do about it? What else could be possible?' Questions can be more effective than straight advice, which rarely works unless asked for. There's a difference between giving advice when requested and telling someone what to do. Almost as a rule, if we tell anyone, not just a teenager, what they should or ought to do, they will be tempted to do the opposite.

Equally, if we express a strong view, adolescents are almost certain to disagree, given their need to carve out their own identity. I've always found seeing things differently challenging, interpreting differences of opinion as something threatening and an attack on me personally as a parent. (Joining a book club was helpful with this. I realized that it was possible to disagree, radically, about a book but still stay friends.) This lesson is especially important when communicating with teenagers who are growing up in such a different world from the one we grew up in. They often hold impassioned views on social and environmental change. We can still adopt a light touch even if the subject matter is serious. And it doesn't always need to be verbal: it could be as simple as sending funny dog videos to each other (though be aware their tastes change with lightning speed). You may want to think of neutral topics to build an initial bedrock of dialogue, or things you agree on – even as banal as your favourite kind of coffee.

How we describe and refer to the changing dynamics of our relationship matters too. My mother-in-law still talks about 'the children' when referring to my fifty-something husband and his siblings, much to their irritation. Instead, interactions may be smoother if we avoid referencing our role as their parent, and abandon childhood nicknames. Be cautious about any ways you have hitherto positioned children in the family, or labels such as 'my girl', 'my boy', 'the oldest', 'the youngest', or other generalizations about them as children in your conversations.

READING BEHAVIOUR

So far, I've discussed what we say and when and how we say it, but their behaviour can also be a way of communicating. It can be both about communicating something loving – your teenager cares about you and shows you this by bringing you a hot lemon and honey when you have flu. Or it might be about communicating something negative: your teenager repeatedly fails to clear the table however often they're asked, because they feel you are controlling and bossy. We may have to become detectives, working out what message underlies their actions or body language.

Reading our teenagers involves seeing if what they say and their gestures line up in any one moment. If your teenager tells you he is happy to join you for supper but does so with a weary shrug of his shoulders and a roll of his eyes, then what he said may not be as reliable as his body-language has signalled.

My life changed when I realized that my teenagers' challenging behaviour was a way for them to communicate what they were feeling. They were just trying to tell us something for which they could not find words. It was not designed to punish me personally.

Here's an example: I cooked one of my son's favourite tomato and prawn dishes for him. He didn't eat a thing. More than that, he scraped the food off his plate into the bin, put the plate in the dishwasher and went back up to his room. A younger version of myself might have seen this as spoilt-brat behaviour. I went to the trouble of cooking supper, and far from being grateful, he was rude. Or, indeed, I might even have imagined that the rejection of the pasta was a rejection of me.

Now I realized that not eating was not primarily to do with me: it was about my child's own emotions. About his relationship with himself. Something was being communicated, in a non-verbal way. I needed to find out what was up.

Perhaps he was feeling angry, or maybe sad. Maybe there was something he needed. Or maybe he just wanted some space. While I was keen to know more, I couldn't force communication between us. I had to accept that at a time of his own choosing he might or might not tell me what was going on. For now, all I knew was that his behaviour meant something was up.

Seeing behaviour in this way – that it is about communicating feelings – helps move away from such behaviour becoming a battle of wills along the lines of, 'I want you to eat the supper I have lovingly cooked for you. You don't want to.' But pitting wills against each other is an exhausting and fruitless way to live. Moreover, if you read the behaviour as a battle, only one of you can 'win'. It is better to wait until you have a chance to talk about what is really going on, including explaining your own responses, so they understand the consequences of their behaviour.

When teenagers feel that they are not being heard, they can behave in attention-seeking ways, interrupting conversations, crying or being dramatic, or playing the victim. (Actually, we adults can do that too.) When our teenagers are attention-seeking in these ways, our first reaction may be to be cross; the behaviour is so challenging we cannot see beyond it. We can find it hard, and may even be unwilling, to sympathize with them because the behaviour irritates us. Far from making ourselves available, our anger means we withdraw still further, and perhaps find something else with which to busy ourselves.

Of course, ignoring your teenager is likely to make their need for attention even worse. So, the next time they try to grab your attention, possibly by engaging in something risky, notice whether you are unconsciously pushing back against your offspring's annoying conduct by neglecting them entirely. You may need to find a new way of communicating.

The trick is to connect and communicate with them in the way that suits them. You too can respond through your actions, not words: get them a cup of coffee in the morning, be their taxi service from time to time, put their favourite snack in their packed lunch. These are small acts of love which speak of your affection, while not infantilizing them by doing everything for them.

Meanwhile there is much to be said for physical communication. Some teenagers respond best to holding, a hug or physical intimacy. Being hugged reduces cortisol, the stress hormone.[5] Boys often can find it easier to communicate through touch, especially with their fathers, be that through mock wrestling or gentle jostling. Nothing much needs to be said: your physical affection can be soft and subtle like a warming blanket. These signals say (obviously, but sometimes we need to be obvious) I love you, I'm with you.

The message that we want to convey in all these different ways of communicating is: 'There's nothing you could ever say or do that I wouldn't want to hear about and help you with.'

ACCEPTING OUR OWN LIMITATIONS

I've discussed ways us parents can reach out and communicate with our teenagers, be it by chatting or by reading and responding to their behaviour. Through these encounters, we need to be aware of our own feelings: particularly what the psychotherapist Geraldine Thomas calls our 'shark music' – what feels frightening to us, like the music from the film *Jaws*.[6] When one of my children criticizes me, my own strong reaction can be a feeling of rejection (sorry, you may have guessed that would be the case, if you've read thus far!). If they contradict me, they don't love me! The solution has been to acknowledge this desire to be liked, and to be honest – and responsible for – my own feelings (another theme that may be familiar by now). A 90-second pause and some deep breathing is usually enough for me to return to calm and not be dissuaded from whatever I set out to do because of my own vulnerabilities.

Nothing can make us feel more vulnerable as parents than teenagers who don't want to talk to us at all. I know I often felt upset by what could feel like a brick wall. I tried to be compassionate to myself: to acknowledge my desire to connect with them, and not think of myself as wrong for wanting to, or indeed trying to. I remember one period when I took to tiptoeing round the kitchen, no longer cooking the eggs I wanted for breakfast for fear that the noise of a spitting frying pan would disturb my teenagers when they were silently listening to their music. They weren't hostile or rude, just unavailable. Things improved when I acknowledged to myself my desire to chat, and that there was nothing wrong in that, but also accepted that I couldn't force the outcome. Trying to force them is not only impossible but makes things worse.

Yes, it's unsettling if we don't know what's going on in our teenagers' lives, and they seem mysterious to us. It's likely your teenager doesn't think you could possibly know the depth of emotion they are experiencing (forgetting that you too were an adolescent once yourself). Who hasn't heard the heartfelt cry, 'You wouldn't understand!'? But we must accept such uncertainty. The less we try, the more likely it is that our teenager might open up. Our constant angst-ridden search to know more about their emotional reality, and our desire for all to be well and for our own peace of mind, is a quest that can never be fulfilled.

Our own constant angst-ridden search for peace of mind is a quest that can never be fulfilled. Our relationships and our communication with our teenagers are mutable, and filled with unknowns, and that's okay. Our teenagers can teach us to accept this not knowing.

COMMUNICATING OUR OWN NEEDS
AND BEING FIRM AROUND BOUNDARIES

Doing our best to discover who our teenager is, and validating and understanding them as far as possible, needs to be balanced with teaching them to respect and appreciate others, including us. It's about talking about our life together, and acknowledging that we have needs too. One mother told me the most useful phrase she employed with her teenagers was, 'Here are my limits, because I care for myself, as well as caring for you. The two go together.' We can be compassionate by being firm and drawing boundaries, and in my case, not letting my need to be liked overcome my need to sometimes disagree.

How do you share space in your family home? What expectations do you have about everyday challenges and interactions, such as what they wear or eat, and generally how they behave around the house? Many believe that communicating rules in such spheres give children security and a safe space to develop, letting them taste autonomy without becoming overwhelmed. But having a lot of family rules to govern personal behaviour and for more minor matters has never worked that well for me. A rule seems made to be broken. The only game everyone wants to play is the one that is forbidden, and it is exhausting trying to defend rules. As parents we may try to control them (often because we think their bad behaviour reflects badly on us). But of course, as we've seen, no-one likes to be bossed around or told what to do.

I've found that teenagers respond best to rough guidelines, or family conventions for everyday issues around sharing space, such as doing the washing up or tidying their room. Others prefer to use the word 'boundaries', which implies some flexibility. All these are gentler and less judgemental than the word 'rule'. After breaking a rule, we feel guilty, a feeling that rarely helps because it is so unpleasant. We can't break a guideline in quite the same way. We need to focus on the behaviour we would like to see, and be an example of it ourselves, rather than focusing on what they are not to do. This is never truer than when it comes to considerate behaviour. It is more likely to ensue if we are considerate to our teenagers ourselves. For example, if we do not check our phones at mealtimes (guilty M'Lud) then they are less likely to do so themselves. Children stick to the established conventions of their family if they realize the conventions have a purpose, that they are not just arbitrary but are about sharing space in a civilized way and behaving sensibly.

Say you would prefer your teenagers not to eat takeaway pizzas or burgers at home. Instead of having a rule that this is always forbidden – the very word makes the prospect exciting! – you might discuss the topic with them, and jointly come up with some guidelines. For example, 'I prefer us to eat healthy, home-cooked food, and we should both try to do so. But sometimes a takeaway is okay. How does that sound?'

This is a guideline, one that allows for some flexibility and wriggle room for both of you (who doesn't crave a takeaway from time to time?) and, crucially, one that lets your teenager have agency in how they choose to interpret your guideline. The more they are involved, and the more they feel that this is not something you are imposing on them, the more they are likely to acquiesce.

GOOD WAYS TO SET RULES

There are a few times, though, when only a rule will do, chiefly when it comes to teenage safety, whether that's physical safety (travelling late at night) or biological safety (not taking noxious substances). Rules are especially needed for younger teenagers, whom we cannot always trust to make good choices about their own welfare. Good rules are about caring for them, rather than trying to control them. A useful phrase could be, 'I have to be honest about my concerns.' And it's about them understanding that their behaviour has repercussions on others – including us parents.

The best approach I found to setting rules was to believe in my own legitimate authority as a parent and as an adult in their lives who cared about them greatly, and who worked hard at staying connected to them. Rules work when combined with warmth, a combination typical of a style of parenting known as 'authoritative'.[7] Authority is built on closeness. While we can all suffer from impostor syndrome, the truth was sometimes I did know best, and clear rules were needed when safety was concerned. This was not the same as being needlessly authoritarian about topics that didn't matter, like how they dressed.

Of course, part of setting rules was accepting that I would not always be popular. My own people-pleasing tendency had to be put to one side, as did a lingering attraction to child-centred parenting. But as Dr Riviere put it to me, 'I would be concerned if my teenagers always thought I was great.' She added, 'Children don't follow rules so much as follow relationships.' Even if they seem to disagree with you, if your relationship is close, your teenagers will naturally have a core of respect for you, one that is not earned through appeasement.

My teenagers knew they must call if they were staying out longer than an agreed curfew time. Another rule was that they must have discussed with us how they were planning to get home safely, and they had to keep their phones on.

As my teenagers got older, there were fewer and fewer rules. I had to trust them to make their own choices within broad parameters. Yes, of course they were going to make mistakes, but that was how they were going to learn, as we've established. It is okay for teenagers to have their own views. Who are we to say what are the right and wrong choices for them? Working that out for themselves is a big part of establishing themselves as individuals and forging their own path.

Often when things go wrong, whether that is a teenager being rude to us, or getting drunk, or breaking a rule, it is because the teenager has been overwhelmed by strong feelings. Ideally we want to know what that emotion is and try to help them with it by perhaps using some strategies I've shared earlier in the book. By contrast, sanctions are often about trying to apply logic to a system run by emotion: but this logic can't always overpower the emotion in question. The next time your teenager is overwhelmed by their emotions, are they really going to be able to pause and think, 'Wait a second, if I do this, I'll be punished.' The immediate gratification of punishment may make a parent feel good, but it is unlikely to lead to any change, and it will just make the teenager feel more like a bad child. Studies by neuroscientists confirm that teenagers are less likely to learn from punishment than reward.[8]

In fact, a teenager may already feel bad from making a mistake – whether that was waking you in the middle of the night, or throwing up over the sofa. They may not need anything that adds more blame, shame or pain than they are naturally experiencing from their actions.

*

In this chapter I've shared some ideas about how we might communicate effectively with our teenagers – an ever more important topic in a digital age when we are all in danger of disappearing behind our screens. There are particular challenges with chatting to teenage boys, but accepting that our conversations may be short and sweet is a good start. So too is learning how to listen, and not giving advice – a bit rich coming from this author, you might think! There's much to be said for gentle questioning, learning how to disagree in a safe way, and not taking things too personally ourselves. And many is the time I've had to play detective, figuring out what my children were feeling based on their behaviour rather than anything they said – which was not much.

Communication is obviously two-way. We have needs too! Guidelines are needed around sharing space, and how we treat each other in considerate ways – guidelines that are more likely to be effective if we focus on the behaviour we would like to see, and are examples of it ourselves. And when it comes to teenage safety, we do need some rules, even though as a people-pleaser I've found it hard to impose many. You might be wondering whether that's really enough. My thoughts on communication and guidelines and the odd rule are all very well for minor indiscretions, and if things are going more or less swimmingly, but what if your children are behaving really, really badly? When they are beyond bloody-minded and selfish? If they are lying or aggressive? When their behaviour feels unacceptable to you; the rows are constant? That there really is nothing to recommend being the parent of a teenager, and actually it's jolly annoying to imagine them as blessings. Never fear! These are the topics of my next chapter.

11

ARGUMENTS AND LYING

I have discussed ways to engage in positive and generally peaceful communication. But despite all our best efforts, conversations will at times be fraught. This is a messy period of separation when it's normal to disagree, as our teenagers forge their own identities (remember individuation).

The conflict is often fuelled by the fact that teenagers have not yet completely broken away from us to form their own tribe. A conversation with one of my teenagers, then 17, about a new eyebrow piercing typifies this confused time. There was no safe answer to whether I approved of her piercing. If I approved, then the piercing would no longer serve its purpose of what psychologists call 'an identity reminder'. She wasn't trying to please me, she actually wanted me to disapprove, to remind her of her independence. But if I disapproved, she would be equally annoyed and a row might be in order.

In this precarious in-between phase, as they forge their own personalities, teenagers are acutely self-conscious: they have an imaginary audience in their minds, watching their every mood, whether that audience is their parents or their peers. They are vulnerable to feeling judged – and quick to flare.

In any fierce exchange of views there may well be emotions beneath what is being said – needs that are not being met, as we've seen. It might be that a spat over coming to the dinner table is actually about a teenager feeling rejected because we failed to honour a promise to go out for a burger. But they might feel ashamed of admitting to such a longing. Instead of revealing how they are feeling, a teenager might start a dispute that is superficially over the fact they can't bear dinner being so late. Facing this behaviour isn't easy.

At times the parent will be the person being unreasonable; at times the teenager will. How then to handle conflict?

DEBATING IS OKAY

Not all disagreement is a cause for concern: we can distinguish between debating (which is a useful skill and even enjoyable) and having a proper row (which tends to leave everyone feeling miserable). I've had to learn not to panic when discussions get heated around our kitchen table, as conversation when I was growing up tended to avoid anything controversial, and we rarely talked about politics or our emotions. Debating was not something we did, perhaps because such discussions can have the potential for serious conflict and misunderstanding if mishandled.

I only learned late in my forties that I need not worry so much when my family argued. I realized that disagreement did not affect our mutual love and respect, even if we all got worked up about our views. After all, we all see the world through our own eyes, and experience it in our own unique way. But despite such differences we could still like each other and enjoy talking. It's worth remembering this, as I've found there's quite some anxiety among parents about even the mildest arguments right now – even the simplest debate can result in young people feeling disrespected and got at. And we can feel the same. So much so, that sometimes, disagreeing with a teenager can be followed by a cascade of proclamations of love and gratitude. We may feel that having a different opinion brings our love for our adolescent into question so we'd much rather not.

The breakthrough for me was to remind myself that it is natural for teenagers to disagree with us, and good that they do. They are working out what they think, and growing up in the process rather than rebelling for the sake of it. The kitchen table can become a good place for debate, a place where we can test our own arguments, challenge bad ideas and exercise our moral muscles. Arguing is about how to disagree while still respecting the other's right to hold a different view. Yes, sometimes discussions get shouty, voices are raised, but there is joy in learning about an opposing view, and in realizing that others hold different views as dearly as we hold ours. This kind of cognitive exercise is crucial for the teenage brain, and our own, especially for the hippocampus. This is a vital brain region for navigation and memory skills; it grows through exercising those faculties and shrinks when it doesn't. It can be stimulated in the real world by finding one's way about geographically, or in the imaginative world by navigating through arguments and ideas, such as by reading challenging and unfamiliar texts or exchanging challenging and unfamiliar views. In short, heated discussions around the table when we swap differing views is good for us and our teenagers.

This is especially relevant because many teenagers talk of their fears of being cancelled or saying the 'wrong' thing. As parents, we can teach them to be sensitive to others – conscious that if, for example, you are a white bloke, you should be careful about pontificating on black feminism without acknowledging your lack of credentials. But we also want the dinner table to be a space where it is safe to bandy around controversial topics, to be flexible and understand the view opposing the zeitgeist of the times, even at the risk of offense. Our children benefit from all sorts of differing points of view, be it from different cultures or different kinds of people.[1] It is especially valuable for children to learn that their parents see things differently, from each other and from them. Indeed, it can be frightening for children if their parents or the adults in their life act as one, uniting in a god-like consensus about the world.

Young people care and know about things – about Black Lives Matter, the planet, being kind. While activism has long been synonymous with youth culture – from the May 1968 protests in France to Extinction Rebellion today – our teenagers are exposed to news in a different way from us, and are able to communicate and mobilize about social justice problems in ways that set them apart from previous generations. We may have a lot to learn.

Both we and our children might find it helpful to remember that these kinds of debates or disagreements are rarely personal attacks. We want to keep communication flowing, as we saw in the previous chapter, and it's okay to disagree. Once again, it's worth reminding all concerned that adults can see things differently – an insight our children need as they navigate a world in which things are increasingly censored. Their views are good for us and can give us perspective on the future; and ours are good for them. Phrases such as, 'That's an interesting point of view' or 'It's possible to see things differently' are helpful. Your teenager may be able to acknowledge that you too have an opinion, your views are not hopelessly regressive, and you are different from them. The aim is to alter the feel of the discussion from an adversarial one to one that is about acknowledging each other's feelings and differences. Many psychologists, including the American professor and author Adam Grant, note that the most creative people grow up in homes where there were lots of heated discussions about general topics,[2,3,4] though he acknowledges that these are safe households, without fistfights or personal insults. Those growing up in properly aggressive households may struggle to be creative because they are too fearful.

MAKING THE BEST OF A ROW

Having a debate is different from a proper row, which self-evidently we want to avoid. Here are some thoughts on reducing the intensity of rows and making them more productive. Underpinning them all is the idea that rowing is not about who is in charge, but about understanding: teenagers understanding you, you understanding them, and understanding that you see things differently. A friend found sticking up a poster in their family kitchen helpful. It showed two plants: one a flowering weed, the other a flower. Another person may see the weed as a flower, even if we don't. Differing opinions are okay – repeat after me.

Naturally it follows that curiosity about their experience, and sharing how you both feel, are in order if there's to be anything fruitful about a row. A better row is about exploring and widening the possibilities of how to do things differently in the future, so that it need not be repeated.

First of all, if you can feel a row brewing, you might want to step out of trouble's way by going into a different room. You could say something like, 'This isn't the conversation I meant to have' or, instead of giving an immediate response, 'Can I have a minute to think?' By which you really mean some time and not just one minute. These phrases can discharge the row's fierceness.

Vent privately before you talk to your teenager – things like going upstairs and punching a pillow can disrupt anger mechanisms. You might return in a calmer frame of mind, able to think and express yourself more clearly. No one can access their highest level of thinking when they are in 'threat' mode. You might even leave the house altogether. Allow your teenager to do the same. Associating what should be the haven of home with aggression and conflict is unhelpful. Suggest that you will talk about the issue later when you are both calmer, and that it is hard for anyone to hear each other in an overheated state. That is something on which you are at least likely to agree.

The psychotherapist Julia Bueno also likes the idea of 'naming your process', or explaining what you are experiencing and why you are behaving as you are.[5] You might say, 'I am sorry but I'm so angry right now I can't think clearly so I'm going to leave the room so as to not say something I don't mean. I wish I could be calmer, I promise we are going to come back to this later.' This is preferable to storming out of the room and slamming the door – though sometimes that's the best we can do when feelings are so big.

Bueno even argues that going to sleep on a row is a good idea! 'Strike while the iron is cold' is her fabulous phrase. 'It's so important to gauge when you are ready to talk, when you aren't clinging on with fury,' she says. 'If you feel a fire simmering, give it more time to peter out, and flag to your teen "I'd really like to talk about this soon" – maybe even name a day.' This is an approach the psychotherapist Esther Perel also adopts in couples' therapy.[6]

(By the way, accepting and formalizing time apart can make life with your teenager less provocative more generally and reduce the overall number of rows all in. You may find, as I have, that you too benefit from time alone in which you can replenish your own resources. I have tried to make a virtue of this extra space, taking time to walk at the weekend. Finding time to read. Maybe you can close your own door for a while. And of course, always remember to knock on theirs.)

If a row is unavoidable, see if you can focus on only the matter in hand. Don't throw in everything but the kitchen sink. If the row is about how late they returned last night, don't also complain about how they never listen, leave their rooms in a mess, and spend too much time on their phones. This is all too common a temptation given that our minds naturally make connections and write negative stories. By doing so, we are once again in danger of giving attention to the behaviour we don't want, rather than focusing on what we would like. Our aim is to solve a problem rather than expand the reasons for arguing. Two techniques help me de-escalate. First, at the end of every sentence, I add a 'power pause'. During this pause, I stop, breathe and notice any escalation. Second, I list any points of agreement or appreciation instead of adding other grievances: a sort of positive escalation. In the case of a late-returning teenager I might say I appreciated the fact that they had kept their phone switched on and that they had been apologetic.

It's also important to be aware of any difficulties that may be coming up for you personally that are nothing to do with your teenager. Remember your own 'shark music' and that you may be experiencing an emotional response that is less about your teen and more something you should address yourself. And mind your language.

HELPFUL LANGUAGE AND PHRASES

The exact words and the tone in which you use them matter, especially when having an argument. Research suggests harsh words and excessive yelling are as damaging as physical abuse.[7] Imagine you are speaking French when you have a row – it will remind you to be careful with the phrases you use.

One magic trick is to begin sentences with 'I'. Let's imagine the argument is about a teenager staying out late, and you didn't know where they were. Start with, 'I might be wrong and maybe you tried to tell me your whereabouts . . .' Focus on your undeniable feelings rather than on what may be disputed facts. Instead of saying, 'You were out until four and behaving in an unacceptable way,' say, 'I don't feel comfortable with not knowing where you are.' Your teenager cannot dismiss the truth of your feelings, whereas they could disagree with your timings. Equally, instead of saying, 'You need to let me know your movements,' you might say, 'I worry about your safety and we've agreed on a rule that you let me know if you are running late so I know you're okay.' The focus is on you, and how their behaviour affects you, rather than labelling the teenager in a personal and critical way.

It can be surprising how well teenagers take it when you tell the truth about your own feelings with sentences beginning with that magical 'I'. I've found they appreciate that we are being honest, and as we have seen, owning our feelings means our child is more likely to own and be open with theirs too. We do not have to be silent martyrs or emotionless robots.

It can also be helpful to use 'we' from time to time, as in, 'When we don't listen to each other . . .' or, 'When we talk over each other . . .' This suggests we are all in this discussion together. Using 'we' also suggests a common humanity and that on some level you are alike.

As we saw in Chapter 10 on ways to communicate, keep asking questions, which perhaps shows your willingness to see the bigger picture. What was going on for them, that they stayed out so late? Was it peer pressure? Did they feel it would be uncool if they didn't stay out as late as their friends? It's worth taking some time to tease out any feelings that underlie their behaviour.

You can also focus on your teenager's positive intentions instead of identifying them with their impulses, actions or failures. You might say, 'I know this isn't what you wanted to happen' or 'It's okay, you'll get there, we all make mistakes.' The more we notice positive behaviour, as we've seen, the more of that behaviour we are likely to get.

COMING TO SOME SORT OF RESOLUTION

Once you and your teenagers have expressed your thoughts, which of course may take some time, emotions should settle down again. You might want to agree on how you would both like to behave in the future and be clear about what you need out of the row. Remember that something good can come out of a difficult situation; no experience is ever without some value. Keep stressing what you like about your teenager, or about anything productive that has happened, not what you dislike. Counterintuitively, this is a time to increase your presence in their lives, whether that's by sending an encouraging text message or amusing meme, or making a gesture such as a hot water bottle in their bed or their favourite food in the fridge. One father said to me, 'When things have been hard is the time to suggest you go out and grab a burger. Step in, not away. You can acknowledge you've had a bad time together, but few teenagers refuse free food.' The message is that their behaviour was not okay, but we still want to spend time with them. We won't be forced out by anything they do.

Crucially, resolution can be encouraged by a simple 'I'm sorry'. It is not our mistakes that matter so much as putting them right with an apology – the notion of rupture and repair I touched on earlier. We can always make amends. We can affirm the validity of our feelings, while acknowledging that the way we communicated them was unhelpful and our own fault. Helpful phrases include 'I was not in a great place', 'I regret that' and 'It was nothing to do with you'.

Good can come from a row. If you think of arguments as discussions that result in something productive, they can feel less damaging and frightening. This allows for the possibility of change. It follows that we do well to avoid expressions such as 'You never' or 'You always' or 'You are', which imply your teenager has a fixed personality and can't change, rather than the possibility of new behaviours.

Sometimes, having an argument leads to discovering a new rule you need to establish. Take one example. I well remember the agony of the time one of my teenagers went to a festival for the day. Of course, as she set off on a sunny July morning, I asked if she had her phone. And would she ring me when she was leaving the festival to come back to London? And what train would she be getting back? These were all the rules we had agreed on, about letting me know she was safe. As she skipped off to the station with a cheery 'Don't worry, Mum!', I had little inkling of the dramas ahead.

All started well: she did text me when they arrived. But then for the next six hours all communication went dead. Despite my own understanding of the need not to catastrophize, and to check my own spiralling thoughts, by the time it got to 10pm and I had heard nothing, in my mind she had been murdered in some West Country field.

Eventually, she limped back into the house at around 1am, having just caught the last train home. Her phone battery had died. We had a row. But something productive came out of our argument. We agreed that next time, things would be different. A new rule to add to our list was that if her phone ran out of power, she would borrow one. We both understood each other a little more after our row, which also made it productive. My teenager realized more deeply that her behaviour had an effect on me. And we both saw that a few practical small shifts in her behaviour in certain situations would have a big emotional impact on me.

Or a second example. We had organized a family dinner. One of our teenagers had made other plans. The row was about forcing him to attend the dinner. He didn't want to join us: I felt rejected, he felt bossed about. We were both trying to force certain behaviour onto the other person – I wanted him to stay, he wanted me to allow him not to attend. Again, the answer to the problem was partly practical. We agreed to move the date so the teenager could come. On one level this was an obvious example of compromising.

On another level, though, it was about both of us understanding the emotions we were experiencing. The breakthrough – for both of us – was feeling understood. He understood that I could feel upset; I understood that his independence mattered to him. Again, this was not about who was in charge, but about understanding. Subsequent discussions about turning up to family dinners became easier.

LYING

Just as we all make mistakes, we all lie on occasion. If you swap the word 'lie' for 'fib' and are honest, all of us probably fib multiple times a day, from saying, 'That's okay' when someone steps on our toe on the bus to telling a colleague that their new hairstyle looks great. Research suggests that teenagers lie more than any other age group. But lying can be about showing kindness, empathy or leadership.[8]

Teenagers lie for lots of reasons. One is in order to protect us from information they believe will worry us. One of my children believed, probably rightly, that if they had told me they were so drunk at a festival their friend took them to the first aid tent, or that they had faked their ID to get into a club, I would have worried and been furious. Yes, I would have.

Another reason why adolescents might mislead us is that they are in the period of their life when they are forging their own identity. Part of creating a new identity is keeping some things private. Perhaps there's also an element of wishful thinking – they lie that they didn't have five vodka shots because they wish they hadn't.

We can all understand that these kinds of lies are not told with the intention to harm. Far from standing in the way of good communication, these white lies lubricate the social wheels. In this sense, lying can have the power to do good; we lie to protect others' feelings. We might say to a teenager that we were stuck in traffic, which is kinder than, 'I didn't think it important enough to leave on time.' We continue to lie to our children as they grow up, usually in this same spirit of making life better for them, as they do to us.

This intention behind a lie matters. If a teenager asks us what we think of their outfit, we might say it looks great. Were we to share the truth – that we are appalled by their short skirt and see-through blouse – we might puncture their fragile self-confidence. Sometimes, deception can be kind and telling the truth can be cruel. Will there be fewer damaging consequences if I lie than if I tell the truth?

So, giving and receiving some amount of misleading information is normal and understandable for both us and our teenagers. But bigger lies are different. They indicate a level of distress, shame or worry that needs to be discussed. Make a gentle start to the conversation by once again trying to acknowledge good intentions. Try gentle comments like, 'Should we look at this another way?' or 'Can we revisit the conversation we had earlier?', which won't box our teenagers into a corner. Unless we take the sting out of the inevitable feelings of shame, the teenager is unlikely to open up about what's really been going on. They are not telling the truth, because they believe their behaviour is transgressive. They may also lie if they fear an overreaction from us parents.

As we've established, teenagers need to know that we can be trusted to keep loving them, whatever they feel or do. If you realize your teenager is lying, see if you can work out what is behind the lie. Is it to protect you in some way? Is it because of their need for privacy and experimentation away from you? Or is it because they are behaving badly and risk being punished?

If we can accept and validate whatever feeling is behind the lying, we may find ourselves more forgiving of it. They will see that we have the capacity to understand and accept their feelings and the reasons they lied. This gentler, more understanding approach may reduce lying more effectively than a punitive one. Only then will they confide in us and tell us the truth of their lives. The more judgemental we are, the less we will know what is really happening to them.

*

Lying and rowing aren't great. But this is a natural period of conflict, and we can be more at ease with our differences if we remember this fact. We can harness the teenage need to disagree with us in a positive way, encouraging debate and discussion, especially at a time when teenagers worry about being cancelled. We can even make rowing more positive, finding ways to make arguments less heated and being examples to our teenagers of how to manage our own strong feelings and our own careful use of language. (Not always possible, I know!) And if we understand why teenagers lie, we may be more forgiving of their fibs, and they in turn may feel less need to deceive us. All of which sounds easy, but of course conflict can be exceptionally painful for us parents. I remember my own mother once telling me I had 'put the knife in so deep' in one heated row – and I still regret my teenage fury to this day. One consolation is that this period of conflict will pass. Intense rowing between adults and teenagers peaks in early or mid-adolescence.[9, 10] Thereafter they no longer feel us, their parents, are letting down what can be considered as their 'brand'. They effectively have their own independent identity now.

Which brings me to the subject of the next section. My last few chapters have been focused on how parents might understand the teenage brain, the adolescent need for connection as well as for independence, and effective ways to communicate. It's been largely about our relationship with them. Now I want to shift to thinking more about their relationship with themselves – what does their brand or identity look like? In particular, how do they feel about their appearance, sexuality and gender? These are the topics of Part Three.

ACCEPTING YOURSELF

YOUR TEENAGER'S CONNECTION WITH THEMSELF

12

THEIR APPEARANCE

How adolescents feel about their looks affects so much else – their gender identity and their sexual lives, as well as their connection with others. Which is why this part of the book begins with this chapter on appearance. The topic has always been of consuming interest to adolescents. I remember my granny asking me, aged about 13, what I wanted to be when I grew up. I answered 'Pretty'. The teenage obsession with looks is even more relevant in a digital age.

While the technology is new, teenagers are still remarkably conventional about what is deemed attractive.[1] Being sporty and athletic makes for male popularity, while being conventionally pretty – such as being slim with long hair – makes for female success. The closer to these stereotypical ideals you are, the more likely you are to be popular; the further away, the more likely you are to be bullied or ostracized. Far from challenging convention, when it comes to looks, teenagers are fundamentally conservative.[2]

Boys can become obsessed with online fitness content, unrealistic transformations from puny to muscular, and the physiques of certain influencers and film stars, all of whom are chiselled from the same marble. Their lives are measured out in how they can increase the size of their quads or up the number of press-ups they can manage compared to their peers. Meanwhile, girls aspire to small waistlines, curves in the right places, large breasts and long legs, a bit like Barbie dolls.

It's true that gender stereotypes are becoming a little more fluid, though this has hardly dented teenage conservatism more broadly. This is partly thanks to the queer community, some of whom defy traditional masculine images of strength and power, while others reject more traditional feminine images in favour of looking young and slim and boyish. Then there is a plethora of androgynous figures like the pop star Harry Styles, himself following in the tradition of David Bowie.

But influencers of both sexes with large followings tend to be tall, sporty – and slim; and our teenagers aspire to be like them. Since the creators of these posts are making money from their content, this restricted set of body types is also equated with worldly success. The message is: if you look like this, then you are not just gorgeous, but you'll also do well in life. It is not just about your appearance, but who you are.

The problem, of course, is that few teenagers fulfil these very narrow conventions of what it is to be attractive, which leads to other problems. As my therapist friend Tara Saglio puts it, dissatisfaction with appearance is 'the hook that anxiety and depression hang their hats on.'[3] This chapter is about how we can support our teenagers to feel good about themselves nonetheless.

UNDERSTANDING THE TEENAGE PREOCCUPATION WITH APPEARANCE

Supporting our teenagers begins with understanding why looks matter so much, what's actually happening to them, and the pressure they are under. Looks are about fitting in, as social exclusion is profoundly threatening to them. They have evolved to attach themselves to a group. Safety comes from being the same as the group; danger comes from being different. The quickest way to fit in is to look and behave like their friends, which is why you will see a group of teenagers all dressed the same, with the same hairstyles and even the same mannerisms.

While fitting in with their friends is a priority, adolescents are also sensitive to whether their looks are in tune with their family. Perhaps they feel uncomfortable about being the biggest or smallest person in their family, or maybe they don't feel they fit in because they became sexually mature more quickly than their siblings, even siblings who are older than them. Most younger siblings are upset at having to step into the shoes of older siblings in the way they dress – literally in some cases if they are expected to wear family cast-offs. Other younger siblings will want to copy the dress and appearance of older family members.

Finally, adolescents want to fit in at school. They can be affected by all kinds of differences, from something as seemingly minor as having brown hair in a class full of blondes, to more important-seeming issues like being of a different race to almost everyone else in their neighbourhood.

As if trying to fit in to all these different environments wasn't challenging enough, there are also dramatic physical changes to contend with that happen through puberty, both to them and to their friends. One minute they are the same height as their best friend, the next he or she has shot up, looking years older and leaving them behind as if they were still at primary school. People treat teenagers differently based on their physical size. One mother told me that many of her teenage son's problems stemmed from the fact that he was already 6ft 2in when he was 14, and thus was often treated as an adult when he was still childish in many ways.

Then, just as they are starting to adapt to one body shape, their body changes. Skin problems, body odour and pubic hair manifest suddenly. Boys may be self-conscious about a growing larynx or Adam's apple, their voices breaking and cracking, having wet dreams, their height and muscularity changing swiftly for some, not swiftly enough for others, and a fear of being puny.

Girls are having to cope with having periods and the physical changes that brings. Having periods is indeed hard, messy, annoying and often painful (and indeed in the past used to be called 'the curse'). It would invalidate much of our teenage daughters' experience if we denied this. However, there may be some space to add that this is also a beautiful, natural event happening because of their fertility. We can frame this as a blessing and have reverence for this rite of passage into womanhood. We might even give them a token like a small piece of jewellery or a handwritten letter to honour menarche and to make it sacred, not shameful. We can be sensitive to the way monthly hormonal changes and differing levels of progesterone and oestrogen can affect their skin, as well as their moods.

Girl after girl told me how ill at ease they felt about their appearance when entering womanhood; it can feel like walking through fire. Their appearance attracts a new wolfish attention: cars slow, boys snigger, adult men stare. Their breasts jiggle during PE and prompt smutty jokes.

So your teenager is coping with a lot: trying to fit in as well as their changing body. And these changes are happening amid multiple pressures to look a certain conventional way. Let's start with teenage boys. There's little room for them to be different. Women alarmed about unrealistic models of female perfectionism have started the Body Positivity Movement, with pictures of stretch marks and tummies online. Plenty of sassy teenage girls talk about the dangers of diet culture on TikTok. However, there is little such support for straight young men.

Meanwhile, many gay young men report a similarly oppressive culture when it comes to their appearance: studies show that gay men tend to be more vulnerable to media influence and tend to have a higher desire to be slim, with more body-image concerns than their straight counterparts.[4] A corollary to this is that homosexual and bisexual men tend to be more vulnerable and prone to disordered eating and negatively impacted body image than straight men.[5]

Such worries can be masked by seemingly healthy habits such as exercise regimes to build muscle mass – which is the kind of positive relationship with exercise that we parents usually encourage. We may also underestimate the challenges our sons are facing as it might seem like puberty involves fewer dramatic changes for them than for girls.

Of course, teenage girls are just as vulnerable to pressure to look a certain conventional way, as we've seen: blond, leggy and slim. Sexualized images of young women (and even of children, wearing high heels and cropped tops) have become more common, as has pornography. Clothing trends that emphasize sexuality can also have an effect, from the rise in wearing lingerie and corsets as normal outwear to crop tops, ultra-low-rise jeans and body-hugging dresses.

HOW SOCIAL MEDIA MADE THINGS EVEN HARDER

Social media, especially apps like Instagram which are more about images than words, makes the teenage obsession with looks even more intense. 'I'm upset if I don't have, say, a hundred likes on my profile picture,' 16-year-old Freya told me at a school talk.

She continued, 'You need your phone continually, for school stuff, for meeting up with friends. So even if you are not wanting to be, you are always on your phone and always seeing this stuff, always thinking about how you look.' Due to the reflex to compare ourselves with others, which is heightened in adolescence, teenagers wish to present the version of themselves that most closely fits conventional 'Insta' beauty. They don't want a normal appearance but a special one. In the same way, they want to be above average intelligence, and feel if they don't achieve these ideals, they are damned to failure.

Yet social media is like a fairground hall of mirrors, where everything is distorted. Teenagers see images of others that are not true to life, making them feeling even more inadequate. Instagram itself acknowledges its platform can be toxic for teenagers. 'We make body image issues worse for one in three teen girls' read one slide from an internal presentation in 2019, leaked to the *Wall Street Journal*.[6]

Photo editing includes digital enhancement and filters to make girls look thinner or curvier, or even create different facial features – whatever brings them closer to the idealized appearance. One in four British women will only upload an image after filtering, or when edited, with the figure rising to two in five in the 16–25 age group.[7] New sophisticated filters like Bold Glamour take retouching to levels that were only previously accessible to the editors of fashion magazines.

Real-life cosmetic procedures that might once have been seen as extreme are now widely on offer on social media: fox-eye surgery to lift and reposition the corners of the eye, lip-flips that use Botox to create fuller, curled-up top lips, and so on.

With our perception of our bodies so far distorted (a phenomenon now recognized by doctors as 'Snapchat dysmorphia'), it is easy to forget that underneath there is a body of skin and bones and a beating heart.

HELPING THEM FEEL BETTER ABOUT THEIR BODY

How can we parents dial down this obsession with appearance, and the inevitable dissatisfaction most teenagers feel about not living up to expectations? First, the online world. Discuss the inauthenticity of digital images and the extent to which these images are curated and edited. See if they can acknowledge that they too may be presenting a sanitized version of themselves rather than all the varied aspects of being a whole human being, their full personality and physical changeability.

Talk in general terms about adjusting their online profile to match more closely with their reality. There is power in being true to ourselves, and not being afraid of showing some depth behind the surface image. And suggest they post something different. Teenagers I spoke to in one West London school talked about the pleasure of first discovering, and then posting, arty images of aspects of the world that strike them, such as sunsets, dramatic buildings or vintage cars, rather than images of themselves. These 'this is what I'm seeing today' posts can help teenagers escape from the tyranny of images being only of themselves.

As well as adjusting their own profile, encourage them to ditch the 'beautiful skinny people in a hammock' accounts, as one of my own daughters, who was 15 at the time, put it to me. They may find themselves inspired instead by social media accounts that show more realistic images from people's lives. Many accounts on Instagram now promote difference and empowerment, often with humour. There are other apps that encourage more realistic shapes, such as BeReal and TruePic. You could search online for accounts that focus on acceptance and positivity, or body positive activists.

It might be worth sharing with them the hard evidence we now have that reducing time on apps such as Instagram and TikTok improves negative body image. During one four-week trial, 220 undergraduates aged 17–25 were asked to use social media as normal for the first week, then half were asked to limit their use to less than 60 minutes a day while the rest carried on as normal. Participants who cut down saw an improvement in how they recorded their appearance.[8]

ENCOURAGING SELF-ACCEPTANCE

There are other ways we can help more broadly. The problem may not be social media as much as the way we engage with it. This is about how our teenagers feel about themselves. The goal is self-acceptance, rather than obtaining the approval of others. The most important person who needs to accept them is themselves. But for many of us, our self-esteem is in the hands of strangers. We try to win their acceptance and validation when we show off our slim figures (girls) or toned bodies (boys). We experience a rush of pride when others compliment us. This is putting a lot of value in what others think of us, and that is something we can never control entirely.

Instead, we should help teenagers to have an independent core of worth – a self-belief – and to take pleasure in their appearance, adopting the kind of supportive and kindly viewpoints discussed in Chapter 4, ones we ourselves now hold (we hope). Trying to backfill this void with the esteem or approval of others is futile. No amount of external validation of how our teenagers look will ever stick. Having a core of self-worth will also help arm teenagers whose appearance is disparaged by others: yes, unkind comments from peers are naturally distressing, but they will take their judgements less to heart if they have a sense of *amour propre*.

Building this kind of self-acceptance about their appearance is less about their trying to change their behaviour, but about their adopting a kindly attitude to themselves. Teenagers might adopt a 'good enough' approach to their appearance, just as we have done to our parenting. This perspective makes it much less tiring to think about their looks; they do not have to convince themselves that they are reaching the heights of physical perfection to be worthy of their own praise.

There's a delicate balance to strike here. It's easy to veer towards invalidating their concerns. Teenagers can be quick to say that we parents don't understand the stress they are under; that there's no avoiding that young people care very much about their appearance, nor the fact that how they look online matters greatly to them. We have to acknowledge the societal pressure they are under. We might talk in general terms about the stress to look a certain way, showing we are aware of the burden they carry, especially in a sexualized world where girls are expected to wax all their pubic hair and boys to have a six-pack.

A healthy weight is different for everyone, based on their build and height. Equally, for both sexes, genitalia come in all sorts of shapes and sizes. It is this understanding that we are trying to encourage: a sense that there are multiple ways to look and be. This diminishes the anxiety that stems from trying to fit into a narrow ideal of having a 'better than normal' appearance.

Our goal should be to encourage the question 'What if . . .?' What if you didn't have to conform? What if you could accept yourself how you are? What if you could accept others how they are? What if you could accept becoming a differently shaped adult? What might life feel like then? How do you question and replace society's and the media's standards of beauty, attractiveness and sexiness?

Some of the ideas I have already shared about questioning our thoughts can contribute to the 'What if' feeling in your exchanges with your teenagers. For example, if you are watching TV together and they make a negative comment about their appearance, you can use it to ask: what if that comment was just a thought? What if they didn't have to believe it? Remind them of ways of challenging their thoughts, beginning with the sentence, 'I am having this thought that I look unattractive' rather than 'I look unattractive', in a calm acknowledgement of an unhelpful way of thinking.

You could go one step further. If your daughter says, 'I hate my stomach' or your son says, 'I'm so small and pathetic', what they may mean is 'I feel unlovable' or 'I'm scared people might reject me because I don't fit in'. Yes, these are uncomfortable and painful feelings to acknowledge. But giving these feelings a voice, or writing them down, may help teenagers work out what they truly need and how to accept themselves, rather than focusing their thoughts solely on bodies they dislike. A hug never goes amiss in moments such as these.

OUR OWN APPEARANCE AND COMMENTING ON THEIRS

How our teenagers feel about themselves and their appearance will naturally be influenced by how we feel about our own bodies. Even if we don't always feel it, try to be positive. As the psychotherapist Susie Orbach has said, 'Never, ever denigrate your own body in front of your daughter. If she sees you look in the mirror, look delighted.'[9]

If you can, be relaxed around your own nudity, be that in the bath or when swimming and getting changed. One study suggests that children who grew up around nudity were more comfortable with their bodies themselves as adults: they had slightly better levels of self-esteem and a more positive body image.[10]

How adults interact with each other about their appearance can also affect our teenagers. One woman, now in her thirties, shared her family's experience growing up and how the way they talked about figures affected her cousin:

My aunt's husband continually made comments about her (for example, that she had let herself go). Sometimes these were made in jest, other times they could be extremely unkind, calling her fat or chubby and commenting on her eating. My female cousin who is only a few years younger than me grew up with this dialogue as the continual background noise to her adolescence, which became the norm. I do not doubt (neither does she) that it resulted in her being a teenager who became obsessive about her physical appearance to the extent she has battled with anorexia and extreme anxiety over food. I think probably she has internalized her father's comments about her mother's appearance as comments that could one day be directed at her. It's really sad.

Just as we need to be careful about commenting on how we or other people look, equally we can be sensitive about how we comment on our teenagers' appearance. One strategy is to avoid compliments altogether, but this is unrealistic for most parents. Sometimes our offspring look so lovely that we can't stop ourselves saying so. Even if our teenager bats the compliment away – 'You're just saying that because you're my mum' – they may be secretly pleased. One teenager told me that her mother never once complimented her on her appearance, and that she was jealous of girlfriends whose mothers told their daughters how pretty they looked. I can remember clearly each and every time my own mother complimented me on my looks. A nice compromise is to give our teenagers a range of compliments, rather than solely focusing on how they look, be that their kindness or courage, or skills they may have, from baking to remembering to feed the dog. This is about celebrating their whole person, in all its aspects, rather than obsessing about sculpting or changing one bit of their physical bodies, which are not commodities.

You are unlikely to be able to alter the way other family members talk about appearance. One of my teenagers was mortified by a comment about her figure on one family holiday, made by a relation, so much so that she stopped coming on trips to the beach. Your best bet is to have a discussion with your teenager about your relations' slightly old-fashioned views in a playful, light-touch way.

There are also good and bad times to have these kinds of conversations. Choose your moment. Avoid triggers when they might feel vulnerable – when they're in a swimsuit, say, in a changing room or on the beach.

ADOPTING SOME HELPFUL PERSPECTIVES ABOUT THEIR APPEARANCE

Teenagers will also be influenced by the way we talk about body image and appearance more broadly. We might be able to weave in some more comprehensive, helpful perspectives. You could share the idea, for example, that there is nothing fixed or permanent in how we feel about our body image. A statement such as 'I am short' might be true or not, depending on what country you are in, or who else is standing in the same room as you at that moment. If you are in Holland, for a simple example – the Dutch are among the tallest people in Europe – no wonder you might feel small. By contrast, on average, people from Asia are smaller than Europeans. Moreover of course, our thoughts will also change as we ourselves change. Time and experience really do change perspectives. One of the best conversations I had with one of my teenagers who was worried about her looks was when I shared my own experience of severe acne. Now, they could see, my skin is okay.

Or we could weave in the idea that it is normal to not always feel confident or one hundred per cent content in one's skin; everyone has insecurities or physical things that preoccupy them. It also may be worth reminding them that most of the time these insecurities are not visible to other people.

More positively, try discussing when and where they feel more relaxed and accepting about their body. Have they ever felt good about their body in one setting, and then taken the same body somewhere else and not felt so good? Often, the time they feel best will be when they are feeling connected and good about themselves, perhaps when they are engaged in something purposeful, or when they are enjoying their ability to dance or swim or use their body doing sport. One of my own teenagers who sometimes felt bad about her body told me that she felt at peace with her appearance on long bicycle rides through the park. Another 15-year-old girl I met when giving a school talk said to me, 'I turned around my relationship with my body when I thought of it as powerful, and something to be respectful of. Starting running was part of this. I realized my body could get me places.'

Wherever they are, encourage them to think of their body with kindness. See if your teenager can think of all the things their body does for them every day, everything from running and dancing to reading a novel. Suggest they treat their body as if it were their friend and say thanks for all that hard work. Ask them to list five things their body does for them. See if they can take a moment to appreciate each one in turn.

PRACTICAL MEASURES
REGARDING EXERCISE AND DIET

Exercise can be a time when teenagers can enjoy and appreciate their physicality, with no thinking required. It is about what their bodies can do for them, be it the splits or dancing or taking a turn in the boxing ring. They can do this without overly worrying about how they look or thinking about losing weight. A body is an instrument, not an ornament.

Encouraging your teenager to take exercise needs to be handled carefully, given the dangers of obsessive exercising. We want to stress how enjoyable movement can be. We want to ditch a results-driven approach – remember, it's about enjoying the process rather than losing weight or developing a six-pack. Instead, we want to think of exercise as enjoyable, with the general aim of feeling healthy, rather than a precise goal of adding a certain amount of muscle mass or creating a 'thigh gap' of a certain size.

One answer is to do this through our own example: remember the ideas we have already looked at about how to motivate ourselves. They are unlikely to join your exercise class, but they are likely to be influenced more by what you do than anything you say, and they will clock your own change in mood when you yourself exercise.

You can be an example of the burst of empowerment and good mood that exercise can give them. A recent review of 38 studies from across the world found that physical activity alone can improve self-esteem in teenagers,[11] while a 2023 study of school sports found that depressed teens were helped by three fifty-minute sessions of sport a week.[12]

We might also remind ourselves of ways to encourage a healthy, even joyful, relationship with food, both for us and our teenagers. A quick recap: rules around eating don't work. Fat shaming doesn't work. Diets don't work – in fact the word should be avoided in favour of a desire to be energetic and healthy.[13] We want our teenagers to follow their own hunger cues and feel in charge of their bodies. This means that nothing is being pushed on them, and that they are creating their own innate cartography of their relationship with food, rather than following anyone else's map, be that their parents' or influencers'. Many who struggle with eating, diet or body image almost always mention something their parents or another significant adult in their lives said in judgement of their bodies.

*

This chapter has been about ways we as parents can support our teenagers through this period when their appearance looms so large in their lives and there is so much pressure on them to look a certain, conventional way, pressures that have been exacerbated by social media. But there are ways to make them feel more at ease about how they look, from adjusting their own profile on social media to reflect a more authentic version of themselves, to ditching accounts that make them feel bad about themselves. More profoundly, we can try to bolster their sense of their self-worth and help them develop a gentle internal voice that tells them they are good, and look good, enough. And nobody else needs to tell them this is the case. It's tricky, as we don't want to seem insensitive to their worries. But we can appeal to their natural sense of independence by challenging conventional thinking about what makes for attractiveness. We can be positive about our own appearance; share thoughts on how perspectives about our looks change over time and in different contexts; and encourage them to be kind to their bodies, nourishing them with exercise and, as far as possible, a relaxed relationship with food. You might find that some thoughts are just as relevant to your own feelings: I know that having to think about the issues facing my teenagers helped me address some of my own difficulties around my appearance and helped me be kinder and gentler to myself. Once again, there are blessings to being the parent of adolescents. My next two chapters look at how we can similarly help them feel at ease with their sexuality and gender.

13

THEIR SEXUALITY

Adolescence is a time of becoming a sexual being. Developing one's sexual identity is a process – one that is quicker for some and slower for others. But for all teenagers there is a precise way in which things happen to the body, orchestrated by the pituitary gland with the release of hormones such as testosterone and oestrogen, changes which are part of the rapid development of the adolescent brain as we saw in chapter 7. These things will manifest in different ways, at different times, but the steps are the same for everyone.

Teens have a new awareness of themselves, and touch itself becomes sexualized. Sex is arguably among the most important aspect of an adolescent's life. Through the ages, teenagers have been preoccupied by the topic. I remember asking one of my teenage sons, aged 17, if he was interested in sex. His astonished response was, 'Yes, of course, that's the only thing I'm interested in.' It is a time for sexual exploration and experimentation;[1] homosexual and heterosexual experiments are common in early adolescence, as is uncertainty over sexual orientation.

But their sexual world is different from ours. First, teenagers today are questioning norms of behaviour in ways it is hard for many parents to imagine, especially when it comes to gender identity, which is linked to sexuality (and the topic of my next chapter). Theirs is a more open and fluid world than ours was. In the UK, almost 9 per cent of young women between 16 and 24 identify as bisexual, while 2 per cent say they are lesbians; 4.1 per cent of young men identify as bisexual with 3.8 per cent saying they are gay, according to the Office for National Statistics' latest population survey.[2] This compares with over 5 per cent of 25–34-year-olds. By contrast, in their grandparents' generation, only 0.7 per cent of 64-year-olds and over say they are gay or bisexual. It feels like a more positive sexual world, in which the explosion of sexual identities reflects a richer culture of personal experience.

Second, for an array of reasons including heavy academic schedules, social media use, unsatisfactory sexual encounters, and an overall slowing in the process of growing up, adolescents today are actually having less intercourse, with fewer partners, than their parents or grandparents did, according to surveys in the US and elsewhere.[3] There's even a culture of 'incels' or involuntary celibates who define themselves by an inability to have sex.

In general, as we've seen, teenagers are pursuing a slower life strategy, hitting markers of adulthood later, including dating and having sex.[4] Research in 2019 found that around 3 per cent of 14-year-olds had had sex, compared with 30 per cent of under 16s in the 1980s and 1990s.[5] In the UK, one survey found the frequency of Brits having sex has fallen with every decade since it began in 1990. As one 19-year-old boy put it to me, there's much talk about sex, but in real life lots of adolescents are prudes. 'Doing stuff is hard. We are focused on how to speak and present ourselves as a brand online but not on having more intimate connections with people.'

Which leads me to the third, and arguably biggest, change in the sexual world in which our teenagers are growing up: the blurring of the online world with the real world. Behaviours online have created new forms of sexual violence and new ways to blame victims. Grammy-winning singer Billie Eilish has spoken about the recurring nightmares she suffered after watching porn, how it affected problems of consent for her: she found herself saying yes to things that were not okay. 'It was because I thought that's what I was supposed to be attracted to,' she said, speaking to an American radio show.[6]

The questioning of norms, the reduction in the prevalence of sex, and the blurring of the online with the real world all make for a new sexual reality. We parents can ourselves feel out of our depth, let alone able to help our teenagers make sense of it. But given that sex remains a central preoccupation, and is something that can add to our teenagers' happiness, this chapter shares some ways we can at least try to do so.

WHY SEX IS SO HARD TO DISCUSS –
BUT WHY WE SHOULD

Most of us parents will probably have received little or no sex education. We only have a vague sense of what we should teach our teenagers, and an even vaguer sense of how to talk about it. By contrast, our teenagers can ask Google anything, and have watched the drama series *Sex Education* on Netflix, which nearly all teenagers I talked to said had had a massive impact on them. The series chronicles the lives of teenagers in the fictional UK town of Moordale. The main character is Otis Milburn, a secondary school pupil. Otis's mother is a sex therapist. Together with a fellow pupil, Otis sets up a successful business advising other students on how to cope with sexual problems in a humorous and light-hearted way. The series, several parents told me, has allowed teenagers to talk about previously challenging topics like anal sex.

For all these reasons, for the most part teenagers may know far more about sex than we parents ever did. Thus it is hardly surprising that teenagers dread the thought of talking to parents who are struggling to tell them things they already know. Parents are often no keener. Some avoid the question, or distance themselves by oblique references to the animal kingdom. When asked to explain sexual relations, one parent confided to me that she was so embarrassed that she explained it was a bit like when one dog was brought to visit another, and they 'were getting married'.

Given these difficulties, it may be that talking about sex is not something that is going to happen between you and your teenager, and another trusted adult might be a more suitable person to chat to. Their developing sexuality is part of their individuation and separation from you. There is nothing wrong with having teenagers who prefer to be private about their sex lives. We need to respect their need for boundaries from us and to trust that they feel secure in their relationship with us, and also are confident in forming relationships with others. All we can do is to let them know we are available to talk about sex, and especially that there is an open door if they need us for troubleshooting, or indeed whatever kind of discussions they want. Which may mean more general chat about relationships, what healthy ones might look like, and even love. Research among 18–25-year-olds in one survey found that 70 per cent of them wished they had received more information from their parents about some emotional aspect of a romantic relationship.[7]

Even if they avoid deep conversations, they may talk to us about particular sexual topics or problems. We can be a safe space if they feel they've made a mistake or misjudgement.

Other teenagers will be more open to discussions: we need a calm and individualized approach, depending on the teenager. Being able to discuss aspects of sex openly is a way we parents can stay close to our teenagers, and instil our own values – crucial now that sex education at school has moved way beyond the facts of biological reproduction and covers relationships and gender identity. The content of such classes is controversial, not least because parents are not always able to know what their children are being taught, and some parents fear that material being shown and discussed in them is explicit and age-inappropriate, and crucially doesn't reflect their own values. All the more reason for us to make sure our voices are heard too. Avoiding the topic altogether means avoiding something that matters to them.

DO SOME HOMEWORK FIRST

Before we can successfully discuss these topics with our teenagers, and maybe even help them negotiate this period of their lives, we might feel better equipped after gaining a broader understanding of teenage development and how sexuality fits into it. I had to do some research, as well as questioning my own assumptions. We might wish that teenagers would place their sexuality at the heart of a committed relationship. But the reality is that sexual relationships take many forms in adolescence.

Once again, their world is different from the one in which we grew up. Their relationships tend to have delineated phases, though of course not every relationship will be following such rigid steps. Teenagers in 'Stage one' of a relationship are having a physical relationship, but with neither party promising exclusivity. 'Stage two' is being in an exclusive relationship; 'Stage three' is committing to be a boyfriend or girlfriend. Many teenagers are exploring their sexuality and can't be categorized: one day they might wake up and feel themselves to be gay, the next, straight. They may not even feel the need to come out. It's more, as one said to me, 'Now I'm getting with this person.'

Sexting is very likely to be part of their relationship even though sharing explicit images is against the law: it's illegal to take, possess or pass on a sexual photo (including selfies) of anyone under 18. Alert your teenagers to the dangers: that what they think is being sent privately may well be shared more widely and at the very least avoid sharing any pictures showing their face. You may need to remind them that even if they do not think the pictures of them, say in a bikini, have any sexual charge to them, others may interpret them in a more sexual way. Sharing nude photos, which can then be more widely distributed, can leave lasting emotional damage.

Many adolescents are not mature enough to have a deep relationship; nor do they want one. Sex can be about other things. Sometimes sex is about a hunger to be desired. It may be an escape from boredom or loneliness. It may also be used as a way of staking out territory or claiming a possession. Sex can be a powerful symbol of status and recognition.

It may also be about dominance or submission. Sex, in some cases, reflects a lack of boundaries and an inability to say no. It can also be about taking risks. From an evolutionary perspective, adolescence is about becoming someone of high reproductive status whose genes will be passed on. Such status can be achieved by being successful with the opposite sex and having a high number of partners. Or sex may be a response to a teenager's exposure to sexual images and pornography, a desire to be like those they've seen on a screen. It could be about exploration and working out their sexuality. And of course, it can also be about enjoyment.

There is pressure for teenagers to emulate and be the same as their friends, so if the norm is to be sexually active in a peer group, then those teens will feel the need to be sexually active too. Sex is primarily about belonging to their tribe. If their peers are already competitive in other spheres, they may also be competitive regarding numbers of sexual partners. As one 16-year-old boy said, 'People are like, oh, what's your body count? It's cool to have a high body count.' On the other hand, teenage girls might be criticized for being promiscuous.

Teenagers are working all these things out, and our role is to support them, whatever their sexual lives look like. At the beginning of all our sexual adventures, none of us knows what we really like: we may have fantasies and preferences, but until we have actually experienced relationships, we do not really know what suits us. Our teenagers are the same. Some things will work with some lovers, not with others. Some desires are too much to admit to until you meet someone who shares them. A loving sexual relationship is unlikely to happen without at least some painful sexual trial and error en route.

Armed with this broad sense of what might be happening in our teenagers' sex lives, let me now share the ways I've found to try to have at least some conversations about sex.

CULTIVATING AN ATMOSPHERE OF OPENNESS

As ever in our communications, tone matters. We might privately be worried about them having sex too young, doubt the idea that it's possible to have a positive casual experience of sex, or be concerned about them using pornography. But if we impose dogmatic views about their sexuality or what we perceive to be right or wrong, they are unlikely to involve us in their sexual lives at all, especially if they feel ashamed that they've made a mistake. If our adolescents do open up to us about their sex lives as they figure things out, we need to avoid judging them. This is the starting point for all conversations about sex. There is already so much shame around our bodies and our sex lives – sexual jokes are 'dirty' jokes, we are accused of having 'filthy' minds – that our aim, first and foremost, should be to reduce the inevitable guilt our teenagers are already feeling. They need to know that nothing they say or do relating to their sexuality can shock us or in any way reduce the unconditional love and regard we feel for them.

As well as being non-judgemental, we can accept that teenagers are unlikely always to be honest with us, probably because they don't want to scare us, and that's okay. Something is better than nothing. And we are more likely to be confided in if we stay calm. The prevailing attitude around many topics to do with sex is at times hysterical, whipped up to alarm us parents and, indeed, our teenagers. Dialling the drama down is a good start. What we read about probably bears little relation to our teenagers' experience and overreacting is never helpful.

We want to somehow keep any conversations around sex light. All teenagers tend to hear about is the risks of sex, unwanted pregnancies, coercion, abusive relationships, rape. All of which have contributed to falling rates of physical contact. If you just talk about all the things that can go wrong, then talk of sex turns into Project Fear. Yes, there are some dark aspects to sex, and coercion, abusive relationships and rape are never, ever okay. But these are the exceptions. Sex can, and obviously should, be more generally a positive experience, an enjoyable not a shameful one. It can be a source of meaning and intimacy. Even a bad experience is something teenagers can learn from: knowing what a bad relationship looks like can help teach them what is a good one. You can adopt a curious gentle tone: teenagers have an ever-evolving language about relationships and sex, and it's good to ask them about it, rather than pretend you know.

This is about having several ongoing chats, because there are many topics to cover. Small, ongoing chats about their ever-changing sex lives will be more effective than 'one and done' even if that's what you would prefer!

THE ART OF BEING INDIRECT

We can be artful. Talking about sex can be disguised as chat about something else. A talk about advertising might segue naturally into one on body image and how sex is used to sell things. Or a discussion about their coursework on *Romeo and Juliet* might lead to a conversation about young love and parental pressure to choose a certain partner. A chat about sexting, for example, might emerge from a wider conversation about their phones and their use of Snapchat, which is the chief social media for sending nudes. Watching *Love Island* together could be a way to discuss how the participants treat each other in their relationships, and whether that is in tune with their own values and if that's okay or not. Even a chat about doing the laundry could lead to talking about wet dreams!

You can weave in conversations linked to what's being discussed in their RSHE classes (Relationships, Sex and Health Education) at secondary school, be that sex education talks or the accompanying videos. We chatted about the sort of content that they would inevitably see online. It was a first gradual nod to pornography, an acknowledgement that it exists, just gently putting sex and everything related to it out there for discussion at any point, rather than preparing for 'the talk'. Rather than a conversation being overly personal, it may be possible to discuss the topic in a more general way.

The existence of sex education at school can be used to your advantage. Say you know they have had sex education lessons at school, but you feel there is more to discuss. You could emphasize the positives, the idea of sexual pleasure, or why people enter sexual relations in the first place, beyond procreation; these are topics up for discussion. Although we may have little technical knowledge of their world, our ability to be honest about our ignorance can elicit information from them. As one parent put it to me, 'One of my teenagers said of their sex ed, "Mum, you have no idea." There was a chance for some playful surprise on my part, and some desire on their part to tell me something new.' One tip: where you talk may be as important as what you talk about. Dispensing with the need for eye contact while going for a walk or being in the car lowers the temperature of a conversation.

TIMING

A natural early topic to cover is when they might have a first relationship, bearing in mind the context that fewer teenagers are having any sex at all, a fact which can reassure them that there's no rush. We want our teenagers to have sex at a time of their choosing and because they want to – and not because they think they have to, or are scared of the reaction of a potential partner, or feel they must because of peer pressure.

This ideally can be a happy experience, and one we need to describe with sensitivity. The phrase 'to lose your virginity', for example, suggests losing something, which someone else has taken, and which could have been preserved. Meanwhile 'popping the cherry' – slang for losing one's virginity, from when the hymen is torn, sometimes causing the vagina to bleed – is a daunting idea for many teenage girls. We want to convey instead that they are gaining an experience when they are ready for it, one that may not be instantly ecstatic (which helps lower the inevitable pressure they feel to enjoy themselves) but something that gets better with practice, especially with the same partner. Using simple language about 'having sex' has the advantage of being straightforward, and isn't freighted with the pressure of a phrase such as 'making love', which is likely to make a teenager go 'Ewww!'

This is what I have most desired for my own teenagers: that they choose to have sex when they feel ready to handle it. This might sound obvious, but studies show that nearly 40 per cent of young women and 26 per cent of young men aged between 17 and 24 feel their first sexual experience didn't happen at the right time.[8] In the study, the right time was judged by various factors, such as whether both parties were willing, whether a reliable method of contraception had been used, whether they felt ready to have sex, and the extent to which they were drunk or felt influenced by peer pressure.

What the right timing is will be different for different teenagers; naturally many of us want our teenagers to have sex when they also have the capacity to develop a relationship in which emotional and psychological intimacy is experienced.

We want to protect our teenagers from getting hurt and from becoming involved in sexual relationships that may not satisfy them, or lead to a teen pregnancy (rates of which are at an all-time low in England and Wales, dropping by 68 percent between 2007 and 2021, from 42 per 1,000 girls to just 13[9]). Sex in adolescence only comes sometimes with the protection of commitment, the promise of exclusivity, the tenderness of consideration, or the support of a community. Instead it is often sex that is unprotected in the deepest sense – psychologically. In their own language, as my teenagers explained, you can 'catch feelings' if you sleep with someone.

That was the experience of one 17-year-old girl I spoke to. Often, she was keen to please others and be part of the cool gang, and on occasion she fell for boys for whom she was not significant. Sex was not about a deep or caring relationship with her but about the adolescent need to belong. She had no idea how painful some relationships – or rather the lack of relationships – would be, or how attached she would become. The simple fact that she was not in an exclusive or loving relationship left her wounded at times.

There are serious difficulties here too, both medical and legal. Sexually transmitted diseases, rates of which are on the rise,[10] can be highly damaging, especially if left untreated. Sex is only legal between people over the age of consent, which in the UK and most of Europe is 16. In some countries it may be higher, but rarely is it lower. Having sex if someone hasn't given their consent is illegal and is rape.

Faced with teenagers having underage sex, what should we parents do? We have to take a firm line. They are breaking the law. To a teenage boy, we might share that there are legal rules around sex and consent, and not brush rape under the carpet. And to a teenage girl, we might say something along the lines of, 'I know when you're having fun, sometimes you can get carried away and forget to stop when somebody is asking you to do something. Could I count on you to remember that it's you who will be breaking the law? To allow yourself to say no, rather than being pressured by others?'

I am not saying that soliciting a good intention in this way will automatically result in the desired behaviour. We all know that good intentions don't always translate into action, though as we have seen our expectations do make a difference. But teenagers have to start somewhere and prioritizing what they truly want is the place to begin. In creating a good intention, we are drawing attention not to our will but to the teenager's. Showing that they have agency, that they need not do anything they don't want to. Instead of saying 'I want you to . . .' or 'You need to . . .', instead try to elicit a declaration of intention, or at least a nod affirming it. Try, 'Can I count on you to take your time . . .?', 'Are you willing to line up with what you really want and not do anything until you are ready and are legally old enough?' or 'Are you ready to look after yourself?'

Meanwhile we can encourage other strong and close relationships for our teenagers which are not sexualized, until they are ready for their own romantic partners.[11] These include relationships with us, but also with their friends, and with other adults – topics I will look at in Chapter 16. This will mean the sexualization of their relationships with their peers more likely to happen in good time, when they are more mature and able to handle their own sexuality. It will help teach them not to be careless of their bodies – and their hearts.

CONSENT

Every teen should be taught that whomever they are having sex with needs to be asked, and their consent obtained. This is especially true in a world where teenagers have grown up witnessing violent sex online, and practices such as spitting, strangling, slapping and 'bratting'(misbehaving on purpose in order to attract discipline) have been normalized but could be dangerous. Such is the sensitivity around the topic that some boys video themselves asking for consent, and some women are expected to make the first move.

Conversations about consent flourish in a broader family culture of respect for others and having open conversations about sex more generally, rather than in a vacuum. Phrases such as 'You have a choice about that', or 'How you respond is your decision', can be used on topics which don't have anything to do with sex, but they introduce the idea of a young person's agency. In a similar way, we can encourage teenagers to seek consent more broadly from others. Introduce plenty of 'Why not ask how so and so feels about that before you act?' into your chats.

The topic of consent is something that most teenagers remember from a short video called *Tea and Consent* which many schools continue to use in their sex education classes. The video compares consensual sex to the act of offering and making someone a cup of tea. Illustrated with gender-neutral stick figures, the video explains, 'If you're still struggling with consent, just imagine instead of initiating sex, you're making them a cup of tea. You say, "Hey, would you like a cup of tea?" and they go, "Oh my god, I would love a cup of tea! Thank you!" – then you know they want a cup of tea.'

'If you say "Hey, would you like a cup of tea?" and they um and ahh and say, "I'm not really sure," then you can make them a cup of tea or not. But be aware that they might not drink it, and if they don't drink it then – this is the important bit – don't make them drink it.'

The video continues, 'If they say, "No thank you" to your offer, then don't make them tea. At all. Don't make them tea, don't make them drink tea, don't get annoyed at them for not wanting tea. They just don't want tea, okay?'

We need to keep everyone safe, and warn them of the risks around sex. But on the other hand, we need to be careful of overdoing it. If we exaggerate a culture of toxic masculinity to girls, then we can risk reaffirming stereotypes that men are insensitive masculine thugs and girls are delicate flowers who need to be careful. Of course they can be vulnerable, but I imagine my daughters as being like trees, who can withstand tough storms and are able to assert themselves. Meanwhile my sons are as sensitive and vulnerable as their sisters. None of them conforms to sexist stereotypes, but both boys and girls need educating about what consent means and its importance.

SETTING AN EXAMPLE

I've discussed conversations you might have about the timing of their first sexual encounter, as well as the need for consent, and your understandable hope that ideally sex happens for them as part of a respectful and loving relationship. Our own relationship with our partner (if we have one) can be influential here. This is not something to discuss with them: I've yet to find a teenager who wishes to know about their parents' sex life! Such personal detail is likely to be alienating if not offensive. But our own example of what an affectionate partnership might look like may be more powerful than anything we say.

This may be hard, if not impossible. You may be a single parent: 23 per cent of households in Britain are headed by a single parent.[12] You may have a difficult relationship with the other parent of your teenager. Even if you are in a steady relationship, you may not always feel romantically disposed to your partner. We can all get tired and grumpy; if you're a menopausal mother, you might find that physical intimacy is the last thing on your mind – in contrast to your own teenager's preoccupation with sex.

Of course, if you have a partner there will be times when you want to show affection to each other – and, by implication, show that sex can be enriching and a great way of communicating. Sexual activity affects health and overall quality of life, with a huge range of benefits.

There are some simple things we can do as couples to celebrate how beneficial physical affection more broadly can be. My own family weren't great huggers. I've tried to be different, whether that's giving our teenagers cuddles (when they let me) or indeed us parents embracing one another. Though few teenagers seem to like seeing their parents touch, in my experience they do like the fact that parents openly love each other. This is not about being insensitive to those who are less lucky in romance, but a simple acknowledgement that touch is a nice way in which humans show affection to each other.

Another way for us to send the right signals is to show that both sexes are equally valuable in our own relationship. As teenage boys in particular embrace their sexuality, they can sometimes devalue the opposite sex and see girls as less empowered than them. Teenage girls can feel undermined. Our job is to mind our own sexist remarks.

Take this example. One day while watching our 16-year-old daughter compete in a match, I said that girls' hockey was not as exciting to watch as the boys'. My daughter shot back that it was not that boys' hockey was better; it was different. Of course she was right: while they are different, both sexes are equally valuable. One is not more powerful than the other, just different. Once again, I learned from my teenager.

If you, the parent, are in a heterosexual relationship, show respect for the opposite sex by putting on a united front, as we saw in Chapter 1. Ideally, both take a fair share of domestic tasks, be that childcare or housekeeping. Build up your partner in the presence of your teenagers, and stress what a wonderful mother or father they have. Teenagers who value and respect members of the opposite sex are likely to have more fulfilling relationships in turn. The best safeguard against your son disrespecting women is for him to see his dad respect his mum, and vice versa.

Even if you are not in a relationship yourself, connecting with other families and adults where physical affection is celebrated in the family, where different genders are equally valuable, and where a teenager's personality is celebrated, can be helpful as your teenagers grapple with their sexuality. With sons, the trick is to have at least a few men in their lives who step up and get involved, be they uncles, grandads, teachers or the gay couple next door.

Affectionate partnerships take many forms, and our own experience is necessarily limited. Heterosexual children never need to 'confess' their sexuality to their parents because, ideally, they were never taught inside or outside the house that it was deviant. Gay or bisexual teenagers may have an expectation of rejection, that you will disapprove of their choices. Instead of focusing on the phrase 'coming out', one helpful approach a parent of a gay teenage boy shared is to think that they are 'letting you in' to their reality. A natural response then is to be flattered they have felt able to trust you. It follows that your job is to be curious and supportive about their sexuality. A simple 'I want to thank you for sharing this with me' establishes that this is about them, not you. Let them know that you wish to know as much or as little as they want to share: they get to choose, and while you might desire to know more, you cannot force them to confide in you. The less you do so, the more they are likely to open up. You may well have concerns, since those on the LGBTQIA+ spectrum often experience challenges to their mental and physical health. Rather than alarm them with what may be your issues, there is plenty you can do as a parent, from educating yourself about the problems they may face, to working on what may be challenging emotions of your own. Try writing things down or using breathing techniques and relaxation exercises to cope with feeling overwhelmed.

PORNOGRAPHY

Phew, you might be thinking. No more chats needed! How I behave with my partner is more influential than anything I say! Yes, but there are more conversations we need to have, if possible, because of the way the world has changed. Take pornography. Its easy availability means that practically all teenagers of both sexes (not just boys, as some parents imagine)[13] will have been affected by it to some extent at a time when they may not have had the maturity to cope with the images they were seeing. The average age at which children see porn is 13.[14] It may play a much larger role in their lives than actual relationships (which as we've seen are happening at a later stage for most teenagers) and can make partnerships in real life more challenging.

We cannot stop our children seeing porn, even if the government in the future attempts to limit access to it via age verification for websites, or other legal means. As one 16-year-old boy said to me wearily, 'Everyone just uses a VPN' (a virtual private network). Furthermore, porn is on social media sites too. Teenagers will always find a way to access porn, just as we did. Studies show that watching porn is widespread and perceived as normal.[15] Prohibition is an act of futility.

So, knowing that our teenagers will have watched porn, we can try to address specific complications it raises. Some teenagers may wish they had never seen porn. Others may wish they had understood it a bit better. We parents can help this understanding.

Porn stars conform to conventional stereotypes, once again upping the pressure on the majority of teenagers who don't, and thus feel inadequate. Male performers are well-endowed and have unrealistic stamina. Boys may worry that their penis is too small, and they can't 'last' long enough. While female comedians, actresses and pop stars have been open with jokes and discussion about female genitalia, there is more of a taboo with talking about penis size, despite it being a preoccupation for many adolescent boys.

Meanwhile, women in porn tend to be both unusually slender and at the same time curvaceous and without body hair. Some teenage girls worry that their body does not look like that. They might also worry that, unlike female porn actresses, they are not willing to have sex of any kind at any time. In the real world, teenagers might as a result turn to drugs and alcohol in order to perform. Girls too may worry that they are not as attractive as porn stars and that the flagging libido of their male partners is their fault, a result of their own supposed lack of sex appeal. This can trigger a sharp decline in teenage girls' self-esteem in the bedroom.

Watching pornography is unlikely to help your teenager be relaxed about their own body, given the narrow range of body types celebrated there. Remind them of some of the ideas we discussed in the previous chapter about being more at ease with their appearance. In real life, there are many more kinds of bodies. They need to be at ease with their own desires and their own bodies, by reducing their consumption of social media and its images of physical perfection, or by helping them build their self-acceptance. We as parents can, too, avoid the urge to comment on other people's appearance.

While porn can make teenagers feel insecure about how they look, it also can make them confused about their sexuality. There is an extra confusion for teenage girls, who may enjoy porn, but feel, as one 18-year-old girl put it, 'weird' and guilty for watching because of their feminist beliefs and the exploitation of the film's female stars, as well as the historic disapproval of women and girls enjoying sex for the sake of it, rather than as part of a committed relationship.

Porn may also mean that teenagers struggle to enjoy themselves in bed. Both sexes can find that they respond physically only to porn rather than to real-life stimulus, especially if they become addicted. Teenage boys who watch porn report less satisfaction with their own sex lives, their own performance in bed and their female partners' bodies than those who don't watch it.[16] Some studies have found a sharp rise in reports of sexual dysfunction – with difficulties achieving or maintaining an erection, or with premature ejaculation – although research on this is inconclusive.[17]

Meanwhile, porn has meant that some teenage girls can feel pressured to respond in a certain way to sex as an expression of masculine dominance, even if they dislike how this manifests, for example, in anal sex or being choked. As one girl put it when she was 19, 'Girls feel pressure to live up to the porn that boys watch even though they know it's ridiculous. They want to please. They know that's what the boy would like. Boys imagine from porn that girls will orgasm with ease, but that's not true. Girls often don't think about themselves or their pleasure. It's sad.'

As a result of porn, teenagers can feel inadequate physically and struggle to find pleasure in their sexual lives. All of this makes it harder for some to maintain sexual relationships, which as we've seen are less common anyway. The messy business of real-life relationships cannot compare to the fantasy of the relationship you can have with pornography, which is why it appeals to so many, and makes it something we have to engage with.

WE'VE GOT TO TALK ABOUT PORN

Before we even begin to raise this delicate topic, we might want to spend time figuring out our own undoubtedly complex responses to porn – whether we enjoy it, do not consume it, object to it, or feel ashamed of consuming it. Our teenagers may find it a relief to realize that we too are trying to navigate what it means for us. Indeed, my experience was that some of my own shame around my relationship with pornography was eased by thinking more deeply about a topic I had previously shunned in an effort to understand my teenagers' experience.

It would be easy to completely vilify porn, given its potential impact on our teenagers. However anxious we may be about it privately, we should avoid doing so. Our aim in all our discussions is to find an accepting stance, as we've seen. The more we look porn square in the face, even with some humour and a light touch, and without being judgemental, the more it loses the capacity to titillate or shock. Reminding ourselves and our teenagers that it is a multimillion-pound business can help dissolve the secret shame around it so we can discuss it in its full complexity.

We need to find nuanced ways to discuss it that don't alienate teenagers who already use porn without any qualms and who may even enjoy it, as well as responding to those teenagers who may feel more ashamed of seeing it and are hungry for ways to understand themselves and their responses to what they are watching, which may well be confused.

The more we can challenge the idea that pornography is viewed secretly, shamefully, the less charge it will have. This could be, counterintuitively, about something as simple as trusting your teenagers to have their phones in their rooms at night, which is when a lot of content is viewed. Ironically, banning phones in bedrooms and bathrooms can make porn feel even more shameful. Sex is good: it increases intimacy, lowers stress, boosts immunity, and helps with sleep. And part of sex is pornography, which has existed since early in human history.

Like any art form, porn has the potential for joy. We can distinguish between porn and erotica. Both deal with sexually arousing subject matter, but there is a difference in intention behind the content and how its creators approach their subject. The creator of erotica, whether in writing or art, views the subject matter as praiseworthy, something to take pleasure in. There is a rejoicing in the human form and an honouring of physical intimacy. By contrast, the intention behind pornography is immediate and intense arousal; it is a money-making venture which often exploits women and much of it is more extreme. Porn actors are at high risk of being coerced or abused and the industry is rife with crime, including sexual crimes against children, committed not just by adults. Fifty-two per cent of reported sexual crimes against children in 2022 were committed by other children.[18] Some content, such as images of child abuse, is illegal.

Of course, this is a subtle discussion. One individual's erotica may well be another's pornography, and vice versa, not least because of the sheer variety of porn on offer, whether that is female-oriented porn, movie sex or the kind of porn available on Pornhub, all of which can be viewed differently by different people. What is banal to one person may elicit a sexual response in others. But discussing some of the differences between erotica and porn might be your best chance of broaching a difficult subject. What role, if any, does it play in a satisfying sexual relationship for them? Is there a distinction between people who have seen porn (nearly all of us) and people who use it? Can they consider the intention behind any porn they watch? And are they aware of the effect pornography may be having on their own ability to have a satisfying relationship? How do they feel about being drawn to porn while simultaneously worried that it exploits those who are involved in its making?

My experience is that we are more likely to have a chance of discussing sex in these ways if we talk in general rather than specific terms about our relationships, or theirs. We are unlikely to get them to talk in detail about their sex lives or their fantasies or what porn they watch. But we are hoping for a broader discussion, which puts porn into the context of other topics that are easier to discuss – general points about the nature of porn, as well as not feeling guilty or judged; and understanding their bodies more generally.

We can agree that porn reflects a relatively narrow version of what a sexual relationship could look like and what sexual fantasies can be – and that their own sex lives can be far richer. We can also agree that pornographic sex bears little relationship to the real thing. Women don't climax right away, nor do they respond only to a man who is unusually well-endowed and able to have sex indefinitely. There are many more ways of finding physical pleasure and intimacy in real life. Gay porn is similarly unrealistic. No porn actor reaches for a bottle of lubricant or a condom. Porn is acting. In real life, there are far more varieties of sexual bliss, as well as many more varieties of body shape and genitalia.

In these kinds of open, non-judgemental chats, we can stress to them that being at ease with their own sexual identity, and sexual orientation, takes time. There is no rush. Working out what makes for a mutually satisfying sexual relationship can be the work of a lifetime – something that we too are still discovering. It's not as if we necessarily have more answers than them. Porn is often about something people do to each other; sex is more about something people do with each other. One answer to pornography is more mindful sex – being aware of sensations, paying attention to them, is critical as it connects brains and bodies. If our brains are elsewhere, that connection is severed. But attention to bodily sensations can be cultivated. All this involves vulnerability, experimentation and curiosity, but also setbacks and disappointments. Feeling inadequate, or struggling for sexual pleasure, are inevitable parts of that discovery – just as in other areas of life.

The more we can share with our children that their own sexuality is something that matters, that their own individual journey to discover it with others matters too, and that it is a journey on which we are there to support them, the more we will be pushing porn back into a less significant place in their lives. One of the lovely things about sex is we grow into these things, one wise friend told me. We find someone – rather than a screen – and we take a journey. And if that journey starts with leaping onto the fastest train possible, we wonder what else is left.

BIRTH CONTROL

Let's assume our teenager has indeed found someone and is in a relationship with them. If so, we need to talk about birth control, especially if we are the parents of daughters' as they are the ones that can get pregnant. If we ignore the topic, our daughter will have to go elsewhere for help and advice. This can be one opportunity for us to help instead and offer to take them to the doctor or clinic.

If we are involved from the start in our child's decisions about contraception, we are more likely to be put in the picture if something goes wrong. Say our teenager gets drunk and finds themself in an unsafe sexual situation; they could have that conversation with us and tell us what happened. But if we have had no conversations about birth control, or sex, ever before, they might not feel able to bring it up. One of my teenage daughters echoed this point, 'If you are on the pill, and your mum knows, then your parents are basically aware you are sexually active. You could tell them if anything bad happens to you. Otherwise, you might not want to tell your parents you are, say, worried you are pregnant. It would be too much of a step.'

In general, because there is generally less sex happening among young people, NHS records found in December 2020 that the number of under-16s asking for the morning-after pill had fallen by 75 per cent in 10 years.[19] Teenagers today are also less comfortable requesting the morning-after pill, which, by the way, is surrounded by frightening myths. One 16-year-old girl told me, 'I was told that it would make me infertile if I used it just once. It's not true. There's lots of shame around this that parents could clear up.'

We are the first generation of mums who also had casual sex. The Family Planning Act of 1967 had made contraception free and easily available to all. This shared experience between the generations bred understanding between me and my teenagers, and made such conversations relatively easy, and good stepping stones to other chats about sex.

TOXIC MASCULINITY

Meanwhile, if we are the parents of boys, we need to talk about 'toxic masculinity'. The phrase was coined in the 1980s by the academic Shepherd Bliss with reference to his own father's military, authoritarian style of masculinity. It has become shorthand for emotional repression, self-reliance and aggression – the kind of image of manhood that can easily lead to violence against others by those embracing it.

Of course not all teenage boys are aggressive. Although there has been much coverage of toxic masculinity, many teenage boys reject its assumptions. Far from being violent, plenty of adolescent boys are affectionate and respectful with girls. They live in fear of being 'cancelled' by their peers, whereby a boy is cast out of social circles for any inappropriate behaviour. In some schools, boys are also now 'allowed' to be close to their male peers and encouraged to let what was traditionally seen as a more female side flourish. By contrast, boys who embrace the values of toxic masculinity are seen as a weird, albeit worrying, minority.

Moreover, overly concentrating on toxic masculinity means that we might miss another phenomenon, one that is arguably now more worrying: that of toxicity among 'mean girls'. Girls can struggle to love each other, or even to be kind to one another. It's almost as if the focus on toxic masculinity has allowed this alternative problem, how girls can sometimes treat each other, to quietly flourish, without the publicity and focus that has been devoted to problems among teenage boys. I will talk more about supporting a teenage daughter struggling with bullying and the 'mean girls' issue in Chapter 17.

So although we should not exaggerate the problem of toxic masculinity, we need to be sensitive to the hormonal changes affecting our teenage sons. The influx of testosterone affects boys in different ways, and is modified by factors such as family structures. But it drives male growth and masculine characteristics, and affects a teenager's confidence and their desire to win. Testosterone also plays a role in impulsiveness and play fighting: high levels can tip into aggression.

This can help explain why teenage boys, albeit a minority, are drawn to models of traditional masculinity. In addition, such figures also make adolescent boys feel they are worth something. Many of them feel under attack in a liberal culture focused on liberating oppressed minorities from under the yoke of white male power. It can feel as if it's wrong just to be a boy right now, especially if you're a straight white boy; that they are to blame for the world's problems. This may explain why some boys are drawn to men who are anti-woke, who say, 'Don't be ashamed! Men are great!' It feels good to rebel against what everyone else is saying about them, in a world in which it can feel as though other groups, and their problems, are the priority.

These stereotypes of masculinity mean that some teenage boys hide their feelings and vulnerability. It is not okay to hug, or to acknowledge your fears. Were they to do so, there's a fear for some that they might be seen as gay. Thus boys can become cut off from their feelings and find that it is easier to express themselves through violence. Boys can clearly be as sensitive as girls, but some of them are trapped in a certain way of being masculine. They are less likely either to ask for emotional support, or get it, though many say they actually hunger for more sustenance.[20]

Some teenage girls I spoke to say how difficult it is to challenge such attitudes. Boys might say that calling feminists 'feminazis' or making jokes about rape is just 'banter'. In the context of sex, some teenage boys focus on their own pleasure because they can be fragile and hungry for status, which, as we have seen, is a way of becoming part of a tribe. Disrespecting women can be a cheap way for them to feel that they have such status.

Other teenage girls feel that sexual pleasure is not equally valued between boys and girls. 'When a girl is seeing someone, or having one-night stands, there's no focus on whether she had an orgasm, or a good time,' a 15-year-old girl told me. 'If a boy was to pleasure a girl on a one-night stand, or focus on her sexual satisfaction, that would be really odd.' Our very definition of sex, she added, is penetrative, heteronormative vaginal sex – in other words more about men, rather than women.

More seriously, boys adopting aggressive stereotypes can lead to sexual assault. It's a problem that will bleed into their future lives. Nearly one in four women in England and Wales has experienced sexual assault or attempted sexual assault, and 85 per cent of assaults are committed by a man known to the victim.[21] Even today, less than 2 per cent of rape complaints result in a charge, while many assaults are not reported to the police – which gives some sense of the scale of the problem.[22, 23]

Raising decent young men

How best can parents support all teenage boys to be young men who respect women? We can be examples ourselves in our own relationships, as we've seen. I discussed earlier how fathers can be powerful examples of men being respectful to women. Their example of being non-violent, unafraid of softer emotions and gentle to women is what our teenage boys need to see day to day – rather than malign influencers. When at puberty a boy feels his explosive new sexual energy, it helps to relate to men who harness that strength and remain equable, gentle, civil and modest. And if there is no father in your boy's life, you may have to specifically ask others, perhaps a brother, cousin or male friend, to become more involved in your teenager's life.

If we do talk directly to them, teenage boys I spoke to warned that parents should be gentle and not come across as preachy. Fathers may be best suited to such chats, letting them know that it's okay to be vulnerable, and perhaps open up that they are too. There's no shame in needing help to figure stuff out, and there are lots of ways of being masculine. It can be worth acknowledging that we understand they face real challenges finding a way to be masculine in their world. Our role as parents is once again not to judge or criticize, which is likely to alienate our teenagers. The reality of most teenage boys is likely to be nuanced. They are neither sexist monsters, nor perfect angels. We must also be aware that, while no assault should ever be minimized, there is an element in the current culture that has the potential to persecute teenage boys and leave young women primed to call out anything, from an ill-judged attempt to hold hands with a girl, to other gentle displays of affection. Boys can be instantly labelled rapists, and online hate in particular can spiral. A lot of unnuanced rhetoric suggests that there is something inherently wrong with them, and that their masculinity is a problem which must be fixed.

The reality is that many boys are actually a bit lost about how they should handle their sexuality. They develop emotionally at a slower rate – some, including Richard Reeves, a scholar who writes on the subject of boys and men, argue that boys need an extra year at school.[24] One teenage boy, aged

16, told me how much more sophisticated and at ease with their sexuality girls seemed to be at the same age. By contrast, he said he felt like a little boy in the presence of mysterious creatures. 'I was totally bewitched by the power girls my age seemed to have.'

Many boys are sitting in their rooms, unsure of how they should behave in a world where, on the one hand, videos preach a message about being masculine and tough, while on the other, they agonize about their stilted attempts at courtship when even a smile can be denounced as a sexist leer. One teenage boy I spoke to said how frightened he was of being accused of being a rapist at his school: perhaps a girl would agree to have sex, but then change her mind, and want to get back at the boy.

This topic came up repeatedly when talking to teenage boys about sex: the terror of having sex with a girl, which they believed to be consensual, only to be subsequently accused of rape. Their social circle and reputation could be destroyed in a second. Boys told me that people would be more likely to believe a teenage girl than boy. One said, 'If a rumour spreads round school, that's it. You're a rapist for life. I'm not worried about the police so much as gossip. And a girl lying.'

The only way a boy will be completely safe from false accusations is when they are having sex in a relationship based on trust and, yes, love – when neither party is drunk, and both are equally willing. Just as sex can be risky for girls with reckless partners, it can also be risky for boys with girls who are equally reckless and irresponsible.

One starting point could be to understand why teenage girls might falsely accuse boys of assault. This might be because they are ashamed of having sex, or fear being punished by their family or their community. Society can still be judgemental about a woman openly wanting sex, resulting in the use of words like 'slag' or 'slut'. In view of this, there are a few practical steps adolescent boys can take to protect themselves.

Obviously, consent is crucial. When it comes to consent, talk about what your teenage boy might do in different scenarios. Remind him that individuals can stop giving consent at any time, and that he's allowed to change his mind too. Discuss with him how a conversation about consent might go. He could ask, 'Are you okay with this?' or 'Do you like this?' or 'May I . . .?' And remind him that consent always remains an issue even if you are in a steady relationship. Talk to him about how certain ways he might behave or assert his physical power might make someone feel uncomfortable or pressured, even if that was not his intention.

The biggest risks often occur when other young people are around, as we've seen when discussing the adolescent brain, or when drink or drugs are involved. The most responsible, loving teenagers can behave differently in social situations – even those who might normally have a clear understanding of difficulties relating to respect and consent. Plan what he would do in the heat of the moment, or if others are around. You might agree an exit plan with him: to have a viable excuse ready, perhaps his need to respect a curfew.

Tell him that keeping his sexual relationships private, with no social media posts, will also reduce peer pressure to behave in a certain way. Moreover, if no-one knows about the relationship, then a teen is less likely to lie about how or why they had sex: there is no judgemental public narrative that needs to be changed.

In conversations around this topic at home, focusing on the problem may amplify it. A better approach might be to draw attention to what we do want: for our teenage boys to treat girls with respect. And if they have done something wrong, behaved in a sexist way, or even forced a sexual relationship, how can we help them step into their new masculinity in a more appropriate way?

How does their behaviour make them feel about other women in their lives? In order to minimize misogyny, encourage teenage boys to ask their mothers, sisters and female friends about their experiences. Yes, the reality of sex differences is rooted in nature, and men can overpower women because of their physical strength. But instead of focusing on these aspects of masculinity, we might stress instead other more positive ways to be masculine. Encourage friendships with the opposite sex, too. Caring relationships allow those of all genders to develop respect for others within relationships that aren't necessarily sexual.

IT'S OKAY TO BE SINGLE
AND FOR TEENAGERS TO TAKE THEIR TIME

This chapter has so far focused mainly on how we can support our children who are having sex. Yes, it's an important topic, but just as important is to instil confidence in our children to reject unhealthy relationships in which they feel uncomfortable for whatever reason. We need to encourage our children to realize they are good enough just as they are. They do not need a romantic or sexual relationship to complete or validate themselves. The narrative that we will live happily ever after only in a romantic partnership is all around us. In fact, it is the other way round. Only when we feel content and at ease with ourselves are we ready to join with someone else. Even then relationships in which both parties retain a degree of independence are more likely to flourish than those in which the partners becoming overly dependent on each other.

It's okay for teens to develop their sexual identities within a relationship at their own pace. Their discoveries and experiences will fire up the brain's reward centre and release feel-good chemicals. These, in turn, will encourage more discovery. Encourage them to work out their own sexual orientation and attitudes about what makes for a mutually satisfying sexual relationship. Feeling comfortable about having sex and developing healthy sexual relations with others is part of their evolution into a healthy and mature adult and they can take it slow, or not at all.

*

Adolescents are more open and questioning than we were, they are in general having less sex than we did, and they are coping with a new blurring of the online world with the real. All of which makes it hard for us to discuss their sexuality, as we know so little about what their lives are like. But avoiding the topic means that we are also missing the chance to stay close to them about something that dominates their thoughts (and screens) much of the time. Our best bet is to do our homework first, and then proceed in an open and non-judgemental way, celebrating the positive aspects of physical intimacy and what a good relationship might look like (ideally modelling one ourselves) rather than alarming them with the darker aspects and risks around sex. We may have to be artful, sharing chunks of useful information which they can take or leave, woven around other topics; and covering – if we can – when a sexual relationship would be appropriate and what consent means. We can't avoid the topic of pornography, as they will have seen plenty of it. Somehow we need to find nuanced ways to talk about this delicate subject, reducing the shame that inevitably accompanies it, if we are to have any chance of discussion.

Then there are conversations to be had about birth control for both sexes, but for girls in particular, and chats about toxic masculinity if we are parents of boys. After quite so many challenging topics, which has made for a long chapter, it can be easy to forget that our teenager may not be in a physical relationship at all, and that's okay too. They are figuring this stuff out. It's also a time when young people are figuring out their gender identity, the topic of the next chapter.

14

THEIR GENDER IDENTITY

What we mean by gender and the way in which it is related to sex is a controversial question these days: different people have different points of view, and one of the dividing lines can be generational. No-one has yet worked out a consensual answer to the topic of whether gender identity trumps biological sex or vice versa, what these terms mean, or an agreed use of language. It is not even that there are two camps, but many voices, some of them loud and fractious, which frequently make headlines as well as causing distress.

As parents, our role is to understand something of what's going on because these debates, while political, are also personal. Even though the numbers of young people experiencing gender distress is small, the topic of identity is affecting teenagers and their families more broadly. A young person's gender identity is mixed in with their racial, sexual and even spiritual character as well as the social and psychological aspects of being male or female. We parents need to understand what this means for our teenagers, ideally to make sure they don't end up in the crossfire, and to reduce any anxiety about offending others. A teenager who misgenders another teenager can be seen as insensitive and disrespectful. They may even be 'cancelled' by their friends. On the other hand, a teenager who is misgendered by a peer when they are exploring their identity can feel invalidated and unheard. Such topics are highly charged, and all of us, teenagers and parents alike, need to navigate them with care. We want to support young people in their exploration of the world and their identities in ways that do not harm them.

One challenge for me has been to understand how discussions around gender have become more prominent since I myself was young. Exploring gender – and indeed identity – has always been a part of adolescent development, at least for some young people. Such teenagers, unsure of where they fitted in and with the collapse of religion and family as sources of identity, have tested norms – whether they are feminine boys, masculine girls, or those who felt androgynous.

But hitherto, such teenagers have largely been under the radar. When I was growing up, few of my contemporaries were openly confused about their gender. One reason is that while some cultures, particularly some Indian and indigenous ones, have traditionally been more accepting of gender fluidity, in the West until recently this has been less true. Until 2013, being transgender as a young person was considered a psychological disorder and some scientists believed in 'conversion therapy' – attempting to change an individual's gender identity or sexual orientation to align with heterosexual norms – which is now widely discredited as inhumane as well as ineffective.

Once in the shadows and taboo, the topic is now far more visible, and this is a good thing: the discourse has drawn attention to the struggles of young people living in the margins, who often face bullying and transphobic abuse, and has caused people to pause and think more critically about who they actually are, rather than who they were told they are, or who they think they should be. Young people in particular have become more questioning about their gender: people aged between 16 and 24 are twice as likely to say they are transgender as older people.[1]

However, as the political debate has become heated, it has become less helpful. More recently, discussion of gender identity, and in particular the topic of trans people in public life, has encompassed women-only spaces, gender-neutral bathrooms and self-identification, with many conflicting views.

Where does this leave us parents? Many of us are confused about how polarized and high profile the topic has become. We are anxious not to offend our teenagers who may have strong views. We want to support them but don't quite know how. We may feel we are not equipped to discuss such nuanced and complex subjects. But we can't just duck out. It's not just that these topics matter to many young people; they reflect an entirely new way of thinking about the world for at least some teenagers – that humans get to choose how they identify. To many – though not all young people – this is not a perspective, but a simple and non-negotiable reality.

So we must find ways to discuss these issues with compassion and factual knowledge, resisting social media tropes and fear-based myths. What is the right balance between a questioning stance about a teenager encountering transgender topics at school, and unquestioning affirmation of a teenager's desire to transition socially or even physically? Are we dealing with gender confusion or something more serious? How can we talk to our teenagers about gender in a way that helps them to open up and be honest and authentic with us, and without making them feel ashamed or judged? Assuming that we get them to talk to us at all, our role is to help our teenager explore their gender identity with curiosity and compassion. No outcome – be that trans, non-trans or anything in between – is preferable, other than what is right for them. These are the topics of this chapter.

DEFINITIONS

If we are going to talk about gender with our teenagers, then we must understand the definitions that some teenagers accept, and the views that have become commonplace in many schools, including among some teachers. That is not necessarily the same as agreeing with them. But if we tell such children that their outlook makes no sense, then we have scant chance of any communication at all, and we are missing the chance to understand their perspective. We need to bridge the rough generational divide between some teenagers who see themselves as more progressive, and some adults who – at least to their children – are more traditional and misguided. Because my aim is to explain this gender landscape to parents, I will be using language that they, in general, are used to – for example, talking about 'daughters'. But I understand that other people may prefer to use other expressions rather than what they might see as gendered phrases.

Even definitions of what sex means are controversial, wherever you stand on the debate and whatever your age group. But for most people, a person's sex describes the kind of body and chromosomes they were born with. These biological differences create female and male sex organs and other secondary characteristics like facial hair. Very rarely, a baby is born with ambiguous genitalia.

Now things get more complicated. 'Traditionalists', or 'sex realists' as they sometimes describe themselves, believe that biological sex is determined at the moment of fertilization, and is unchangeable. Others take the view that sex is changeable: it is not fixed, but 'assigned' at birth by parents. Still others do not consider sex to be changeable as such, rather that a person's gender and sex may not align.

If your gender matches up with your biological sex, this is known as being cisgender, or cis, which is the case for most people. However, some people identify as girls or women although their biological sex is male, or as boys or men though their biological sex is female. Some identify with neither gender, and not everyone assumes that there are only two genders. You can also be gender fluid, for example meaning you do not identify as either male or female, but as one or the other depending on the day.

A person who feels deeply upset that their sex doesn't line up with their gender can be diagnosed with gender dysphoria in a clinical setting. It's important to understand that gender dysphoria is far rarer than gender nonconformity or experimenting with gender identity. Gender dysphoria is distress at the sexed body and is described by the NHS as 'a sense of unease that a person may have because of a mismatch between their biological sex and their gender identity'. It is included as a health condition in the Diagnostic and Statistical Manual of Mental Disorders, Fifth Edition (DSM-5), which is the principle diagnostic tool for psychiatric disorders within the US and is considered a worldwide standard. It is also included as a health condition within the International Classification of the World Health Organization (WHO).

In the UK, legally changing one's gender is a well-established procedure, currently requiring a medical diagnosis and that the applicant live as the gender they identify as for a certain period of time. No medical intervention, neither hormone treatment nor surgery, is required. Methods of treatment, and the ages at which those are provided, continue to be topics of controversy for some. Our gender is not the same as our sexual orientation, which is who we are attracted to.

It's complicated! The main thing to understand is whether it is about sex, gender or sexual orientation – the common theme in all cases is that many teenagers do not want to be put rigidly in a box, forced to live in a way that feels inauthentic to them, or classified in simplistic ways.

HOW GENDER BECAME MORE HIGH PROFILE

Having acquainted ourselves with definitions some teenagers may be using, and a little of their perspective, our next challenge is to understand how gender diversity went mainstream. It has always existed; it shows up across cultures and is not unique to today's youth. But in the past, and certainly when I was growing up as I've said, gender was something personal, and rarely discussed or understood.

But over the past ten years, trans people have become more high profile and accepted, similar to the way gay, lesbian and bisexual people did a generation before, when they also faced discrimination. The battle moved on. In general, there is now more societal acceptance of diversity, helped by the ubiquitous smartphone and explosion in social media use, and because, some say, many schools have introduced these topics via Relationship and Sex Education (RSE) and Personal and Social Health Education (PSHE). There is also an element of boundary-pushing – teenagers like to rebel against their parents' norms and have done for millennia. Each generation needs a new challenge.

The result of this social change meant that, in her first year as prime minister in 2016, Theresa May announced that she wanted to update the law to allow people to change gender by self-identification without a medical diagnosis. One by one, schools and other institutions began to adjust and teaching about the topic was introduced, with teachers becoming more aware of the concept of 'misgendering' and how this can feel invalidating to some young people.

Meanwhile, clinics began giving puberty-blocking hormones to an increasing number of teenagers. Such hormones have been used since the 1980s to delay precocious puberty, but prescribing them for young people who identified as trans was a newer phenomenon. The number of children and young people being referred to the Tavistock Gender Identity Development Service in London, where the NHS provided gender-related healthcare, rose year by year, from 250 in 2011–12 to 5,000 in 2021–22.[2] In some high-profile cases, some of those who took puberty-blockers later regretted it. More recently, the NHS closed the Tavistock Gender Identity Development Service and announced that it will be replaced with multiple regional centres to support young people. In 2020, the National Institute for Health and Care Excellence (NICE) described the quality of the evidence to support using puberty-blocking drugs to treat young people struggling with their gender identity as 'very low'.

HOW PARENTS OF GIRLS ARE ESPECIALLY AFFECTED

A majority of patients at the Tavistock Gender Identity Development Service were gender-confused girls rather than boys. Girls tend to reach puberty earlier than boys, so distress at their changing bodies can manifest when they are still living at home. Confusion around gender identity in boys may happen at a later stage, often when they are in their twenties, when parents may be less involved in their decisions, and they have had the opportunity to explore the wider world.

One possible reason is that there is a lot of rhetoric and information, especially online, suggesting that transitioning is one answer to what may in fact be ordinary adolescent problems for girls. Our teenage daughters might dislike their appearance and developing bodies in an increasingly sexualized world or feel uncomfortable in their skin. Many women can remember some degree of discomfort during sexual development. Puberty can result in a girl's body being perceived as a woman's before she is psychologically ready, especially as puberty is happening at a younger age than in the past. Budding breasts change a girl's relationship with the world. Men treat them in an inappropriately sexual way. The iPhone in their pocket shares unattainable ideals of slimness and sexiness as well as graphic pornography in which women are debased, as we have seen.

As a result, some people believe that identifying as transgender might offer one kind of freedom that some young girls are seeking. The girls are freed from one type of sexual identity when they are liberated from their feminine body by transitioning – in the same way, some argue (albeit controversially) that anorexics might also reject their femininity.[3]

One gender-confused teenage girl, who was aged 17, told me, 'All I wanted was for someone to make me feel less horrified by my body.' The dislike of their female appearance is something that social media has exacerbated for many teenage girls, whose gender confusion may be linked to body dysmorphia.

The alternative perspective is that trans people are now more aware that they do not have to live in the gender they were believed to be. Younger trans people, rather than suppressing their identity, can see others like them and believe it might be possible for them, too, to live openly as the person they know themselves to be.

BECOMING A BETTER-INFORMED PARENT

Parents trying to support gender-confused teenagers are thus more likely to be parents of daughters than sons. What then should we do? Before we talk to our teenagers (which may or may not be possible) it's important to be better informed. Here are some questions we might ask ourselves in this quest.

First, how intense are my teenager's feelings on the topic? Is my child just generally confused about their gender identity and what it means – because there's so much noise about the topic? Or are they among the much smaller group of youngsters experiencing gender dysphoria, which could potentially lead to transitioning? And if this is the case, is their gender dysphoria an extension of body dysmorphia, which can affect teenagers as they enter puberty? Or are they distressed because they cannot relate to the gender everybody believes they are? Are they afraid that, if they come out as their true selves, they will experience prejudice or bullying? Are they worried about how we will react if they are trans? Or are they unsure themselves about what they feel, or how strongly they feel it – which is the case for most youngsters in this situation?

Second, do gender difficulties result from mental health problems, which clearly have greatly increased, or the other way round? One girl, aged 13, said her mental health problems and identity questioning were linked. 'They definitely were,' she said, 'because once I actually started working on things, I got better, and I didn't want anything to do with gender labels – I was fine with just being me and not being a specific thing.' On the other hand, lesbian, gay, bisexual, transgender, queer or questioning, intersex and asexual people (known as LGBTQIA+, with a plus to represent other sexual identities) do experience mental health problems disproportionately, including increased incidences of self-harm and feeling suicidal.

Gender dysphoria or distress may be a symptom, not a cause, of wider mental health issues in teenagers (which I will address in Part Six), or the distress may be caused by uncertainty and not being accepted as the gender they know themselves to be. It is difficult to know the exact link: the 2024 Cass Review (the final independent investigation of gender identity services in the UK for children and young people, which followed an interim report published in 2022 and was compiled with diligence and care) found there was limited evidence of routine mental health assessment taking place within the Gender Identity Development Service (GIDS) at London's Tavistock Clinic.[4] The correlation between rising referral rates to GIDS and rising mental health problems among young people needs to be better understood.

Finally, could it be that what seems to be about gender is actually about something else? Is a child identifying as trans because of bullying, post-traumatic stress or sexual abuse? Or the shock of discovering online porn at a young age? This is undoubtedly harmful to children. Have they been subject to social contagion or online grooming? Or might questioning their gender be the way for a shy child with few friends to be cool in a class where being cisgender is the most boring thing you can be?

Or might a teen be confused about their sexual orientation? This may, or may not, be linked to gender identity: many lesbian, gay and bisexual teenagers who are gender nonconforming may be exploring their sexuality, rather than exploring their gender.

There's no doubt that some children who have been sent down the path of transitioning would have grown up gay. Similarly, there are people who identify as gay when they are truly trans, but saying they are gay feels a little easier. But whether our children are cis, trans, gay, straight, pansexual, asexual or anything else, we want them to be happy and it is our job to guide and advocate for them to help them access the support they need.

Nonconformity to sexual stereotypes among young people may be no more than a challenge to the overwhelming conservatism of adolescents when it comes to looks. If a teenage daughter wants to have short hair or a son to grow his hair long, parents must not assume this means they are trans. Children should not feel they have to conform to regressive sex stereotypes in order to feel comfortable in their own skin, nor should it be assumed that they are questioning their gender identity if they choose to defy the stereotypical norms associated with their sex.

Alternatively, do you have a child who knows they do not align with the gender they have been brought up to be and is afraid of rejection, bullying, hate and even murder, following the brutal death of Brianna Ghey, a 16-year-old transgender girl who was murdered in 2023?

As parents, we need to figure out what's going on and why, and not get muddled by all these different though related topics. Tricky indeed! Adolescence is a time when young people are questioning their identity more broadly, and playing around with different gender identities can be a part of that. It is naturally a carefree and explorative time and our safest bet is not to put labels on things immediately but to watch, wait, and become more informed ourselves.

PROCESSING YOUR OWN FEELINGS FIRST

Having played detective and tried to understand your teenager's state of mind and the issues that may be at stake, what of yours? How are *you* feeling? Parents vary. Some are relieved, happy that their teenager has the freedom to discover who they truly are in a way that was impossible for many of us. Young people get to choose their gender, and hooray for that. For others, it's hard. They might long to be relaxed and understanding but instinctively feel worried.

If this is the case, you may also need to calm down and address your concerns. A parent described the moment their teenager said to them, 'You've misgendered me since I was born,' as if they had been hit by a juggernaut. They felt they were being blamed. While they were trying not to be judgemental, it was as if their teenager was judging them. Our children often know exactly what to say to make us feel defensive and under attack. It's understandable you might feel panic: not so much because you don't accept them, but perhaps from a deep-seated fear that your child may want to put themselves on an irreversible medical pathway or may face discrimination and challenges if they live their life as an 'out' trans person.

There may be sadness because some aspects of the way they feel seem to us a rejection of our choices. They may adopt a new name; their previous name becomes a 'dead' name. Some parents say how wounding this moment can be for them. It's hard to unlearn the name you carefully chose for your child and sang in a thousand lullabies. Calling it a dead name can feel cruel, too, forcing parents to think of their children in such emotive tones. Remembering why this change is important to our teenager can help, and focusing on the happiness and acceptance they feel when we call them by their new name can be beneficial. It's perhaps less of a rejection of our choices and more of an assertion of their own.

We may experience a sense of loss regarding the expectations we have been holding onto for our teenager. Countless family and cultural traditions, from coming-of-age rituals such as bar and bat mitzvahs to graduation ceremonies to roles at weddings, are inextricably tied to gender. We may also be fearful about being accused of bullying or even domestic abuse if we don't affirm our children's identities. Or that our rejection of their disclosure may cause more damage to their potentially fragile mental health. If we are upset, we need to get to the point where we can set aside our own emotions and judgements. Our feelings may be complicated, and it's our responsibility to manage them, not our teenagers'. This is about them, as well as us: who they are, as humans with autonomy and self-determination.

RE-ESTABLISHING A CLOSE CONNECTION TO OUR TEENAGERS

The next step is to re-establish a close and loving connection with our teenager before talking to them about their gender. If we don't do this, they may not be willing to talk to us at all. If we have already reacted negatively to their disclosure, we may well have been cast as the villain: someone who doesn't understand their difficulties and is trying to force them to be someone they are not. And even if we have been positive, many teenagers think asking them about their or their friends' gender is off the table and indeed offensive.

It's likely your teenager is being more open about their gender confusion with their contemporaries than they are with you (though they may also be subject to bullying because of it). And they may or may not be talking to supportive teachers.

Us parents can be left in the dark. It's not just that our teenagers are not talking to us. No-one in their world is being open with us either. One mother I spoke to shared her feelings of being gaslit by her child's school, therapists and even, in some cases, doctors. 'They completely deny the parent their "lived reality" of giving birth to and raising a child as one sex, only to be told as parents to a teenager that they've got everything wrong,' she said. Sharing the fact that they feel confused about their gender may be a teenager's way of making friends with the cool group in a class, or of winning the approval of like-minded teenagers and becoming part of a gang for people who feel isolated. Or it may be that they are telling them who they truly are.

In particular, those who lack safe and secure attachments to mature adults naturally turn to their peers instead, and there are many online communities that teens might seek to become a part of. This fits with what we know about the developing teenage brain, which is more susceptible to peer influence, more impulsive and not as good at weighing long-term outcomes and consequences as the fully developed adult brain. Due to its anonymity, online support can be crucial if teenagers are unable to talk to real-life peers or family about their difficulties. However, it can also be exploitative or put a child at risk.

The key is belonging. Instead of being part of our family, gender-confused teenagers may join a 'glitter family' – a group of friends, sometimes online, who make up a 'chosen family' for LGBTQIA+ people who feel rejected by their biological family, and who give them a sense of belonging. Teen girls tend to be more avid consumers of social media than boys, which some believe could lead to an increase in gender confusion. Trans influencers on TikTok and YouTube, who talk about their experiences and explain ideas like breast binding and taking hormones, are increasingly popular.

We parents must get back into the picture. If you suspect that your teenager's gender questioning has arisen as a result of peer-to-peer influence and is their answer to feeling isolated, then surprise them with invitations to interact and establish routines where you can connect with them – be that a weekly trip to pick up a coffee or a regular bedtime ritual. Be curious in conversation about what really makes them content and how they might line up with that, rather than needing the approval or affirmation of others.

And tell them how much you love them. One mother I spoke to said how painful it was to be portrayed as the opposite: someone who would be knowingly cruel to her daughter. Her answer was to reassure her daughter how much she adored her and to ask her child if she could acknowledge that, as a parent, she only had her daughter's best interest at heart. It took a few weeks to reconnect before any other conversation was possible.

TALKING DIRECTLY ABOUT GENDER CONFUSION

Here are some ideas that may ease conversations about gender confusion, now you have graduated to a point where this is possible (I hope!). In general, we can follow our children's lead and allow them to talk to us without fear that we will reject or invalidate their thoughts and feelings on these topics. Listen to what they have to say with an open mind. While we might not have anticipated having a gender-confused teen or a teenager who wants to transition, and while it might not be what we had hoped for, it may yet be the case, and it's up to us to decide how to respond.

We can acknowledge how grateful we are that our teen has found the courage to trust us with their news and their feelings. If they have confided in us, it is a testament to the closeness of our relationship. We can still support them to be happy, even if it's not quite in the ways we expected to.

We can thank them for speaking to us in what is likely to be a daunting moment in their life and reassure them that we love them whatever their gender. We want to encourage them to learn about themselves and live an authentic life. We want to know more about what our child may have been facing, and about any bullying or discrimination they've experienced. Ultimately, we want our child to be true to themselves. Just as we would hopefully encourage a gay teen to feel confident and cherished, we want to treat a gender-confused or trans teen (who may also be gay!) with love and support.

Make it clear that your family is accepting of gender nonconformity – and indeed all sexual orientations. Ideally, you will have been relaxed about your child behaving in whichever way feels natural to them, no matter their sex, from an early age by ensuring that they know that our sex does not define our behaviour. You can also talk openly and without judgement about any LGBTQIA+ or gender-nonconforming people in your own life or in the media. You might say something like, 'It's great that they felt comfortable coming out to their dad.' The unsaid speaks volumes: that you would also be pleased if they wanted to talk to you about their gender or sexuality.

Many parents are already conscious of avoiding gender stereotypes. In the past, fathers might have played rough games with their boys, and quieter ones with their girls, but now such distinctions increasingly feel outdated for many. The message of empowerment of women and girls is getting through loud and clear, although this is sometimes at the expense of similar attention being paid to boys. One father told me there weren't many boys in the Penrith ballet class when his son started in 2013. By contrast, the Penrith girls' football club is thriving. It is encouraging when we see some teenage boys carrying pink rucksacks or wearing skirts, make-up or long hair, for instance, but there is still rigid social pressure for boys to be 'tough' and 'masculine' outside most big cities.

Reinforce the person your teenager is, rather than their sex or gender. Try to take cues from your teenager as a person first. The more your growing teenager is comfortable with themselves as an individual, the more they are likely to be comfortable with their sexuality and gender identity, and the more confidence they will have in expressing their needs. If, for example, your daughter is distressed by her appearance, ask 'What if?' questions. 'What if they didn't have to conform to other people's views of what makes for physical attractiveness?' 'What if they could accept how they are?'

Our role is to help our teenager to explore their feelings carefully and gently, with open-ended, broad-sweep questions, to believe in them and to figure out whether any other issues are involved. Could them questioning their gender identity be simply part of normal development? Or is there something more to it? How distressed are they by their situation and feelings? Keep focused on your whole child, not just their concerns about gender. Talk about what they're reading, or anything else they are drawn to. Otherwise, a teenager may end up feeling as if their whole experience is reduced to being about gender distress, which is not helpful.

Supporting our teenagers doesn't have to mean agreeing with them about everything. We owe them honesty, even if it's painful to hear, and we owe it to them to hear their honest feelings, too, even if that causes us pain. We need to tell them that there are many things that could make them feel uncomfortable in their developing body, and gender dysphoria is one of them. Just because an explanation feels right now, it might not forever. Adolescents change significantly and rapidly; they may view themselves and their place in the world differently at 17 than they did at 14, and we know their brains are still developing until their mid-twenties. We need to show them that we can tolerate this questioning and that we'll help them take their time to work out what's true for them. While some gender-distressed children may go on to be trans adults, most won't: only 20 per cent of youth engaged in gender-nonconforming behaviour before puberty will report a transgender gender identity as an adult.

SPECIFIC DILEMMAS: SOCIAL TRANSITION

Such supportive chat is all well and good, but what about thornier topics? Should we take steps to support our teenager's social transition, like using a preferred name and pronoun and letting them express themselves through their clothes, hair and make-up? As we've seen, we may find this hard, even if it makes our teenager happy. Unfortunately, there is not enough careful research as to precisely what helps or hinders teenagers, although overall familial support is known to be important. Dr Hilary Cass, the paediatrician who chaired the eponymous Cass Review, argues, 'Social transition is not a neutral act, and better information is needed about outcomes'.[5]

Parents in this situation told me that the best course is neither to encourage nor discourage social transition. There will be conflicting voices in a teenager's mind. Bullies, and transphobes on social media, may resist social transition, while queer-supportive communities may encourage it. A parent's neutral voice can be valuable as an alternative perspective at a time when teenagers are in the crossfire and working out what they really want: the more points of view they experience, the better. While remaining calm, our best approach is to provide information: we can share that there is little current consensus on the best way forward.

MEDICAL TRANSITION

What if your teenager wants to medically transition by taking hormones or having surgery? Far fewer parents find themselves in this situation than those supporting gender-questioning teens, and clearly the stakes are higher – both in terms of having surgery but also in terms of having untreated gender dysphoria. Such teenagers deserve empathy and support because we know that trans people are far more likely to experience mental distress. Theirs is a long and challenging path. There are still gender stereotypes to contend with: not least the societal image of the 'perfect' relationship as a heterosexual one, with a perfect family, living in a beautiful house.

A two-step approach can make sense. Start with trying to understand what might be going on for your teenager. Only then attempt to talk directly. How does it feel to experience such levels of gender distress? Someone born female may experience sharp psychological discomfort with their first period; someone born male may struggle to reconcile their internal self with the first sprouts of facial hair. This distress combines with a desire to be rid of the characteristics that don't match what they feel inside, whether that's their name, clothes or physical features.

One trans teenager has described their experience as feeling they were carrying a 'worry backpack full of rocks that is going to make everything in my life harder, and in many cases is going to make things impossible'. Another said it was like constantly feeling at war. 'It is the "battle of the beliefs": hanging on to your belief that you are who you are despite how others may define you, while also challenging yourself not to compare your insides to other people's outsides. It's a constant effort to align yourself externally with how you feel internally.'

Gender dysphoria is hard to describe, even for some people who experience it, and it can be especially challenging for cisgender parents to make sense of. Teenagers have described a sense of being disconnected from their bodies or feeling as though the reflection in the mirror or what they see when they look down doesn't match who they are. The pain of such incongruence has been likened to the body dysmorphia of those with anorexia.

And remind yourself that, while we still need more research, according to GIDS data published in 2018, 35 per cent of children referred to the service presented alongside autistic traits.[6] Even this isn't simple: as the authors of a 2020 study exploring this crossover put it, 'We want this study to really demonstrate that both of these things can co-occur, and just because these things co-occur does not mean that one should be denied.'[7]

Thus armed with some sense of what being trans feels like, you could suggest that you and your teenager research the matter together and that both of you look at the evidence, insofar as it exists. Researchers still don't know what causes gender dysphoria. Though we've established that gender dysphoria may interact with mental health conditions such as depression and anxiety, there's little agreement about how or why. Trauma, particularly sexual trauma, can contribute to or exacerbate dysphoria in some patients, but again, no-one yet knows exactly why. We don't want to treat people for gender dysphoria if their core difficulty is something else. However, having experienced trauma or mental health problems does not preclude somebody from also being trans and feeling dysphoric.

You will find there are more ways to be trans than being on a medical pathway; your teenager may be able to express their gender identity in different ways, and medical interventions will still be an option in the future. Looking at the evidence together means you can both be aware of the potential positive and negative outcomes of treatment, including the risks and side effects. Suggest you both listen to trans people tell their stories. The presence of detransitioners suggests that some go ahead with medical intervention without proper investigation of their problems beforehand (although detransitioning is not always about regret; sometimes, it is discrimination, rejection by family, and a lack of acceptance that causes a person to detransition, even if they still believe they are trans).

Alternatively, a minority will be making decisions for their futures that will assert their sense of self and allow them to lead a happy, self-determined life. Being trans can be a positive, life-affirming experience. LGBTQIA+ people often find a community and sense of freedom, taking strength from having rejected pressure from a world that had tried to make them fit into an unsuitable box. The LGBTQIA+ pride movement has grown out of centuries of oppression, but as well as being a protest, pride is a celebration of living an authentic life, of supportive communities and of people knowing you and loving you for who you truly are, not who they want you to be. Coming out as trans is undoubtedly a difficult path, but it does not mean inevitable tragedy, for either a teenager or their parent. Many people, when their child comes out as queer or trans, see that child blossom and grow in confidence since having been brave and self-aware enough to understand themselves and tell others their truth.

While some outcomes are positive, the overwhelming problem is that there is a distinct and profound lack of data about the consequences of transitioning, a view confirmed by the 2024 Cass Report.[8] We do not know enough about children who have transitioned, mainly because of the failures of the Tavistock Gender Identity Development Service to collect data on this cohort. It is vital that your teenager knows this – that what they may feel they want to do to themselves has no evidence of success, or indeed failure, and that they are potentially going to make life decisions that they may later regret, some of which are irreversible.

WATCHFUL WAITING

While much is uncertain in this area of medicine, we know one thing for sure: many children who experience gender distress find it is resolved without transition.[9] In one of the largest studies to date, 87 per cent of such children who were followed up after 13 years had desisted. Thus, the best answer seems to be 'watchful waiting'. This is the name given to the approach of observing these conditions without active medical intervention, and it is deployed in many other different child mental health situations. Parents of teenagers in this situation told me again and again to take your time. Ask questions, and do so again the next month, and the next month, and the next. This is about an ongoing conversation with teenagers who have a complex range of conditions, of which gender questioning is one part, and how we might provide holistic support. The answers are rarely black and white, and we need to talk openly, without any name calling.

Dr Erica Anderson is a clinical psychologist who urges caution for any young person considering transitioning.[10, 11] Her words have weight, as Dr Anderson started hormone treatment to transition from male to female in her late fifties and had surgery aged 61. She warned that teenagers seeking to transition may not be transgender but may be cycling through the ordinary problems of adolescence. The one certainty is that no-one should rush into medical treatment.

AND FINALLY . . . GET PROFESSIONAL SUPPORT

Given that this is an area of great complexity, accessing support from doctors, counsellors or gender specialists can make sense. We wouldn't rely on ourselves to differentiate between whether our child had IBS or Crohn's disease, so we must resist the temptation to make similar differentiations within these complex mental health spheres. Teasing gender queries apart from other concerns ideally requires a clinician who will conduct an in-depth evaluation of the child's identity, experience and mental health, and help them explore whether their discomfort is gender-specific or reflects broader teenage angst with a changing body. Referring a young person for specialist treatment does not inevitably result in hormones or surgery: such services should spend time initially exploring with your teenager what is really going on for them rather than starting them down a pathway of prescriptions and surgeries. The problem is that there are years-long delays in getting this kind of clinical help and indeed treatment through the NHS. Of course, many people cannot afford or are opposed to private treatment, in which case peer support groups, primary care support and Child and Adolescent Mental Health Services (CAMHS) or organizations offering free counselling can be helpful.

*

As we've seen, we need to understand something of the debate that has been raging around gender and sex. Gender identity affects our teenagers, even if they are not confused about themselves. We do well to understand the definitions that many teenagers accept of words such as sex and gender. We also need to understand how the topic became so politicized and high profile, even though the numbers involved are small, and how much the ferocity of this debate can harm all involved. It's difficult for many parents to work out whether a teenager really is uncertain about their gender, or if something else is at play. Recognize that our role is not to figure this out but instead to support our teenager to work it out for themselves, or to get them professional help when needed. What's really going on? Do they have a mental health problem? Could they be confused about their sexual orientation? Or is this a child who really knows they do not align with the gender they have been brought up to be? We need to discuss these issues with compassion, re-establishing a close connection if one has been lost.

If a teenager is confused about their gender, supporting them does not mean agreeing about everything. While many teenagers may experience gender confusion, some may be experiencing gender dysphoria. They may wish to medically transition, but that process takes a long time, so there is room to explore. The distress they are experiencing is valid and real. We need to try to work out what's going on, ideally with professional help.

I had much to learn about this interior landscape our teenagers are navigating, and in doing so inevitably learned more about myself. I also realized that a teenager who is at ease with how they relate to themselves in these intimate ways is more likely to be at ease in their relationships with others, which is the topic of the next part of the book.

DEALING WITH TRICKY RELATIONSHIPS

PART FOUR

YOUR TEENAGER'S CONNECTION WITH OTHERS

15

THEIR SIBLINGS

I n Parts One and Two, we focused on parents and our relationship with our
teenagers, before turning in Part Three to our teenagers' feelings about
themselves and their interior world, especially their appearance, sexuality
and gender. This next part of the book is about our teenagers' relationships
with brothers, sisters, peers, friends and other adults. As parents, we would
like to think that we are the most influential people in our children's lives, but
we shouldn't underestimate the role of their other relationships, beginning
with their siblings.

The sibling relationship is likely to last longer than any other relationship
in a child's life, and plays an integral role in the lives of families, right from
birth. I remember one of my older children asking, when their younger sibling
was born, if we could send the baby back now. Another asked, full of fury,
if I was his mummy too? Yet despite its importance, in comparison to the
wealth of studies on parent-child relationships, relatively little attention has
been devoted to the influence of siblings and their impact on one another's
development. Nonetheless, a few results are clear.

In general, parents are more influential when it comes to teaching teenagers
how to behave in public and with other adults, and in social aspects of family
life. But siblings may be more influential role models for how teenagers act
informally at school or around friends.[1] Understandably, younger siblings
are more likely to be influenced (positively or negatively) by older siblings
than by parents.

Studies have also found that the quality of the sibling relationship, as
well as siblings' influence on each other, naturally influences teenagers'
emotional development.[2, 3] This has implications for us parents. Ideally we

want our children to get along! Siblings can support each other when we are absent, and help each other grow. It's worth making an effort to encourage collaboration between siblings, as the odds are against us. We know that the more siblings an adolescent has, the more likely they are to be depressed, anxious and have low self-esteem.[4] While children with more siblings seem to have better social skills, as siblings provide 'practice partners' for negotiating complex relationships, those in larger families can suffer because they are competing for parental time. This chapter is about what you can do to foster positive sibling relationships in your home, especially for anyone with a big family (like me).

UNDERSTANDING SOME CHARACTERISTICS OF OLDEST AND YOUNGER SIBLINGS

Helping our children get along begins with understanding how their birth order typically affects their character and interactions. Oldest children tend to be more 'parent oriented' than their younger brothers and sisters. Without any other offspring with whom to compare themselves, oldest children are inclined initially to measure themselves against their own much older and wiser parents, and understandably can feel inadequate. They can develop a powerful need to achieve in order to compensate, and this is only exacerbated when new siblings come along, as eldest children can feel dethroned. This may be one of the reasons why older children are likely to be more anxious, and more driven, than their younger siblings.[5] If our eldest child is like this, we can stress that there is no such thing as a mistake, only chances to learn, encourage them to focus on processes rather than goals, and help them become less judgemental (discussed earlier in my thoughts on perfectionism and rethinking mistakes, see page 51). They may also need extra support getting along with their siblings, whom they see as competition.

Younger siblings are different. Some are minded to be 'older-sibling oriented', looking to their brothers and sisters for information on how to behave and relate, rather than their parents, and minded to get along with their siblings, especially if there is a bigger age gap. As a result, they have a smaller developmental gap to overcome, less to prove, and so less self-imposed pressure to achieve. This is often true regardless of parental influence.[6]

Younger siblings often imitate their older brothers or sisters, particularly when it comes to antisocial or risky behaviour, be that drug-taking or promiscuity. Laurie Kramer, professor emerita of applied family studies at the University of Illinois, says that if older children drink and smoke, their younger siblings are more likely to do so.[7] The power of the older sibling is magnified in families where parents aren't much around, and the siblings spend a lot of time together. Given the powerful influence of older siblings on younger ones, we are lucky if our eldest child is a good role model – something we might try to encourage.

Having said that, the opposite can also be true. Some younger siblings can sometimes be desperate to be different from their older siblings and carve out their own path. Researchers call this 'de-identification'.[8] If your eldest teenager is sporty, your next one might deliberately avoid sport, particularly if they worry they won't measure up. Or if one sibling has a mental or physical health problem, or a disability, the other child might try to be 'perfect', or minimize their own problems, in order to compensate. They might imagine they can't be a normal, stroppy teen because they don't want to add to our parental worry.

How then can we try to foster a good and supportive relationship between our teenagers – one where they get along, resolve disputes and support each other through the trials of the outside world?

UNDERSTANDING WHY TEENAGERS FIGHT AND WHY IT'S NOT A DISASTER

Fighting goes with the teenage territory – with us (as we saw in an earlier chapter) and with their brothers and sisters. This is because children start to compete for dominance, parental attention and household resources – especially if your children are close in age. The 'resource dilution model' posits that the more children there are in a household, the less resources available to any one child.[9]

Part of this rivalry also reflects a wider sense of scarcity in our competitive culture – the feeling that we must fight to get our share. Who goes first? Who gets the most? Who's right? Who's best? Who wins? The most common areas of conflict between teenage siblings in my experience are sharing personal space, possessions and friends. What is most often at stake is a sense of equality.

There can also be rows about fairness. The older child might, for example, resent the younger for getting away with more or being allowed more freedom at a younger age. Meanwhile, the younger child might resent the older for being bossy or enjoying freedoms the younger one is denied.

While a parent's first instinct might be to stop their teenagers from arguing, actually not only is some degree of conflict normal, it actually has some virtues, as we saw in my earlier discussions on rows and lying between us and them (see page 148). The first of these is that it is a safe way of learning how to manage relationships in general. How better to learn how to have a fight than with someone who is still going to be your brother or sister the next day?

A second virtue of conflict between siblings is that it's one of the ways in which teenagers establish themselves as separate people with distinct likes and dislikes. This is part of their developmental journey towards autonomy. Fighting is not always a sign that siblings do not get along. It is often how they get along: using conflict to test their power, forge their identity, learn life skills, establish differences and vent emotions with a familiar adversary. It's how they manage their relationship, and we do well to keep out of it. In healthy sibling rivalries and arguments, teens can be both good companions and good opponents.

If a younger teenage child sees an older sibling as another authority figure, fighting can increase as the younger child tries to become independent from both their parents and sibling. Some parenting experts argue that, when handled well, the struggle for dominance between siblings can act as a spur for development.

DIALLING DOWN THE ROWS AND THE IMPORTANCE OF TREATING SIBLINGS EQUALLY

Still, as you will remember, I'm not one for conflict, and nor was my mother: I never forget her cautionary tale of how her sister once pulled out her hair during a fight, including a bit of the skin off her scalp! We ideally want our children to row in the most constructive and least painful way possible: remind them of tricks like 'naming their process' – saying what they are experiencing, taking time out, using helpful language and beginning sentences with 'I' – all methods you by now are using! Whenever there is a row, make it clear to them that both parties are jointly responsible for the conflict. Sometimes therapists call this 'co-creation'. If you try to determine 'who started it' you will only go backwards. This is as true for us as it is for our teenagers.

It's proved especially helpful to teach my own teenagers to focus on the issue rather than the person: emotions run so high among rowing teenagers that things can turn nasty and personal, I've found. If, for example, the row is over borrowing a sibling's clothes, rather than focusing on character – 'You're so selfish!' – encourage your teens to focus on answers. For example, they could take turns to wear the disputed item of clothing. When they row, see if they can avoid personal character assassinations and find a solution together.

Your children can learn that even if they disagree, family connections still hold strong. Have your children talk about ways they could show love to each other following a conflict. Your job is that of a relationship triage nurse. Don't let wounds go untreated. Make sure that forgiveness is sought, and amends are made. And don't have favourites. Rates of sibling rivalry are lower in families where teenagers feel this to be the case.[10]

However, it is difficult, if not impossible, to treat your children the same. We ourselves, as parents, keep changing and inevitably we will interact differently with each child at different times. Differential treatment is also often the result of age, developmental differences and gender. A 16-year-old, for example, might naturally feel they can go to bed later than their younger sibling. For reasons of safety, you might find yourself being tougher on a teenage daughter than a son going out to a club. Or you might be stricter with a teenager who is behind on their homework compared to one who is on top of their work. Your treatment might vary if one teenager is physically unwell or has special needs and the other doesn't.

All you can do is to be aware of favouritism and address any real or perceived incidences of it by adopting a few approaches. First, explain your reasoning, and reassure them that they are much loved. One psychotherapist said to me that jealousy was ultimately insecurity. Establish a principle of fairness and be prepared to explain it. Try to make sure they get similar treatment at similar ages. But explain to your children that there are lots of criteria which can explain different treatment for different children – not just age, but gender, health concerns and school performance. All of these might mean a difference in what they're allowed to do and what responsibilities they have.

Second, encourage them as individuals. It might feel as if celebrating one child comes at a cost to the others, and thus it is easier to avoid it. This was the case in my family growing up. At times it felt as if my parents found it hard to celebrate any individual child among the three of us for fear of upsetting the others. While this had advantages in terms of a scrupulous lack of favouritism, there were times I felt needy for my parents' praise and approval but it seemed to be unforthcoming. I no longer feel the need for so much external affirmation, and I feel good enough as I am – most of the time! But I might have been less needy if, when I was growing up, my parents had been more at ease with celebrating each of their children in turn, even if they risked a moment of inequality. I've tried to involve my other children in the success of one of them, be that with a raised glass or a celebratory meal.

A sense of equality among siblings can also be fostered by not comparing them, which tends to happen if you find one child easier to deal with than another. It's tempting to say things like, 'Why can't you be more like your brother?' or 'Your sister never did that.' But these messages can naturally spark rivalry, as well as dissatisfaction.

Third, spend time with each child individually, which may require resources you haven't got. But I found doing so – thanks to family help – mitigated a sense of scarce resources that need to be fought over among my children.

For many years, I created a system of a 'Special Day' with each of my five children, a moment every few weeks when just the two of us went out for a coffee or a walk together, often after school. Part of its success was the sense of ritual. I tried to be fully present, switching off my phone, parking my own worries and tuning in to what mattered to them. Often we saved up tricky conversations during the week, agreeing that the 'Special Day' would be the best time to address them. We both could relax knowing we had set aside that time. Being in a neutral space out of the house contributed to an openness that was harder to find at home where others might overhear us or interrupt. The option of being able to choose food added to the sense of occasion.

Children don't have as much need for rivalry when they get their fill of your attention, and when they don't feel they're being lumped in with their siblings. This is especially the case if you, like me, are a parent of boy and girl twins who develop at different times. One twin may already be dating, the other not. In girl twins, one may start their periods well ahead of the other. All these differences mean that twins, even more than regular siblings, benefit from time spent alone with you when you can celebrate them as individuals away from their twin. Separate spaces can be helpful too: a room that other children can enter only when invited, or individual nooks for families living in tighter quarters. This is also true with belongings that they don't have to share.

TEAMWORK

Aside from avoiding conflict between siblings by treating them equally, parents can encourage sibling closeness by building a sense of their joint identity away from you. There are several ways of doing this. One is to encourage mutual interests and discourage isolation. If you are negotiating with one teenager about being allowed to go to a festival for example, then the price of going might be to take a sibling along. You could give your teenagers a joint task to work together on – for example, cooking a special meal for the family or planning part of a family trip. Encourage occasional joint interests or activities, too, like exercising, going shopping or watching movies together, and get them to plan things on their own, perhaps with their own WhatsApp group. Nothing gives me more pleasure than when two or more of our teenagers team up together, perhaps because it's something I rarely did myself growing up. My greatest pleasure, now most of my children are in their twenties, is that they have a WhatsApp group together, independent of our family's group.

There are many other ways children can establish relationships with each other and help one another. I remember asking an older teenager to talk to a younger one who was struggling with their exams. An older sibling may be reminded of their younger self when helping a younger sibling. They might also be far better at remembering what a particular phase of adolescence felt like than you, especially as the landscape has shifted so radically since the time when we ourselves were adolescents. A sibling might provide support during stressful family experiences or share how they navigated their relationship with you, their parent. You could encourage them to build that supportive relationship that will last into their joint future.

ONLY CHILDREN

What if your child has no siblings, which is the case in 44 per cent of UK families?[11] One common narrative is that only children can be at a disadvantage: spoilt, selfish 'little emperors'. Our culture has maintained this view since the late 19th century, when writers such as G Stanley Hall (a pioneer of American psychology) famously wrote that 'being an only child is a disease in itself'. His view was supported by another writer-psychologist, EW Bohannon, who through questionnaires sent to schools in New Jersey found that in 191 of 266 cases, only children were 'excessively' indulged.[12] Although these writers did not use credible research practices, for decades these negative conclusions remained entrenched among everyone from child development specialists to advice columnists.

Happily, we now know otherwise. Since the early 1970s, researchers in psychology and sociology have studied only children and their families, finding that 'onlies', as they are known, have far more similarities to other children than differences. While there is no absolutely typical only child, in general only children demonstrate many of the same traits as first-born children. Research has also found that only children are also similar to first-borns in their relationship to their parents, who often hold higher expectations for achievement, and focus more attention on them.

Only children are often high achievers as adults, enjoy high self-confidence and self-esteem, appear more mature than their age, and maintain high standards for themselves when compared to children with siblings. Because these teenagers do not compete for their parents' attention, parents are more likely to notice and praise achievements. Parents of onlies might have more time to help with homework and support other activities, such as music or sport. Couples with one child also report more marital satisfaction.[13] This could lead to less conflict in one-child families, which might help their teenagers' emotional development. These children spend more time interacting with adults. Because of this, they model adults' emotional maturity.

Nonetheless, parents of onlies need to be careful not to ramp up expectations: first-born children and only children are more likely to have anxiety and depression than later born ones.[14] An only child, without siblings to compete or compare themselves with, will often compare their skills and achievements to their parents'. Your focus needs to be on allowing mistakes and failures and praising efforts, not results, thoughts I shared earlier on being good enough (see page 51).

Obviously, many parents of only children may have been unable to have more children for various reasons. Parents may also have to be careful if they suffered fertility problems or lost a child in pregnancy. The psychotherapist Julia Bueno says, 'It's super important for that to be honestly talked about and known in the family narrative rather than a buried grief. We need to do this with care too – as you don't want your living child to bear the "burden" of being a miracle.'

While only children benefit from the advantage of not sharing parental attention with their siblings, their parents might have to work a little harder to provide opportunities for them to play and grow independently and to have some of their social needs met. Studies have found that onlies reported fewer overall friends – but similar numbers of close friends – and joined fewer clubs than those who had siblings.[15] Other research has concluded that adolescents and young adults without siblings are more cultured and socially sensitive, more likely to engage in intellectual and solitary pursuits and extracurricular activities. By contrast, those with siblings gravitated towards group and practical activities such as school leadership roles and team activities.[16] Knowing this, parents of onlies might encourage the sorts of activities that their teenagers might otherwise miss out on.

Parents of only children may therefore need to create a socially balanced life for their offspring since the companionship of siblings is unavailable. An only child will need help in developing close friendships – the topic of Chapter 16 – and learning to manage the give and take of being in a relationship. Having play dates, sleepovers and bringing friends on family holidays all contribute to your only teenager's ability to navigate social relationships.

*

This chapter has been about understanding a bit more about siblings, notwithstanding the lack of research on the topic. It's in our interest to foster the relationship between our offspring, as the quality of sibling interactions impacts our teenagers' emotional development – as you might expect. Siblings matter. We can help by defusing rows and not over-reacting ourselves when they squabble. I love the phrase therapist Kristen Gygi used when I discussed the topic with her – she said to 'Pass the popcorn' when rows start and to observe them with humour and detachment, as if I were in the cinema watching a film. Naturally we have to guard against favouritism, and instead encourage solidarity between our offspring, by helping them build a joint identity away from us. Perhaps this feels painful or as if we are somehow losing intimacy with our children ourselves, but this is about building a supportive relationship which will last into their future when we ourselves will be gone. Those of us with large families may have to be artful with our time to mitigate a lack of resources, but it can be done. The quality of our interactions matters more than their quantity.

There are different issues at stake for only children. But we need not overly worry about them: it turns out they are more like children with siblings than we previously thought. Nonetheless, we can help onlies develop social relationships with others, given the absence of siblings. Fostering these relationships, whether with friends or significant adults in their lives (and whether your teenagers are only children or not), is the topic of my next chapter.

16

CREATING A VILLAGE

W e have looked at the importance of the relationships between sibling birds in their little nests. This chapter is about nurturing other significant relationships in their lives, both with other adults (especially extended family) and with their friends. This matters, as social interaction stimulates the reward system in the brain and makes us feel happy, because it gets the endorphins and 'happy hormones' going.[1] Fun is too often dismissed, but it is a crucial part of how our teenagers (and indeed we) build and maintain a psychologically fit mind. Sadly, loneliness, once more the preserve of the elderly, is now a problem among the young too. There is much to be said for seeing the raising of teenagers as a collective endeavour rather than an individual one; and for realizing that we can act as family to others in the community, and they can do the same for us.

This is no longer inevitable in the way it once was. It has become hard to get others involved with our teenagers. In traditional societies, children were looked after in large groups, typically of around ten members. Teenagers grew up with plenty of relationships without trying. In a similar way, in the past bigger families meant that older children and adolescents were involved in caring for infants.[2] But smaller families, the disruption of the pandemic, the mass closure of youth community groups and the growth of social media mean that connecting with others and building relationships are no longer inevitable. This is especially true among teenagers from disadvantaged backgrounds. The prevailing zeitgeist is to be suspicious of strangers and wary of their involvement.

If you are working, you may feel your time with your children is something so precious you don't want it to be diluted. Some needier parents may be jealous of others getting involved. All of us naturally feel that we hold ultimate responsibility for our children. Especially if we have planned lots of activities for our teenagers, which we may not trust others to fulfil. We may or may not be relaxed about how our own parents, for example, engage with our teenagers and what they allow – or don't allow – them to do, the roots of which may have started years ago when we handed over our child as a baby.

And if we reach out to others, does that mean we are not proper parents, unable to cope on our own? Why can't we sort things out ourselves without needing help? It can feel hard to share the difficulties we are encountering with our teens. It's as if we are being disloyal to them and our family, especially if those problems are not obviously earth-shattering but are 'just' day-to-day challenges when we don't feel as if we're good enough. For all these reasons, it can be hard to ask for help, but that doesn't mean we shouldn't try. This chapter is about ways to find and connect with others as best we can.

WHY INVOLVING OTHERS IS GOOD FOR PARENTS AND TEENAGERS ALIKE

We can begin by consciously deciding that reaching out to others is a good idea for us parents. It may assuage some feelings of guilt if we are not always present. Like most mothers, I often felt at fault for not always being at home. Yes, we parents are important. But even if we are sometimes absent, others can be present and important for our children, including what sociologists call 'weak' as opposed to 'strong' ties: friends of friends, those they meet at their local hairdresser or bike shop, the staff in a local café, members of the wider school or sporting community.

Part of helping our children to find these people involves giving them the space to form other relationships – to allow them to develop as people. This involves us putting aside any of our own fears that forming other relationships might involve meeting some dodgy characters, or in some way diminishes our own intimacy with our children. This is especially true at this stage of being a parent, when we are no longer needed in the same way to wipe bottoms, cook pasta or run baths. If we are not needed in this way, we can sometimes be left thinking: what is our role? But need is not the same as love. We can still have a loving relationship with our teenagers, even if they do not need us in the practical ways in which they relied on us when they were younger. And others can have a loving relationship too.

Enlisting others to talk to and support our teenagers can feel a blessed relief; we are not the only adults looking out for them. I remember the joy I felt when one of my teenagers began talking regularly to their godmother, who did seem to have a magical effect.

Nor do we need to feel guilty. Allowing others to be involved gives us time for ourselves. If we neglect ourselves, we are less able to look after our children. In the past, I would be embarrassed to say I was off to see a friend or going away for a few days of 'me' time. My inner narrative was that looking after myself meant I was neglecting my children. It was somehow selfish. I now believe the opposite is true, as I discussed at the beginning of this book. The best way to be present, to be alongside others and able to support them, is first to be in good spirits ourselves. Think of the plane safety instructions: put your own oxygen mask on before you attend to that of your child. Remember, teenagers may also find it a relief when we return refreshed from our time-out. It is not their role to mother or look after us.

Adult attachments are just as important for our teenagers. When pushing away from us, their parents, as maturing adolescents tend to do, having an alternative adult to turn to can keep the adolescent from turning to inappropriate peers. While some of their peers may have our children's best interests at heart, responsible adults with mature emotional responses are likely to be better guides than many teen contemporaries. Around three million families in the UK are single-parent households, most of them headed by women,[3] and there is a predominance of female teachers across all age ranges in the UK.[4] Teenage boys in particular can be helped by male mentors.

There is also much to be said for teenagers absorbing alternative viewpoints. This is especially relevant in a world where, as we've seen, schools have increasingly taken responsibility for children's emotional health, moral values and political views, whether that is schools dictating travel arrangements or the contents of lunch boxes, to sex education classes where teachers comply with government directives on relationships, sexuality and gender identity. Young people need to make up their own minds, and the more they hear from a diverse group rather than just their teachers or indeed us, the better.

Doing so also means they will have to make the multitudinous compromises and accommodations that getting along with others entails. They can find solace and wisdom in the realization that different adults bring different perspectives. Other adults can offer a space to help our teenager offload their feelings. They can offer reassurance in a way that we parents cannot always deliver. By spending time in different environments, they will realize there is no such thing as a perfect family. The sooner our teenagers realize this, from their exposure to other families who face different challenges and meet them differently, the better. They may even decide their own family is not so bad after all.

Hearing other viewpoints is especially relevant if they are facing a problem. They may not always want to talk to us or a family member. They might worry we will be indiscreet. Or they might fear that we will be distressed by what they tell us, and we will be unable to deal with our own emotional response, given that our emotional lives tend be so enmeshed with theirs. (This kind of 'co-dependence', as it's called, whereby the moods of others dominate our own, is something to try to resist. Better for our teenagers if we can remain calm in the face of whatever emotional turmoil they are dealing with.) They might even be furious with us and need to talk to someone else about our relationship together. They may well wish to talk to someone nearer their own age, or just a little bit older, who has more first-hand experience of their problem.

We parents may need to give teenagers 'permission' to look elsewhere for advice – making it clear that they are not being disloyal to us or any less appreciative of us. We can agree that certain conversations can be better had with others rather than us, and respect the need for confidentiality. Teenagers must not feel other adults will immediately feed back what they've said to us parents.

Conversations with others from a wider world can loosen up their thinking. If a teenager can look at things from many angles, they might make more confident choices. It is easy for a young person to develop tunnel vision, to think that the way they picture things is the only way, and that the people they thought were good for them are the only option. Psychologists know that patterns of thought like these are at the root of a great deal of distress. We can become fixated on one outcome and cannot picture another way of seeing a situation. Sometimes we as parents are not the best people to suggest different viewpoints and options.

WHERE ARE WE GOING TO FIND OTHER ADULTS?

All very well, you might be thinking, and yes, it's a good idea, but where am I going to find all these people? And do they even want to get involved with my teenagers? Won't it be an imposition on them? The last few decades have seen the erosion of what Gabor Maté calls the 'attachment nexus' in which child development ought to take place. We no longer live in villages or even neighbourhoods where other adults can mentor and help us raise children. The extended family is, for many teenagers, geographically or emotionally distant. Covid threw a new spanner into many families' support systems and the sense of a wider network. It can feel as if we are increasingly parenting in isolation.

It's tricky, I agree. My own answer has been to encourage teenage altruism: volunteering or selfless acts get them involved with other adults and create a sense of belonging, without them being an imposition on others. Before you know it, adults they've met may help them in turn. This happened to several of my own teenagers who became volunteers at local charities, perhaps because they were on good form away from home. Numerous studies confirm that acts of kindness cheer us up, benefit society, as well as healing some of the damage of isolation. Focus outwards, not inwards.[5, 6]

The best way to encourage immediate family members and grandparents to play a role, I've found, is to withhold any criticism I might feel about inappropriate jokes or how they choose to interact (though, as we've seen, we could tip off our teen to their eccentricities). And certainly don't offer any advice – hard for me, as you can imagine. No other species of animal has members who outlive their reproductive usefulness by as long as humans do. Having grandparents, according to some theories, was evolution's way of letting mothers do other things: it is easier for us to go back to work, forage for food, or have more babies if our own parents are there to mind the children.

I have also widened my net to encourage relationships between my adolescents and school psychologists, sports coaches or teachers, trusting that on the whole they mean well (though clearly we need to be sensitive here).

Intimacy can be found in unexpected places. I remember a guitar teacher once telling me that he saw his role as offering psychotherapy while teaching his charges to strum chords too. If a friend takes a particular interest in your teenager, perhaps elevate them to being a godparent to encourage their involvement still further.

Another way of building a village of caring adults is to cultivate relationships with the parents of our children's friends. In a pre-existing village of attachment, we would already have a connection with the parents of the children with whom ours are interacting. If we are not living in such a world, the only option we have is to build the village from the ground up – from our child's peers to their parents. We may not be able to control who our children's friends are, but if we can make friendly connections with their parents, we may bring some coherence to their attachment world. Can we always succeed in doing this? Of course not. The differences may be too great to bridge. But we should, at least, try.

MAKING FRIENDS – DO WE HAVE A ROLE?

While other adults may support our children, another crucial aspect of teenagers' emotional life is their relationships with their friends. Hang on. Is it even possible to help our teenagers find a supportive friendship group? You might be thinking this is a lovely idea but completely unachievable, as the last thing a teenager wants is for their parents to be involved in their choices.

There is a good argument that it is not a parent's role to be involved with their teens' selection of friends at all. Their friends are theirs: an important part of building a life away from us and their family. More than that, attempting to manage their friendship circles undermines our teenagers, taking away their ability to feel competent in life, so they develop poor coping skills, doubt themselves and develop a fear of failure. This is an area where they need independence. In addition, our motives may be suspect. One mother I spoke to admitted, confidentially, that her concerns about her child's friendship group were based on snobbery.

While it is true that it is not our job to decide who should or shouldn't be our child's friends, we are nonetheless an interested party. We naturally wish for our teenagers to fraternize with supportive, suitable and loving peers at a time when many teenagers are lonely or addicted to technology.

Somehow, we are aiming for balance – to stay involved, but in an age-appropriate way as our teenagers mature, until they are ready to handle their own relationships as they see fit. We can cultivate relationships with our teenager's friends, ensuring that we remain in the picture and that our teenager's connections also involve us. We might imagine this is not about us, but our role as parents matters. Making and maintaining friends is as good for our children's emotional wellbeing as it is for our own. If our teenagers have friends they can rely on, the less we will worry. It is a pleasant feeling when our children's peers reach out to support them; again, we know we are not the only people keeping an eye out for them.

THE NEUROLOGICAL CONTEXT

One way of supporting our children in their friendships is to understand the social environment in which they are operating and the social challenges they are facing. There are three in particular: the neurological context and their need to find a tribe, what it means to be popular, and how teenage boys and girls make friends in different ways.

First, neurology. From an evolutionary point of view, we are programmed to be part of a gang, and adolescence is when our teenagers are finding theirs. What happens in the teenage years, say some academics, is a kind of perfect neurological storm when it comes to friendships and popularity.[7]

As we saw in Chapter 7 about the teenage brain, at the start of puberty, the brain grows dramatically. The quantity of myelin, the fatty substance that coats the neurons and allows the brain to function efficiently, increases, affording the child a sustained burst of neural activity. Those shifts, along with others, aid the brain's gradual transition from childish ways of thought (impulsive and relatively unselfconscious) to adulthood's more logical and ruminative modes.

One effect of these brain changes is a newfound teenage self-consciousness and self-awareness. The adolescent brain is primed both to take in the world around it more than ever before, and to process that information with more self-awareness than ever before. Teenagers are particularly aware of their identity and whether they are popular. Having friends, and being part of a group, really matters to them more than it does to us.

Teen friendship is so crucial that going without it hurts: a brain-imaging study from the University of Michigan indicated that social rejection activates the same parts of the brain as physical pain.[8] There is an evolutionary reason for this. Friendships are vital for life. Teenagers are going to have to rely on friends when they leave home. In the wild, some mammals without an adolescent peer group are as good as dead. No wonder friendships can feel like a matter of survival.

A teenager can feel desperately vulnerable if someone does not sit at lunch with them one day, for example. They will respond as if their life is in danger, even though it quite clearly is not. For us, the best way to imagine how a teenager might be feeling is to imagine being mugged. The feeling is that intense. It gets worse. The more times that they feel rejected, the more quickly their nervous system responds to the perceived threat.

This fear of being socially excluded leads naturally to an associated syndrome: the urge to fit in. Given the strong urge to be part of a group, teenagers will adjust their behaviour to fit in, wearing the same clothes, adopting the same mannerisms, habits and attitude as those in their friendship group, as we've seen. Their overwhelming incentive is to conform; sticking out from the crowd is truly frightening to them. Linked to the desire to fit in is a longing for approval and status.

The age at which teenagers want to become part of a tribe is different for every person. True friendship is based on a solid foundation of mutual respect and individuality, and therefore needs a certain level of maturity and a capacity for social integration in our teenagers. We want our teenagers to make friends and find their tribe, but not at the expense of neglecting their true natures, their need for self-development and an ongoing strong and stable relationship with themselves. Relationships with others ideally develop alongside an increased understanding of oneself.

We may be able to support our teens in their relationships with their peers, helping them keep this balance between enjoying their friendships but not overly pleasing others. One 13-year-old told me that she wanted to be part of a horsey gang of teenagers, even though she lived in London and had never ridden a pony. Indeed, she was actually frightened of horses! It makes one exhausted on her behalf.

POPULARITY AND STATUS

A second context we need to understand is what makes for popularity among adolescents. There are few things that are more painful than being a parent of a teenager who feels they are unpopular and don't enjoy any status at all among their peers, either because they feel they do not look the part (athletic and sporty boys, tall slim blond girls, as we know) or cannot play the part.

But we can reassure them that this is only a phase. Academics distinguish between two types of popularity: status and likeability. Likeability is based on our charm, friendliness and inquisitiveness. It's the charisma that draws other people to us, and it is largely independent of status or physical attractiveness. Status, meanwhile, is based on our perceived place in the social hierarchy: our power, influence and notoriety, and becomes more relevant in adolescence. Awareness of likeability starts from around the age of three, whereas status becomes important in adolescence.

Popularity in adolescence is based more on being of high status than on being likeable. Though popularity takes different forms in different cultures – aggressive behaviour can raise your popularity in the West, while in China, the exact opposite is true – the problem is that in general teenagers are conventional and traditional in what they perceive as high status. Even if our child was popular at primary school, they may find making friends in adolescence more challenging if they score less highly on conventional status markers such as being good at sport, being successful with the opposite sex, and being thought of as good-looking and, crucially, funny. One teenage boy I spoke to said that, as he was not sporty, his ability to be humorous was a saving grace. In his view, social ranking among boys was almost entirely about being funny. Only about 35 per cent of people who have 'high status', one study found, are also likeable.[9] In other words, our teenagers are in a world where successful adolescents are not necessarily also pleasant.

For less popular teenagers, these years of finding their tribe can be painful, firstly because it matters so much to them, and secondly, because they may not have the high status that ensures that friends will come easily. Luckily, by late adolescence, status and likeability merge. Instead of status, confidence in who we are becomes more important. If they are sure of themselves, most teenagers will, over time, encounter so many different groups that they will find others with whom they connect and feel at home – their tribe – which no longer needs to adhere to the narrow conventions of what makes for popularity among adolescents. More introverted, contemplative, or less conventional teenagers may take time to build their own tribe of friends and find this kind of confidence in themselves.

Meanwhile we can help by challenging the prevailing model of what makes for conventional high status. In adults we often see these individuals move into high-status jobs or roles mirroring these capacities. But in reality, this model of what it is to be successful may be as much about our own desires as adults projected onto our teenagers than what is helpful for them. Supposedly high-status teenagers can, counterintuitively, find life challenging, not least because of the pressure to live up to all these expectations. I remember talking to one such 15-year-old during lockdown. She told me that it was a relief to be at home, as it was a break from having to be a certain kind of 'successful' person. She had been able to line up with what suited her rather than with the expectations of her peers and her parents. In her case, she had discovered a fondness for sewing and making hair scrunchies: impossible in her previous life.

HOW BOYS AND GIRLS MAKE FRIENDS

We've considered how teenagers want to be part of a tribe, and what makes for popularity. A third context to consider is that of gender differences in the ways adolescents meet up and spend time with each other. Anecdotally, girls tend to make more plans to meet up with their friends, often making dates and arrangements outside their everyday lives at school and home. They prefer to meet face to face, often chat on the phone, and are obsessive about remembering each other's birthdays. Boys by contrast tend to see their friends in less formal ways. Their friendship groups are the boys they travel to school with, the boys they play sport or other games with, the boys in their classes at school. Boys' friendships are more incidental, and less diary-focused – more side to side than face to face, and more based around doing things together.[10, 11]

Teenage girls and boys also tend to communicate in different ways. On average, boys are less chatty, preferring to connect in a more physical way: loafing around in large groups, with fist bumps in the classroom, or jostling in the corridors. As one of my teenage sons put it to me, you wouldn't ever ask a friend to come and have a talk. 'It's more like do you fancy doing something – playing footie or going to the pub.' Girls by contrast tend to do more one-on-one chatting.

Finally, there are differences in what the different genders talk about when they communicate. In general, girls are more at ease with admitting their needs and sharing their vulnerabilities as well as their strong feelings for their friends. Which is generally a good thing, though psychologists warn of the dangers of 'co-rumination', whereby girls get caught up in anxious feedback loops, overly fixating on negative thoughts and feelings and projecting them back onto one another. Girls can be in danger of talking endlessly about how unhappy they are without arriving at any solutions.[12] If this is the case, you could share with them some of my earlier strategies to manage pessimistic thoughts and feelings, which hopefully you are already doing yourself and are thereby being an example to them! Boys are different. While younger boys can admit they love each other, around 16 or 17 this changes. One psychologist calls it the 'guy code': not to betray any vulnerabilities or dependence or talk about feelings, which is seen as effeminate.[13] Masculinity, or a version of it, gets in the way of intimacy. Being in control means being unemotional, unless that emotion is anger. One boy I spoke to aged 17 said he had 'literally never had a conversation' about his emotions.

An ability to open up about feelings for boys can be especially problematic if they are going through periods of depression, anger or isolation. These differences are relevant if we are the parent of less physically confident, less sporty boys who are less able to communicate in this more physical way. Or, if we are parents of a teenage girl who doesn't fit the mould and prefers less intimate and less diary-focused relationships. These kinds of adolescents may find social interactions even more challenging.

SUPPORTING TEENAGE FRIENDSHIPS

A knowledge of some of the social challenges that our teenagers are facing, and the social context in which they are operating, means we can at least be a good sounding board for them, should they wish to talk to us about their relationships (unlikely for boys, more likely for girls). Even better is to know some of the characters involved. This may entail welcoming their pals through the front door, as it were, of the family's life. Allowing our children's friends to enter by a metaphorical back door enables them to escape the normal rituals of family greetings and introductions. Likewise, while it is unrealistic to stop them retreating to their rooms, and we all need privacy, it's nice if teenagers and their friends are greeted and made to feel welcome in the sitting room and kitchen, rather than isolating themselves from us. We want to get them into the common living areas where we can maintain connection. This subverts the mentality that it is us versus them.

This applies to teenagers hosting social events at home. Yes, they can have parties, but we parents will be around, especially for younger teens. Later, this may not be realistic and there could be a danger of our teenager feeling we don't trust them if we never let them have their friends round without us. But sometimes even with older teens we can still be active hosts, putting names to faces, making eye contact and introducing ourselves and showing an active interest in their lives. The message is that relating to our teenager also means relating to us, their family. Our adolescents are a package deal. Our teenager might be mortified at such plans, but they may also be secretly relieved, and even pleased that we care about them, their relationships and their friends.

My previous comments assume your teenagers have friends in the first place. Plenty of teenagers don't feel they have enough friends, of any kind: they have no-one to sit next to, are left out of social media groups, and are not being invited to events. As we've seen, teenage loneliness is a real and growing problem.[14] One mother told me that her teenager had become so shy during Covid that she would send her to the shop with a written list to hand over to the shopkeeper in case she was struck mute with nerves.

For this group, we can reassure them that making friends takes time. Being a companion and keeping friendships going are skills we can learn, like any other skill, and our personalities aren't fixed. It turns out we can, for example, learn to be more extrovert (more ideas on how to do so coming shortly) and become happier as a result.[15] We parents need to build our teenagers' belief that they will win on the friendship front eventually. One woman in her early twenties said this approach was helpful to her when she was younger.

'I didn't foster extremely close friendships at school, only when I got to university,' she said. 'What I didn't realize is that your year group at school is completely out of your control and it's the luck of the draw whether there will be people you connect with (more so if it's incredibly small). It sometimes happens that due to assigned classes or sets, which can be quite defining, teenagers can struggle to forge meaningful friendships.' Remind them that the conventional standards by which their contemporaries judge what is attractive or popular will change rapidly. More options open up. Meanwhile, we adults can remain significant in their lives.

How else can we support our children if they do not make friends easily, but want to do so? Academics such as the psychologist Ray Crozier, who has studied shyness, say we can learn strategies to cope with it. He reassures us that shyness is part of the human condition – a state as well as a trait: we all of us can feel shy from time to time, whether that's on a first date or going to a party where we don't know anyone.[16] There are even some upsides to shyness, he says – shyness can convey a sense of modesty, and shy people are often good listeners.

As with any worry or fear, our instinct is to stop doing the scary thing. This is especially true in social situations. It is all too easy to avoid meeting up and spending time with others, especially as we spend more and more time online. But the less we do, the more socially awkward, hyper-sensitive and quick to take offence we can become.[17] Far from avoiding challenging social situations, the best strategy is to embrace them. The more a teenager stops going out, trying to make friends or reaching out to others, the worse their social anxiety will become.

Begin with baby steps. If they are frightened of asking a friend to go shopping together, first suggest they go to the corner shop on their own, then progress to going with a friend, then when they feel comfortable with that, they can try the mall. If they get no response from a friend, an important step is for them to realize it's not about them; the other person might have had a bad day. See if they can see things from the other person's point of view and shrug it off. They can choose their own reaction.

Low-pressure activities can work well. Suggest they meet up with someone for nothing more threatening than a walk in the park. They might try certain types of exercise with others – endorphins released by doing something physical boost mood and ease conversation. Team sports make particular sense: being on a pitch together allows teenagers to strike up conversation about a common pursuit. Connections with others can be boosted by, quite literally, having a shared goal. Meanwhile boxing or karate, for example, can help teenagers feel physically powerful and learn to hold their body in a different way. Whatever exercise they choose, a regular commitment means they avoid the challenge of reaching out to others more randomly, with the possibility of rejection.

Shy children are often perfectionists – you'll know by now my belief in feeling good enough, a philosophy to share with them. Share thoughts on what makes friendships easier. For instance, you could stress that friendship is about finding common ground in terms of interests and preferences, and a shared sense of purpose. One shy teenager I know, a boy aged 16, joined the St John Ambulance cadets. He found a purpose, new confidence and, along with it, friends.

A 14-year-old girl who felt isolated at school was encouraged by her teacher to join the school debating club, due to her love of politics. Her mother told me, 'Debating and joining the club gave her a sense of achievement and status at school (allowing her to shine), which really in turn improved her overall confidence and her relationship with herself (she had difficulties with food and her body image), and then in turn led her to make more friends.'

LEARNING THE ART OF CONVERSATION

In the past, any self-respecting teenager might have baulked at the suggestion that they could learn how to engage in discussion. But some teenagers told me they now need help as phones have killed the art of conversation for many. So here goes. One simple way to keep a fledgling chat going is the 'Yes – and' rule, which the journalist Caitlin Moran recommends in her book *What About Men?*[18] If someone asks if you want a drink, Moran writes, instead of saying no (at which point the conversation is stone dead), you would say, 'Yes – fizzy water please, and could you get me a packet of crisps. Someone told me this place sells the worst crisps they've ever eaten and I want to see if it's true. Which of those flavours do you think will be the most unpleasant?' As she points out, there are now myriad possible topics to pursue, from crisps, to pubs, to why someone wanted water rather than an alcoholic drink. You could even prepare conversation lines and topics to discuss ahead. As a teenager myself, I remember sometimes having a list of topics handy on an envelope, if I was nervous about meeting someone. It sounds rather clinical and prepared, but it worked – it made social interaction much smoother.

There are a few other tricks. Good conversationalists naturally mirror body language in what is known as 'echo posture'. If the other person sits with their arms open and their legs crossed, we can do the same. When approaching a group, check the body language: see if it feels open before approaching. We can also match conversational styles. Breezy matches breezy, playful matches playful. These strategies give the other person the message that we are like them, and being alike is attractive as the other person feels understood. It also gives the message that we like them, because it is flattering to behave in a similar fashion.

Then there's the ping-pong rule: for every question we get asked, ask one back. If in doubt, 'What about you?' returns the ball to the other person's court. It might sound formulaic, but by asking questions about the other person, in time we may hit on a topic we both feel passionate about. Then the conversation is likely to take off with a life of its own, especially if we smooth its passage with plenty of compliments. It can be as simple as beginning a chat with, 'What a treat to see you. You always cheer me up.' And seeking recommendations or advice makes the other person feel validated.

Meaningful conversations can work better than more surface ones. In an experimental method known as the 'fast friends' procedure, participants gradually open up about their hopes and fears, with increasing levels of self-disclosure. Research suggests participants enjoy the conversations far more compared to standard small talk.[19] Teenage girls may need less help than teenage boys who, as we've seen, may struggle to move beyond what Caitlin Moran calls 'bloke chat' and banter. Yet boys can obviously benefit emotionally from sharing their anxieties and fears with their other male friends, as much as girls do with theirs. One of my sons made the point that it was a revelation when he realized, aged 18, that he could also be emotional and vulnerable with his male friends, who it turned out were willing to listen to his problems. Hitherto, he had felt that was only possible with a girlfriend, and given he didn't have one, he felt lonely.

Another teenage boy, a 19-year-old who had had therapy, told me he borrowed some of the questions and phrases his therapist had used with him to say to his own friends when he sensed they were finding life hard but wouldn't open up to him. Comments like 'That sounds really hard. Tell me more', 'What would make it better?', 'What's going on for you?' and even a simple 'What are you worried about?' had led to deeper and more meaningful conversations. 'It's hard to admit this but I think some teenage boys feel jealous of the girls, of the way they can talk openly when we can't.'

It may be easier for teenagers, especially boys, to talk to someone when they are doing something else – which explains the appeal of gaming side by side. They can concentrate on what they are doing and talk about that if it comes naturally. It can also be easier to enjoy companionable silence when they do something together, rather than feeling they must make polite conversation the entire time. Any takers for assembling some flat-pack furniture? I remember one of my children finding affable companionship in doing so.

Another idea is to suggest our teenager thinks of a 'five-minute favour' they could do for somebody else: we've already seen the benefits of being altruistic (see page 233). They could make time to do something small but meaningful – pick up a coffee or tea for someone else, lend someone a book or share some notes. It is a great way of connecting and is used by many universities to break the ice between new students when they first arrive.

It can be relaxing for teenagers to realize that they need not always talk but can focus on paying attention to what someone is saying instead. Sometimes teenage anxiety about what people think of them can make it hard to listen. They are busy thinking of the next thing they might say to impress others. They feel responsible for keeping the conversation going. But lulls in the conversation need not be frightening. Reminding them that we have two ears and one mouth can be a good visual prompt to remember to listen twice as much as we talk (which of course we parents are adept at doing too, given my chapter on communication skills!). Another good rule of thumb is to allow the person to finish what they have to say. We could even add, 'Is there anything else you want to add?' This worked well for one of my shyer children who found that others love talking about themselves; and he loved listening.

TROUBLE-SHOOTING

A few thoughts on keeping friendships on track – which of course is another skill that can be learned. Teenagers told me how helpful they found it to use 'I' messages, such as 'I feel sad when you don't return my text messages', rather than the accusatory 'You make me feel sad by not returning my text messages'. Using limiting words like 'sometimes' and 'on occasion' make any criticisms less charged – so 'Sometimes I feel sad . . .' This reflects the reality, which is that there are good bits about their relationship too, otherwise they wouldn't be trying to reach out.

Suggest they use open-ended questions, ones we are hopefully using ourselves. This means their questions start with words like 'What' or 'How'. So they might say, 'What was going on when you didn't reply to my text messages? How were you feeling?' The person cannot answer just yes or no, thus ending the discussion, but can respond to the invitation to share their emotional state. The closed version of the question might have been 'Do you want to tell me what you were feeling when you didn't reply to me?' The answer could simply be no, and that's the end of the conversation.

To decide if a falling-out is small or big stuff, we can ask our teen to think whether the topic of the argument will still be relevant in a week's time. If not, let it go. If so, they can talk about it. Or, if this is a repeated pattern, or a painful friendship, it may be time for them to end the relationship (which I will discuss in a later chapter), or to walk away.

UNSUITABLE FRIENDS

What about teenagers who have unsuitable friends? Teenagers who have difficulty making friends may also find themselves attracted to objectionable confidants – even more so since they've found someone who will accept them.

Despite our best efforts to stay involved with our teenagers' choice of mates, they may choose peers who make poor choices, especially when it comes to drinking and taking drugs. Status among their peer group can come from recklessness and not caring about the consequences of their behaviour.

Fight the urge to criticize your teenagers' friends; the more you do so, the more alluring they will become. Also, don't blame their friends for your teenager's bad behaviour. You may want to believe it's wicked peers who are leading your teen down the wrong path, but the truth is, there are no bad teenagers, only teenagers making poor choices. It could well be that they choose to get drunk or take drugs with a group of pals because that is a way of overcoming their shyness. Instead of blaming them, ask yourself what your teen's reasons for choosing these peers might be. The chances are that they feel accepted and understood by that group.

Might they find that acceptance elsewhere? Try listening rather than lecturing. Seek to understand your teenager's way of thinking without judgement. Spend time with them. And then share your concerns without criticizing their friends. You might say, 'I understand that your friends are important to you. But I worry that you might make bad choices if you spend time with them. And I care very much about you.'

Or you might try to encourage a new activity, away from the gang. One mother explained, 'My boy became a bit of a party animal at school, mixing with the wrong crowd, and that started to have a knock-on effect on his grades. He had always been good at art so we suggested he started it up again, which amazingly started to calm him down, allowing him time to immerse himself in something else away from unsuitable friends and peer pressure.'

*

I've dwelt on our teenagers' relationships with others, as this is a subject of such consuming relevance to them in lonely times, and so important for their sense of wellbeing. It's not just about mitigating the corrosive effect of isolation. More positively, encouraging other adult relationships can bring fresh viewpoints, and the possibility of male mentors for teenagers brought up in single-parent households, most of which are headed by women. Easier said than done, I agree. But there are ways – perhaps getting your teenagers to volunteer is one route: they meet the adults involved by default and can often forge meaningful connections. Then there are relationships with their peers. I found it helpful to understand a little more of the context in which they are making friends – how their brains are wired to be part of a tribe, what makes for popularity, and the different ways in which the sexes make friends.

Some teenagers don't feel they have friends of any kind. It might seem odd and old-fashioned, but we can play a role here teaching them the art of conversation in an age of mobile phones. I know of few topics that have preoccupied my own children more than their friendships and how to foster and maintain them, yet such social skills are rarely discussed or taught at school or elsewhere. All these conversations about the significant relationships in our teenagers' lives, whether they are with other adults or their peers, can be had in an upbeat spirit, reminding ourselves and them that things can change if they feel left out or friendless, because everything is indeed continually changing, including what makes for adolescent popularity. Sometimes, however, optimism can desert us parents, if unsuitable friends turn into bullies, a topic I turn to next.

17

BULLYING

We know in our bones that bullying has always mattered. The problem is even more serious now: the rise of online bullying means a teenager can never escape. If your child is bullied for too long, and too seriously, it can lead to anxiety or depression.[1] A teenager can go from being chatty and guileless to silent and bitter. It is as if they give up on anything in the world being fun or good.

But there is a way through. The best way to help a teenager who is being bullied, whether online or in the playground, is to understand the dynamics of what's going on, how bullies abuse power, and the different roles we all play: the bully, the bullied and the rescuer (which might be you, the parent). Though it might seem a good thing to be the rescuer, as we shall see, this is a role we want to avoid. Understanding these dynamics, as I had to do myself when one of my teenagers was bullied, makes it easier for anyone involved to avoid falling into unhelpful patterns.

UNDERSTANDING HOW BULLIES OPERATE

One respected Norwegian academic has defined bullying as an intentional and repeated behaviour involving an imbalance of power.[2] We can all be bullies, including us parents. When we are a bully, we assert our strength over others, whether that means the power to slap a child, call someone an unkind nickname, tease someone about their appearance, exclude them or start a rumour about them. Difficult as it is to acknowledge it, parents inevitably have moments of power over their teenager, which are all too easy to abuse.

Our teenager might be a bully too, much as we might be loath to admit such a thing. Maybe they have witnessed bullying at home, perhaps if one parent is being unkind to the other and they are repeating that dynamic. Or having been bullied themselves, they have subsequently turned to tormenting others.

Bullies crave power because they feel powerless which, again, is something we can all feel at times. Their way of having power is to make others feel powerless, sometimes physically so. Several boys I spoke to evoked regular fighting in the playgrounds, some of it violent, especially between those from deprived backgrounds given the link between poverty and youth violence.[3] One 15-year-old boy told me at a school workshop that he lived with a constant awareness that violence might be round the corner at any time, whether that was being spat at, being given a dead leg, or another boy deliberately careering into him fast, smashing into an arm or a leg. He had once been picked up by his hair and thrown down.

Among teenagers, power can also come from being popular and a ringleader in a gang because of high status, which we know results from sporting prowess or popularity with the opposite sex. Bullies are often attractive and popular figures, and even favoured by teachers. I was astonished when a teenager who had bullied one of my own children was made a prefect at their school. Bullies of this sort work by excluding others, and girl bullies are especially adept at doing so. One 16-year-old girl explained that she was bullied verbally for being nerdy and odd, and not fitting in with the cool crowd. 'It felt as if I was some weird organism that they had to repel from their group. I just wasn't the right kind of girl.' Ostracizing others is about being unfollowed online or excluded from a social media group; or approaching a table at lunch to join a group of girls you thought were your friends, only to find that they are picking up their trays and leaving.

While bullies can be individuals, they usually don't operate alone, given their social success. They enjoy being at the top of a hierarchy, with a network of supporters below them, some of whom passively support their behaviour for fear of being bullied themselves.

The problem is that the bully rarely self-identifies as a bully and does not take responsibility for their abuse of power. They do not think they are a persecutor. They imagine the other person is socially inept and they are just the one who cracks the jokes. Sometimes, later, the bullies will send friend requests or make contact on social media, as if confirming that they never identified themselves as bullies.

Take the example of a teenager in an English class who puts their hand up to answer a question. The bully throws a book at them, narrowly missing their head. Their supporters laugh. The banter is seemingly benign, but is actually about excluding someone, with an element of performance to the jollity. Or the bully who grabs a girl's bag and starts tossing it around to their mates, as if it's all a joke. Or the persecutor who begins to throw snowballs at one particular child, snowballs with stones in them, and gets their friends to throw snowballs too – all the while laughing as if what is happening is funny.

Most people who are being bullied are unable to help themselves. If they were, they would not be bullied in the first place. Particularly vulnerable are those from ethnic, racial and religious minorities; young people with special needs or learning disabilities; and lesbian, gay, bisexual, transgender and other queer young people. One study found intelligence was a risk factor for bullying, as well as being overweight.[4] Some psychologists call this 'bias-based bullying'.[5]

However, even those with no noticeable vulnerabilities can be bullied too. Some of the literature about bullying is so keen to stress the pieties of minority oppression that they seem to leave no allowance for sheer wanton childhood nastiness. Just being perceived as 'different' in some way can be enough.

Those who are being bullied feel they have little room for manoeuvre and cannot confront their persecutor. It is awkward, often nearly impossible, for them to accuse someone of bullying them: the bully will then use that against them, label them a snitch, and there may be reprisals. If they were to tell a friend that they were being bullied, and that friend tells a friend, who then tells the bully, the bully would be indignant. They might even respond, 'Why are you badmouthing me? We're friends!' – which is also a useful line if the bully fears recriminations from a higher authority. Or they might make jokes about the accuser being oversensitive or lacking in humour, or that they are over-reacting to normal banter to be expected to some extent, and even a rite of passage between older and younger teenagers. For the same reasons, it can also be just as hard to find the courage to report bullies or abusive posts on a social media platform, or tell parents what's going on.

FINDING OUT WHAT'S GOING ON, AND GETTING HELP FROM SCHOOL

A study of 15,000 secondary-school children in 2022 found that 80 per cent of girls were hiding their distress from their parents and teachers.[6] They worry that we, in turn, will inform the school, which again can make things even worse for them. They may worry we will be so upset that in addition to coping with the bullying, they will have to cope with a distraught parent.

One teenage girl who was bullied when she was 15 told me how hard she found it to tell her parents. 'Everyone enjoys telling their parents good news, so having to confide painful stuff feels bad. You know you are involving parents in it too. You feel responsible for their happiness and as if you are making them sad.'

I myself couldn't find out what was happening to one of my own teenagers when they were being bullied. We used to have a tradition of going out for a hot chocolate once every few weeks, after the school pick up – my aforementioned 'Special day'. It was our special time together when we would chat and relax. At the height of the bullying, one of our sons almost stopped talking altogether. We sat there in the café in silence. I never did discover exactly what the bullying involved, but I know it was largely online. He wouldn't tell me any details.

Parents can be left with a sickening sense that something is wrong but have practically no information about what is happening. Perhaps we suspect something: our teenager may be sleeping badly, or feeling sick, or crying. But then our teenager will assure us that it is just 'banter' and nothing to worry about. In other cases, our teenager may not tell us directly that they are being bullied, but they might say that they feel isolated, worthless or lacking in confidence. I have never felt more worried, depressed or powerless than when I worried my own children were being bullied, as several were at different times.

For some teenagers, being heard, and really listened to, can be a huge help on its own. They no longer have to pretend everything is okay. But depending on the seriousness of the problem, which is sometimes difficult to judge, we may need to do more than listen. If it is serious, though, the obvious answer would seem to be to jump in, complain to the school, and make sure the bullies are punished. Most schools trumpet their anti-bullying policies and try as hard as they can to have protocols in place to stop bullying. In my experience, however, this rarely works.

The first problem is that our teenager is likely to beg us not to tell the school, assuming they have confided in us in the first place. They may threaten that if we do, they will cease to share with us what is happening to them. This puts a parent in an impossible situation. Yes, we can get the school involved. But we risk no longer knowing what is going on and breaking our child's trust.

Those who are being bullied often have little faith in adults to sort out the problem. As one of my teenagers put it, 'Bullies don't care what adults say.' Nonetheless, suggest they write down what has happened and how it has made them feel, and sign and date the document. At a time when they feel powerless, this is something they can do. Not only is this useful if the difficulties need to be investigated at school, but it also allows the child to get feelings out of their head and onto the page.

What of teachers? Ideally, parents, schools and children will work together to deal with bullying – and this does indeed sometimes happen. Some schools have welfare professionals who will help the children involved at an early stage, rather than trying to act as police and intervene with or punish the bullies once the problem is entrenched. Teachers can and do discipline bullies, though often even if one group of bullies is chastised at school, or an individual punished, then the bullies can regroup and operate in a new way. Again, as one of my teenagers put it, 'If the main bully is caught, then those around the bully will come for you.'

This happened to one of our children. The school and its teachers did try to interview the bullies, but the bullies closed ranks and covered for each other. I hoped some of them would be expelled. They weren't. Sometimes it is the child being bullied who changes school, rather than the bullies.

I felt even worse, having tried and failed to help. Like so many parents I started out enthusiastic, trying to get the school involved, but this initial hopefulness gave way to cynicism. In retrospect, the only adults I didn't approach were the parents of the bullies, something I regret as that might have helped.

NO LONGER BEING THE RESCUER

Given the difficulties, it can feel as if dealing with bullying is an insurmountable problem. But there are ways to help your child. As challenging as it can be not to jump in and fix the situation, somehow, you need instead to help your child step out of the classic bullying 'triangle', and do so yourself. As I've explained, this consists of the bully (or bullies), the person who is being bullied (your child), and the rescuer (possibly you). The aim for all three is to step out of their role.

It can be really hard for you to step away from being the rescuer. Naturally, you are likely to be frantic to help. But the more you define yourself as the rescuer, the more your child is put in the role of being vulnerable and broken. The more you try to fix the situation, the more you entrench the view that your child is a defenceless victim and that you, their powerful parent, can sort things out for them (which, as we have seen, may well not be the case anyway). This, in turn, can make your child even more vulnerable.

One way of stepping away from the rescuer role is to see if you can dial down your own reactions. It can be a relief to the child in question that their parent is able to stay calm since they can't cope with your emotional health as well as the bullying. Strange as it sounds, you might even introduce an element of humour: laughing at the bullies and their latest antics makes them ridiculous. To make bullies seem less frightening, you could draw parallels with characters like Draco Malfoy, a major antagonist in J K Rowlings' Harry Potter series, who is frequently accompanied by his two cronies, Vincent Crabbe and Gregory Goyle, who act as henchmen. I remember one of my teenagers, 15 at the time, describing that a new group of younger children had joined the older generation of bullies in his own year group. We were driving at the time. I remember bursting out laughing, saying how outrageous that was, and how I could hardly believe his description of such ridiculous characters. He laughed too. Later, when the crisis had passed, the same teenager told me the moment we laughed in the car was a turning point.

A second way to escape the rescuer role is to believe in your children's power, and that they will be part of the solution. Bullying almost always relates to school life, and your teenagers understand the situation and context better than you ever can. Their own perspective is key to finding answers. By removing obstacles for them, you remove opportunities for them to develop independence.

When I stopped seeing one of my children as a victim and had confidence in their own strength instead, I could see that they felt better. Our aim as parents is to restore our teenager's self-respect and to believe in their resilience and ability not just to recover, but to emerge even stronger. We all grow through exposure to challenges and figuring out how to deal with them, and this is no different. No one likes being seen as a victim, least of all by their parent, who is the one person who should always believe in them. Bullying involves a loss of dignity and control, and involving them in finding answers helps them regain that. Phrases we could use might include, 'I'm really sorry that's happening', 'What was that like?', 'How did you manage that?' and 'What can you do?'

BUILDING UP YOUR TEENAGER: HELPING THEM OUT OF THE BULLIED ROLE

Bullies exploit weakness. As our teenagers discover their own strength, bullies may cease to engage with them or bully them in the same way. Our child may start giving off a different sort of energy; this means the bully will be less likely to target them. It may even become the case that a bullied teenager answers back and 'questions' the bully. One 16-year-old girl I interviewed initially felt there was nothing she could do. But she began to change.

She recalls being in a boarding school environment which she described as 'incredibly cliquey'. One lunchtime a few girls in her house (one in particular) made it clear they didn't want her to sit with them, together with some snide comments muttered quietly. 'I said loudly, "Excuse me, I didn't catch that. Would you mind repeating it?"' She told me she thinks questioning can be extremely disarming for bullies and makes them falter, because they're not expecting it. (And, she added, even if they did repeat what they've said, it means they are doing what you say!) Responding with humour or sarcasm can also show a more determined, less victim-like demeanour. Another time she said, 'Thank you! A lovely compliment. How kind of you to say!' Or 'Do you feel better about yourself now?'

She thinks that what stops bullied teenagers from defending themselves and stepping out of the victim role is a fear that challenging the bullies will make matters worse. The bullied hope that the problem will go away by itself, which might be true, but only if they're near enough to the end of attending school, or at least a school year. The reality is that it is unlikely to get better by doing nothing, so it's worth answering back, but with thought and tact. Doing so could perhaps give some power to the victim and a sense that they are capable of overcoming the bullying, or at least calling the bullies out on their behaviour.

All of this relies on strengthening our teenager's self-belief. This can be exceptionally challenging, but it is worth persevering. As one bullied teenager told me, 'Bullying makes you feel rubbish, and that makes you question yourself.' Share with them the idea that while they can't control someone else's behaviour, they can control their own reaction, question their own negative thoughts, find ways to allow and soothe their feelings of sadness and shame, and build their strengths.

It is hard for someone who is being bullied to find any kind of empathy for the bully, as most of the time they are too miserable to develop compassion for others. But there is a chance that by understanding a bully's behaviour and the reason for it, they might see that, while they seem powerful, a person's bullying usually comes from a place of insecurity. They wish for power because they feel miserable themselves or are acting out behaviour they themselves have suffered, perhaps at the hands of their parents. One question you could ask a bullied teenager is, 'What kind of suffering do you think could lead to someone doing something like this?'

Probably the only time someone who is being bullied can find this kind of sympathy for others is when they are momentarily feeling happier about something else that's going on. That can be our moment to have that discussion. Another approach is to share with our teenager that, often, a bully doesn't realize they are being a bully. They think it's normal. It's the behaviour they know and may have witnessed at home. They think it is just about making jokes.

The key insight to get across is that the bully's behaviour is about them, not the victim, who needs to fully realize that the bullying is not their fault. They have nothing to be ashamed of: overcoming a sense of shame is crucial to recovering. 'When you are being bullied (from my experience as a teenager at school) there is a huge factor of shame involved, as everyone wants to be liked,' one teenager told me.

In the meantime, we can help our children to strengthen other social networks, to ensure they do not become socially isolated, and so that they continue to learn about good social communication – all topics discussed in Chapter 16. This was the strategy that helped one of my own children the most when he was 14 and being bullied. He said, 'I managed to forget that I was being bullied when I had had a good time with a friend from a different school at a football match.'

Conceptual strategies can help. One technique is to ask our teenager to imagine an invisible shield protecting them from other people's behaviour. The shield is covered in some of their favourite things that make them feel safe – maybe a treasured possession, words from a book or film or song they love, or a picture of someone who makes them feel strong. I use this technique myself if I am entering a daunting social situation, using the image that I am surrounded by a protective light, perhaps – as I am a Catholic – with a cross in front of me (though I know this kind of religious imagery wouldn't be appropriate for all readers). We could suggest they bring to mind their favourite place, or a jug of cool water slowly being poured – whatever image induces a feeling of calm and space between them and the bullies.

Other teenagers say that focusing on looking after themselves is a good antidote to being bullied. This could involve exercise; one report found that teenagers who took part in sport felt less stressed and better able to handle confrontation.[7] Engaging in activities that provide reward and positive feedback is helpful. Do whatever small thing makes life a bit better. Here's how one of my children who was bullied puts it: 'You can make it not as bad as it could be. You can do more things for you. Like enjoy stuff you like to do. Like yoga or running. Live your life to the maximum level of enjoyment you possibly can.'

This kind of self-care can help, as being bullied activates the threat mode in our nervous system; we are threatened by not belonging and by having our social selves attacked. Ideally, we want our teenager to activate their soothing system instead – an idea you may have already perhaps shared by now and one discussed on page 75.

As well as nurturing themselves, our teenagers might be helped by hearing of others who have been bullied and have survived, gone on to great things and come through stronger. One of my own teenagers who was bullied said the turning point was hearing a charismatic and much-admired teacher, who had been bullied as a schoolboy, address the school. He described how he was locked in a cupboard and beaten up. Yet now he's a successful teacher; bullying hasn't ruined his life.

ONLINE BULLYING

All these suggestions are about trying to help a teenager who is being bullied in person. But what if our teenager is being bullied online? While the overall trends in school bullying have remained stable since 2018, cyberbullying has increased, with boys more likely to report cyberbullying than girls, and one in six school-aged children experiencing cyberbullying in Europe.[8] Other research from America suggests that as many as half of all teenagers have been bullied or harassed online,[9] which comes with new challenges given the potential audience is huge and beyond the school walls. Bullies can be even nastier online than in face-to-face interactions, where people tend to be more co-operative and sensitive to others' feelings. According to psychologist Dr Twenge, an in-person conversation is 'more honest, but it's also more agreeable. People have a very strong tendency online to say cruel things they would never say to someone's face.'[10]

To give some background, some types of cyberbullying include harassment, the sending of offensive and insulting messages, being abusive in posts, and posting photos, memes and videos on social media sites, chat rooms and gaming sites. Then there's 'denigration', when someone sends information about another person that is false and damaging. Photos can also be altered for the purpose of bullying. Sometimes online bullying is even simpler: it's about insulting someone's photo online. One of my teenagers, then 14, described how upsetting it was when two other friends of theirs discussed a photo of them which had been posted on social media. Their posts were supposedly humorous but actually were deeply upsetting, as they implied that my teenager had weird and disgusting personal habits which could be inferred from the photo. The effect was more devastating for being couched as a bit of fun that all could enjoy online.

Meanwhile, 'flaming' involves the use of extreme and offensive language and getting into online arguments and fights. This is done to spark reactions, and to enjoy the fact it causes someone to become distressed. Other bullies hack into someone's email or social networking account and use the person's online identity to send or post vicious or embarrassing material to or about others. Bullies may also create fake accounts to cause harm.

'Outing' and 'trickery' are more weapons in a bully's online arsenal. Private, personal information is shared, and forwarded to others. This may include private images and videos. 'Cyberstalking' is repeatedly sending messages that include threats of harm to make a person afraid for his or her safety. 'Exclusion' is probably the most common kind of online bullying: others intentionally leave someone out of a group, such as group messages, online apps, gaming sites and other online engagement. The Snap Map function on Snapchat shows where your friends are in real time – leaving the uninvited devastated. So too does Snapchat's feature that allows you to select your eight best friends with special 'Friend Emojis', making it a source of misery for those who don't make the cut.

All of these multiple ways of being bullied online are worsened by the most obvious point about cyberbullying: you can never escape what's on your phone, even if you move school or change area.

As well as the impossibility of escape, there is also the potential anonymity of online bullies. Anonymity means that targets may believe more people are witnesses to the abuse than is actually the case, which can compound their pain. In addition, online bullies can be more vicious than in-person ones, as they can't see what their actions are doing to their victims and tend to feel little remorse. This is something psychologists call the 'online disinhibition effect'.[11] Nor do online bullies feel there will be any consequences to their behaviour.

Our teenagers may be more worried about online bullying than bullying in person. They might feel that we as parents are out of our depth. Most teenagers believe their elders know less than they do about technology. We may not know about new bullying trends online, which move at bewildering speed. This perception can make them feel we could not possibly understand the seriousness of cyberbullying. For them, their digital identities are essentially the same as their real-world identities. They are unlikely to think that we parents can be of much help.

But we can, especially if we start early. Ideally before any bullying starts, talk about the topic. It may be better not to use the word 'cyberbullying'. Teenagers themselves use other terms to describe a range of behaviours that don't necessarily fit into our adult definition. We might ask our teenager about what they already know about bullying online, or whether a friend has experienced it. We need to get ahead of the idea that we are out of touch or don't care. We do.

As soon as we give them a phone, teenagers need to protect their accounts. Ideally, they should not share their passwords with anyone – not even their closest friends, who may not be close for ever – and password-protect their phone so no-one can use it to impersonate them. Suggest they use unusual passwords (using a combination of lowercase and uppercase letters, symbols and numbers) and avoid using any part of their name, email address or birth date because that's easy for people who know them to guess. Don't let anyone see them signing in, and if they do, they should change their password as soon as they can. Make sure that they turn their location settings off and set their accounts to private.

If they are using a public computer, such as one in a library, computer shop, or even a shared family computer, be sure they sign out of any web service they are using before leaving the computer, so as to protect their privacy. Encourage them to think twice before they post anything online, because once it's out there they can't take it back. It is easy for any comments or posts they make online to be taken out of context, and these could be damaging to them in the long term.

These are all sensible preventative steps, but what if our teenager is already being bullied? Cyberbullying is still rooted in relationships and there is still usually a connection to life offline, so my earlier thoughts on how to tackle the problem are relevant: stepping out of the bully/bullied/rescuer triangle. The only good news about bullying online or by text is that posts and messages can usually be captured and shown to someone who can help (though Snapchat messages disappear after 24 hours).

We can advise our teenager to use the available tech tools for reporting content to the tech provider, which they may be savvier at using than us. We can reassure them that these reports are anonymous, so there's no need to fear reprisals from the bully. Most social media apps and services allow users to block perpetrators, whether they are being harassed via an app, texting, posting comments or tagged photos. If a teenager doesn't feel able to block someone, suggest they try muting them. The bully won't know they've been muted, and the teenager won't have to see their posts or messages. They can also use the privacy settings on their social networks to limit what others can see on their profile. Even though that may not end the bullying, by taking these steps the teenager regains a sense of agency. If they're getting threats of physical harm, they should call the local police (with your help).

*

I've shared some ideas on how to deal with bullying, whether it's online or in person. Tackling this most serious of problems begins with understanding how bullies operate, and then trying to persuade our teenager to share what's going on in their life. Which is hard. Even harder is to know what to do next. Stepping out of playing the rescuer role, and helping my teenager in turn step out of the bullied role, is an approach that helped me. There are sensible preventative steps we can suggest to reduce bullying online, a new and terrifying version of more traditional in-person abuse. For all its differences, cyberbullying is still connected to relationships in real life, be that with the bully or your teenager's feelings about themselves. My earlier chapters about ways to counter negative thinking might be helpful and worth a second look. So too perhaps are my earlier thoughts on handling challenging emotions: while these were aimed at parents, the techniques can just as well be used by teenagers, especially if they are grappling with the horror of being bullied. It's hard to think of anything good that can possibly come of any kind of bullying, but my experience is that I was left with a few positives. The first was that I became closer to my teenager who had been bullied. And the second was that I understood more about the topic, an understanding that has since proved relevant in my adult interactions. Once again, I was lucky enough to be taught by my children.

18

ENDINGS

This part of the book has been about relationships with other people in our teenagers' lives, with their siblings, other adults, friends or enemies who bully them. Those relationships have their ups and downs: and sometimes they end. Endings can be important yet are often neglected by both adults and teenagers. They can be especially harsh in our digital age, when a friendship or romantic partnership is terminated by text, or worse, by 'ghosting' when all communication is withdrawn without explanation.

It is possible for parents and teachers to help bring relationships, exam periods, school years and other transitions to a close for teenagers, emotionally and physically, in a way that leaves the young person feeling fulfilled and supported. One teacher told me his constant mantra was 'How can we end it well?'[1] He was amazed the topic didn't get more focus, given its importance to adolescent wellbeing. What then makes for a good ending? How can we mitigate the agony of breaking up with friends or lovers for our adolescents? And smooth the dramatic gear-shifts of teenage life? Reflecting on endings may provide lessons for us parents too, as we navigate our own shifting and ever-changing relationship with our teenagers, as phases begin and end with bewildering speed.

ENDING FRIENDSHIPS

For young people, breaking up with a friend can feel like a bereavement, or a divorce. There is terror in no longer knowing who they will sit with in the dining hall at lunch, or on the bus, or with whom they will join in sport or for a science experiment. So much of school life happens in pairs.

Girls in particular can feel utterly abandoned if they fall out with a best friend. One teenage girl I spoke to, aged 17, said, 'You can feel like you've been stabbed.' But here we may have one advantage, that our daughters may confide in us; we've established that girls tend to talk more about their feelings than boys. After she broke up with a best friend, one of my teenage daughters, aged 16 at the time, told me that nobody would ever be a friend again, and that she would have to change schools: classic catastrophizing! The sheer intensity of her declarations helped me realize how deeply she felt about the break-up. Meanwhile, boys may not vocalize their loss in such dramatic terms, or indeed they might mask what is happening. However, losing a close friend for a boy may be equally traumatic and can be revealed by changed behaviour, be that introversion or outbursts of unexplained anger. If these ordeals take place at already traumatic times such as during exams, it will only add to the sense of overwhelm.

Break-ups can feel so devastating because this is a time when, as we have seen, teenagers are searching for their tribe and often riding a roller-coaster of emotions as their brains change. A close friend gives a teenager a sense of belonging, that they are valued and accepted and supported, that they have someone to embark on adventures with, that they are not judged or criticized. Typically, my own teenagers would return from school, having seen their friends all day, only to instantly want to be back in touch on their phones.

Such friendships now exist in an online world too. Thus, when a teenage friendship ends, our child will also face being bombarded with pictures of their ex-friend on social media, hanging out with other (often mutual) friends, having a good time. No wonder it feels devastating when a friendship suddenly ends, whichever party calls time.

As parents, we are naturally upset to see our teenagers so miserable. We may be sad, angry about whoever has ditched them, if that's the case, and shocked by how deeply they seem to be affected. Before we engage with them (once again, I'm afraid!) we need to regain a degree of emotional calm ourselves. We can remind ourselves of the inevitability of difficult feelings and use practical strategies such as writing stuff down and using breathing exercise to regain our equilibrium.

We can then turn to our teenager. Perhaps recall a time when we lost a friendship in adolescence, or more recently, and what that felt like. A simple statement acknowledging how painful the break-up must be for them will validate their emotions, and what their relationship meant. Our message is: 'I will pay attention to your needs. I will be there to comfort you. I will talk to you in ways that make you feel safe and secure.' Suggesting instantly they can find new friends may trivialize the friendship break-up when we want to show that we understand what they have lost.

Only after our teenager has had a chance to grieve might the conversation pivot to more philosophical thoughts on changing relationships: that not all friendships are meant to last and this is as inevitable as snakes shedding skins; connections come and go. Given that others are continually changing, it may be that in due course they will reconnect with this particular friend; we can remind them that both parties are responsible when relationships sour, as all relationships are co-created, and neither party is likely to have been their best self. Finally we can remind them that the reasons behind a break-up might sometimes be unclear, and that time spent figuring out what went wrong could be time better spent cultivating new relationships. No experience is without value, including the pain of a break-up. The experience can lead to conversations about what else is possible. How would they like a good friend to be? Where can they find this person?

A few practical points can make this painful period go a little more smoothly. Help them come up with a fixed line, ready to handle questions from mutual friends (as well as those gossiping about them). Something neutral along the lines of, 'We don't spend much time together anymore. Life moved on.' Plan ahead who they might sit next to on the bus or in the dining hall.

Throughout this period, remind them that their own emotional wellbeing comes first and that their main relationship is with themselves. Only when they look after themselves will they be available as a friend to others to whom they are better suited.

ROMANTIC BREAK-UPS – UNDERSTANDING THE CONTEXT

We may also need to remind ourselves how devastating a relationship break-up feels to a young person, given the overwhelming power of romantic love at that age. One study found that when young people are shown images of someone special to them, their brains became active in areas that are rich in dopamine, the so-called 'feel-good' neurotransmitter. This has multiple effects: it triggers the teenage reward system, it makes falling in love addictive[2] and it leads to physical and emotional reactions including fast-beating hearts, sweaty palms and anxiety as the stress hormone cortisol rises to adjust to the new drama in their lives. Recall your own young love to find sufficient empathy for them: how it felt so new, like nothing in the world could go wrong, and that no-one else in the history of the planet could have felt as deeply as you.

We may also need to recollect that the teenage romantic time frame is different from the adult one. What we might think of as brief and inconsequential may, to a teenager, feel like a significant long-term relationship, not least because a few months is a greater proportion of their lifespan than for someone older. We know the teenage brain is undergoing cognitive and emotional changes so relationship break-ups feel more prominent and powerful for young people than they do for adults. If I ever felt in danger of minimizing the significance of their feelings or telling them to 'get over it', I found it helpful to imagine what they were feeling as physical pain.

One new sensitivity to be aware of is the painful and impersonal ways relationships can end digitally. Sending a text message or changing a relationship status on social media can all hurt more than a face-to-face ending. Ghosting gives no chance for closure or discussion. Endings are especially painful if it is a teenager's first relationship. One minute they are flying high on the wings of love, the next they've crashed into a sea of heartache.

Anecdotally, there might also be gender differences in the way teenagers experience romantic break-ups. While both sexes can be left devastated, boys may be hit particularly hard, if for example they are less able to lean on or open up to their friends about their feelings. In some cases, their girlfriend might have been someone who helped them manage difficult emotions. After a break-up, teenagers (of both sexes) without an emotional outlet can resort to drinking and self-harm.[3, 4]

HOW TO SUPPORT A TEENAGER
THROUGH A ROMANTIC BREAK-UP

Teenagers are likely to need support in the run-up to a break-up, as well as the break-up itself. Psychologists say that adolescents who are struggling with an impending separation tend to behave in one of three ways.[5] They may avoid their feelings, not sharing them with their parent or others, and become increasingly self-reliant, withdrawn and guarded. When one of my own teenagers was in the throes of a break-up and went silent, I found it helpful to imagine a circle of light and love around myself, and to imagine them entering the circle and being bathed in love. It was something I could do even when we couldn't communicate verbally, and I felt helpless at the immensity of their suffering.

A second response for a teenager is to express self-doubt, questioning what they did wrong and feeling an intense need for a perfect relationship. Or finally, they may become disorganized, unpredictable and, while appearing confident, become unexpectedly anxious.

However they respond, once again this is about our teen and their feelings, not ours. While we may have adored our teen's former partner, or indeed despised them, this is about acknowledging our own child's feelings, and is a time to give them the gift of attention. They should feel that their needs will be met, even if a romantic partner is no longer there for them. If our teenagers feel secure in their relationship with us and safe in other relationships, they are likely to navigate break-ups with more ease and less fear. Being single doesn't mean being alone. The ending of a romantic attachment means a chance to re-engage with friends they may have neglected, with other significant adults and with us.

Supporting a teen in this situation may be as simple as letting them know we are around, or being in the same room. We might cook their favourite food. We can share our own stories of first love, making our teen feel validated and assured that we have been in their shoes. Yes, we are their parent, but we too have tales to tell, and we too are individuals whose hearts were broken but eventually recovered. I remembered my own mother sharing a poem, *Apple Blossom* by Louis MacNeice, which begins: 'The first blossom was the best blossom / For the child who never had seen an orchard,' when I was heartbroken as a teenager. Over time, your teenager may be able to cherish the intensity and beauty of having experienced love so deeply and be reassured that they will feel love like that again.

Teenagers might feel sad, but also humiliated and angry, at a break-up. Psychologists talk about emotional 'granularity', or the ability to be specific about different emotions happening at the same time. This leads to a better understanding and more accuracy about describing the experience. Some people naturally can engage in this descriptive process, while others rely on broader emotional strokes. Helping a teenager adopt this 'granular' approach and name their different emotional states helps their prefrontal cortex regulate them, and we've already seen how identifying feelings can be helpful. Or they might like to write or draw how they feel. We could remind them of the ways in which free expressive writing, and listing their fears, can be helpful.

All of which may take time. Lots of time. During the first weeks of various heartaches among my own teenagers, I was taken aback by the fact that they couldn't stop obsessing over their break-ups. I needed to remind myself of the intensity of their feelings, which those of us in long partnerships may have forgotten. Maybe this is a chance to try to become more patient ourselves.

It can be helpful to abandon the idea that our teenager will 'get over it'. The grief is akin to an open wound that heals with time but the scar never goes away. Instead, another way to think of it is that their loss stays the same, but their world grows bigger around that loss. Over time, the sadness will remain but life will continue, new experiences and new relationships will come along, and the grief will take up less space in their view of the world.

While we are unlikely to be able to stop them sharing thoughts online, we might remind them that they may be able to be more flexible and have more options in the future if they share less. It's possible, for example, that they become friends with the ex-partner, but this would be less likely to happen if they have been negative about them online during the break-up.

IF THEY ARE THE PARTNER WALKING AWAY

There can be separate challenges if our teenager is the one walking away from a relationship. They may need our support to find the courage to do so. Some teenagers I spoke to said they ended up staying with their partners for longer than they wanted, whether due to pressure from them, or fears of hurting them, or their own fears of being single.

There is room for practical help with this, too. How exactly are they going to end the relationship? Help them plan what they want to say. Remind them that they need to say clearly that they want to end things, pick a neutral place, and plan how they will get home safely before they meet up. Encourage them to let a friend or family member know when and where they are going, as the encounter may prove upsetting. Afterwards, stress the need to take care of themselves, and to try not to go out too much or drink too much. They may be tempted to contact their ex or feel vulnerable.

SHARED ENDINGS

Hitherto, this chapter has concentrated on individual endings, particularly in the context of teenagers' relationships with others. But there are shared endings to consider too, such as the end of a school year, moving schools, the transition between school and college or college and university. These transitions are often where young people feel lonely and vulnerable: they are moving to a new place, away from familiar friends and surroundings. Teenagers can be surprisingly resistant to change: like most of us, they fear the unknown. Even this simple awareness can be helpful. We might help them reflect on the end of one stage and consider the new beginning in an optimistic frame of mind, 'What else could be possible?' being an ever-useful question. Only by emptying their hands of one thing can they receive something new: an end is simultaneously the beginning of a space for fresh discoveries. They have a chance to re-invent themselves, away from familiar expectations. (And so do you!) Yet more often than not they are plucked out of one pool and thrown into the deep end of another. We need to try to find time together to consider their strengths and achievements as one phase of their life closes, and discuss the challenges and opportunities of the upcoming new situation and how they might handle them. They might write themselves a comforting letter talking about how they are feeling, and how their future selves would reassure them. Remind them how they have handled other transitions. Or (my favourite) a quick series of columns – a list of changes, how they feel about them, and then ways they might cope. This can help to ground young people, lessen anxiety and foster a sense of preparedness.

*

It is easy for us more sanguine adults to underestimate the sheer intensity of emotional break-ups in adolescence, as many of us have forgotten the charge of first love. But reminding ourselves of quite how deeply teenagers experience loss, both of friends and lovers, can equip us to support them through such dramas. Our help can be both practical – how might they rehearse ahead what they will say to others about what's happened – as well as more philosophical. We can share the perspective of time: while it might feel as if they will never recover, we are living proof that this too will pass. We need balance here, though. There is nothing more tiresome, as one of my daughters told me when she was 16, than a parent who tries to minimize their experience. Learning to be with difficult feelings is a skill I discussed in the first section of the book: these are helpful lessons to share with our adolescents if they are in the throes of a break-up, when we might find them unusually receptive to our wisdom. We can talk together about endings more broadly, as a teenager's life is full of fairly abrupt transitions, more so than it is for us adults. But endings can be opportunities as well as times to take stock: even being aware of their prevalence is a good place to start.

This part of the book has been about our teenagers' relationships with others, both the highs (such as making and cultivating friends) and the lows (such as how to survive being bullied). It's also been about handling change and navigating endings. In the next section I will turn from these personal relationships and transitions to the environment in which our teenagers are growing up. Their world can seem daunting for both us and them, due to global warming, academic pressure and knife crime, to give three examples among many pressing issues. At least we can approach such concerns together.

STAYING PROTECTED

PART FIVE

YOUR TEENAGER'S CONNECTION TO THE WIDER WORLD

19

AN ACADEMICALLY PRESSURIZED
AND UNSAFE WORLD

We are not bringing up our teenagers in a vacuum. We are influenced by parenting trends and the prevailing culture as much as by our own biology, psychology and personal circumstances. We are affected by the zeitgeist, even if we are not always aware of it, as being a parent is so profoundly cultural as well as personal. We are shaped by a world that is changing at lightning speed. The same is true for our teenagers: they pick up on the spirit of the times as much as we do, and the spirit of our age is largely one of turmoil.

Right now, it might seem that the world is a frightening place in which to come of age. Even without distressing global events, parents often fear that the world is dangerous. We naturally feel we need to keep our children safe from threats, which range from being mugged on the way home from school to being groomed online.

Certain minorities and ethnic groups are at a higher risk of violence, in particular getting into fights in which they are injured, compared with white people.[1] The writer Christie Watson has written movingly about her own mixed-race children's experience of violence and racism. 'No group of grown men have racially attacked me when I was a young child, or surrounded me when I was a teenager, shouting monkey noises, threating to kill me. Nobody has spat on me at a bus stop. But these things have happened to my children.'[2]

Even if as parents we can control the environment at home, at school our children face other causes of stress, such as bullying and academic competition. Again, the landscape facing adolescents of certain minorities and ethnic groups is especially challenging, in a world where accomplishments and achievements may be more about race than talent and merit, and they face discrimination and disadvantages. We feel pressured to get our children into the right schools, and they feel pressured to do well in exams. Studies show that, on average, young people see exams and their fear of failure as the biggest causes of stress in their lives. Yet clearly, not all children can achieve high marks, or gain a place at a Russell Group university (if that is what success looks like to you, as it does to many parents). This chapter deals with how we might think about three particular aspects of society that particularly frighten many of us parents: the pressure for academic success, our teenager's safety, and being concerned about the environment, which affects young and old alike. These are common drivers for many of us becoming 'helicopter' parents, who fret about our children more than our parents did about us, or theirs before them. I share some ways that could make us, and our teenagers, feel less anxious. I also share some practical ways to help our teenagers with their specific fears.

ACADEMIC PRESSURE

Since I first became a parent in the mid-1990s, life at school has become more and more competitive. It began with the introduction of performance tables in 1992. Children had to jump through more exam hoops, passing more tests at younger ages. Life in the classroom today is not comparable in terms of pressure to the classroom of even ten years ago.

We parents have added to this pressure. Many of us harbour hopes that our child will achieve, with a fistful of good grades – a sign of success in this newly competitive system. Others of us have real fears that our children will not get into prestigious schools or universities, and some of us are influenced by a desire for our offspring to go to the same prestigious schools we ourselves have attended. Consequently, some of us in a position to afford to do so pack our children off to tutorials, extra-curricular activities and work-experience placements. I have done it myself. I cringe at the memory of a parent-teacher meeting in which a teacher told me our child would not be able to get into the school we had chosen. I felt a red mist of anger rising and forced our child to try for the unsuitable school, nonetheless. The truth can hurt, but only if we accept society's focus on academic achievement.

At the time, I was unable to line up what really suited my child with the expectations of society, and indeed my own hopes.

The danger of such an approach is often that teenagers then find themselves, later down the line, in schooling environments that don't suit them and they can struggle to keep up. In a poll conducted for Mumsnet in 2019, nearly two-thirds of parents surveyed said that exam pressure was affecting their children's mental health.[3] A teenager who is feeling too much pressure may show classic signs of someone striving for perfection: tending to be fearful of risks, finding it hard to see their successes, focusing on their mistakes at school, setting high goals that are hard to achieve and therefore feeling upset when they fail, having a rigid viewpoint about how things should be done, being critical of their own supposed failings and those of others, being sensitive to criticism or finding it hard to finish their work.

These fears that our teenagers are being left behind academically have been long in gestation but worsened when a cohort of children fell behind at school during the pandemic. Teenagers themselves fear they are ill-prepared for the future, and that financial instability lies ahead. Us parents fear that we can no longer take for granted a reliable improvement in their living standards compared to ours, thanks to globalization and economic crises. Social mobility has stagnated too. Indeed, millennials are the first generation to be worse off than their parents at the same point in their lives.[4]

This perilous economic landscape fuels the pressure this generation of parents feels for their adolescents to succeed academically. Of course, not all children are destined to get a string of A*s. Measuring success only in terms of academic achievement may be one of the great problems of our education system. Once our teenagers leave school, they might be the happiest we have ever known them as they come to realize that life is about so much more than just passing exams.

Practical ways to help teenagers who are sensitive to academic pressure

How can we translate some of these thoughts into practical support for the kinds of teenagers who aspire to be academic high achievers, and will be upset if they fail? Of course, some parents may be reading this and thinking,

'Gosh, I wouldn't mind one of them!' and have the opposite problem, of which more later.

For parents trying to calm anxious strivers, the first step is to question our own assumptions: our notion of success, and our choice of schools. Do we see our own lives in terms of results and academic achievements? Without realizing it, we often live by a set of prejudices that conform to society's expectations of what it means to be successful. These prejudices need exploring. Play around for a bit to see if you, without realizing it, have any prejudices yourself that you have conveyed to your teenager. Ask yourself where your own views came from. Perhaps it was a perspective you imbibed from your own parents? What does success really look like to you? What are your own values, and your family's values? Where do love, honesty or creativity fit into your world? Or are you caught up in the need for exam success? Is your child's academic success about validating you, rather than anything to do with them?

This is not about you or your need to look good in the eyes of others. It is all too easy to conflate your success in the world with their success at school. You may feel that if your teenager does not do well, then it reflects badly on you as a parent.

A clue that you may have fallen into this mindset is if you find it hard to be open to well-intentioned criticism of your children. I remember being furious with a critical teacher at a parents' evening, before I realized I was taking the criticism personally. I needed to learn that I was not my teenager. They may be struggling with more academic subjects and prefer sport or art. Maybe when concerns about their academic progress are raised, even concerns voiced out of love, your knee-jerk reaction is to shoot the messenger because for you academic results are paramount. Check how you respond to their choice of subjects, and for any prejudice you may be harbouring about high-status academic subjects such as physics or maths. Show an interest in your child's schoolwork in the subjects they love. This can be motivating for them. The key aspect to this is choice: support them in the subjects and areas in which they choose to be interested.

A second practical step is to keep a close eye on their school. Be curious about what the school's priorities are and if it has developed more inclusive approaches and space for your child's emotional wellbeing. You can distinguish between a school's curriculum, which can be broad-ranging, and a school's exam-based assessment. While exams are inevitable, they may be less pernicious if combined with a more inclusive curriculum which provides a wide range of subjects and plenty of extra-curricular activities. You may even need to switch schools if, despite your good intentions, the academic pressure on your child is overwhelming.

A third approach is to be clear there's nothing they need to achieve to please you, including top grades. You might ask them to come up with one or two expectations they have made for themselves. If they are truly in line with their own desires, all is well and good. But if they are about pleasing you, you could ask them to imagine a different approach. Stress to your teenager the importance of their own individuality. Yes, they are a member of your family, but they are first and foremost their own person, with their own destiny and their own likes and dislikes. They get to choose.

It follows that you should avoid praising teenagers purely for good grades. This can exacerbate a fragile sense of self-worth because results are not entirely in their control, however much work they have done. They may be unlucky on the day or misread a question. Instead, praise the effort they made. We want them to believe in simple perseverance, which is something they can affect. Discuss how hard their heroes worked to get where they wanted, whether they're footballers, musicians or whatever.

Stress that friends and family love them for who they are, not what they have done. The danger of praising only achievements or successful grades is that teenagers may think they are only worthy of approval if they accomplish something. Instead, remind them of their other gifts. These include their character strengths. For example, you might praise how they problem-solve, or how kind they are to others. You could ask them what they feel are their strengths. They have many skills and qualities that are not assessed by schools. Suggest that these are gifts with which they are born; they do not require any effort and come easily and naturally without the striving that academic work can involve.

Why is this emotional support so important? It is because we estimate the gradient of a hill to be less steep if we have someone we trust standing next to us. We want stressed teenagers to feel supported by our physical presence and emotional connection. Hugs, encouraging Post-it notes, or supportive texts will help your teenager know you're alongside them and you love them whatever.

Helping teenagers who are struggling at school

While some parents will be worried about too much pressure, others will be concerned about too little: their teenagers may not be engaging with their schoolwork, or struggling with it, or indeed may be uninterested in going to school all the time, or in some cases any of the time. School refusal has been more common since Covid and is most common among children with additional or special educational needs. Others may fear being bullied or be suffering from anxiety. Teachers told me that the key was for parents, working with them, to act swiftly at the beginning of term to give children the habit of going to school, and find ways of supporting them.

Boys are more likely to underachieve at school compared to girls.[5] They are also more likely to be excluded from school and are less likely to go into further education. There are many academic studies setting out why modern education is more of a challenge for boys than girls.[6] One reason is that female students fear failure more, and thus study harder. A second reason is that coursework, rather than last-minute exams, favours the ways girls rather than boys perform. In addition, as we saw earlier, girls' brains reach physical maturity ahead of boys, at around the age of 11 as opposed to 15, which may mean that boys struggle more than girls with some aspects of schoolwork. Another factor might be the predominance of female teachers across all age ranges in the UK: boys might respond better to being taught by men.

Encouraging teenagers, and boys in particular, at school is less about stressing that exams are everything, and more about building skills of concentration, ideally with subjects they enjoy. I like using the 'Pomodoro technique' to help with focus. This is named after a red tomato-shaped kitchen timer which lets off an almighty ring after a set time, thus breaking down study time into short bursts of concentrated activity. The science of learning has found that focus is helped by spreading out study sessions over time, followed by testing – hence the Pomodoro. It has also been found that motivation follows achievement, rather than the other way round (so if in doubt attempt the easier work first), and that multi-tasking is best avoided. Each time the brain adjusts its focus, there is a small cognitive cost.

To encourage educational engagement, we can also hitch a ride on the passions of the teenage brain and make the most of some of them (as well as nourishing their minds with enough rest, wholesome food, and plenty of exercise). As we have seen, teenagers' brains have a set of drivers that are unique to them. Among these drivers are the desire for novelty and autonomy, being social and conscious of their peers (less helpful!), and being highly emotional.

To appeal to their love of novelty, suggest they change where they study from time to time and mix it up: maybe go out to a café to study, or to the local library. Rote-learn in the bath rather than their desk! Revise while walking – exercise is good as it introduces more oxygenated blood to the brain. Movement stimulates the hippocampus for good evolutionary reasons. If we leave our camp on the savannah, we've got to know how to get back, so our memory systems are stimulated by exercise.

As for their need for autonomy, play a consultative role, rather than telling them what to do. Ask them what they think they should do to motivate themselves. What distractions, such as their phone or Xbox, might they remove? How might they reward themselves if they stick to the plan? Ask what you can do to make this plan go smoothly. You are a support system. You are not in control: they are. Your suggestions can come across as criticisms. See if they can come up with their own. As one 16-year-old boy who was preparing for exams put it, 'I don't want to be told to "tick off my syllabus", "work work work" . . . I want to be trusted that I am doing my best.'

Linking their passions with study can deepen this desire for autonomy: perhaps a teenager who loves running could listen to something educational on headphones as they run, an adolescent who enjoys cooking could cook while listening to an audiobook of the Shakespeare play they are studying. This is about developing their internal motivation and agency. Studies show that when patients have some agency over their healthcare, and get involved with their treatment, their outcomes improve.[7] The same is true for our work-shy teenagers.

There may be ways we can harness the social, collaborative bit of the teenage brain to encourage study. However, we want to avoid the competitiveness that can accompany it. My teenage daughter talked about the stimulus and comfort of connecting with others while working, but not in a competitive way. 'It's really easy to assume that everyone else has got a grip and is sorted on their work. For the most part, everyone else is trying to get by. When I talk to my friends or someone I'm close with, it's quite bonding. They really understand my position: they're going through the same thing. Sometimes it helps all to go to the library together and enjoy their company in study breaks.'

Given how emotional teenagers are, timing is key to any of our conversations with them. 'I can only have these kinds of chats if I'm in a good mood,' said one of my daughters. 'If you are in a bad mood, you're just going to delete in your head any advice from your parents. You don't want the parent in your face. I don't want to be dealing with all my notes and subject syllabus and dealing with my mum and dad on top of it if I'm not in the mood.' Pick your moment, and adopt a gentle voice to suggest ideas; best of all, of course, is wait until you're asked.

Even if the results don't follow, these strategies mean it is more likely that work-shy teenagers will have adopted disciplined habits. This will be useful whatever kind of work they choose to pursue in the future.

Exams – there are other options

Whether our teenagers are perfectionists or in need of a pep talk, they will all in due course face exam season. Some don't care. Others do. For them, exam time can feel like months in an adrenaline-fuelled brace position. The exam season has its own added pressures, including plenty of unsupervised time and no teachers easily available. Support from us may be particularly welcome if they have yet to develop their own autonomy.

Here are some approaches more anxious teenagers might welcome. The stress of exams comes from the feeling that there is only one narrow gate through which they must pass. And if they fail to do so, then life is effectively over. It would be trite and unconvincing to say that exams don't matter. That might be true for the super-privileged who have myriad other routes to advancement, but for most students from a normal background, exams do matter.

The antidote is to change that narrative in a realistic way; the world offers other possibilities. The American psychologist Adam Grant talks of the importance of 'equifinality': there are multiple routes to the same end.

He argues that the only thing we have to do for sure to be successful is to be open to different ways of achieving success.[8] Even if our teenagers don't get the exact grades, that doesn't mean life will end. There are opportunities open to them. Some will be determinedly set on a non-graduate career, due to aptitude and passion (as opposed to low ambition). This is not about dismissing their fears as ridiculous, or saying, 'Don't worry, it'll be fine,' but about redefining failure. There's no such thing.

We can embed this approach by using supportive statements, or affirmations. These might include, 'You may not do as well as you want to, but you will be able to move on and learn from that experience.' We could encourage them to have some of their own affirmations to hand too. These could include, 'There will be problems to solve if it does not go well this time, but there are people to help with that.'

'I know it sounds a bit culty to have these kinds of affirmations,' said one 18-year-old girl who found them helpful. 'But say I'm having breakfast. I'm nervous. I've got another maths exam. I like to leave the house with one line as I leave the front door. I want my parent to say something like, "Whatever happens, it's going to be okay." Weirdly that's what I keep repeating to myself.' Parting lines of wisdom can have more impact than we think.

We can also reinforce this notion that the world is replete with options by discussing what they would like to do after their exams. Suggest they make a list. You could do this together. This is a subtle way of reminding them of all the things in life they want that don't involve exams.

Helping with their wonky brains

We can remind our teenagers of the glitches in our brain structures, which mean we are drawn to negative thoughts which tend to spiral. Instead, suggest they imagine the exam going well. They might play out the best scenario in their head. Seeing themselves coping well makes their brain believe that it is indeed possible.

Exams are a time when teenagers can so easily fall into the trap of catastrophizing and predicting the future. Ideally, we can help them build an awareness of their inner thoughts, and ways to challenge them. Simply say (without criticism), 'There you go writing stories again; it's just what all of us humans are designed to do,' or something equally neutral. In other words, this is completely normal for all of us. It is just not always helpful.

Here's how one 15-year-old girl learned to challenge her own thoughts. 'Sometimes when I go to sleep, I think things over too much. Like I think I'm rubbish at school. I'm going to fail the exams. I say, do you actually have legitimate proof? What's the evidence? If I think of exams, I think that if I don't do well, I'm going to die. Like, wait – I'm not going to die if I don't do well in exams.'

They can become observers of their thoughts, reminding themselves that thoughts are not facts. The stories they write about not being good enough don't have to be left to thrive unquestioned. This kind of self-criticism can develop into shame: teenagers may start feeling not just that they have done something wrong, but that they are wrong. Remind them instead that we all have different gifts and that succeeding at exams may or may not be something at which they excel, nor which they can always control. Yes, they can control how much effort they put into their work, but they cannot control how well others around them do, or how difficult this year's exams are. Encourage them to stay in touch with their intention to do their best, rather than the outcome. Either way, they are good enough.

During exam season, naturally young people's thoughts veer towards comparisons. What grades will I get compared to my friends? Again, stressing the existence of a bigger world, full of options, can be helpful here. It is only in the narrow confines of school that these comparisons feel urgent.

Elsewhere, kindness matters. Help them develop their capacity to make a difference to others. A recent study showed that children performed better in school tests when they had parents who valued kindness over achievement.[9] Ask them to help a neighbour take in their shopping. Or suggest they cook a nice meal for the family, even if they feel they don't have the time. Here's how this suggestion helped one teenage girl, aged 16:

If you are feeling really stressed about exams, it's good to be distracted. A really nice thing is helping other people. You don't need good grades to help someone. At school I did what the school calls 'service' – in my case working with little children at primary school, helping them how to read. It's now like, 'Wow, I'm smelling the air and helping people.' I felt really

*purposeful and like I made a difference; I could see that the children were
actually getting better at reading. I was doing my mock exams at the time.
It was one hour when I didn't have to worry about exams or revision.
My attention had to be on helping a child to read a sentence.*

If we can, we should weave these kinds of different activities and ways of
being into our teenagers' timetables and make a point of focusing on these
aspects of their character in subsequent conversations.

DEALING WITH PARENTAL ANXIETY
ABOUT CHILD SAFETY

Stressing about our teenagers achieving at school pales in comparison with
fears about dangers to our children's safety lurking in the wider world
(though if we ask teenagers themselves, these are largely parental concerns,
rather than worries our teenagers share). We fear they will be the victims of
crime. We worry about our teenagers' social lives. There are tales of spiking
with hypodermic syringes in clubs or being 'roofied' – having a drink spiked
with Rohypnol on a night out. We panic that our teenage daughters are
vulnerable to violence. In a variety of ways, parents have received a consistent
message that life is dangerous.

One reason we are likely to believe in this frightening world is because bad
is stronger than good. We mind losing money more than we like winning it.
We hate criticism more than we're cheered by praise. Bad things tend to be
more memorable than good ones. Pessimism makes evolutionary sense. In
a Stone Age village, stories would tend to be about possible dangers. Tales
about how nice the fellows in the tribe over the hill were wouldn't have
improved your chances of survival, but news that they were sharpening their
axe heads and planning to set off to murder you would grab your attention,
as your very life was at stake. The DNA of the tribe with a preference for bad
news was more likely to be passed down the generations than that of the tribe
who listened to uplifting stuff.

It's understandable that we are scared – but how well founded are these
fears? Social psychologists have documented 'safetyism': the overprotection
of children that began in the 1990s[10] even though the perception of lurking
danger is not really borne out by the facts. Fear of violent crime is rampant,

yet actual levels of violence, burglary and car crime have been declining for 30 years – and by close to 90 per cent, according to the Crime Survey for England and Wales (CSEW), our best indicator of true crime levels.[11] Unlike police data, the CSEW is not subject to variations in reporting and recording. There are, of course, exceptions. Some crime types have had a less pronounced decline, or even an increase, and some groups including LGBTQIA+ youth, are more vulnerable. There are risks in the virtual world, and a disturbing increase in sexual abuse against teenage girls, including rape, thanks to the rise in violent pornography. But in general the real world is not as dangerous as we parents might imagine.

That's not to say we won't worry, especially if our children are particularly vulnerable to violence. Sometimes we are right to do so. Allowing our teenagers to return home on their own from a party speaks to the courageousness we need as parents – nerves of tungsten, as one parent said to me. Again and again, we have to release our teenagers into the unknown world where we don't have the means or control to protect them. We have to accept that on occasion bad things will happen. But in general this remains the exception. More likely is that they might miss the last bus and have to abandon their agonizing high-heels to walk home in bare feet. They may meet dodgy characters and have to scarper at high speed, or get lost, or even break a limb. Or, as happened to one of my sons, navigate a group of drunken youths who were spoiling for a fight. His solution was to kiss his girlfriend – introducing this romantic gesture threw the lads off their violent stride. Somehow it wasn't cool to pick a fight with a young couple who were evidently enjoying a night out. The gang melted away in search of someone who was more obviously interested in having a fisticuff.

But we must balance our own fears with the sure knowledge that, as we saw in Chapter 9 on building independence, overcoming adversity leads to confidence and resilience and is the way they will learn to survive, just as germs fortify children's immunity. Yes, at times they will be frightened. But to quote Marjory Allen, the landscape architect who campaigned for children's rights and who spearheaded the adventure playground movement, 'Better a broken bone than a broken spirit.' They need to be at risk of harm in the world to learn how to manage peril. They are also having adventures and learning to read a situation or a street. Painful though this is for us, it's good for them.

ACKNOWLEDGING TEENAGE CONCERNS

So far, I have addressed some thoughts for adults worried about child safety. What about worried teenagers? Many of us share their fears about climate change, for example, and take our teenagers' part here. As King Charles recently said, we've got a dreadfully long way to go to reverse climate change.[12] You don't have to be Greta Thunberg to see that growth in renewable energy isn't going to stop deforestation. That said, the more apocalyptic eco-anxiety that young people are often quoted as expressing – that the world will end, and the human race will shortly be extinct – is more along the lines of our generation's nuclear worries. Eco-anxiety affects 84 per cent of 16–25-year-olds, one report found,[13] while another found that climate change was the single biggest concern among adolescents, with 75 per cent feeling worried about it.[14] Which young person really cares about exam results when the world is going up in smoke?

We might be able to help, by giving perspective of our own experience, sharing more positive news about the planet, or encouraging them to get involved in local schemes to preserve nature or to work hard at science, as scientists will provide the best answers. The psychotherapist Philippa Perry cautions against getting carried away with strong feelings of panic, instead staying close to the facts.[15] 'People think their feelings are so real now that they're not worried about facts at all . . . Yes, what you feel is true, in that you do feel it. But how you're talking to yourself, to make you feel what you're feeling, might not be true . . . As panic rises, people feed it by having more pessimistic thoughts.' We can remind our teenagers of sensible ways to handle their strong feelings and challenge their negative thoughts, letting go of ones that don't serve them (see page 43). We can help them find room for joy too, so they have the robustness to make a difference. The stronger they are, the better they manage their dark thoughts and strong feelings, and the more difference they can make.

*

I have shared some possible ways of responding to our parental concerns about the world in which our teenagers are coming of age. Some of us need to dial down the academic pressure; others of us need to encourage our offspring to attend school in the first place. A knowledge of how the teenage brain is growing and changing (ideas discussed in Chapter 7) can be helpful here – we can work with the grain of neurological change to engender an enthusiasm for schoolwork. Few teenagers welcome exams, but affirmations about redefining failure can help them through an inevitably stressful period. So too can teaching them ways to challenge their negative thoughts, in particular ditching the tendency we all have to catastrophize and to compare ourselves with others (some favourite themes of mine, as you will know by now). This tendency is not helpful at any time, and especially unhelpful in exam season.

We parents can also benefit from challenging our own negative thoughts when it comes to child safety. It's understandable that we are scared, and I'm not arguing for complacency in the face of a big, bad world. But teenagers need to learn to manage risk themselves. We can't always be there in a heated car, waiting for them to exit a party. Nor do we have all the answers to existential fears about climate change. But we can be sympathetic to their concerns, which are shared by many of us, and figure out some answers side by side. All well and good, you may be thinking. But these days much of what we might call the world is digital rather than physical, equivalent in mountaineering terms to the North Face of the Eiger compared to the hillocks I've focused on in the last few pages. Quite how to navigate what is arguably *the* challenge of our age is the topic of my next chapter.

20

THE DIGITAL WORLD

F ew of us are unaware of the challenges of the digital world in general, and of smartphones in particular, challenges that worsened during the pandemic when teenagers spent even more time on their phones. The move to online platforms such as Zoom for everything from appointments to school lessons has remained in place long after the lockdowns have ended, and with no signs of a return to pre-Covid days.

No more than a paragraph is needed to remind you of what you already know: the adolescent online world is, by and large, an ugly place. Yes, there are pockets of fun, and of course that must be true or it wouldn't be so appealing to our adolescents. But it's also full of dark and violent content, insidious misinformation and unrepresentative images, of bullying, grooming, sextortion (criminals posing as teenagers to make online contact, then blackmailing them by threatening to share sexual pictures or videos) and gaming. (This has become such a problem, especially for boys, that it is now seen as a mental health condition, a topic I turn to in Part Six.) It's an addictive world of obsessive scrolling where young adults (aged 18–24) spend on average four hours, 36 minutes a day.[1] One parent I talked to spoke for nearly all of us when she said, 'I just want to smash their phones into a thousand pieces and flush them down the loo.'

In the past, we weren't sure exactly how all these aspects of phone usage influenced teenage mental health. The usual line was that we didn't know if phones were at fault, because the evidence correlations were small. Are teenagers already depressed, and then they go online? Or do they become depressed because of what they discover on the internet? There is still some uncertainty and we need more research: one study found that there is no evidence that the global adoption of Facebook is linked to psychological harm.[2] It's also true that mental health problems are triggered by multiple factors, including abuse, stress, family history, drinking and drug use, and having a long-term physical health condition. Many mental health problems, such as eating disorders, pre-dated the arrival of the smartphone. The prevailing culture of empathy and openness with which teenage mental health is now, rightly, treated means we may be in danger of over-medicalizing normal teenage angst.

However, the extent to which phones, and social media in particular, can exacerbate mental health problems is now clear. It is probably best summed up in Jonathan Haidt's recent book *The Anxious Generation*.[3] The American psychologist argues that there is a link between the rise of smartphone use and mental health problems, especially for girls, who consume more social media than boys, and are more vulnerable to social comparisons and perfectionism as we saw in an earlier chapter. New research published since 2019, especially about the damage caused by Instagram (as opposed to Facebook), and a recent convergence of views among the leading commentators and researchers, suggests that the more time adolescents spend online, the higher their levels of depression and other adverse consequences.[4] Phones block normal human development by taking time away from sleep, play and in-person socializing. Every day sees new evidence of all these damaging impacts. Haidt talks about 'the great rewiring of childhood' which happened between 2010 and 2015 and believes that social media is a substantial cause, not just a tiny correlate, of depression and anxiety, and therefore of related behaviours including self-harm and suicide.[5]

We are now 13 years into the largest epidemic of teen mental health problems on record, and its rising curve neatly correlates with the launch of various social media platforms. One survey, an American one, found that the majority of girls (57 per cent) now say that they experience persistent sadness or hopelessness (up from 36 per cent in 2011), and 30 per cent of teenage girls now say that they have seriously considered suicide (up from 19 per cent in 2011).[6] Boys are doing badly too, but their rates of depression and anxiety are not as high, and their increases since 2011 are smaller. Why is this happening, and why did it start so suddenly around 2012? There is one giant, obvious, international and gendered cause: social media. Instagram was founded in

2010, in the same year that the iPhone 4 was released – the first smartphone with a front-facing camera. In 2012, Facebook bought Instagram, and the latter's user base exploded.[7]

What should parents be doing, specifically about social media rather than lumping together all screen-based activities such as watching YouTube or Netflix, or playing games? Studies that look at all screen-based activities, including television, for kids (of all genders) and their links with worsening mental health generally find only small correlations.[8, 9] However, as you zoom in on social media, for girls the correlations rise. TikTok in particular reduces the ability to focus, and studies suggest it has the worst impact on teenage intellectual development.[10]

UNDERSTANDING WHY SOCIAL MEDIA APPEALS TO TEENAGERS

Teenagers, as we have seen, are more vulnerable to peer pressure, given the way the teenage brain is developing and their longing to feel connected. One American 2023 report showed how teenagers who habitually checked their social media accounts experienced changes in the way their brains responded to the world, including becoming hypersensitive to feedback from their peers.[11]

Acknowledging the adolescent need to belong and feel attached explains the appeal of the digital world to young people – the seduction of 'friends and trends', as Dr Jane Gilmour, a clinical psychologist at Great Ormond Street Hospital, puts it. It is less about the entertainment social media provides, or the information it yields, than its power to offer social connection. The internet can be a powerful force for good in this process. Young people can find their tribe online: for example, others who dress, act or think like they do. This might involve stumbling across a comedian on TikTok who shares their sense of humour, or finding a poster on Pinterest with the same taste in nail varnish ideas.

It's a need that seems to be answered by the number of likes their posts receive or the number of followers they attract. As Gabor Maté says, 'The technology may be new, but the dynamics are as old as humankind.'[12] Adolescents have always wanted to look and be part of the gang, and social media is where the gang is now to be found. Smartphones feed what can be a bottomless adolescent desire for affirmation of their identity.

But these upsides come with downsides. One problem with being able to see so many other people doing so much is, well, exactly that. Because teens are acutely aware of social status and FOMO (fear of missing out), their internet browsing can make them feel like there's a whole world out there which they're not part of. In general, as we've seen, people are more likely to be affected by losses than by gains, something psychologists call 'loss aversion'. I remember this when we went on holiday with our teenagers. While there were nice aspects to spending time together, the perception that they had missed out on parties or gatherings with their friends at home (witnessed on their phones) outweighed many of the pleasures of being away.

In their quest to become part of the gang and to be attractive to their peer group, the temptation for teenagers is to either post only what speaks of a perfect existence, or to become more outrageous in their posts in desperation for more followers, likes, laughs and hits online. They may end up posting more and more unsuitable material.

In order to fit in, our teenagers may cultivate an easily graspable identity: one that is social-media friendly and designed to be seen by others. They end up with what one commentator called a 'double self-image'.[13] One minute they are dressed to kill, posing in their bedroom, before curating and posting the picture that is their online image; the next they are in torn pyjamas, covered in spot cream, eyeing up what's in the fridge. This can even lead those whose identities are not yet fully formed to forge a new false identity, even a negative one. It may even be one forged on a shared illness. Anorexia, for example, can provide one such defining online identity.

This is an exhausting way to live: everything is continually chronicled, and the self-presentation of this identity never stops. The amount of time spent online by teenagers is daunting: in the UK, nearly one-fifth of 16–24-year-olds spend as many as seven hours online every day.[14] Social media is built to keep users locked into it – endless feeds that keep users scrolling manipulate the brain's dopamine delivery mechanism to intensify use, incessant notifications encourage repetitive checking of accounts, and metrics exploit social comparison.

A key part of fitting in is bound up with appearance, as we saw in Chapter 12 on the teenage preoccupation with looks. Social media's differing effects on the different genders may be partly explained by the fact that, generally, boys use technology more for gaming and girls use their phones more for activities that involve comparing looks.[15] One 19-year-old girl explains how social media's visual nature is at the heart of its appeal:

For my generation, there is less use of Twitter and Facebook. There's more use of Instagram, Snapchat and TikTok. They are all platforms that are based on filming yourself or taking pictures of yourself. It's about being part of the group, looking the part. Facebook and Twitter are a bit wordier. With images, there's more pressure. I didn't know what insecurities were until I got my first iPhone.

All of this was just as true for us growing up. Many of us cared about being asked to parties. We wanted to look the part. Social media in its early days was another step in the long progression of technological innovations that helped people achieve the eternal goal of maintaining social ties, from the postal service to the telephone, email and texting. But social media now involves over-exposure to other people's lives, as well as over-exposure of our own lives, at entirely new levels of intrusion and exhibition. Our teenagers are exposed to this stuff all day, every day, in a way that is utterly new and that few of them can handle. They have levels of detailed information about exactly what their peers are doing that was unimaginable in our day.

While it might seem as if a phone-based social life offers the validation and belonging that teenagers seek, more often than not it fuels negative, fear-based narratives. They drown in social comparisons, and feel vulnerable. A particular fear is being ostracized from the dreamed-for tribe by tripping up in today's culture wars. If they blunder they can end up buried in hateful comments. Teenagers tell me how anxious this has made them, to the point they self-censor for fear of expressing a socially unacceptable view, especially on topics such as gender identity.

HOW TO RESPOND

Taking away our teenager's phone isn't going to work. The online world has clearly brought with it some massive advantages and teenagers understandably want to benefit too: there is nothing inherently wrong with digital connection. The internet is not innately satanic, any more than Gutenberg's printing press or the first transatlantic cables were. Accept that your teenager needs a phone to run their life, make plans with friends, book a train ticket, arrange their journey and so on. They rely on their phones, again just as we do. They need to read online, whether that's sources of news or books or for homework. In addition, they listen online to podcasts or videos, use Citymapper to navigate round town, and Uber to get home safely just as we do. None of this kind of interaction is necessarily damaging (indeed, it can actually reduce the burden on us parents!). Nor is the connection that phones provide for young people. When teenagers talk to their contemporaries online, they feel they belong. They can show they care about each other, and intimacy can be important for those who find communication in real life more difficult.

The problem is that these useful phone functions are inseparable from accessing social media. And this tends to happen before many teenagers are mature enough to manage astonishing new levels of social connectivity. We cannot just assume the necessary level of maturity in their decision-making when they click, send, share, like, block or mute to thousands of others.

What about digital parental controls? (Which, by the way, have been made so deliberately cumbersome and inaccessible by the tech firms as to be unusable for most parents, myself included.) Even if we do figure out how to use them, teenagers will find a way round such controls, whether through back-up phones or by using VPNs (virtual private networks, which can hide who the users are), just as they find ways round age verification. They are almost certainly more tech-savvy than us. Coercion and punishments will only magnify the problem, adding fresh layers of resentment and frustration to the dynamic between us and our teenagers.

But don't despair! Some approaches do help, especially those that tap into teenage psychology and work with teenagers rather than against them. First, their need for connection: we must ourselves try to stay close to our teenagers for as long as possible, given the deep allure of social media as a way to link with others. Second, their love of autonomy: reducing phone use needs to be their idea, not ours.

Connecting more with our teenagers

The best immunization against using digital devices for social connection is a teenager who feels understood, communicated with and connected to us.

The earlier contents of this book may have given you practical ideas for how to stay close to your teenager in these ways, whether that's one-on-one time, 'special days', five-minute chats or prioritizing quality moments, by which I mean focused and meaningful engagement.

To protect times when a more fulfilling connection is possible, we need to create digital-free zones in our homes and in our schedules, including holidays off grid (ideally) involving climbing, swimming or any physical activity in which it's impossible to be on a phone. One parent told me her teenager was surprised how relaxing she found such a digital detox, even though she had resisted the idea originally. 'I think of it as a "stealth health" holiday,' the mother told me. 'You subtly weave in digital-free times.' Mealtimes, family times, evenings and bedtimes are the most important periods to keep free of digital activities, both to create the space to provide the connection our children really need, and to slow down the obsession with phones. Put your own phone aside to encourage your teen to do the same. If you're typing while talking to them, even if you're actually working, they'll interpret it as social media use. You are giving the message that they are less important to you, so they might as well hang out with their peers online – just as you are hanging out with your peer group. We can't restrict them from having their need for connection met by their peer group online if we are not available to answer that underlying need ourselves. Sometimes we have to put our own work aside. We must be present if we can be, or accept that their phones will be.

Appealing to their love of autonomy with cunning questions

Once again, we want to tap into the teenage desire for autonomy. Telling them what to do may be less effective than asking questions so they figure things out themselves and take ownership of the problem – the 'Big Fat Greek Wedding' approach, so named after the film in which the heroine falls in love with a non-Greek man against her father's wishes, but the various family members plot to make him think that the wedding was his idea all along. Ask exactly how much time they spend on social media. This is so simple, but effective. Many teenagers are concerned about the time they spend, but haven't actually totted up the hours. When they do, they can be quite shocked. One teenager who carried out this exercise said, 'I realized I could have done so many other things – forged better connections with friends in person, quality time with my family, time spent doing more worthwhile things. I just hadn't realized how many hours were involved.'

A second question you could ask your teenager is, 'How does social media make you feel?' You could ask why they are drawn to social media in the first place. Is something else going on? Are they anxious, or being bullied, or looking to social media for answers about something? Or to distract from their negative thoughts? (In which case you could remind them of other, healthier ways to do so – see page 75.) Does it feel like they really are connecting with others, or more like they are performing? Is the experience an active one, or more passive, vicariously viewing the curated experience of others rather than actively living life? The likelihood is that the answers will be negative. Digital intimacy does not deliver on its promise. In fact, it makes things worse; psychologists have found increases in loneliness reported by 15- and 16-year-olds in most parts of the world.[16] The data often seem to show these problems taking a turn for the worse after 2012.

Ask them to experiment. Do they feel happier when they spend less time on their phone? What might feel better? One study randomly assigned college students (there are fewer studies on adolescents, as it's hard to get parental consent for studies on minors) to either greatly reduce the use of social media platforms for a period, or not to do so. The researchers then measured the students' depressive symptoms three weeks later.[17] They found that 'the limited use group showed significant reductions in loneliness and depression over three weeks compared to the control group'. Trust them to work this out for themselves, and equally trust their ability to apply some critical thinking to what they're seeing online. Is there another point of view? Is what they are viewing curated to the point where it bears no relation to reality? Hopefully, given my earlier thoughts on the joy of debating (see page 146) such critical exchanges are already par for the course.

Teens themselves seem instinctively aware of the fact that too much sharing and absorbing of the world through an Instagram filter is bad for the soul. Many teenagers are worried about their own social media use. Platforms such as BeReal invite them to post during a two-minute period, inviting teenagers to be themselves online rather than using curated images of themselves with filters. 'Less make-up, more mess' is how one teen described it to me, though others say it can be just as grim as other social media.

Some describe how they have embraced an offline 'flip phone revolution': one 18-year-old told me that when she goes out, she takes with her a basic flip phone with no internet access, because 'everything that leads to us having a bad time stems from our phones'. Many adolescents yearn for a time when they can leave the house and meet up with friends and be present in each other's company, not continually checking their messages or hitting refresh on Instagram and Snapchat to see how many people are thinking of them. They are self-aware about how phones affect them. One 17-year-old girl told me that if she is lonely or stressed, she uses her phone more. 'Obviously it worsens these things,' she said. But the good news is that she has that awareness. The more they figure out this stuff for themselves, the better.

Collective action

I'm not suggesting keeping teenagers off phones or creating digital-free zones will be easy. Or that we can stop our teenagers using social media altogether. Individual efforts to resist its lure will be hard, given that a teenager will naturally argue that all their friends are on social media. For instance, take a teenage girl who stops using social media completely. If all her friends continue to spend five hours a day on the various platforms, she would be completely out of the loop and socially isolated. Social media creates a cohort effect among teenagers: something that has happened to all young people, including those who don't use social media.

It also creates a trap – a collective action problem – for girls and for parents. An individual girl might be worse off quitting Instagram, even though all girls would be better off if everyone quit. She would be cut off. This social media paradox explains why at times researchers find that teenagers don't feel better if they digitally detox. This research previously confused me as it is counter to all the evidence that social media causes harm. Teenagers realize this. 'I think lots of my friends just want those simpler times, but they also realize that there is no going back to it unless we all try together,' one 16-year-old girl told me. We need collective action for real change, so talk to other parents in your teenager's circle to see if you can work together in creating guidelines. But meanwhile we need to find ways for coping: agree that they can be on it but they must time their use, or just use it less. Or when they make a new friend, perhaps they could agree to only communicate with their new friend the old-fashioned way. Norms do change over time but as the history of smoking, for example, shows, this can take decades.

*

To end on a positive note: connecting more with teenagers ourselves, encouraging them to find their own answers, and working together with other parents can help reduce phone use. Collective action will be more powerful than anything we can achieve as individuals, but this is still a way off. Meanwhile, if we understand the pressures teenagers are under to engage with social media, and are sympathetic to their plight, we are more likely to have an impact on their engagement with the digital world. This is about understanding their reality, rather than trying to close the stable door after the digital horse has bolted.

There are tentative signs about a more positive future. Tech companies are shifting the balance in parents' favour, with the introduction of Instagram 'teen accounts' for 13–17-year-olds. These use AI age verification, are private by default, have content and messaging restrictions, and enable parents to see who their children have been communicating with (though not what is said). This is good news – although it is parents who are being recruited to moderate their children's accounts. It's also true that such controls have limitations, in particular the fact that teen accounts will still show a teenager's list of followers, which is key for blackmailers. Ideally there will come a time when tech giants take full responsibility. Governments such as Australia's are acting too: in November 2024, it announced that it will ban children from using social media. Meanwhile, the Wild West of the internet remains a challenge which is arguably more daunting than the more traditional trials of teenage life – namely the lure of drinking and drugs, which is the topic of my next chapter.

21

DRUGS AND DRINKING

F irst, the good news. Young people in general are drinking less than we did: around one-quarter of 16–24-year-olds don't drink at all, compared with just over one-fifth of the broader adult population[1] (though there seems to be a blip in the trend among younger children, perhaps because of lockdown, with one in three 11-year-olds having had a drink).[2] Drug use is also down: around 17.6 per cent of 16–24-year-olds took drugs in 2022–23, compared to 21 per cent in 2019–20.[3] This has been driven by a drop in cannabis use since 2020: a total of 15.4 per cent of people aged 16 to 24 used cannabis in 2023, compared with 18.7 per cent three years earlier.

The overall reduction in drinking and drug use could be because teenagers in general are more health conscious. They are smoking less (though they are vaping more: by the age of 15, 40 per cent of girls and 26 per cent of boys have tried e-cigarettes[4]), and they are fearful of 'hangxiety' – a combination of 'hangover' and 'anxiety'. They are also more self-conscious of how they appear on social media: they don't want their exploits plastered(!) over TikTok or Instagram. It might also be because the pandemic meant some teenagers skipped going to school, which is often where they begin experimenting. Nor do they go so often to sticky-floored nightclubs to find love – they swipe right, thus missing opportunities to meet in real life over a glass of wine, or indeed to take drugs together. As we've seen, in general teenagers are hitting adult milestones later than we did – if taking drugs and drinking can be deemed adult behaviour!

This general decline is of little consolation to many middle-class parents, whose children are more likely than their poorer counterparts to drink, take drugs and vape before they turn 16, given access to funds, and a certain 'breezy entitlement', as one teenager put it to me, which sees them wangle their way into clubs and bars with fake IDs.[5] Nor is the overall decline any comfort to a parent whose teenager has got into difficulties. While such activities may be enjoyable and relatively harmless for roughly 90 per cent of young people, they can be catastrophic for around 10 per cent of teenagers, whose delicate adolescent brains may never recover from taking toxic substances – and as parents we find out our adolescent is in the 10 per cent too late. Talk to parents with children in rehab and you'll find much more caution around drink and drugs, despite the reduction in use. This is especially true, I found, for the distraught parents of troubled teenage girls, who are more likely to drink, take drugs and vape than their brothers.[6]

Understanding the world of drugs is tough. Few parents – certainly not this one – are likely to fully grasp the ever-increasing and changing array of drugs on the market. Any attempt to do so will almost instantly be out of date. Take something familiar like cannabis. We might think we know what it is. But the cannabis available now is a different product from what it once was. In the old days, most hashish grown under sunny African skies contained low amounts – about 2–5 per cent – of the main psychoactive component, tetrahydrocannabinol (THC). In the past 10 or 15 years, a UK-farmed substance has taken over, leading to a concentration of THC that is about five times higher. This more potent form is skunk, which now dominates the market. Pretty soon some new drug will emerge. We are not going to keep up, and there's not much point in trying.

Our drug policy and how we use drugs is confusing. Obviously, drugs have allowed uses – for example, we give heroin (diamorphine) to people in pain. Most drugs are bad for us; some are less bad for us than others, but legislation does not always reflect this, or always take into account how prevalent usage is. Legal drugs, including alcohol, do harm; ecstasy and LSD are arguably less dangerous than alcohol but are illegal.[7] Or take the mixed message on vaping: vapes – which heat up nicotine and produce a vapour that can be inhaled – are lauded as a healthier alternative to smoking for adult use, but only now are we realizing how addictive and dangerous they can be for teenagers and indeed children.

It's hard to understand why drugs might appeal. Psychologists that I spoke to stressed how complex substance misuse is, and mentioned the limitations of our knowledge about exactly why it occurs. Nonetheless, there are some clues.

THE LURE OF RISK-TAKING

Drug-taking is influenced by young people's economic circumstances and where they live, whether that is inner-city poverty where gangs, drug-taking and crime are commonplace and young people may have little choice; in smaller towns where there is little else to keep young people occupied, especially given the lack of funding for youth services; or among wealthy children who have money to burn, literally. Several factors underpin the appeal.

There's the attraction of something new, illicit and risky. Experimenting is normal in teenagers, and many of us will have experimented and pushed boundaries in the same way. As we saw in Chapter 7, the teenage brain is drawn to novelty as well as risk-taking as young people strive for independence and their own identity.

Then there's the way drugs ease the process of finding their tribe and interacting with others. Parents talk about teenagers breaking their trust if they take drugs. But this is partly why they are doing it. There is a link between getting closer to school friends and distancing from parents. Drugs can be both the cause and the symptom of that process. Trying out supposedly adult pastimes, and seeing which ones fit, is part of that process.

One of my teenagers' friends explained why the urge to connect with others by being cool was behind her decision to start smoking when she was 13:

Most people start smoking to look cool. I began by practising how to inhale without coughing. Then I practised rolling cigarettes. It was like learning how to look glam. I wanted to be able to roll them in front of people at parties. Smoking makes you look fun, carefree, risky and older. That's why it's cool and that's why people start. It's because of the image it gives you.

The steps to taking harder drugs follow a similar process, though a teenager I spoke to emphasized how nuanced being 'cool' is. 'There are layers to being cool. There's being cool between you and your best friend; and then there's being cool in a group or among overlapping circles socially. That's where I think there's more of an overlap with drug-taking.'

Drugs and drinking are used by teenagers as ways to reduce anxiety around the inevitable social challenges they will encounter. They constitute what psychologists call 'negative coping strategies'. The present moment can feel unbearable. A teenager feels anxious about meeting friends or coping with relationship problems. Others may be suffering from attention deficit hyperactivity disorder (ADHD) or mental health problems. Drugs distract them. They don't have to feel those unpleasant emotions. Drugs make them feel, at least temporarily, more carefree, alert or excited.

And they are easy to get hold of – easier to acquire and cheaper than alcohol in many cases. As one fifteen-year-old teenager put it to me:

Parents do not seem to even realize how common it is. It's so easy on your phone. You just text. It's like a website. The website puts the name of the drugs, there are lots of emojis. There's a price list, the numbers of grams. They come in a car, you get in the car with them, exchange the drugs and money, you get out of the car a few streets later. It's called 'picking up'. Or you just meet them in the street and just brush hands. You walk past someone and high five. They decide a meeting point and you text. It doesn't feel illegal, or sordid – there's not a meeting in a shady alleyway.

Perhaps most obviously of all, drugs are pleasurable and addictive. I asked one former addict, now in his twenties, why he had begun taking drugs, earnestly enquiring if he had suffered from anxiety? He laughed. 'I took drugs because they're great!' The baseline level of dopamine is lower for an adolescent than an adult, so teenagers have fewer feelings of mild pleasure – 'Oh that is nice' – in the course of a day. When novelty and excitement release dopamine in the teenage brain, the kick is greater. The reward centre – the bit of the brain called the striatum, found in the cortex – shows marked changes in adolescents generally. It is highly reactive at a time when, as we have seen, the prefrontal cortex is not fully developed. Drug-taking (and drinking, which I'll discuss later) trigger this reward centre. Your teenager's brain learns that drugs are an effective way to boost feel-good hormones in the brain. Soon it becomes what psychologists describe as 'learned behaviour'. The brain remembers that last time they needed a high, drugs worked to deliver the result.

The problem is that, over time, this behaviour can become addictive. The same brain synapses that are being reformed to develop learning at this time are also involved in addiction.

Taking drugs floods the brain with surges of dopamine, creating a desire to repeat the experience. When these behaviours develop into habits, the brain starts to produce less and less dopamine each time, which is why addicts often explain that their drinking or drug use no longer actually provides them with as much pleasure as before. Dopamine works on a key-and-lock principle. For dopamine to work, it needs a lock to attach itself to. If the floodgates of a teenager's brain keep opening because of drug use, then the brain is forced to manufacture more locks. In turn, the locks require feeding with their favourite drug, dopamine – which means they need another fix of drugs to satisfy their changing brains. They may therefore, over time, take more drugs to get the same impact and satisfy those demanding locks. The stakes slowly and inevitably get higher. Finally, the requirement to take drugs ramps up in an addictive way because it can become a way of coping with the lows after a session of drug-taking.

If you add together those reasons – the desire for experimentation, the fact that drugs make teenagers feel part of the gang as well as easing their social anxiety, that drugs are a means of reacting against parental control, and that they are easy to get hold of and addictive – it's no surprise that practically all teenagers have taken drugs of some kind. You might be thinking, well, I might as well give up then. But no. Once again, I do have some ideas of what to do, you'll be relieved to hear.

BEING SYMPATHETIC TO THE PRESSURE THEY ARE UNDER

To reduce the appeal of drugs, we can first acknowledge how alluring they are. If we say, 'Drugs are bad, drugs will kill you,' our teenagers are unlikely to listen. The conversation will be over before it has begun. Instead, we might say, 'I understand why you might want to do this.' We get the pressures they are under.

We are trying to establish an authentic connection with them on the topic, through active listening and validating their feelings, in this case especially their need to belong, and their belief that they will only be okay and make friends if they take drugs. Given that the secrecy surrounding drugs is probably at least as damaging as the drugs themselves, we have to try to keep the conversation open and transparent. It's a secrecy that can lead to criminal behaviour and a complete disassociation from our teenager.

We can be honest and share that we may ourselves have felt pressurized to take drugs – and indeed found them alluring. We were young once! (Though I had a sense that this concept was hard to grasp when one of my teenagers asked me how I had found it growing up in the war.) One parent I spoke to said their most effective strategy to deglamorize drugs was to tell their teenagers that they had taken drugs themselves. 'Nothing made drugs seem less exciting to my adolescents than the idea that someone as uncool as me, their dad, had taken them when young.' Such a conversation is another opportunity to point out that these days, the contents are far more risky.

'I have friends whose parents offered to partake alongside their children so as to create the safest environment in which to experiment. This is too radical, and I don't think it makes sense,' said one 19-year-old boy who had previously taken drugs. He continued, 'But I think the sentiment behind it is valid, namely that as much transparency between parent and child is the most effective way to prevent disaster. Secrecy and deception is the killer.'

Our role is to make them feel that they are known, that we are on the same side as them and are non-judgemental, that they matter to us – and that we care deeply about them and the damage that drugs can cause.

SHARING INFORMATION IN A STRAIGHTFORWARD WAY

We want to share reasons why drugs are a bad idea in a non-dramatic way that acknowledges our ignorance of specifics, while sharing our broad concerns – the damage they can cause to developing brains, that people can become aggressive when high on drugs and not realize what they are doing to others, the danger of getting into debt and crime, the mental health implications. Our tone ideally should be one of 'Let me pass on some information, so you make good decisions.' Most effective can be stories of individuals who took drugs: a friend's child who became psychotic after taking drugs at a festival, or another young person who has developed schizophrenia since taking drugs. The stories are more impactful without any advice from us about the conclusions they might draw. Sharing the less alluring side of drug-taking can be powerful too. Ketamine, for example, causes the bladder to shrink to the size of a 4-year-old's, and a life of incontinence pads. The damage may be so severe that it is irreversible, and a person may require a stoma bag to bypass the bladder. It was this kind of distasteful physical detail that made an impact in my own discussions. 'It's suddenly not so cool to take something that might make you incontinent,' one of my teenagers said.

Keeping calm (because being hysterical will alienate them), we need to point out that drugs are in a different category of risk because we don't know what's in them, or what a drug has been mixed with. This is the key difference compared to alcohol. A dodgy drug could be lethal. Take ketamine again. As far as many teenagers are concerned, 'Special K' is seen as something recreational and relatively harmless: it's relatively hard to become dependent on it, and it's cheap, costing as little as £3 a dose. Young people see it as something to help them cope, a bit like alcohol or cannabis. Yet taking ketamine can lead to heart attacks, especially if combined with other drugs such as opioids or benzodiazepines.

While we may be struggling to keep up with the ever-shifting reality of the drug scene, the same may be true of our teenagers. Those I spoke to said how little real information is available to young people. Here's one 16-year-old boy:

The last time you have a conversation about drugs is when you are about 15. Your teacher will have a conversation like 'Drugs will kill you', just like they say 'Sex leads to pregnancy'. You might be lucky and be shown a video about a heroin addict. The drugs you are told about at school are often removed from the drugs that teenagers are involved with.

APPEALING TO THEIR DESIRE FOR AUTONOMY AND SOCIAL JUSTICE

We can stress their autonomy, too, taking advantage of their natural desire for independence. They don't have to do what everyone else does. What strategies can they employ for themselves not to be tempted? We want to position them as responsible and independent. Ask them what they would do if one of their friends has overdone it. It casts them as the sensible one.

This approach may appeal to the rebellious side of our teenagers: they may not like the concept that drugs and their dealer could control them, rather than the other way round. Their life could quickly revolve around drugs and making sure they can get them. This may sound odd, but in this vein you could try asking them to imagine that drugs were a friend. Would a friend be someone who followed them around, took their money and wanted them dead? Encourage them to celebrate the death of this enemy who is trying to kill them rather than grieving the loss of a friend. It will no longer be a sacrifice to avoid drugs.

We can also appeal to their concern for the environment and social justice. Wide-scale drug production is environmentally damaging. Cocaine production, for example, leads to soil erosion as large areas of forest are cleared for coca cultivation. The use of highly toxic and unregulated pesticides (because of the clandestine nature of drugs) can severely affect the environment, while the production of chemical drugs such as crystal meth leads to the dumping of toxic waste.

Drug-taking also means endorsing an economy that wreaks utter misery on the poorest, most disenfranchised communities. It leads to gun and knife crime, prostitution, gang violence and people smuggling. The same teenagers who support Black Lives Matter may see the hypocrisy involved in their drug-taking, which leads to disproportionate numbers of deaths among young Black men.

We can also address the challenges they are facing as they engage with their peers. Sometimes these will be because of a lack of confidence in their social abilities, a painful shyness that they may feel drugs will answer. If the appeal of drugs is because the present moment feels too agonizing for them, then remind yourself of ideas about staying present with, and allowing, uncomfortable emotions. If they can realize that even the most intense moments of social anxiety pass, and that they need not be afraid of their feelings, again they are less likely to be drawn to drugs.

IF YOUR CHILD IS ALREADY TAKING DRUGS

Establishing a connection, being honest ourselves, sharing information in a straightforward way, appealing to their desire for autonomy and social justice as well as acknowledging the pressure they are under, can all help defeat the lure of drugs. But what if you realize or find out that your teenager is already taking drugs? And that their drug use is not just a bit of fun at parties or festivals, but something more serious that is happening regularly? Such news is clearly devastating for any parent.

The problem is that we don't have enough evidence about serious drug addiction – exactly why it starts, or what treatment helps. If they are heavy users we may need to get them medical support or intervention (which I address in Part 6). Taking a supportive and non-judgemental stance, we can help them find an addiction treatment programme, assist in scheduling and getting to appointments, and attend therapy sessions and support groups with them. Medication may be used to manage withdrawal symptoms, prevent relapse, or treat any anxiety or depression which may occur at the same time as drug addiction.

DRINKING

And so to alcohol, a drug that appeals to teenagers for many of the same reasons that other drugs do: it is enjoyable, addictive and widely available. Natural ingredients in alcohol act on GABA receptors – pleasure receptors in the brain – to give a warm, happy feeling. Teenagers feel uninhibited and more interesting to people. Teenagers and adults alike are culturally conditioned to associate being sober with being dull.

While teenagers drink for many different reasons, just as with drugs the chief appeal of drinking is fulfilling a desire to belong and feel connected, or even to feel happy and loveable. As one of my children said about why they began drinking, 'I rely on drinking in social situations. I will always "pre" [when you drink ahead of an event]. If I've had some drinks, I'm way less self-conscious. Or if I'm nervous before a date, I will take a shot.'

As we've seen, repeatedly, banning something makes it more alluring, so once again we are trying to help them make good decisions by sharing the facts as best we can in a calm and non-judgemental way. After all, we ourselves may well drink, possibly more than them, and we need to be careful of lecturing about something we ourselves consume. The more we over-react, the more our teenagers will be drawn to alcohol, given their need to experiment and rebel, in the same way that telling teenagers not to take drugs rarely works. But we are hoping they consume alcohol in sensible ways and are mindful of the law.

Alcohol is not taboo in the same way as drugs because it is not against the law, at least after 18. The legal minimum age for drinking in a pub with an adult and food is 16, though a teenager cannot buy a drink themselves then. A teenager can be stopped and fined or arrested if they're under 18 and drinking alcohol in public.

Teenagers respond in very different ways to alcohol. Some get instantly drunk (especially if they are smaller) while others don't; some are more risk-averse than others. The symptoms of getting drunk include slurred speech and feeling emotional, drowsy, nauseous, happy and uninhibited. This is different from the much more serious signs of alcohol poisoning, when in addition to the symptoms of being drunk, a sufferer may also be severely confused, seriously vomiting, falling unconscious and turning pale or bluish. At which point they need to go to hospital. If they pass out, they could choke on their own vomit. So your teenager is going to need a friend, someone with whom they have agreed in advance that they will both keep an eye on each other's drinking. The friend will need to try to keep the alcohol-poisoned teenager awake if possible. And if they do pass out, they need to turn their friend's head on its side to prevent choking. And then they need to get help, fast. Serious stuff, all of which your teenager needs to know – for their sake and for that of their pals.

Regular drinkers can suffer from bad breath, skin problems and weight gain. Alcohol damages adolescent brain development in three main ways: it affects decision-making and impulse control because it slows down the brain; it affects memory, learning and emotional regulation; and finally it affects movement, balance and coordination, which is why accidents and injuries are common among young people who drink.

YOUR OWN DRINKING CULTURE

How do you behave around alcohol at home? The average age to have a first supervised alcoholic drink in the UK is 13.4, unsupervised is 14.7.[8] But since 2009, doctors have recommended an alcohol-free childhood: no alcohol until 15, and no unsupervised drinks until 18.[9] Given the medical advice, a sensible approach is to wait as long as you can before you allow teenagers to drink at home. Psychologists stress that the earlier children are exposed to drink, the more likely they are to go on to misuse it[10] and the more likely they are to have alcohol-related problems as adults.[11]

There's something to be said for normalizing drinking in moderation in a family context, at mealtimes (though few self-respecting teenagers drink wine, in my experience) or at family celebrations (when they might get tiddly on a cocktail). If we don't, drinking may happen in secret, with teens necking a bottle of Baileys out of our sight at a friend's house, or on the street. If we offer alcohol, teenagers get to choose if they accept, and they may not if the offer comes from us, as parental endorsement naturally makes alcohol less desirable.

If we decide to embrace this normalizing approach, our own behaviour is crucial. Teenagers are likely to mirror our attitudes to alcohol. If they see their parents drink most days, or see us drunk, or notice that we turn to the Chablis every time we're disappointed, we cannot be surprised if they do the same. Be aware of the extent to which you as a family drink; while some are households of moderation, others are not, especially richer families where money is no object, and sporty families where drinking is part of the culture and its dangers disguised by its association with something wholesome. British families are in general less skilled at handling alcohol at home compared to their European counterparts. 'Drunkenness is just embedded in British society in a way which it is just not in other countries,' says Dr Joanna Inchley, an expert on drinking from the University of Glasgow,[12] perhaps because we are more buttoned-up than our European neighbours, and less ashamed at appearing drunk around our kitchen tables.

While we need to be honest about how we behave, we can have high expectations about their behaviour which, as we've seen, makes a difference. I found the work of Robert Rosenthal, a German-born American psychologist and professor, and Lenore Jacobson, an elementary school principal, helpful.[13] They are best known for formulating the Pygmalion effect, also known as the Rosenthal effect: the psychological phenomenon that the greater the beliefs and expectations on individuals – including children and students – the better they function. This is self-amplifying in both positive and negative directions. If we have the expectation that our teenager will be a moderate and responsible drinker when they are 18, then that is more likely to happen. By contrast, if we expect them to be out of control, drinking when 13, and criticize their drinking behaviour as well as alcohol in general, then they are more likely to be irresponsible.

Given that even responsible teenagers tend to experiment, the best place for this to happen is somewhere safe and supervised, but realistically we are not always going to be at home ourselves. One teenager told me that the first time they got properly drunk was indeed at home, with a small group of friends for their 16th birthday, but their parents weren't there. They threw up and had to be put to bed by a friend. They at least slept in their own bed and woke up in their own house. Thereafter, they had a better sense of their limits – especially when out and about, which is when naturally most of their drinking was happening.

DRINKING RESPONSIBLY WHEN NOT AT HOME

Given that most drinking will happen out of sight, teenagers told me that the best thing we parents can do is to arm them with some sensible strategies to minimize the harm alcohol can cause. Here are some ideas, many of them suggested by teenagers themselves. Encourage your teenager to agree on responsible drinking with a friend if they are going out, as outlined above. Should there be trouble, then you as their parent have an extra number to call, assuming your teenager shares who their friend is.

Suggest your teen makes their first two glasses alcohol-free; maybe they will find they are having a good time without alcohol, and no-one need know they are not drinking. Challenge the idea they will get a feeling of relaxation the instant they take that first sip of an alcoholic drink. Alcohol doesn't instantly get into the bloodstream. In fact, it takes around 10 minutes: we learn to associate the effects on our brain with the first sip, but we can unlearn this.

Another practical tip is to drink from a small glass. Go at the speed of the slowest drinker. See if they can restrict themselves to the drinks they really want and forget the rest; the best drink is the first drink. Subsequent drinks attempt to recreate the feeling that the first drink gave them, and it doesn't work. With each extra drink, the benefits diminish, and potential harms increase.

Examine their thinking around drinking: if they've had a difficult time with a friend or in a relationship, do they feel they deserve a drink? If they are nervous at a party, are there other things they can do to help? Are there other ways of bonding with people? If they've had a good day, and are drinking to celebrate, are there other ways to have a good time? If they have had a boring day, again, are they distracting themselves from that? Teach them to notice their excuses. Can they find other ways of answering the needs that alcohol satisfies?

Even so, it is all too easy to binge-drink at parties, given the extra social pressure. What might they do if they feel such pressure? Share ways that they can stay present in those moments, in their bodies, and not seek to distract themselves with drink. They may experience unpleasant feelings of social anxiety. Some of the breathing techniques and mindful approaches can help them stay with difficult feelings until they pass, and not reach for the bottle. 'Urge surfing' is a term for when we notice an urge, rather than fighting it; your teenager could imagine they are on a surfboard riding with the feeling. Notice the shifting sensations and ride the waves.

List the reasons they might regret drinking to excess on a night out: how they will feel the next day, how they might feel about something they said or did, the problems that may arise with sex or relationships when drink is added to the mix, how sick they might feel, how they will lose motivation to continue with that healthy eating or gym regime. Suggest they write notes on their phone and set an alert or look at the list when they go to the bathroom at a party to remind themselves of the consequences of heavy drinking.

They could use visualization too: not an ice-cold lager garlanded with condensation, but a half-empty can, warming and smudged by greasy fingers or lips. A wasp or two might be buzzing around it. Focusing on this image instead of the first could help.

Agreeing a time a teenager will return from a party may reduce alcohol consumption for some, although for others it might encourage it as they feel pressured to compress alcohol-induced fun into the timeslot provided. By imposing a time limit, you are also demonstrating a trust in them. This sense of trust can extend to how they behave with regard to alcohol. Remember the golden rule: the more you treat them as responsible adults, the more likely they are to behave as such. Let them know they will be greeted when they get home, that you are waiting up for them and that their behaviour influences the family, especially if you have younger children who may be woken by late-night returns. Above all, let them know that you care. If you don't care, who does?

A final PS on drinking, but a crucial one. How can our teenagers avoid becoming the victim of other people's drunkenness? Having a pre-rehearsed response to challenging situations can minimize danger, while preserving your teenager's social standing. For example, they might feel pressured to get a lift with someone who is about to drive while intoxicated. A prefabricated excuse can be helpful: perhaps, 'I've ordered a taxi to pick me up at 10.30, so I need to wait for it' or 'I've agreed with my friend that they are taking me home.'

*

Once again, the world in which our teenagers are growing is different from ours. While in general young people are drinking less and taking fewer drugs, substance abuse is a real and present danger. Our best bet is to understand the appeal of both alcohol and drugs, and talk openly about the topic in a straightforward, non-judgemental way, trusting our teenagers to work out their own conclusions. No-one likes being bossed around, least of all our adolescents. Trying to ban all alcohol or drugs is likely to be counter-productive. The more we say no to something, the more appealing it becomes. Instead, we can arm them with sensible information, and alert them to the dangers of peer pressure and situations that elicit emotions and arousal. Thus equipped, and knowing their desire for autonomy, they may make better decisions. Engaging their natural desire for social justice can help with drug use in particular.

We can address our own behaviour too, especially around drinking, and share some practical ways to reduce the amount they drink. Sometimes it's a case of being able to be present to difficult emotions. I shared some thoughts on how to do this in Chapter 5, ideas that can help our youngsters as much as us parents when feeling daunted at a party and wanting to down three drinks in quick succession. Sometimes though, things go more seriously wrong, and our teenagers need professional help with their mental health, the subject I turn to in Part 6.

ADVICE ON GETTING
PROFESSIONAL HELP

PART SIX

CONNECTING WITH HELP

22

UNDERSTANDING AND IDENTIFYING
A MENTAL HEALTH CONDITION

S o far, this book has concentrated largely on the more commonplace
range of experiences that most parents come across at one time or
another: less serious drug addiction for example, more the everyday
ups and downs of raising neurotypical teenagers, and ways to help us deal
with them and enjoy the ride. Sometimes, though, it feels as if something
more serious is going on. Our teenagers are in trouble. Their bad feelings
don't settle down.

All mental health conditions have been increasing among young people,
the most common mental problems being anxiety and depression. The
highest prevalence is among 17–19-year-olds: one in four of them have a
mental health disorder.[1] The NHS found that 18 per cent of children aged
7–16 in England were identified as having a probable mental health disorder
in 2022, up from 12.1 per cent in 2017.[2] In 2022, 1,239,838 young people
aged under 18 were referred to Child and Adolescent Mental Health Services
(CAMHS), compared with 812,070 in 2019[3] – the figures show a 53 per cent
increase in yearly referrals.

While boys are more likely to experience neurodevelopmental disorders
such as autism,[4] girls are more vulnerable to eating disorders, self-harm and
suicidal thoughts. One study found that girls are more than twice as likely as
boys to suffer mental health problems by the time they are 18.[5] In England,
40 per cent of 16- and 17-year-old girls describe themselves as unhappy
with their mental health.[6] Suicide is the biggest killer of under-35s in the
UK – more than five people in that age group take their own lives each day
on average.[7]

A final point is that around 50 per cent of mental health problems emerge by the age of 14 and 75 per cent by the age of 24.[8] This means that interventions during childhood and the teenage years offer a critical window of opportunity to address these concerns and help prevent lifelong difficulties.

KEEPING PERSPECTIVE

Given these numbers, it's easy to panic (not least because that's what our wonky brains do). There are some points to remember that may give a sense of perspective. The first is that less stigma means that teenagers are more likely to admit they have problems: yes it's true that the numbers of those suffering are higher than ever, but this may be a less dramatic shift if we consider the heightened awareness around this topic.

Second, medical terms are now stretched to cover standard ranges of low mood. Take anxiety, the most common mental health condition worldwide for children. Anxiety is a normal feeling that everyone experiences. But when it is severe enough, it constitutes a mental health condition, known as generalized anxiety disorder. It is easy to confuse the two. We seem to have gone from one extreme of internalizing and repressing difficult emotions, to oversharing and catastrophizing them.

This is done not least by teenagers themselves, who are fluent in the language of mental health, despite not always understanding the phrases they bandy about, from 'boundaries' to 'gaslighting'. Some young people pathologize their moods, encouraged by the prevalence of self-diagnosis online. Having a psychological condition of some sort or other can make a teenager feel special, given that a diagnosis is now almost par for the course for many celebrities. The psychological and social challenges facing teenagers (as we have seen) are especially acute, given their need to feel connected and part of a tribe. Identifying as having a mental health problem is one specific way of fitting in. Diagnostic labels are in some ways attractive as they confer validity to symptoms and provide the comfort of belonging to a family of fellow sufferers. They provide a way for teenagers to ascribe their inchoate distress to something, anything, beyond their own control.

Third, we need to remind ourselves that serious mental health conditions are still the exception rather than the rule: there is a glossary on page 357 of this book with details of the prevalence of mental health problems to give some kind of perspective on the numbers. The kind of mental distress that requires professional help is rarer than you might imagine, given the headlines that suggest almost all young people have a mental health condition. In fact, this is not the case for most teenagers. The numbers still mean that more than 80 per cent of teenagers would not meet the criteria for diagnosis.

Nonetheless, parents who fear that their teenager has a serious mental health problem can understandably descend into a cascade of dread, especially as such problems can blow up with alarming speed. What are the reasons for mental health problems? How do we know if our teenagers are suffering from a mental health condition, or if this is a normal reaction to the inevitable challenges of adolescence? Is it our fault? What did we do wrong? What should we do? Where can we get support? While these daunting topics are the subject of this chapter, we need to stay calm: most teenagers will emerge from this period of their lives in good psychological shape and without a diagnosable condition.

UNDERSTANDING WHY MENTAL HEALTH PROBLEMS HAVE WORSENED

The reasons for mental health problems are not fully understood, and are made more complex by the range of problems and differing degrees of seriousness. We don't understand everything about how our brains work, even when all is going well. So, it is unsurprising that we also don't know everything about what happens when our brains work less well. It's easy just to blame social media but there are other legitimate reasons for problems. One factor has been fairly constant for decades now: those living in difficult circumstances are more vulnerable: 40 per cent of those most disadvantaged suffer problems, compared to 13 per cent of the population overall.[9] This has arguably worsened more recently with the cost of living crisis and the rise of financial anxiety.

Alongside this constant are some new developments. In rough chronological order, psychologists believe a fresh approach to parenting took hold in the 1980s: we began to see children as precious possessions rather than as resilient and responsible individuals.[10] Numbers of primary school pupils who walk home alone from school has plummeted from 86 per cent in 1971 to 25 per cent in 2010.[11] Since the 1980s, children tended to be supervised at home rather than left to play in the local wilderness as we worried about child molesters and rapists; at school they were sheltered from coming last in competitions or on sports day. When such coddled children left for university, researchers found they demanded safe spaces, trigger warnings and the non-platforming of speakers. Good intentions to protect children were carried too far, robbed them of these experiences and made them more fragile, a view I share and one that underpins much of what you've read so far. I discussed ways we can encourage our teenagers to develop their independence by doing and saying less as parents, and reframing stumbling blocks as stepping stones in Chapter 6.

A second, related psychological trend in the 1980s was the rise of the self-esteem movement, and a competitive need to feel special. Its essence was to stop linking ourselves to contingent variables, or in the words of the rugby player Jonny Wilkinson, a world in which we are 'only as good as our last rugby game'.[12] Instead, the answer was to assert our own worth. The problem was that we cannot all be special, and belief in the benefits of the self-esteem movement has largely died out in the psychological science literature, though it has remained prevalent in popular culture.

Wanting to feel special, and the related trend of perfectionism, which I discussed in Chapter 4 and which you know is a bugbear of mine, could be one reason why more girls than boys seem to be suffering from mental health problems. It could also be that girls seek more help. Or they engage in social media in different ways from boys, as we've seen. Teenagers who see themselves as religious seem to be less susceptible to mental health problems: girls raised in secular liberal households are twice as likely to have problems, according to research[13] (focused on the US but whose findings are relevant in most Western societies) into how likely teenagers are to say they are 'no good' or 'can't do anything right'. Figures for teenagers with mental health problems started rising ten years ago, except for boys who identified as conservative and said that religion was important to them. White liberal girls seem the most depressed.

The rise of liberalism and the self-esteem movement has coincided with the rise of a phone-based childhood – the third factor that has led to poor mental health and one I discussed in detail in Chapter 10. In particular, the need for attention or acceptance within an online community may have led some teenagers to assume a mental disorder.

A fourth factor that has shifted over the past few decades is family structure and stability. Studies have concluded that in general children who grow up with continuously married parents have better health outcomes than children who grow up with single or separated parents. This is consistent for health and development outcomes, including physical health, psychological wellbeing and educational attainment. Possible explanations include higher poverty and time limitations of parental engagement within single-parent families.[14]

In addition to these four factors, many of the problems I've written about in earlier chapters can escalate to the point they become so acute they create mental health conditions. These include the pressure to succeed, traumatic personal loss, and drink and drugs, especially the links between weed, skunk and psychosis. Sometimes mental health problems are secondary issues, attendant on something else that is not technically a mental health problem, such as having a trans identity or being neurodiverse, but which can cause mental health difficulties.

All of this adds up to the sense that teenagers are growing up in a world they don't much like. The writer Hadley Freeman has written about her experience of anorexia.[15] Stopping eating seems to stop time. A girl delays puberty and interacting with other teenage girls if they go to hospital. By starving or stuffing their bodies, teenagers show their unhappiness: anorexia is not about food, but more about anxiety at the world around them.

The final complicating factor in this mental health landscape is the aftermath of the pandemic. The picture is nuanced: some teenagers said they actually preferred being at home with their parents,[16] while others felt isolated and disorientated, feeling they had lost control over their lives. Starving or harming themselves can be seen as a way to regain power. Girls suffered in particular because they missed close friendships even more than boys. Most students had their education disrupted. Teenagers were often left to their own devices, in every sense. Lessons were taught online, and some had no lessons at all. Problems such as online bullying became rife, and attendance at school post-pandemic has plummeted.

DISTINGUISHING ORDINARY UNHAPPINESS FROM MENTAL HEALTH PROBLEMS

Living in difficult circumstances, being over-supervised, the need to feel special, the rise of mobile phones, the breakdown of traditional families, and the spanner Covid threw in all these works have all played their part in worsening adolescent psychological health. How can we decide if our teenager really has a problem, or if they are just dealing with what at times, we can all agree, is a tough gig?

It's tricky. The current diagnostic system is still largely based on symptoms reported by the patient, in this case already anxious teenagers saturated in the language of mental health from social media. We have (as yet) no blood test, or brain scan, that can say for sure whether we are suffering from a mental health disorder. Although mental health problems are often compared to physical ones – 'it's no different from breaking a leg' – actually, that may not be true when it comes to the complexities of diagnosis. Diagnosis in mental health is more an art than a science: the doctor is forming impressions, reading nuances, listening to silences.

Psychiatrists are trained to arrive at diagnoses, and are guided by manuals such as the American *Diagnostic and Statistical Manual of Mental Disorders* (DSM) and *The International Classification of Diseases*, works that have largely been developed through research and clinical consensus and which change as the research itself changes. Psychiatrists also rely on their own skilled assessments, and ways of asking questions about an individual and how they are functioning, to decide on a diagnosis. However, in the absence of physical diagnostic tests, it remains the case that diagnosis in mental health is always going to be less certain than in other fields of medicine.

One sign of this uncertainty has been an expansion in the number of possible mental health conditions, described by the psychologist Lucy Foulkes as 'prevalence inflation'[17] and by others as 'diagnosis creep' – the American DSM now runs to 1,000 pages; the first edition in 1952 was just 100 pages long. Critics say we now pathologize normal human experience, and I began this chapter by stressing the need for us parents to keep a sense of perspective given all the bad news. Whereas once a person was shy, now they might be diagnosed with 'avoidant personality disorder'. There is also a trend in the DSM of lowering the threshold of what it takes to be diagnosed with a given disorder. In earlier editions, someone might need to have shown symptoms of a condition for six months. Now the duration has been reduced to three.

Saying our child has a mental health condition assumes that there is a precise threshold they have reached, when there is no such clear-cut line when it comes to mental health problems. Many doctors in the field acknowledge this and find it more helpful to talk about whether a teenager has more severe symptoms and needs more help. This acknowledges the blurred boundaries: some dispute whether most diagnosed conditions are illnesses at all. Even if we can successfully group clusters of symptoms, it doesn't mean there is any biological basis – which is what diagnosis implies.

Deciding on a diagnosis is trickier still when dealing with sufferers who are naturally volatile, which means sometimes the nature of an adolescent's symptoms (and therefore any diagnosis) will change over time. One minute teenagers are seemingly fine, the next so desperate that we fear we are out of our depth and need specialist help to cope with their distress. More than with adults, their problems can settle down naturally through this process of change, but equally it is easy to miss how bad things can be.

Tim Owen, whose 19-year-old daughter Emily died by suicide in March 2020, says she was on fine form in the days before she died, and indeed suicide is often preceded by a good or better mood than usual. Owen, who with two other bereaved parents has set up the fundraising and campaigning group Three Dads Walking,[18] recalls how Emily had visited her grandparents, singing Taylor Swift on the way home, and did a food shop for her parents and three siblings as lockdown loomed. The next day she was agitated, leaving the house and slamming the door behind her. Her parents found her after a quarter of an hour. She was taken to hospital and died five days later.[19]

A RISE IN TEENAGE NEURODEVELOPMENTAL DISORDERS

Just as there has been a sharp increase in incidences of mental health conditions and 'diagnosis creep', there has also been an increase in teenage neurodevelopmental disorders including diagnoses for ADHD (those who are impulsive and have difficulty concentrating, see page 358) and autism (those who have problems communicating and interacting with the world, see page 361).

ADHD used to be diagnosed mainly in children. Now it is becoming more common (and cynics would say, fashionable) in adulthood – in 2024 there was a 28 per cent increase in adults on ADHD medication. But what concerns us parents is that there was also a 10 per cent increase in child prescriptions, with 120,000 children given drugs.[20]

Doctors such as Sir Simon Wessely, former president of the Royal College of Psychiatrists, have expressed worry over what some see as ADHD over-diagnosis. Just as it is complicated to make mental health diagnoses, it is also tricky to make neurodevelopmental ones.

A hasty diagnosis can stop medics making in-depth assessments and analysing properly what is happening in a child's life – how they are being parented, for example. Writing in *The Spectator* in 2024, Dr Max Pemberton, a psychiatrist and medical columnist, echoed Sir Simon's concerns, saying, 'It's easier to whack a label on a child – to medicalize their behaviour – than to confront parents with the idea they might be in part to blame for the way their offspring behave.'[21]

Dr Pemberton was also concerned about the side effects of ADHD drugs – powerful stimulants such as methylphenidate. The evidence around the effectiveness of the medication is not clear, though drugs such as Ritalin are seen as fun: 'like cocaine, but better', as one patient put it to Dr Pemberton.

There are incentives for parents to get ADHD diagnoses, which are more prevalent in affluent areas where middle-class families know that a diagnosis secures a child additional time in exams. Ofqual figures from November 2024 show that 27 per cent of pupils at non-selective state schools got extra time, compared with 42 per cent of those at private schools (though this may be because private schools are better at spotting those who are struggling).[22]

It's tricky. Youngsters being diagnosed with ADHD are floundering, so this is not to deny their difficulties. But it may be that the reason is not ADHD, but that their problems lie elsewhere, the most likely culprit being constant online stimulation. The answer might not be Ritalin, but less screen time.

For others, a smaller minority, medication can be helpful if not essential. Dr James Kustow, a consultant psychiatrist and author of *How to Thrive with Adult ADHD*, says ADHD can lead to a real feeling of shame among teenagers, who are assumed to be misbehaving or lazy at school, and who are more likely to turn to alcohol, gambling, overeating and gaming as answers to their distress.[23]

The number of teenagers being diagnosed as autistic is also increasing. Eighty years ago, autism was thought to affect one in 2,500 children. That has gradually increased and now one in 36 children is believed to have autism spectrum disorder (ASD), with a notable rise in diagnoses among girls.[24] Once again, the same debates are taking place: is the increase due to over-diagnosis, or do more children have the condition?

Whether we suspect our children are autistic or have ADHD, we parents naturally wish for expert help to navigate these tricky waters. Unfortunately, we face long waits – several years in some cases.[25] Often we are left trying to figure out if our teenager has a neurodevelopmental problem or a mental health one, or neither.

Many of my thoughts on navigating the world of mental health difficulties below also apply to parents whose children are coping with neurodevelopmental disorders, though clearly these are not the same and my focus here is on mental health problems.

HOW TO JUDGE IF YOUR CHILD NEEDS HELP

The dangers of over-medicalizing ordinary teenage angst, the difficulties of psychiatric diagnoses, and the volatility and secrecy of teenagers themselves mean that it is challenging for us parents to judge the extent to which a teenager needs professional help. A sensible approach is to ask yourself – and others involved with your child, such as their teacher – a series of questions, while bearing in mind some of the confusion around this topic more broadly: how intense are the symptoms, and how long have they lasted? Does the problem feel overwhelming, to the point where the issue is dominating your teenager's life? Is it putting your teenager's physical safety in danger? And: would they like to get some help?

You might also look out for the following warning signs that your teenager might need professional help: changes in school performance (teachers are again relevant here); a drop in grades; changes in sleeping habits; changes in eating habits; excessive worry or anxiety – to the point of refusing to go to school, for example; hyperactivity; persistent nightmares; persistent disobedience or aggression; getting into trouble at school; and showing less interest in the things they used to enjoy.

Even if a teenager is showing many of these symptoms, many parents resist getting help. It is hard to accept that our youngsters are suffering. What have we done wrong? Why is our love for them not enough to make them happy? We might not get help because it makes us feel like failures wracked by guilt and shame. And we might be wary of stepping into an unknown world of professionals, possible medication, and doctors who might disrupt our relationship with our beloved offspring, or who might suggest an approach with which we disagree. Surely we are enough for our teenagers, as the people who have invested in and loved our children for longest?

But this is about them, not us or our relationship. There's a problem that needs addressing. It is okay to get help, and many of us need help with our children's psychological health from time to time. If our child had a physical problem, we would get help rather than blame ourselves. (On which note: we might also book an appointment with the GP in case there is a physical issue affecting our teenager, perhaps low iron levels explaining lassitude, or an off-kilter thyroid explaining mood swings.)

You probably feel it is 100 per cent your responsibility to fix the problem, but others can help. Try making a pie chart in your head. Who is responsible, for example, if your child is refusing to go to school? Naturally the school's culture will be relevant, as well as your teenager's peer group. Your partner? Another chunk. Your teenager themselves? Yes, another bit. Mental health services? Say another part of the pie. Yes, you too are involved, but you are not the only person responsible for your teenager's welfare or getting them the support they need.

Be gentle on yourself. No one is a perfect parent: we all make mistakes that may or may not have contributed to our teenager's distress. While you may be able to help your teenager deal with some of the reasons for their psychological misery, other causes of mental health problems may leave less scope for your involvement or ability to help. There is only so much that any parent can have power over. There are times when life can be against us. For all our best intentions, sometimes our teenagers' lives are affected by something beyond a family's control, and we need help from others.

GETTING A DIAGNOSIS: SHOULD YOU OR SHOULDN'T YOU?

While it might seem obvious that getting a diagnosis is helpful, I would advise a careful weighing of the pros and cons. As we've seen, a diagnosis might disempower our teenager, and indeed us, their parents (known as 'labelling theory'). We may hide behind a diagnosis, resisting setting boundaries ourselves, blaming instead a child's 'sensitivity' or 'anxiety'. There are problems with putting someone in a box, defining them as a patient suffering from a pathology which is fixed and from which they can't recover, rather than seeing them as a whole person who is continually changing. There are concerns too about the prescription of medication, and that psychiatric diagnoses are not always reliable. Even talking therapies can do harm.

Psychiatry's critics say that a diagnosis can create the misleading impression that a teenager's feelings are caused by an inner pathology, such as a known chemical imbalance. This can limit the treatment options and can contribute to stigma, and the loss of a teenager's feeling of their own agency. This approach may overlook the possibility that a teenager's low mood is a maladaptive response to the problems of life, rather than an organic disease.

Take depression, for example. We still don't know the inner mechanisms that cause it. A teenager diagnosed with major depressive disorder may have a certain number of symptoms that can include low mood, excessive feelings of guilt or worthlessness, fatigue or sleep problems. A diagnosis can create the false impression that their low mood is caused by an inner pathology, akin to diabetes or heart disease. This could lead us to overlook other treatment options. For example, many mental health professionals think depression, far from being a disease or pathology, is the brain's attempt to show us that something in our lives needs to change.

Ideally, if a mental health provider and your teenager still chose to use a diagnosis, they would do so only after discussing with you the pros and cons of using it. At the least, doctors who choose to use psychiatric diagnoses ought to be clear with young people about what these labels do and don't imply, lest they mislead them about the nature of their problems. Yes, they have a diagnosable list of symptoms, but that doesn't necessarily add up to an 'illness'.

On the other hand, even though they cannot possibly convey the full story of an individual's experience of their difficulties, diagnoses such as 'bipolar disorder' perform some valuable functions such as summarizing symptoms, improving communication between specialists and guiding treatment.

Change is only possible when challenges are named, normalized and understood; for some, diagnoses can remove the guilt and shame around thoughts, feelings and behaviour by enabling an understanding of problems that aren't unique to them. One teenager told me that getting a diagnosis was similar to the satisfaction that comes when you find the lost piece of a jigsaw puzzle.

A diagnosis can be a useful shorthand for your child's doctors and other professionals. Doctors tend to be trained to use diagnostic terms; they use these when speaking to other professionals and to patients about their collection of symptoms. Giving a name to what your child is suffering can lead you to the correct treatment more easily. Sometimes it can mean your teenager's school is more easily able to provide appropriate support.

Finally, a diagnosis can be useful for your teenager as it can help other people to understand a bit more what they are going through. They can connect with others suffering the same set of symptoms, whether they do so online or through friendship networks, while you too can connect with other parents whose teenagers are also finding life difficult, and swap notes on what is helpful.

*

While it is understandable that many of us are worried about mental health problems among the young, this chapter has partly been a plea for calm and perspective. Yes, there are problems, and indeed serious ones for some, but we need to stay steady and be cautious of assuming that our teenager has a mental health condition. Diagnoses for mental health conditions can be tricky, not least because teenagers themselves are changing with lightning speed, and what might be true for them one month is no longer the case the next. There's a good argument – one I've had multiple times with different parents, doctors, psychologists and teachers – that we are over-medicalizing what Freud called 'ordinary human unhappiness'. Nonetheless, some teenagers *do* need more help than we parents can provide.

There are pros and cons to getting a diagnosis for your adolescent, but there's no doubt that a diagnosis is the way to get professional help. As I know from experience, this can become an obsession in the face of a teenager's suffering. As I've become an older parent whose children have faced multiple challenges, I've become less focused on reasons why – which are always hard to know for sure – and more interested in answers to problems: ways for teenagers to feel well and what might help look like. And how on earth we might find it. What exactly might intervention involve? Assistance is available, in different shapes and forms, though waiting lists can be long – this is the subject of my next chapter.

23

HELPING A TEENAGER WITH A MENTAL HEALTH CONDITION

I f you are seeking help, the first step is for your teenager to be assessed by the NHS. You will need all your resources to stay calm through this process, given the paucity of services both in private care and the NHS, delays in getting help, and a widespread feeling that the only way to do so is for your child's mental health problems to be extreme. Parent after parent I spoke to told me how frustrated they were that their teenager was seen only months after their problems began, when it would have been far easier to help them had they been seen sooner. It takes on average 21 weeks for a first appointment with Child and Adolescent Mental Health Services (CAMHS) – the average waiting time recorded in February 2023 had increased by two-thirds in two years.[1] General helplines like Childline, or support lines from charities dealing with specific issues, such as domestic abuse, phobias or OCD, can be invaluable during a long wait for NHS support.

Parents also told me of the exhaustion of having to justify to those around them how ill their teenagers really were. Anorexia, for example, is life-threatening. One parent of a daughter with anorexia said her teenager's hospitalization was a relief as others could grasp how serious her illness was. It's not just that it is difficult to get help in the first place; parents report that it is a struggle to keep getting support. Sometimes this is because teenagers themselves don't engage with services, either because they are not feeling up to it, because the services they are offered do not feel helpful, or because they don't want to. There are no easy answers, but understanding about the services on offer within CAMHS and how it is structured is a start.

CHILD AND ADULT MENTAL HEALTH SERVICES (CAMHS)

It is hard to offer definitive statements about what is offered on the NHS through CAMHS. Services are rapidly changing and depend on where you live. Most local CAMHS teams have a website where you can look up how to access their services. This might be via a mental health officer in schools, a mental health support team in the community, via a teacher or GP, or sometimes via a parent themselves. The assessment involves a chat, usually with one or two members from a CAMHS team, to consider a teenager's circumstances and social situation. Usually a CAMHS team includes nurses, psychotherapists, family therapists, counsellors, psychiatrists or clinical psychologists. The assessment can happen at home, at school or in a clinic. If a teenager is under 16, you the parents (or carer) will be invited to join for at least part of the meeting. Under 16s who are judged to have sufficient capacity can sometimes also be referred for mental health support by a GP without parental involvement. Teenagers over 18 need to move from CAMHS to adult mental health services.

The assessment will cover most aspects of your teenager's past and current experience and should give a realistic picture of whether they have a mental health problem or if they are struggling to deal with life's everyday ups and downs. The assessment will also cover what sort of treatment plan they need, if any, and whether that will involve medication.

Your teenager may be referred to a psychiatrist or mental health team working in a community specialist clinic, who will assess whether your teenager has mental health difficulties. The specialist doctor makes this assessment based on:

The level of distress your child is feeling

The severity of problematic or challenging behaviours

Their ability to function day to day

Whether their symptoms and struggles match up with those of a mental health problem

What else is going on in their life that might help explain the seriousness of their feelings

It can be a complex process for a doctor or mental health team to diagnose a mental health problem in a young person, as we saw in the previous chapter. But in general, early intervention is key because it can change the trajectory of a child's life. A psychiatrist friend said that's why she enjoys adolescent psychiatry. It is easier to intervene effectively when people are young, rather than years later, when the problems have gone on so long that they are harder to address.

This is what intervention might look like:

Tier 1 services are provided by your GP, teachers, social workers, school nurse or nurses in GP surgeries, all of whom can give mental health advice for more common problems and decide if a referral elsewhere is needed.

Tier 2 services offer therapies for milder problems and assess whether things are getting serious for your child. School counsellors, educational psychologists and special education needs coordinators (SENCOs) all work in Tier 2 services, as do counsellors and psychologists in GP practices and paediatric clinics. You can also find Tier 2 support workers in local children's centres. They are there to help students with educational problems that are causing them stress.

Tier 3 services involve a team of experts coming together to coordinate your child's treatment. The experts could include psychologists, counsellors, nurses and family therapists, and are usually headed by a psychiatrist. If it is decided your child is experiencing problems that require a formal treatment plan, you and your teenager will have an assessment with a CAMHS professional. Tier 3 services offer many kinds of help and often coordinate with Tier 2 workers at your teenager's school. They may offer one-to-one help, family help, group help, or medication.

Tier 4 provides specialist services which tend to see children with complex needs who sometimes need to be looked after in hospital. These may be young people experiencing severe episodes of depression or psychosis, or who have experienced a trauma. Specialist eating disorders services are also available in Tier 4. Your child may be seen in Tier 4 if their safety is of concern.

Given that CAMHS is so stretched, it is a good idea to keep a log of interactions with the service and to try to maintain a relationship. Agreed actions should be documented and followed up. If things get worse while waiting for treatment, don't be afraid to contact CAMHS again. Of course this is particularly true of self-harm or any attempts at suicide. In these cases, you can also access CAMHS by going to the Emergency Department (ED) in hospital – the new name for Accident and Emergency – where there are always paediatric liaison teams and psychiatrists available.

Your local council or local education authority may also be able to help while you wait for help, but the truth is that, for a long while, parents may have to turn to voluntary help or work with a private therapist, of which more shortly.

WHO'S WHO

These are some of the many professionals you might find in CAMHS services, all of whom can help your teenager recover in different ways, depending on their training and skills.

A **clinical psychologist** is a mental health professional trained to assess and treat the symptoms or problems that are often linked to a mental health condition. They do this by talking and listening, by suggesting behavioural changes your child might want to try out, and by helping them to notice thinking patterns and habits that may be harming them. Psychologists are not medical doctors, so will never prescribe medicines as a treatment for your child's problems. They are often less definitive about diagnoses, and usually talk in terms of a psychological formulation.

A **psychologist** may be an expert in CBT – Cognitive Behavioural Therapy – which as we have seen, helps people adjust the way they think, and they may also be trained in other approaches. They will suggest a treatment plan based on your child's needs and on psychological research. A psychologist might be the right option for your child if they are looking for solutions to a set of feelings or particular set of difficulties in their life.

A **clinical nurse specialist** is a nurse with specialist mental health training. Sometimes their training includes CBT and counselling. As they are nurses, they can help administer medications and perform other clinical tasks such as weighing and other checks that may be needed to assess your child's condition.

A **psychiatrist** is a medical doctor who specializes in psychiatric, behavioural and emotional problems. They look at how somebody's body and brain are working, diagnose mental health conditions and prescribe treatments such as talking therapies or medication. Some psychiatrists, especially when they are specialists in working with children, are trained in other therapies too, such as CBT, counselling or mindfulness. The approach of a psychiatrist is in some ways similar to that of a psychologist, but with more of a medical focus. They will also use research to guide them to the best treatment plan.

A **psychotherapist** (or **family therapist**) is a professional who counsels people experiencing emotional or mental health problems. They may also be trained in the emotional impact of relationships on an individual's mental health, or specialize in working with particular groups of young people, such as those with eating disorders, those from marginalized groups or particular age groups. They usually focus on your child's family life and how things are between you and your child, as well as the patterns your child's relationships tend to follow, whether with their family or friends. They may discuss the impact of difficult early experiences on your child's current state of mind. A psychotherapist may work with a teenager on an individual basis, reflecting on the shape of their emotional life in one-to-one sessions, or less often in group therapy. In children's services this may include using methods like drawing and play. A family therapist, meanwhile, will want to work with the family too, because they see a teenager as part of a family system.

A **social worker** is a professional who supports people to improve their lives and cope with problems, including those that stem from their community, whether that is because of poor housing or because of a difficult family situation. They become involved in your child's mental health care if it seems as though they might benefit from more support in their everyday life, if there are safeguarding concerns, or if you as a family need help as well. A **family support worker** might also provide help, in particular practical support.

Although you won't necessarily be offered a choice, I would encourage any parent with a troubled teenager to first work with a psychologist or therapist before a psychiatrist unless their child is at risk. A formal diagnosis given by a psychiatrist can lead to your child accessing appropriate treatment that is not otherwise available, but as have seen in my previous chapter, psychiatric diagnoses are complicated for multiple reasons.

TREATMENT

As we've seen, it may be challenging for teenagers to accept getting help, either medical or therapeutic. Doing this means acknowledging they have a difficulty. Some would rather push away help than accept that something is wrong. They may feel they are to blame and talking about their feelings solidifies that feeling of blame. But for most teenagers, there is also another voice, albeit a quiet one, that wants to get better and knows that things are wrong. We need to win their trust that, with help, they will indeed recover.

Medication

There is an important debate about the merits of medicalizing and providing drug treatment to teenagers. Although this varies depending on the medication itself, in general professionals tend to avoid drug treatment except as a last resort, because all pharmaceutical treatments come with risks as well as benefits, and this is especially true when dealing with delicate developing teenage brains. Teenagers change so quickly we risk medicating them for conditions that disappear in the rear-view mirror. However, appropriate treatment may help your teen to manage conditions like depression, OCD, PTSD or anxiety disorders, and can help if there is a long wait ahead for therapy. Parents told me that they credited medication with giving them the time to find other longer-term strategies.

With any medication though, there is the risk of side effects. Studies into whether antidepressants increase the risk of suicidal thoughts are contested, but it seems that those risks are higher in young people than in adults. One study found a 38 per cent increased risk of suicidal thoughts and attempts in young people who had taken certain antidepressants.[2] Other side effects include nausea, anxiety, headaches, weight loss or gain, and sexual dysfunction, and less commonly, psychotic episodes.

We also don't know enough about how many of these drugs impact the brain when used in the long term.

There are also some disputes about the efficacy of drugs. The studies on how well they work often seem contradictory and frightening to those of us who are not clinicians.[3] Finally, some people suffer discontinuation symptoms when trying to come off medication and these tend to be more pronounced in young people.[4]

Given these concerns, the National Institute for Health and Care Excellence (NICE) states that children given medication for mental health problems must be monitored closely, the drugs should be prescribed by a psychiatrist rather than a GP, and the person being treated should also be given counselling. Ideally, if your teenager is given medication, it should be regularly reviewed, ideally for short-term use, and stopped when no longer needed.

Therapy and counselling

Therapy can give a teenager a space to talk with someone sympathetic who feels safe and whom they can trust, especially if they are frightened of opening up to us parents, for fear of shocking us, or because they do not feel understood at home. Therapists respect client confidentiality as a core tenet of their professional principles, as long as their client is not a danger to themselves or anybody else, in which case there are systems for therapists to report concerns to somebody else. But knowing quite how much you are likely to be worrying, counsellors have ways to keep you the parent informed in a manner that does not compromise their relationship with your child, their promise of confidentiality, or the needs of your teenager. Therapy happens in one-to-one, group and family sessions.

Typically, the NHS offers around six to eight session of counselling, often CBT, for those being treated in the lower tiers of CAMHS, because there is some evidence base that it delivers quick relief from symptoms. Each week your child will be given 'homework' designed to relieve some of their symptoms and to help them understand their problems a bit better, and the links between their feelings, thoughts and behaviour. In their therapy sessions they will reflect on this homework and add to it the following week. Much of the work is about identifying unhelpful thinking patterns, such as catastrophizing or black-and-white thinking, patterns that us parents can harbour too. I found awareness of such negative thoughts helpful and did CBT myself, but the data for its efficacy among children is mixed, and the evidence as to whether the change is sustained is also unclear, not least because of the numbers of youngsters who give up on counselling altogether and whose experience goes unrecorded. For those that persist though, evidence suggests that for young people with anxiety disorders, CBT shows better results when compared to no treatment, and that benefits were lasting.

Other kinds of therapy include Compassion-Focused Therapy (CFT), which concentrates on developing a kinder inner voice – an approach I've emphasized in this book. Psychoanalytic therapists have the most intense training compared to other approaches. Unfortunately, these other therapies are generally not available on the NHS, and you would have to pay for them privately. The cost of a private therapist varies, but it is usually upwards of £60 for a 50-minute session. Some therapists charge less, and there are charities, such as the Counselling Foundation, that provide help with counselling.

Young people's charities can also be a reliable place to go to get free or low-cost counselling for your teenager. Many focus on those who need extra support, such as those living in difficult circumstances or those who have been in care. What they offer varies, but it may include support groups or one-on-one counselling.

When choosing a therapist, check they are a member of a professional body such as the British Association for Counselling and Psychotherapy (BACP), the UK Council for Psychotherapy (UKCP) or the British Psychoanalytic Council (BPC). The best thing is to try one session – many therapists offer a free introductory session – and see how it goes before committing, and ideally get a personal recommendation.

The effectiveness of therapy varies: There's bad as well as good. How can you know the difference? Well, good therapy can teach teenagers to let go of their unproductive anxiety and rumination, and help them believe in the possibility of change and that a different life is possible. It can allow them to share secrets and traumas they have never felt safe to share before, with somebody objective who can provide perspective. Through therapy, young people can learn that even if they have been traumatized, or feel hopeless, they can learn to cope, and even emerge stronger. It is the opposite of self-absorption. In my experience, good therapists want their clients to live life independently, without becoming over-reliant on their help: Beware the therapist who doesn't have a plan to end their sessions. All of which depends on the relationship between a therapist and the teenager in question. Is there a good fit? Does communication flow? Does your teenager trust their therapist? Feel safe with them? That they can open up? It may take several goes before you find the right person to help.

SUPPORTING A TEENAGER WITH A MENTAL HEALTH PROBLEM – IF THEY'LL LET YOU

As we've seen, not all teenagers will share their mental health difficulties with their parents, who may be part of the problem. If they they are LGBTQIA+, they may be scared to confide in you in case you reject them. If they have suffered abuse, they may be afraid such a revelation would destroy your relationship (or, alternatively, afraid that it wouldn't). Perhaps they feel you will not listen, or they see you as unavailable or distracted. Or often, they simply do not believe that we parents could possibly understand what their lives are like.They may feel you will not be able to cope: your teenager is already overwhelmed with their feelings and cannot deal with you being overwhelmed too. Children may worry that you will blame yourself or get angry with them. They may prefer to talk to a teacher or another adult friend.

One of the most difficult periods of my life was when one of my teenagers was suffering and they chose to talk to others rather than me. I longed for that connection and communication. But much as I desired to stay close to them, I couldn't force that outcome. I worked on honouring and acknowledging my desire, while accepting the limits of what I could do. I felt proud that my teenager trusted me enough to be truthful about what they needed and was able to tell me I wasn't helping without fearing my reaction. I tried to be happy that they found others more helpful: I needed to trust their instincts.

I could offer practical help instead. I busied myself with sorting a therapist for them and organizing food that they liked, even as I wished I could do more. It also helped assuage my guilt that I wasn't the best person for my teenager to talk to at the time. I used some guided meditations in the middle of the night, when I would sometimes wake worrying about my troubled teenager. I would bring to mind a circle of light around me, and imagine my teenager being bathed in the light and love. I would bring to mind all their strengths and qualities, believing in their own ability to get better. It felt better that I was at least doing something rather than lying awake worrying.

And I imposed the rule that I wouldn't call them: they would call me if they wanted to discuss their emotional wellbeing, saving the heartbreak of unanswered calls for me, and additional pressure on them. Making it their decision was empowering, and our relationship became more intimate the more I allowed them to choose how and when they communicated with me. Eventually, they did. One challenge was how to talk about their treatment.

Open questions such as 'What did the therapist say?' might elicit more responses than 'How was your session?', which is quite likely to get the monosyllabic answer 'Fine'. Equally if you say, 'Did therapy go well?' the answer could be a simple yes or no. Instead you could say, 'What were your feelings when you had therapy?'

You might wish to acknowledge how hard it is for them to discuss mental health problems with you. Sometimes sharing a book about the struggles of young people finding their way can be more effective than anything you do. Or a simple 'That must be really tough' may be all it takes. In turn, this acknowledgement can mean much to the teenager who has found the courage to confide in you. They may also find it hard to share the fact they are actually feeling a bit better. One of my teenagers told me that they were worried that if they did so, their support would be removed.

In my own experience, and that of other parents I spoke to, there's a need for patient endurance, never believing in a simple 'They are on the mend' trajectory, which can put pressure on both you and your teenager. More likely, their return to improved mental health will be bumpy: some days will be better, some worse, with mood swings even within a day. A mountaineering image maybe helpful. Your teenager will clamber with difficulty to a peak on the mountain, or mental health challenge, but then drop down again into the valley of despair soon afterwards. Overall, however, even if the ups and downs of this mountain journey seem unchanging, over time the peaks and troughs will begin to even out and the landscape will become flatter and easier to traverse. Eventually they will hopefully be moving at a steadier pace.

Your teenager may be confused as to what is happening to them and it may take them time to properly explain their mental health issue. As one of my teenagers said to me, 'Just keep quiet, and I will get there in the end.' You may have to repeatedly reach out. One mother shared that it was on the eighth – eighth! – time of trying that her teenager responded. It is not necessarily anything personal against you if a teenager does not respond. Talking to you may require huge courage on their part. As one teenager said to me, 'If she hadn't kept trying and trying, I'd probably still be sitting in that deep pit of depression now.'

A simple 'How can I support your mental health?' can be powerful too. First, it shows your teenager that you care and accept they are struggling. Second, that you can support them and they are not alone in their trials, crucial given, as we've seen, the long waiting times to get professional help which mean you may be their main support for months.

You could also ask them 'How can you support your own mental health?' As parents, we often long to be able to fix all their problems; to be knights in shining armour rescuing them from hardship. A more helpful approach, I found, was to help them gradually take responsibility for their own lives without us being cast as their saviours: in other words it is less about us than them. Let's not assume that they are broken, and only we can help. Yes, they are feeling terrible, but at times that's their body and mind telling them that their behaviour isn't helping them. I remember having this conversation with a teenager of mine. At the time, they were not exercising, nor eating or sleeping well. Naturally they felt awful.

The breakthrough came when they believed they could change their behaviour. The first step was to get outside, the next was to begin exercising, then to quit junk food, then to examine their thoughts and assumptions. While as parents we can share ideas and strategies that may help their mental wellbeing, teenagers themselves still need to take responsibility for their psychological health. This can actually be positive. Feeling passive and powerless to do anything about a mental health condition can make teenagers feel worse. Instead, teenagers can train themselves to notice their negative thoughts and allow their feelings, in short they can help themselves to flourish, and should not rely exclusively on experts or the other professionals we have discussed in this chapter. Neural plasticity means teenagers can rewire their brains and create new neural pathways, which is encouraging.

Somehow, we have to believe in their agency and strength. I remember chatting to one parent whose child had been hospitalized with anorexia. What, I asked, had led to her recovery? 'Well,' he replied, 'she decided to get better.' We need to be alongside our adolescents, to be supportive, to get them the help they may need and of course some conditions require more specialised support and treatment, but at the same time we need to step back from being rescuers. The same father told me that his only advice to other parents was to be themselves. 'By being honest and showing up as who you truly are, they can be who they truly are.'

Try not to be shocked – or at least not to show it – whenever your teenager tells you some frightening detail of their experience or treatment. Keeping eye contact is one way of doing this, rather than looking away, if they share the reality of being in hospital, or of the thoughts and feelings they've been having, or experiences they have been through that you knew nothing about. Panicking doesn't help anyone. But showing that you are dropping everything to focus on them does. One teenager I met at a wellbeing workshop described to me how his mother had, in front of him, called her boss to say she wouldn't be available to go to a meeting, and someone else would have to go in her place, because her child had a serious mental health problem. It was at that point the teenager knew that his mother cared, and wanted to help.

This is about trust: about establishing it, building it and keeping it, both with you and with any professional help. Part of trust is about respecting confidentiality. This is complex: ideally you need to honour your teenager's request not to share information. They may have talked to you only on this basis. But we may have to borrow from the guidelines used by therapists, namely that there are times when we break their confidentiality. If your child has an active plan to take their life, or if they are being sexually exploited by a teacher for example, or might be a danger to others, then such exceptional circumstances mean you may be justified in passing the information to professionals, with or without your teenager's consent, though clearly you should always try to get their agreement first. Being reliable is a second element of building trust, and more straightforward. You need to deliver on what you have promised. If you commit to taking them to the doctor, then show up. Having said that, life intervenes. We parents can't always deliver. If you cannot meet a commitment, it is better to say so honestly, in an upfront way.

We don't need to pretend we understand exactly what's going on. Their world is so different from ours. It's all too easy to think that it's reassuring to say you understand their mental health issue. As another teenager I spoke to put it, 'I think all parents got taught on some course somewhere to say, "I understand how that must feel" the moment you open up.' But more appropriate might be to acknowledge if you don't understand mental health conditions, or the specific dynamics of what is troubling them. As the same teenager put it, 'It's not helpful, it's insulting.'

Beyond all this, you will also need to stay up to date with your child's treatment and recovery. This may involve making sure they follow specific instructions from a medical professional, such as taking medication or attending counselling.

LOOKING AFTER YOURSELF
AS WELL AS YOUR TEENAGER

Faced with such challenges, we need to look after ourselves. Imagine if you heard that a friend was in a similar situation. You would most likely say something like 'Poor them, they must be having a difficult time.' Try to find compassion for yourself in the same way that you would for any other parent in the same situation.

You may struggle to find anything joyful in your own life, or even feel you have a life at all. One mother whose teenager was unwell told me she felt like a worn-away bar of soap: all that was left of her was a discarded scrap which needed to be thrown away. When one of my teenagers was unwell, I found the best approach was to aim low. Take a moment to enjoy the small things, be it a good cup of coffee or arranging a jam jar full of daffodils. Remind yourself how to use breathing exercises to calm yourself. Remember to nourish your brain with rest, nutrition and exercise; check your own thoughts with kindness; use mindfulness; write things down; and focus on your values as well as the goal of making your teenager better. This has the added benefit of modelling healthier ways of coping to your teen, who can see you learning to help yourself when you're struggling.

No parent with a child in crisis can be totally separate from the teenager in question, nor would they want to be. Your world naturally narrows to you and your child. One parent told me he felt like a puppet on a string, his every move determined by his child. Another mother whose daughter had anorexia put on two stone herself trying to encourage her daughter to eat. But as far as you can, do not be sucked into the quicksand with them. You may need a degree of acceptance that there are problems we parents can't instantly solve. We are not in control of all that is happening. Nor is it helpful to blame ourselves; being accountable and taking responsibility for our role in any distress is not the same as berating ourselves and being full of self-hatred. The reasons for mental health problems are complex and multi-faceted, as we've discussed. We can honour and acknowledge our desire that our teenager might feel better, but we can't force any outcomes or the pace at which they will recover. Acceptance is not the same as giving up.

Our responses can be complicated. One parent admitted to me she liked the attention of having an unwell child, and even enjoyed the feeling that people thought she was coping magnificently. But this is about our child's recovery, not us. One technique that helped me was to say positive statements about the teenager in trouble. It could be something like 'I believe in so-and-so's strength' or 'I have faith in so-and-so's gifts and powers to recover'. I would repeat these statements, and feel into them, using deep breathing as I did so, so that mind and body lined up and I really believed what I was saying.

As well as looking after yourself, you need to keep family life going, despite the tension that comes with having an unwell teenager. Somehow, you must do your best to maintain routines because the human brain loves regularity – which is why going on holiday can be so difficult if a teenager is unwell, because of a change of routine and the lack of freedoms they are used to at home. This is easier said than done if your teenager will not come out of their room and the normal rhythms of night and day and family mealtimes have disappeared because your teen is not sleeping and getting up at three in the afternoon. My own answer was to tempt them into daylight, to try to restore their circadian rhythms with a trip to a coffee shop or somewhere they wanted to go, even if that was a brief trip outdoors. Little by little, a sense of routine did return.

Anything social can be helpful. We love to do what other people are doing, because we're social creatures who evolved to be part of tribes. So, they do homework; you do admin at the same time. They take control of the more ambitious bits of making supper while you chop vegetables and clean up around them. I found that asking a sad teenager for their help sometimes worked. They regained a sense they could make a difference to others. Anything to avoid them being stuck up in their room on their own.

You also want to be keeping an eye on your teen's siblings, who have sometimes been dubbed 'glass children' – siblings of a disabled or unwell child who feel they are invisible to their parents.[5] Understandably they can feel ignored and become resentful. There's only so much pressure a parent with a mentally unwell child can take, and you may have to acknowledge to other children that at least for a while, your attention is elsewhere, while making a real effort with them when you can.

Naturally, your time may be consumed with numerous appointments with doctors and therapists, and you may worry that your other children are taking on more responsibility than they should at their age. We don't want to force these siblings to grow up too quickly or to hold them to developmentally inappropriate expectations. We still need to carve out time specifically for them. I know when I was worried about the mental health of one or other of my own children, I had to stop myself looking for confidential insights and support from their apparently healthy siblings. I learned that to do so distanced me from them, as they naturally felt as if I was less interested in their problems and only those of their sibling.

A NOTE OF OPTIMISM

I want to conclude these two rather daunting chapters on mental health on a more positive note. Yes, mental health problems are frightening, and we should not diminish the challenges for parents and teenagers alike. Even if a person fully recovers from their mental health problem, there can be long-term physical health implications, especially if their struggles included disordered eating, self-harm, substance misuse or behaving recklessly or dangerously. There are a lot of families and young people in need of long-term support.

But we need balance here, and to stay calm, as that's our best hope of helping. With professional support even the most serious conditions can be managed or treated, and indeed many problems right themselves even without psychologists or doctors. Teenage patterns of behaviour, however negative, are often relatively short-lived, with relatively shallow roots, and can be reversed more easily than in an adult. Do not lose heart. Recovery rates are good.[6, 7]

Hmm, you might be thinking. All very well, but where is the gift in experiencing a teenager with a mental health problem? What is positive about the agony of those dark times? Living through the crisis of an unwell teenager is perhaps the hardest thing any parent will ever have to experience. The problems can feel so profound they overwhelm any other issue. I remember waking at night, a sickening feeling in my stomach, fearing the worst. It was a far more devastating time than when I myself was unwell.

Well, no experience is without value. We parents may emerge from this period with a new perspective on what matters. Our views about what success means – prestigious universities, high-powered jobs – may evaporate in the face of a new understanding of what truly is important: a person's psychological health. I remember talking to another parent when one of our children was struggling. He was talking about a famous university and why it meant a lot to him that his teenager was going there. I remember thinking that what mattered to me was that my teenager stayed alive.

While it may feel like we have lost any closeness to our teenager when they are unwell, we may both emerge from these desperate times with a much stronger relationship, where we understand them, and know how to support and love them, in new and profound ways. This may require a certain humility from us: we may have to accept that we have not always been the parent we would have liked to have been. But our relationship can reflect the additional knowledge and appreciation we now have of each other.

While a teenager has a serious mental health problem, it seems as if nothing good can come from this painful period, but a teenager who emerges from dark times is often someone with a new sympathy for others who struggle. A childhood without stress would mean a lack of opportunity to develop inner strength and the ability to bounce back from adversity and trauma. They have been granted a passport to a land that not everyone will visit. They have a deeper understanding than their peers of what it is to find life hard.

Meanwhile, the lessons they learn about how to look after their own wellbeing can last a lifetime. They have grown new muscles at the psychological gym, muscles that only they could develop, much as we parents would have liked to have been able to do the heavy lifting for them. Through the period of ill health, they may have discovered what works for them, whether that's exercise, or routine, or challenging their negative thoughts. By learning these lessons relatively young, they may face a calmer future than a teenager who has never struggled. Those of us who, like me, faced mental health challenges later in life can find it harder to move on, because our minds have been working in unhelpful ways for longer than our younger peers. Teenage agony is real, but it can also be quite short-lived;

negative patterns and lifestyle habits can be easier to shift as they are, relatively speaking, less entrenched.

Teenagers who have struggled may even become role models for other young people. They realize the importance of mental health and that there are steps you can take to foster a sense of wellbeing. The sooner all young people prioritize their mental health, and we adults support them in that endeavour, the better.

*

Getting help for mental problems is a challenge, but it can be done. This chapter has tried to set out a road map of the services on offer, the professionals involved and the kinds of treatments that may be suggested for your teenager. Supporting a teenager who is finding life traumatic can be gruelling for parents – but somehow we have to survive and remember that it's not all about us. Ideally, we need to stay connected as best we can with our youngsters, and look after ourselves too. Of all the life lessons my teenagers have taught me, perhaps the greatest has been the need to stay calm myself in the face of their ups and downs. To borrow from the American-Lebanese poet Khalil Gibran in *The Prophet*, we need to be like a stable bow, from which our children shoot forth into the world like arrows.

> You are the bows from which your children as living arrows
>   are sent forth.
> The archer sees the mark upon the path of the infinite, and He bends
>   you with His might that His arrows may go swift and far.
> Let your bending in the archer's hand be for gladness;
> For even as He loves the arrow that flies, so He loves also the bow
>   that is stable.[8]

EPILOGUE

I am lying on a mat on the sitting room floor, catching the last rays of evening sun, and attempting some stretches. One 21-year-old daughter rushes in. 'Mum, can I borrow your gold pumps please?' she asks. 'Yes, that's fine,' I answer, reflecting with pleasure that whereas once she might have simply taken my shoes, now she asks politely. 'Where are you going?' I wonder. 'Oh, I'm just hanging out with K' – her 25-year-old sister. 'Do you need me to drop you anywhere?' I venture. 'No, we're good, I'm going with K.' I return to my mat, and pause to reflect on my years as a mother of teenagers, as I turn 59 and this period is vanishing, as if in a rear-view mirror.

I've had a continuous run of 15 years of living with teenagers. My eldest son became a teenager in 2008; my youngest teenagers turned 20 at the end of 2023. Another way of looking at it is that each of my five children spent seven years of being a teenager, so I've had five times seven years of experience – that's 45 years if I count the time in this way. Now this period has come to an end.

Once I was the sympathetic coach, the annoying encourager, proffering advice and my latest learning, whether that was about how their brains were functioning or what negative thoughts might look like. They were the ones needing support. Now they're the ones offering me a lift. I might be the one sharing my vulnerability, adult to adult, when a child asks what I am working on – what indeed! – a new grown-up question from a fellow grown up.

We always remain parents, but at least for now, I'm hanging up my teenage parenting hat (though young adults have problems too – but that might be for another book). There's no more being woken up in the night; gone is the need to ferry a child to a friend's house or football match. Gone too are those gut-wrenching moments when I feared for the mental health of my adolescents.

Parenting teenagers has been both the hardest thing I've ever done and the best. The emotional roller-coaster has been extreme. Love and hate, resentment and joy, have lived side by side throughout this period. I've had to dig deep to cope with my own powerful thoughts and feelings, and not be overwhelmed. There were plenty of mess-ups on the way, but I've managed to reframe them too as stepping stones rather than stumbling blocks.

Adolescents have energized me, with their fun and their crazy clothes and the fresh ideas tumbling out of them; with their new ways of looking at the world, whether it's about sex or gender or what matters. They are the ones who've sorted out my phone when I haven't been able to make it work. They have taken me to new parts of town and introduced me to new ways of seeing, they've encouraged me to care about what is happening in parts of the world of which I know little. They have even learned to tell their granny they love the Christmas socks.

And, through all these adventures, and over the course of my parenting years, I've turned down the worry dial and had more fun as the years have ticked past. I have learned at least some tricks of the parenting trade, and become a calmer, happier mum. Me and the five – we've grown up together. Of course there will always be multiple routes to psychological growth: being a parent is only one among many. But it's been a good ride for me.

And how would I sum up my role? Well, I've attempted to be the bamboo cane to their clambering sweet pea, hoping to remain a steadfast frame, a structure they can cling to when they face fierce storms; to stay happy while they are sad; to be the stable bow from which they can shoot forth into the world, to return to the poet Gibran's wonderful image.

And now what remains? A connection that will last into their adulthood and beyond, I hope. Our relationships with our teenagers, the people they have become, are among the most precious we can have. I remember the first time I really laughed at a joke that one of my children cracked, and I found myself giddy with the realization that now I didn't just have a teenager, I had company. We can feel levels of connection we didn't know were possible, having journeyed with our youngsters through their adolescences. To borrow the phrase from E. M. Forster that began this book, we live in fragments no longer. Now that really is a gift.

FURTHER RESOURCES FOR TEENAGERS AND PARENTS

Childline (run by the NSPCC charity)
www.childline.org.uk
Freephone: 0800 1111 (24 hours)
If you're under 19, you can confidentially call, email or chat online about any problem, or sign up for a Childline account on the website to be able to message a counsellor any time without using your email address. It's also possible to chat one-to-one with an online advisor.

Youth Access
www.youthaccess.org.uk
Email: admin@youthaccess.org.uk
Provides information about counselling in the UK for those aged 12–25.

The Mix
www.themix.org.uk
Freephone: 0808 808 4994 (13.00–23.00 daily)
Text: 85258 (24-hour Crisis Messenger)
The under-25s can talk to The Mix for free on the phone, by email or on their webchat. You can also use their phone counselling service or get more information on support services you might need.

Samaritans
www.samaritans.org
Freephone (UK and Republic of Ireland): 116 123 (24 hours)
Email: jo@samaritans.org

For those in distress and needing support, you can ring Samaritans for free at any time of the day or night.

No Panic
www.nopanic.org.uk
Helpline: 0300 772 9844 (10.00–22.00 daily; charges apply)
Youth helpline for 13–20-year-olds: 0330 606 1174
   (Mon–Fri 15.00–18.00; charges apply)
Email: admin@nopanic.org.uk
For those suffering from panic attacks, OCD, phobias and other related anxiety disorders. Having a panic attack? Try their crisis number with a recording of a breathing technique: 01952 680835 (24 hours)

SHOUT
Text: SHOUT to 85258 for urgent help
Texts are free from EE, O2, Vodafone, 3, Virgin Mobile, BT Mobile, giffgaff, Tesco Mobile and Telecom Plus.
Provides free, 24-hour crisis support across the UK, via text, for young people experiencing a mental health crisis. All texts are answered by trained volunteers, with support from experienced clinical supervisors.

Papyrus (Prevention of Young Suicide)
https://papyrus-uk.org/
Hopeline UK: 0800 068 41 41 (24 hours)
Text: 88247
Email: pat@papyrus-uk.org
Confidential advice and support for young people who feel suicidal, 24 hours a day, every day of the year including weekends and bank holidays.

Family Lives
www.familylives.org.uk
Helpline: 0808 800 2222
Email: askus@familylives.org.uk
Provides support with parenting and family challenges, with a helpline, live chat and email services.

NHS support: Child and Adolescent Mental Health Services
www.nhs.uk/mental-health/children-and-young-adults/
Information about Child and Adolescent Mental Health Services (CAMHS).

Particular issues

Gamble Aware
www.gambleaware.org
Helpline: 0808 8020 133 (24 hours)
Provides free help 24 hours a day by phone or live chat on their website.

Talk to Frank
www.talktofrank.com
Helpline: 0300 123 6600 (24 hours)
Text: 82111
Email: frank@talktofrank.com
Provides free help 24 hours a day and useful advice for parents and guardians about drugs and alcohol.

Beat
www.beateatingdisorders.org.uk
Helpline for under-25s: 0808 801 0711 (Mon–Fri 15.00–20.00)
The charity's mission is to end the pain and suffering caused by eating disorders. Email support is also available.

GLOSSARY OF MENTAL HEALTH CONDITIONS

As we have seen earlier in the book, getting the correct diagnosis can require persistence, and only a qualified professional can judge what is or is not a mental health condition.

The descriptions of mental health conditions and symptoms that follow are introductions to the topics for the general reader: always consult your doctor for more detailed medical information on these conditions. There are also sections on developmental conditions, such as autism, which are not the same as a mental health condition.

These introductions briefly explain how a condition manifests itself, its salient characteristics, why a teenager might experience it, and the symptoms they might have. They do not include detailed thoughts on treatment, which will tend to reflect an individual treatment plan, in most cases involving a combination of therapy and medication.

I've also included how common these conditions are, though the old adage 'There are lies, damned lies, and statistics' is particularly true when it comes to working out how common mental health conditions are in young people. As we've seen, this is tricky. Has the increased awareness of mental health conditions inflated the numbers? Or have the numbers really increased? What is the prevalence in your teenager's age group? These are key questions to ask your teenager's doctor.

Another difficulty in calculating the prevalence of each condition is that young people themselves decide on whether they have a problem: as we've seen there is no blood test or scan to say for sure whether a young person is suffering or not. Yet another issue is how 'young people' are defined – what exact age group are we discussing? Sometimes the figures measure numbers of those aged, say, 12–16; at other times 16–25. A final problem is the way that mental health problems are categorized. A young person is described as 'probably', 'possibly' or 'unlikely' to have a mental health condition – all of which reflect the difficulties of diagnosis.

Despite these reservations, I have included statistics to give at least a sense of the prevalence of the problem your teenager might be facing, which will give some perspective. Yes, there are many teenagers who are suffering, but the majority are not.

ADHD AND ADD (DEVELOPMENTAL CONDITIONS)

Attention deficit hyperactivity disorder (ADHD) is a condition where teenagers are restless, easily distracted, impulsive and have difficulty concentrating. Those with ADHD also find it hard to control what they say and do: they might speak without thinking first, talking a lot and interrupting others. They often have poor organizational skills, finding it hard to get to school on time, to start or finish homework, and risk losing things and zoning out.

Attention deficit disorder (ADD) has similar symptoms to ADHD, in that sufferers of ADD also have difficulty concentrating, but children with ADD are not as hyperactive. Symptoms usually start early in life, before the age of six.

Other people's confusion about these conditions can exacerbate difficulties for ADHD and ADD sufferers, who may wrongly be believed to be deliberately challenging. This can make them feel isolated and can lead to feelings of low self-esteem.

The worldwide incidence of ADHD is 7.6 per cent in children aged 3–12 years and 5.6 per cent in those aged 12–18, according to 2023 figures.[1]

Why might your teenager suffer?

Experts think ADHD might run in families and that sufferers have a genetic predisposition. A second explanation is that the chemicals in your teenager's brain are organized in a different way. Specifically, researchers think people with ADHD and ADD respond differently from non-sufferers to stimulation of the brain. In some rare cases, the condition could be triggered by environmental events, brain damage or head injuries, but a neurodevelopmental predisposition is the main factor.

ANOREXIA

Anorexic teenagers have disordered thoughts about their weight: consequently, they exercise a lot and do not eat much, and often take laxatives to empty their stomachs. They worry about eating in front of others and feel fat even if this is not the reality. Other psychosocial signs of anorexia are when a teenager compares themself to others and suffers from low mood.

The physical effects of anorexia are serious. Sufferers become so thin that their periods and other bodily functions can stop. They can also feel cold all the time and grow new downy hair on their bodies; end up with weakened bones; and may be left infertile because of hormonal changes. Worse, their organs organs can be damaged and the condition can be fatal. Anorexia has the highest mortality rate of any mental health condition.

The diagnostic criteria for anorexia say you have to show significant weight loss, but you can be normal weight and have anorexic thoughts. Starvation can become an addiction.

A second eating problem is avoidant or restrictive food intake disorder. Sufferers avoid and restrict food but do not seem concerned with weight and body shape.

In 2023, 0.2 per cent of 11–16-year-olds in England met the criteria for anorexia, as did 3.3 per cent of 17–19-year-olds.[2]

Why might your teenager suffer?

For some young people, an eating disorder may begin as a way to feel in control of their lives, especially if everything feels chaotic around them. For others, eating disorders are an extension of feeling sad. People sometimes reduce what they eat as a way to punish themselves and add to their feelings that they are not good enough.

Though it affects girls more than boys, it can also happen to boys. Harriet Frew is a psychotherapist who works part-time at an NHS trust in Cambridge and believes that many more boys suffer from eating disorders than we realize. This is because, first, they tend not to get any help as they feel there would be a stigma in doing so; and second, because boys with eating disorders often first develop them by going to the gym an excessive amount. 'This normalizes certain disordered practices, so people don't realize they have a problem,' Frew says.[3]

Treatment involves possible hospitalization for severe malnutrition, and then therapy aimed at returning your teenager to a healthy weight.

ANXIETY

All teenagers feel anxious on occasion, whether they've had a bad day at school, are facing an exam, or they have missed their train home. Typically, they will produce more adrenaline, feel more alert, focus on the threat and stop thinking about other things. They breathe more quickly, to get more oxygen to the muscles so they can run faster from an imagined threat. Some people feeling stressed will also have a dry mouth, sweat, feel hot, or have stomach cramps or diarrhoea. Afterwards, these symptoms cease, they calm down and feel better.

The mental health condition of anxiety is different. It is when a teenager feels these stressful, panicky feelings much of the time and they are no longer connected to a particularly stressful event.

There are different kinds of anxiety. Separation anxiety occurs when a child doesn't want to separate from parental figures or significant adults. Generalized anxiety disorder is when a person has a sense of constant non-specific worry. Phobias, such as being unreasonably afraid of heights, lifts or bridges, are another kind of anxiety. Social anxiety disorders are characterized by an exaggerated fear of strangers and unfamiliar social situations. Panic disorders are marked by extreme bouts of anxiety that are not usually linked to any obvious stressful triggers. Panic attacks come unexpectedly.

Teenagers who have anxiety also tend to have other emotional symptoms, including feeling nervous, overwhelmed, full of dread or out of control, or finding it hard to concentrate.

This is by far the most common mental health problem: 34 per cent of young people aged 18–24 feel anxious most or all of the time, according to 2023 figures.[4]

Why might your teenager suffer?

Teenagers can suffer from anxiety because of bullying, traumatic events, the death of a loved one, or because of difficulties at school, including academic pressure.

AUTISM (A DEVELOPMENTAL CONDITION)

Despite its inclusion in this glossary, autism is not a mental illness. It is a developmental condition that affects how young people see the world and how they interact with others. Although the difficulty of processing information seems to be a cognitive disability, more broadly an autistic person suffers from poor communications skills.

You will undoubtedly have heard the phrase 'on the autism spectrum'. As the word 'spectrum' implies, autism affects people in different ways and to varying degrees. However, there are certain traits that most autistic people experience to some extent. The first main feature is finding social situations challenging, especially those in crowded, noisy spaces. An autistic person may have difficulty understanding emotions, especially when reading body language and facial expressions in others, as well as having difficulty expressing their own emotions.

The second main feature is a difficulty with communication, and the third is a tendency towards repetitive activities and interests, including what are known as 'repetitive motor actions' – hand flapping, clicking of fingers, head movements, swaying and rocking.

Other characteristics of autistic people include being over- or under-sensitive to loud noises and bright lights, and developing an intense and specific interest in a particular topic.

Just like anyone else, people who have a diagnosis of autism can have mental health problems. However, the complications this developmental problem causes mean that people with autism are more vulnerable to psychological problems. A study found that 70 per cent of people with autism also have a condition such as anxiety, depression, ADHD or obsessive-compulsive disorder.

The main treatments are finding the right school and getting parental support. Home- and school-based programmes can reduce difficulties and foster better-adjusted development. Very rarely, medications may have to be used, although there are no specific medications for the condition. One per cent of children in the UK have a diagnosis of autism spectrum disorder.[5]

Why might your teenager suffer?

The causes of autism are still being investigated, though we know that there is no link between the condition and the measles, mumps and rubella (MMR) vaccine, a theory that began with some flawed research published in Britain in 1998. Autism often runs in families, and scientists are trying to work out which genes might be implicated.

BIPOLAR DISORDER

People who suffer from bipolar disorder have big mood swings from one pole of manic highs to the other pole of depressing lows. Episodes can last for days or weeks on end. The symptoms of bipolar may not necessarily be present all the time. Although it is often true that those suffering from mental health conditions will have little insight into their behaviour and their need for help, this is particularly the case for those who are suffering from bipolar disorder.

During manic episodes, a sufferer will talk a lot, experience racing thoughts, overconfidence and increased mental activity, and have difficulty concentrating. Their physical symptoms include increased energy, hardly needing sleep or having difficulty sleeping, reduced appetite, thoughts of self-harm and believing they have special powers or abilities.

When on a low, a sufferer will feel down, upset or tearful, tired or sluggish and uninterested in things they usually enjoy; have low self-esteem and a lack of confidence; and feel guilty, worthless or hopeless, agitated and tense, unable to concentrate on anything and suicidal.

In 2014, 3.4 per cent of 16–24-year-olds who were screened for mental health problems had bipolar disorder.[6]

Why might your teenager suffer?

The exact cause of bipolar disorder is unknown. However, research suggests that a combination of factors may contribute to the illness, including a genetic likelihood.

BULIMIA

Bulimia is an eating disorder. Those afflicted have episodes of eating a great deal and then trying to get rid of the food they have eaten by making themselves sick.

This process is known as bingeing and then purging, often with the help of laxatives. It harms a sufferer's physical health, as vital nutrients are lost every time someone is sick. Regular vomiting can lead to sore throats and bad teeth because of the presence of stomach acid, as well as dehydration. People with bulimia often end up being malnourished and frequently feel weak and tired. They can suffer either from weight loss or gain.

Mental health professionals define a binge as an episode of eating that feels out of control to the person. It also happens within a short space of time (around two hours). This behaviour needs to happen at least once a week for a period of months to be considered a problem.

The teenager usually feels uncomfortably full after a bingeing session. Often sufferers also feel miserable and embarrassed by this behaviour, which happens in secret because they feel ashamed. Other psychological symptoms include feeling helpless, low and losing interest in other people.

Eating disorders were present in 0.4 per cent of 5–19-year-olds in 2017.[7] In 2023, 0.5 per cent of 11–16-year-olds in England met the criteria for bulimia, as did 1.7 per cent of 17–19-year-olds.[8]

Why might your teenager suffer?

Those who suffer from bulimia may have previously struggled with anorexia. Although the illnesses are different, some of the reasons for them are similar: bulimics may feel that parts of their life are out of control, and purging or restricting what they eat gives them back a sense of agency.

Many people with bulimia also find that overeating helps reduce strong negative feelings. They then feel guilty for this overeating, and purge. Some people binge without then purging. This is called binge-eating disorder.

CONDUCT DISORDER

Conduct disorder is a mental health problem that involves disruptive or defiant behaviour. These who suffer with this disorder tend to be in trouble at school much more frequently than their peers.

These young people find it difficult to respect the boundaries of others and can behave in an antisocial way. They might display aggressive behaviour such as fighting or bullying and may even harm animals. They will sometimes break the law, stealing or vandalizing property. Sometimes those who suffer will stop going to school or run away from home.

Most children with behavioural problems do not have a conduct disorder: everyone is naughty or breaks the rules from time to time. Occasionally acting out is not conduct disorder either. To be considered a conduct disorder, the problems need to be persistent over several months, with frequent aggressive or destructive behaviours including burning or stealing, as well as lying or shoplifting, drug and alcohol abuse, sexual activity which is not age appropriate, and anger and hostility tinged with cruelty. If left untreated, conduct disorder can lead to more serious personality disorders of adulthood. The prevalence of conduct disorders is 5 per cent among children and young people aged 5–16 years according to various surveys.[9]

Why might your teenager suffer?

There seem to be several factors rather than any single one that make a teenager more likely to suffer, but problems in their home environment and other social factors are most likely.

Sufferers are often under other types of psychological strain as well. For example, they may be struggling educationally or have trouble managing emotions such as anger. Sometimes people with this problem also have difficulty maintaining attention levels and with hyperactivity.

Treatment involves parental programmes, parental support, anger management and classroom-based interventions.

DEPRESSION

Depression is a feeling of emptiness and low mood: you feel down all the time. This kind of continuous misery, whatever is happening, is not the same as an understandable sadness related to a particular event. Language is confusing here, as teenagers can often say they feel 'so depressed', when they do not mean they are suffering from a mental health condition but just that they feel temporarily flat.

Emotional and cognitive symptoms include no longer finding enjoyment in what was previously pleasurable; avoiding friends or social situations; feeling irritable, upset, miserable or lonely; being self-critical; feeling guilty or hopeless; and experiencing suicidal thoughts or acts. Physical symptoms include sleeping more or less than normal, eating more or less than normal, and not having any energy.

Normally, a teenager will have to have many of the symptoms that are listed above for at least two weeks before a doctor will diagnose them with depression.

About 4.8 per cent of children aged 17–19 have a depressive disorder.[10] Major depressive episodes and other depressive episodes have been shown to be present in 1.5 per cent and 0.6 per cent of children respectively.

Why might your teenager suffer?

Depression can happen as a reaction to abuse, bullying or family breakdown. It can also run in families. It may develop alongside anxiety. Often, however, a teenager feels they cannot explain why they feel as they do.

There is also a problem called adjustment disorder that is more short-lived than depression. This is when a teenager feels low, but they suspect it is because they are getting used to something new. Perhaps they feel sad because they have lost a loved one, moved schools or their older brother has left home. This 'event-related' bout of low mood is different from the kind of ongoing low mood that is characteristic of depression.

GAMING ADDICTION

Moderate amounts of gaming (around three or four hours a week of games involving others) can contribute to wellbeing because it helps people connect. Appreciating youth culture is always a challenge for adults. Many dismiss online gaming as an indulgence or waste of time. However, for many young people (especially boys) it provides an important social connection with each other. As long as the content is appropriate and it is alongside other activities, playing a game together online can be good for stress, social engagement and happiness.

However, non-stop gaming can be highly addictive. 'Stickier' – more addictive, 'time-thief' – games have graphics and storylines that have become so realistic that video games can start to take over a teenager's life. Some games replicate gambling-like behaviour. There is also the problem of who your child is interacting with through gaming. In some cases, excessive gaming may lead to more violent behaviour.

Many boys would rather play games with other players online than interact with real people. Very quickly, teenagers or children can find that their social lives revolve around playing online games.

A related topic is online gambling addiction: in the old days, you needed to go to a bookmaker to gamble, and that would have been difficult for young people. However, easy access to gambling online has changed that. Problem gamblers show many of the same characteristics as those addicted to games: they isolate in their bedrooms.

Signs of a gaming addiction include a preoccupation with gaming to the point where a teenager is agitated when away from a screen, talking about a game continuously, being uninterested in other things, downplaying or lying about the amount of time that they are spending playing games, coming up with excuses as to why they need to be online, and being unable to limit the amount of time they spend playing games (they may plan to spend an hour online but realize hours later that they are still playing). They often neglect other areas of their life, including friends, family and personal hygiene. They may become defensive when questioned about the amount of time spent playing games.

Gaming addiction can also cause physical symptoms, including migraines, carpal tunnel syndrome, trouble sleeping and backache. Consequences

GAMING ADDICTION

include low school achievement, social isolation and relationship problems with family and friends.

Treatment for gaming addiction usually involves a gradual reduction in screen time, though sometimes the best strategy is a period of abstinence (no gaming at all) as well as a gradual return to activities in the real world. It may also be necessary for the person to work on social skills which have been neglected while they were glued to the screen.

A recent review of studies on gaming disorder found that the prevalence of gaming disorder was hard to quantify, putting it at anywhere between 0.7 and 15.6 per cent, and it was mainly among young men.[11]

Why might your teenager suffer?

Games are designed to be addictive, by being just challenging enough to keep young people coming back for more, but not so hard that they give up. Teenagers are drawn to these addictive games by a desire for escapism. Playing gives them a sense of euphoria, or at least a sense of relief from unpleasant feelings, be that bullying, feeling lonely and having no friends, or the experience of a traumatic event.

MANIA

Mania occurs when someone feels on a high, with lots of energy and enthusiasm. It is different from experiencing a normal good mood, because the feelings are intense and go on for a long time. Hypomania is a milder form of mania.

These conditions might not sound like an illness, but those with mania and hypomania suffer, as they can feel disconnected from everyone else. They are in their own world when they are on a high, full of ideas, bursting with confidence and feeling more sociable, as well as experiencing more sexual desire and intense happiness in this state of heightened awareness. By contrast, everyone else can seem to inhabit a less exciting world.

Less positively, mania also comes with feelings of increased irritability and aggression, being easily distracted, talking a lot and very fast, and having poor judgement. Sufferers might also take risks with drink and drugs. They are unable to look after themselves properly, not washing or eating well.

Since such behaviour may be unusual for them, after a hypomanic or manic episode, people can feel ashamed and hopeless about how they have behaved. They can also need a lot of sleep after the energy it has required to be on a high. Prevalence figures among teenagers are hard to establish.

Why might your teenager suffer?

As with some other mental health conditions, we do not know exactly why people suffer from mania and hypomania, but possible causes include high levels of stress, changes in sleep patterns and use of drugs and alcohol. It is likely that a chemical imbalance in the brain is linked to mania as well, and there may be a genetic link. Mania can appear as part of bipolar disorder (see above) or on its own.

OBSESSIVE COMPULSIVE DISORDER

Obsessive-compulsive disorder (OCD) is a specific type of anxiety disorder. Sufferers have repeated thoughts, images or feelings that are distressing, and by which they become obsessed. They carry out rituals or habits – known as compulsions – to help themselves feel better temporarily.

OCD rituals can involve practical activities, like checking door locks or repeatedly checking on loved ones to make sure that they are safe. They can also involve obsessive tidying and organization. Often the negative thoughts are about dirt and contamination, which is why one common OCD behaviour is frequent washing of hands or taking repeated showers. Brain imaging studies have shown that the act of cleaning can help regulate emotions like shame, fear and disgust. Other common rituals include tapping to reduce anxiety.

OCD rituals can also happen inside a teenager's head. They might count to themselves. The emotional symptoms include feeling as if their mind is being invaded by repeated thoughts of fear, self-disgust, guilt or self-questioning. They might have a powerful urge to do something to stop the feelings – this is the compulsive element of OCD. Sufferers find some temporary relief after performance of chosen rituals. They may feel the need to ask for reassurance or get people to check things for them.

OCD affects 1.2 per cent of the UK population.[12]

Why might your teenager suffer?

What predisposes a teenager to OCD is complex, but research suggests that the condition involves problems in communication between the different parts of the brain. It can also be caused by environmental triggers, such as events a child feels are beyond their control.

Research shows that OCD does run in families, and that genes are likely to play a role in the development of the disorder. OCD can exist as a part of other disorders too. For example, people with anorexia can sometimes have OCD-type symptoms.

PSYCHOSIS

Psychosis is characterized by losing touch with reality, and those who suffer share many of the same symptoms as those who have schizophrenia (see opposite). They might hear voices, see or feel things that aren't there, imagine that there is a conspiracy against them, or believe things that don't rationally make sense.

Other symptoms include feeling that they are being followed or that their life is in danger, muddled thinking and difficulty concentrating, or feeling like time speeds up or slows down. One parent said, 'It feels as if a teenager with psychosis exists on a different, inaccessible planet and you can't have a rational conversation with them.'

Psychosis can occur in its own right, but often occurs as a symptom of another serious mental health problem such as bipolar disorder or schizophrenia. Other people might notice symptoms before the sufferer does; psychotics are not always even aware of their psychosis.

Some people have one episode of psychosis and never have another. This type happens shortly after a trauma or major stress, such as the death of a loved one, an accident, assault, or a natural disaster. It's usually a reaction to a disturbing event. Other sufferers might need ongoing treatment with therapy and medication.

Psychosis is rare: in 2002, the prevalence of psychotic disorders in children aged 5–18 years was 0.4 per cent.[13]

Why might your teenager suffer?

A teenager might suffer psychosis as part of a specific mental health condition such as bipolar disorder. Substance abuse or extreme stress or trauma are also possible causes.

SCHIZOPHRENIA

Schizophrenia is often misunderstood and thought to mean someone with a divided personality. In fact, a person suffering this serious mental health problem finds it difficult to distinguish between their thoughts and ideas, and what is happening in reality. The sufferer sees, feels, smells or hears things that aren't there, and suffers delusions, when they believe things that seem unreal to other people. Their muddled thinking can include fixed bizarre beliefs. Sufferers' thoughts are confused and interrupted; they may feel like someone is 'stealing' their thoughts and as if they are being controlled by something outside themselves. Understandably, all of these symptoms often mean that a sufferer is unable to perform normal activities like washing, dressing or seeing friends. The illness usually appears between the ages of 15 and 35. Other people might notice symptoms before a teenager does, because the condition means that a young person doesn't always know that they are suffering from it.

Schizophrenia can be treated with medication and therapy, but there are challenges. A sufferer's withdrawal from society and diminishing interest in their surroundings are always relevant when treating mental health problems, but are among the greatest difficulties that patients face when trying to recover from schizophrenia.

The Royal College of Psychiatrists says that while 1 per cent of people will develop schizophrenia over their lifetimes, it is extremely rare in younger children and usually begins when someone is in their late teens.[14]

Why might your teenager suffer?

A teenager is more likely to experience schizophrenia if their parent has suffered psychosis, if their developing brain was damaged when they were younger, or if they have associated drug and alcohol problems.

SELF-HARM

Self-harm is when a teenager hurts themself on purpose. They usually do it because their emotions feel overwhelming. It seems like there is no other way to let the strong feelings out. Often self-harming brings temporary relief from these feelings. People who self-harm can be helped to find other safe ways of coping.

Self-harm can make people feel ashamed and fearful that no-one will understand their behaviour. Being secretive, feeling low, expressing a wish to punish themselves, being withdrawn and feeling suicidal are all characteristic feelings of someone suffering from self-harm.

Physical signs of self-harm can include someone cutting their skin, typically on their wrists, arms, thighs or chest, or burning or punching themself in the same places. They may well need quick treatment for injuries from self-harming to avoid infections. They may also poison themself with medication. Sufferers are often fully clothed, even in hot weather.

Among those aged 12–16, 27 per cent reported thoughts of self-harm and 15 per cent reported at least one act of self-harm, according to 2013 figures.[15] Numbers are likely to have risen considerably since then, but reliable figures are hard to find given low levels of reporting among teenagers themselves.

Why might your teenager suffer?

Self-harm can happen if a teenager is feeling anxious, depressed, stressed or bullied. Self-harm is most often described as a way to express or cope with emotional distress: those that are being bullied, for example, are unable to turn on the bullies themselves, who seem more powerful than them, so turn on themselves instead.

SUICIDAL FEELINGS

Your teenager might have been feeling down and sad for a while – certainly for several months. If those feelings have deepened and intensified, and they don't know what to do about them, they might think the only solution is to end their life.

Here are some warning signs of suicidal feelings: a teenager who is always talking or thinking about death, showing deep sadness, losing interest in daily life, having increasing trouble sleeping and eating, feeling helpless or worthless, self-harming, and feeling angry and as though things cannot change.

These feelings can get in the way of everything else – so much that it might be hard for the sufferer to believe that they can feel better. Around 200 teenagers are lost to suicide in the UK every year.[16]

It can be hard for a teenager to talk about these sorts of feelings. But sharing their worries with someone they trust can help them see their problems in a different way and understand that suicide is not the only option. The person in question might be a family member, friend or teacher.

It is common for people with suicidal thoughts to say that the thoughts come and go like waves. Talking to others when the wave has come, even a brief chat, can give time for the wave to settle down and for them to set their thinking down another path.

If your teenager doesn't feel they can speak to anyone they know, there are confidential helplines like the Samaritans, and safe online forums like The Mix, where they can get support from trained people. Research shows that talking to others helps.

The Samaritans provides free and confidential advice to anyone suffering from suicidal thoughts. Your child can speak to them 24 hours a day, 7 days a week. If your teenager is talking about suicide, go straight to your local Accident and Emergency service, where they should be fast-tracked to the right help.

Call: 116 123

Website: www.samaritans.org

Why might your teenager suffer?

The reasons for feeling suicidal can include being depressed or having another mental health problem, struggling with low self-esteem, using drugs or alcohol (especially when they're upset), feeling anxious about pressures today or in the future, and feeling under pressure from family or peers. Young men are three times as likely to take their own life as their female peers, according to the Samaritans.

ENDNOTES

INTRODUCTION

1. Kahneman D, Krueger A B, Schkade D A, Schwarz N and Stone A A, A survey method for characterizing daily life experience: The day reconstruction method. *Science* (2004) 306(5702), 1776–80
2. www.nhs.gov/about/news/2024/08/28/us-surgeon-general-issues-advisory-mental-health-well-being-parents.html (accessed October 2024)
3. Gibran K, 'On Children' from *The Prophet* (2020) Alma Classics, London

CHAPTER 1

1. Wilkinson K, Ball S, Mitchell S B, Ukoumunne O C, O'Mahen H A, Tejerina-Arreal M, Hayes R, Berry V, Petrie I and Ford T, The longitudinal relationship between child emotional disorder and parental mental health in the British Child and Adolescent Mental Health surveys 1999 and 2004. *Journal of Affective Disorders* (2021) 288, 58–67
2. www.webuyanycar.com/about-us/press-centre/taxi-of-mum-and-dad/ (accessed October 2024)
3. Segal J, Teachers have enormous power in affecting a child's self-esteem. *The Brown University Child Behavior and Development Newsletter* (1988) 10, 1–3
4. Golombok, S, *We Are Family: What Really Matters for Parents and Children* (2020) Scribe Publications, London
5. Simmons C, Steinberg L, Frick P J and Cauffman E, The differential influence of absent and harsh fathers on juvenile delinquency. *Journal of Adolescence* (2018) 62, 9–17
6. Saglio T, in conversation with Rachel Kelly (2023)
7. Cui M and Donnellan M B, Trajectories of conflict over raising adolescent children and marital satisfaction. *Journal of Marriage and Family* (2009) 71(3), 478–494
8. Scharrer E, Warren S, Grimshaw E, Kamau G, Cho S, Reijven M and Zhang C, Disparaged dads? A content analysis of depictions of fathers in US sitcoms over time. *Psychology of Popular Media* (2021) 10(2), 275–287
9. www.ons.gov.uk/employmentandlabourmarket/peopleinwork/employment andemployeetypes/datasets/economicactivityandemploymenttypeformenand womenbyageoftheyoungestdependentchildlivingwiththemtables/current (accessed October 2023)

375

10. www.theguardian.com/lifeandstyle/2022/dec/25/number-of-stay-at-home-dads-in-uk-up-by-a-third-since-before-pandemic (accessed January 2024)

11. Atzil S, Hendler T, Zagoory-Sharon O, Winetraub Y and Feldman R, Synchrony and specificity in the maternal and the paternal brain: Relations to oxytocin and vasopressin. *Journal of the American Academy of Child and Adolescent Psychiatry* (2012) 51(8), 798–811

12. Willems Y E et al, Out of control: Examining the association between family conflict and self-control in adolescence in a genetically sensitive design. *Journal of the American Academy of Child and Adolescent Psychiatry* (2020) 59(2), 254–262

CHAPTER 2

1. Bowlby J, *Attachment and Loss: Attachment* (1969) Basic Books, New York

2. Byng-Hall J, *Rewriting Family Scripts: Improvisation and Systems Change* (1998) Guilford Press, New York

CHAPTER 3

1. Shan Xu C et al, A connectome of the adult drosophila central brain (2020); www.biorxiv.org/content/10.1101/2020.01.21.911859v1

2. Siegel DJ, *The Developing Mind: How Relationships and the Brain Interact to Shape Who We Are* (1999) Guilford Press, New York

3. Hanson R, *Hardwiring Happiness: The New Brain Science of Contentment, Calm, and Confidence* (2013) Harmony/Rodale, New York

4. Leahy RL, Holland SJF and McGinn LK, *Treatment Plans and Interventions for Depression and Anxiety Disorders* (2011) Guilford Press, New York

5. Siegel DJ and Payne Bryson T, *The Whole-Brain Child: 12 Proven Strategies to Nurture Your Child's Developing Mind* (2011) Random House, London

6. Gilbert P, *The Compassionate Mind: A New Approach to Life's Challenges* (2009) Little, Brown, London

CHAPTER 4

1. Nazari N, Perfectionism and mental health problems: Limitations and directions for future research. *World Journal of Clinical Cases* (2022) 10(14), 4709–4712

2. Winnicott DW, Transitional objects and transitional phenomena: A study of the first not-me possession. *International Journal of Psychoanalysis* (1953) 34(2), 89–97

3. Hewitt PL and Flett GL, Perfectionism in the self and social contexts: Conceptualization, assessment, and association with psychopathology. *Journal of Personality and Social Psychology* (1991) 60(3), 456–70

4. Hewitt PL, Flett GL, Turnbull-Donovan W and Mikail SF, The multidimensional perfectionism scale: Reliability, validity, and psychometric properties in psychiatric samples. *Psychological Assessment: A Journal of Consulting and Clinical Psychology* (1991) 3(3), 464–468

5. www.self-compassion.org/what-is-self-compassion/ (accessed October 2024)

6. Freeman H, *Good Girls: A Story and Study of Anorexia* (2023) Fourth Estate, London

7. Neff K, *Self-Compassion: The Proven Power of Being Kind to Yourself* (2011) HarperCollins, New York

8. Cleese J, *Creativity: A Short and Cheerful Guide* (2020) Cornerstone, London

9. Claxton, G, *Hare Brain, Tortoise Mind: Why Intelligence Increases When You Think Less* (1998) Fourth Estate, London

CHAPTER 5

1. Biddulph S, *Wild Creature Mind: The Neuroscience Breakthrough That Helps You Transform Anxiety and Live a Fierce and Loving Life* (2024) Bluebird, London

2. Starr LR, Hershenberg R, Shaw ZA, Li YI and Santee AC, The perils of murky emotions: Emotion differentiation moderates the prospective relationship between naturalistic stress exposure and adolescent depression. *Emotion* (2020) 20(6), 927–938

3. James W, *The Principles of Psychology Volume 1* (1890) Henry Holt, New York

4. Izard CE, *Human Emotions* (1977) Plenum Press, New York

5. Rosenberg M, *Nonviolent Communication: A Language of Life* (2003) PuddleDancer Press, Encinitas

6. iGrok app, download online at https://groktheworld.com

7. www.kristengygi.com (accessed October 2024)

8. www.ted.com/talks/brene_brown_the_power_of_vulnerability (accessed September 2023)

9. www.filialplaytherapy.co.uk/about_geraldine.html (accessed October 2024)

10. Gilbert P, *The Compassionate Mind: A New Approach to Life's Challenges* (2009) Little, Brown, London

11. Koschwanez HE, Kerse N, Darragh M, Jarrett P, Booth RJ and Broadbent E, Expressive writing and wound healing in older adults: A randomized controlled trial. *Psychosomatic Medicine* (2013) 75(6), 581–90

12. Ibid.

CHAPTER 6

1. www.who.int/europe/initiatives/health-behaviour-in-school-aged-children-(hbsc)-study (accessed October 2024)

2. Kelly R, *The Happy Kitchen: Good Mood Food* (2017) Short Books, London

3. Singh B, Olds T, Curtis R et al, Effectiveness of physical activity interventions for improving depression, anxiety and distress: An overview of systematic reviews. *British Journal of Sports Medicine* (2023) 57, 1203–1209

4. Sudo M and Ando S, Effects of acute stretching on cognitive function and mood states of physically inactive young adults. *Perceptual and Motor Skills* (2020) 127(1), 142–153

CHAPTER 7

1. Blakemore S-J, *Inventing Ourselves: The Secret Life of the Teenage Brain* (2018) Transworld Publishers, London

2. Ibid.

3. Foulkes L, *Coming of Age: How Adolescence Shapes Us* (2024) Penguin Random House, New York

4. Somerville LH, Jones RM, Ruberry EJ, Dyke JP, Glover G and Casey BJ, The medial prefrontal cortex and the emergence of self-conscious emotion in adolescence. *Psychological Science* (2013) 24(8), 1554–1562

5. Chein J, Albert D, O'Brien L, Uckert K and Steinberg L, Peers increase adolescent risk taking by enhancing activity in the brain's reward circuitry. *Developmental Science* (2011) 14(2), F1–10

6. Silva K, Chein J and Steinberg L, The influence of romantic partners on male risk-taking. *Journal of Social and Personal Relationships* (2020) 37(5), 1405–1415

7. www.gov.uk/government/publications/young-peoples-alcohol-consumption-and-its-relationship-to-other-outcomes-and-behaviour (accessed October 2024)

8. https://cls.ucl.ac.uk/wp-content/uploads/2018/01/Determinants-of-risky-behaviour-in-adolescence-Evidence-from-the-UK.pdf (accessed October 2024)

9. Barry JA, Do men take too many risks in relation to the environment and Covid-19? *Male Psychology* (2022) 1(6), 7–11

10. Friedman HS, Tucker JS, Tomlinson-Keasey C, Schwartz JE, Wingard DL and Criqui MH, Does childhood personality predict longevity? *Journal of Personality and Social Psychology* (1993) 65(1), 176–85

11. Logue S, Chein J, Gould T, Holliday E and Steinberg L, Adolescent mice, unlike adults, consume more alcohol in the presence of peers than alone. *Developmental Science* (2014) 17(1), 79–85

12. Foulkes L, Leung JT, Furhmann D, Knoll LJ and Blakemore S-J, Age differences in the prosocial influence effect. *Developmental Science* (2018) 21(6), e12666

13. Rosso IM, Young AD, Femia LA and Yurgelun-Todd DA, Cognitive and emotional components of frontal lobe functioning in childhood and adolescence. *Annals of the New York Academy of Sciences* (2004) 1021, 355–362

14. Diener E, Sandvik E and Larsen RJ, Age and sex effects for emotional intensity. *Developmental Psychology* (1985) 21(3), 542–546

15. Larson R, Csikszentmihalyi M and Graef R, Mood variability and the psychosocial adjustment of adolescents. *Journal of Youth and Adolescence* (1980) 9(6), 469–90

16. Barber BL, Jacobson KC, Miller KE and Petersen AC, Ups and downs: Daily cycles of adolescent moods. *New Directions for Child and Adolescent Development* (1998) 82, 23–36

17. Cole DA, Peeke L, Dolezal S, Murray N and Canzoniero A, A longitudinal study of negative affect and self-perceived competence in young adolescents. *Journal of Personality and Social Psychology* (1999) 77(4), 851–62

18. Nook EC, Sasse SF, Lambert HK, McLaughlin KA and Somerville LH, The nonlinear development of emotion differentiation: Granular emotional experience is low in adolescence. *Psychological Science* (2018) 29(8), 1346–1357

19. Barrett LF, Gross J, Christensen TC and Benvenuto M, Knowing what you're feeling and knowing what to do about it: Mapping the relation between emotion differentiation and emotion regulation. *Cognition and Emotion* (2001) 15(6), 713–724

20. Mogilner C, Kamvar SD and Aaker J, The shifting meaning of happiness. *Social Psychological and Personality Science* (2011) 2(4), 395–402

21. Foulkes L, Leung JT, Furhmann D, Knoll LJ and Blakemore S-J, Age differences in the prosocial influence effect. *Developmental Science* (2018) 21(6), e12666

22. Akshay S, Krishnan DA, Reichenberger SM, Strayer L, Master MA, Russell OM, Buxton LH and Chang A-M, Childhood sleep is prospectively associated with adolescent alcohol and marijuana use. *Annals of Epidemiology* (2024) 98, 25–31

23. O'Loughlin J, Casanova F, Jones SE et al, Using Mendelian randomisation methods to understand whether diurnal preference is causally related to mental health. *Molecular Psychiatry* (2021) 26, 6305–6316

24. Lund L, Sølvhøj IN, Danielsen D et al, Electronic media use and sleep in children and adolescents in Western countries: A systematic review. *BMC Public Health* (2021) 21, 1598

25. https://foodfoundation.org.uk/sites/default/files/2021-10/FF-Broken-Plate-2021.pdf (accessed October 2024)

26. Neri D, Steele EM, Khandpur N, Cediel G, Zapata ME, Rauber F, Marrón-Ponce JA, Machado P, da Costa Louzada ML, Andrade GC and Batis C, Ultraprocessed food consumption and dietary nutrient profiles associated with obesity: A multicountry study of children and adolescents. *Obesity Reviews* (2022) 23, e13387

27. Trafford AM, Carr MJ, Ashcroft DM, Chew-Graham CA, Cockcroft E, Cybulski L, Garavini E, Garg S, Kabir T, Kapur N, Temple RK, Webb RT and Mok PLH, Temporal trends in eating disorder and self-harm incidence rates among adolescents and young adults in the UK in the 2 years since onset of the Covid-19 pandemic: A population-based study. *The Lancet Child and Adolescent Health* (2023) 7(8), 544–554

28. Musick K and Meier A. Assessing causality and persistence in associations between family dinners and adolescent well-being. *Journal of Marriage and Family* (2012) Jun 1;74(3):476–493

29. www.oxfordshire.gov.uk/sites/default/files/file/virtual-school/adoptedandsgochildren ineducation.pdf (accessed October 2024)

30. Hopper SI, Murray SL, Ferrara LR and Singleton JK, Effectiveness of diaphragmatic breathing for reducing physiological and psychological stress in adults: A quantitative systematic review. *JBI Database of Systematic Reviews and Implementation Reports* (2019) 17(9), 1855–1876

31. Shahbaz A, Zaheer U and Abbas J, Parental expectations, self-control and risk taking behavior in adolescence. *Advanced Psychological Research* (2023) 1(1), 1–17

CHAPTER 8

1. www.civitas.org.uk/publications/teachers-or-parents-who-is-responsible-for-raising-the-next-generation/ (accessed October 2024)

2. Twenge JM and Park H, The decline in adult activities among US adolescents, 1976–2016. *Child Development* (2019) 90(2), 638–654

3. Erikson EH, *Identity and the Life Cycle* (1968) International Universities Press, New York

4. Neufeld G and Maté G, *Hold On to Your Kids: Why Parents Need to Matter More Than Peers* (2013) Knopf, Toronto

5. Ishizuka P, Social class, gender, and contemporary parenting standards in the United States: Evidence from a national survey experiment. *Social Forces* (2019) 98(1), 31–58

6. Dotti Sani, GM and Treas, J. Educational Gradients in Parents' Child-Care Time Across Countries, 1965–2012. *Journal of Marriage and Family* (2016) 78: 1083–1096

7. https://nurturescienceprogram.org/nsp-team/martha-welch/ (accessed October 2024)

8. Gibran K, 'On Children' from *The Prophet* (2020) Alma Classics, London

CHAPTER 9

1. Akhlaghi F, Transformative experience and the right to revelatory autonomy. *Analysis* (2023) 83(1), 3–12

2. https://matthewfray.com (accessed October 2024)

3. Gray P, Lancy DF and Bjorklund DF, Decline in independent activity as a cause of decline in children's mental well-being: Summary of the evidence. *Journal of Pediatrics* (2023) 260, 113352

4. Vigdal JS and Brønnick KK, A systematic review of 'helicopter parenting' and its relationship with anxiety and depression. *Frontiers in Psychology* (2022) 13, 872981

CHAPTER 10

1. Abrams DA, Mistry PK, Baker AE, Padmanabhan A and Menon V, A neurodevelopmental shift in reward circuitry from mother's to nonfamilial voices in adolescence. *Journal of Neuroscience* (2022) 42(20), 4164–4173
2. www.danielledick.com (accessed October 2024)
3. De Lillo M, Foley R, Fysh MC et al, Tracking developmental differences in real-world social attention across adolescence, young adulthood and older adulthood. *Nature Human Behaviour* (2021) 5, 1381–1390
4. Lorenz-Spreen P, Mønsted BM, Hövel P et al, Accelerating dynamics of collective attention. *Nature Communications* (2019) 10, 1759
5. Dreisoerner A, Junker NM, Schlotz W, Heimrich J, Bloemeke S, Ditzen B and van Dick R, Self-soothing touch and being hugged reduce cortisol responses to stress: A randomized controlled trial on stress, physical touch, and social identity. *Comprehensive Psychoneuroendocrinology* (2021) 8, 100091
6. http://filialplaytherapy.co.uk (accessed October 2024)
7. www.ncbi.nlm.nih.gov/books/NBK568743/#:~:text=Authoritative parenting is characterized by,tool rather than as punishment
8. Palminteri S, Kilford EJ, Coricelli G and Blakemore S-J, The computational development of reinforcement learning during adolescence. *PLoS Computational Biology* (2016) 12(6), e1004953

CHAPTER 11

1. Howard LH, Carrazza C and Woodward AL, Neighborhood linguistic diversity predicts infants' social learning. *Cognition* (2014) 133(2), 474–9
2. www.nytimes.com/2017/11/04/opinion/sunday/kids-would-you-please-start-fighting.html (accessed October 2024)
3. Koestner R, Walker M and Fichman L, Childhood parenting experiences and adult creativity. *Journal of Research in Personality* (1999) 33(1), 92–107
4. Mackinnon DW, Personality and the realization of creative potential. *American Psychologist* (1965) 20(4), 273–281
5. Bueno, J, in conversation with Rachel Kelly (2023); www.juliabueno.co.uk
6. www.estherperel.com/blog/letters-from-esther-36-fighting-with-your-partner-about-values (accessed October 2023)
7. Dube SR, Li ET, Fiorini G, Lin C, Singh N, Khamisa K, McGowan J and Fonagy P, Childhood verbal abuse as a child maltreatment subtype: A systematic review of the current evidence. *Child Abuse and Neglect* (2023) 144, 106394
8. Debey E, De Schryver M, Logan GD, Suchotzki K and Verschuere B, From junior to senior Pinocchio: A cross-sectional lifespan investigation of deception. *Acta Psychologica* (Amst) (2015) 160, 58–68

9. Allison BN and Schultz JB, Parent-adolescent conflict in early adolescence. *Adolescence* (2004) 39(153), 101–19

10. Eisenberg N, Hofer C, Spinrad TL, Gershoff ET, Valiente C, Losoya SH, Zhou Q, Cumberland A, Liew J, Reiser M and Maxon E, Understanding mother-adolescent conflict discussions: Concurrent and across-time prediction from youths' dispositions and parenting. *Monographs of the Society for Research in Child Development* (2008) 73(2), vii-viii, 1–160

CHAPTER 12

1. Dummer GM, The role of sports as a social status determinant for children. *Research Quarterly for Exercise and Sport* (1993) 63(4), 418–24

2. www.thetimes.com/life-style/parenting/article/teenagers-lost-generation-z-lucy-foulkes-interview-85pkw0kzh (accessed October 2024)

3. Saglio T, in conversation with Rachel Kelly (2023)

4. Himanshu, Kaur A, Kaur A and Singla G, Rising dysmorphia among adolescents: A cause for concern. *Journal of Family Medicine and Primary Care* (2020) 9(2), 567–570

5. Parker, LL and Harriger, JA. Eating disorders and disordered eating behaviors in the LGBT population: a review of the literature. *Journal of Eating Disorders* (2020) 8, 51

6. https://www.wsj.com/articles/facebook-knows-instagram-is-toxic-for-teen-girls-company-documents-show-11631620739 (accessed March 2025)

7. https://origympersonaltrainercourses.co.uk/blog/body-image-study (accessed October 2024)

8. Thai H, Davis C et al, Reducing social media use improves appearance and weight esteem in youth with emotional distress. *Psychology of Popular Media* (2023) 13(1), 162–169

9. Orbach S, *Bodies* (2009) Profile Books, London

10. West K, Think of the children! Relationships between nudity-related experiences in childhood, body image, self-esteem and adjustment. *Children and Society* (2023) 37, 1187–1202

11. Liu M, Wu L and Ming Q, How does physical activity intervention improve self-esteem and self-concept in children and adolescents? Evidence from a meta-analysis. *PLoS One* (2015) 10(8), e0134804

12. Recchia F, Bernal JDK, Fong DY et al, Physical activity interventions to alleviate depressive symptoms in children and adolescents: A systematic review and meta-analysis. *JAMA Pediatrics* (2023) 177(2), 132–140

13. www.bath.ac.uk/publications/talking-to-your-child-about-weight-a-guide-for-parents-and-caregivers-of-children-aged-4-11-years/attachments/talking-to-children-about-weight-guidance.pdf (accessed October 2024)

CHAPTER 13

1. Halpern CT and Haydon A A, Sexual timetables for oral-genital, vaginal, and anal intercourse: Sociodemographic comparisons in a nationally representative sample of adolescents. *American Journal of Public Health* (2012) 102(6), 1221–8

2. www.ons.gov.uk/peoplepopulationandcommunity/culturalidentity/sexuality/datasets/sexualidentityuk (accessed October 2023)

3. Herbenick D, Rosenberg M, Golzarri-Arroyo L et al, Changes in penile-vaginal intercourse frequency and sexual repertoire from 2009 to 2018: Findings from the national survey of sexual health and behavior. *Archives of Sexual Behavior* (2022) 51, 1419–1433

4. Twenge J M and Park H, The decline in adult activities among US adolescents, 1976–2016. *Child Development* (2019) 90(2), 638–654

5. Kelly Y, Zilanawala A, Tanton C, Lewis R and Mercer CH, Partnered intimate activities in early adolescence: Findings from the UK millennium cohort study. *Journal of Adolescent Health* (2019) 65(3), 397–404

6. www.howardstern.com/news/2021/12/13/billie-eilish-performs-2-songs-live-in-studio-and-opens-up-about-surviving-covid-and-hosting-snl/ (accessed November 2023)

7. https://mcc.gse.harvard.edu/reports/the-talk (accessed January 2025)

8. Palmer MJ, Clarke L, Ploubidis GB et al, Prevalence and correlates of 'sexual competence' at first heterosexual intercourse among young people in Britain. *BMJ Sexual and Reproductive Health* (2019) 45, 127–137

9. www.nuffieldtrust.org.uk/resource/teenage-pregnancy (accessed January 2024)

10. www.gov.uk/government/statistics/sexually-transmitted-infections-stis-annual-data-tables (accessed January 2024)

11. Gazendam N, Cleverley K, King N, Pickett W and Phillips SP, Individual and social determinants of early sexual activity: A study of gender-based differences using the 2018 Canadian Health Behaviour in School-aged Children Study (HBSC). *PLoS One* (2020) 15(9), e0238515

12. https://assets.childrenscommissioner.gov.uk/wpuploads/2022/12/cc-family-and-its-protective-effect-part-1-of-the-independent-family-review-.pdf (accessed January 2024)

13. www.bbfc.co.uk/about-us/news/children-see-pornography-as-young-as-seven-new-report-finds (accessed January 2024)

14. https://assets.childrenscommissioner.gov.uk/wpuploads/2023/02/cc-a-lot-of-it-is-actually-just-abuse-young-people-and-pornography-updated.pdf (accessed January 2024)

15. Thurman N and Obster F, The regulation of internet pornography: What a survey of under-18s tells us about the necessity for and potential efficacy of emerging legislative approaches. *Policy and Internet* (2021) 13, 415–432

16. Kuan H T, Senn C Y and Garcia D M, The role of discrepancies between online pornography created ideals and actual sexual relationships in heterosexual men's sexual satisfaction and well-being. *SAGE Open* (2022) 12(1) 21582440221

17. Park BY, Wilson G, Berger J, Christman M, Reina B, Bishop F, Klam W P and Doan A P, Is internet pornography causing sexual dysfunctions? A review with clinical reports. *Behavioral Sciences* (Basel) (2016) 6(3), 17. Erratum in: *Behavioral Sciences* (Basel) (2018) 8(6), 55

18. https://news.npcc.police.uk/releases/vkpp-launch-national-analysis-of-police-recorded-child-sexual-abuse-and-exploitation-csae-crimes-report-2022 (accessed January 2024)

19. https://digital.nhs.uk/data-and-information/publications/statistical/sexual-and-reproductive-health-services/2019-20/emergency-contraception2 (accessed September 2023)

20. Sheikh A, Payne-Cook C, Lisk S et al, Why do young men not seek help for affective mental health issues? A systematic review of perceived barriers and facilitators among adolescent boys and young men. *European Child and Adolescent Psychiatry* (14 July 2024)

21. www.ons.gov.uk/peoplepopulationandcommunity/crimeandjustice/articles/natureofsexualassaultbyrapeorpenetrationenglandandwales/yearendingmarch2020 (accessed August 2023)

22. https://rapecrisis.org.uk/get-informed/statistics-sexual-violence/ (accessed August 2023)

23. Perry L, *The Case Against the Sexual Revolution* (2022) Polity, Cambridge UK

24. Reeves R, *Of Boys and Men: Why the Modern Male is Struggling, Why It Matters, and What to Do about It* (2022) Swift Press, London

CHAPTER 14

1. www.ons.gov.uk/peoplepopulationandcommunity/culturalidentity/genderidentity/articles/genderidentityageandsexenglandandwalescensus2021/2023-01-25 (accessed October 2024)

2. https://cass.independent-review.uk/home/publications/final-report/ (accessed December 2024)

3. Freeman H, *Good Girls: A Story and Study of Anorexia* (2023) Fourth Estate, London

4. https://cass.independent-review.uk/home/publications/final-report/ (accessed December 2024)

5. Ibid.

6. https://www.england.nhs.uk/wp-content/uploads/2024/08/PRN01451-ehia-cyp-gender-service-service-specification-national-referral-support-service.pdf (accessed March 2025)

7. Warrier V, Greenberg DM, Weir E, Buckingham C, Smith P, Lai MC, Allison C, Baron-Cohen S. Elevated rates of autism, other neurodevelopmental and psychiatric diagnoses, and autistic traits in transgender and gender-diverse individuals. *Nature Communications* (2020) 11, 3959

8. Ibid.

9. www.washingtonpost.com/outlook/2021/11/24/trans-kids-therapy-psychologist/ (accessed October 2024)

10. www.reuters.com/investigates/special-report/usa-transyouth-care/ (accessed October 2024)

11. Wallien M and Cohen-Kettenis P, Psychosexual outcome of gender-disphoric children. *Journal of the American Academy of Child and Adolescent Psychiatry* 47(12), 1413–23

CHAPTER 15

1. Kramer L, Conger KJ. What we learn from our sisters and brothers: for better or for worse. *New Directions for Child and Adolescent Development* (2009) Winter (126): 1–12

2. McHale SM, Updegraff KA and Whiteman SD, Sibling relationships and influences in childhood and adolescence. *Journal of Marriage and Family* (2012) 74(5), 913–930

3. Stormshak EA, Bullock BM and Falkenstein CA, Harnessing the power of sibling relationships as a tool for optimizing social-emotional development. *New Directions for Child and Adolescent Development* (2009) 126, 61–77

4. Downey DB and Cao R, Number of siblings and mental health among adolescents: Evidence from the U.S. and China. *Journal of Family Issues* (2023) 45(11), 2822–2850

5. Franklin B, Higgs E, Bartelt K and Sandberg N. Firstborn Children and Only Children More Likely to Have Anxiety and Depression Than Later-Born Children. *Epic Research* (2024) https://epicresearch.org/articles/firstborn-children-and-only-children-more-likely-to-have-anxiety-and-depression-than-later-born-children (accessed March 2025)

6. Whiteman SD, McHale SM and Soli A. Theoretical Perspectives on Sibling Relationships. *Journal of Family Theory & Review* (2011) Jun 1; 3(2): 124–139

7. Kramer L and Conger KJ, What we learn from our sisters and brothers: For better or for worse. *New Directions for Child and Adolescent Development* (2009) 126, 1–12

8. Whiteman SD, McHale SM and Soli A. Theoretical Perspectives on Sibling Relationships. *Journal of Family Theory & Review* (2011) Jun 1; 3(2): 124–139

9. Whiteman SD, McHale SM and Soli A. Theoretical Perspectives on Sibling Relationships. *Journal of Family Theory & Review* (2011) Jun 1; 3(2): 124–139

10. Loeser MK, Whiteman SD and McHale SM, Siblings' perceptions of differential treatment, fairness, and jealousy and adolescent adjustment: A moderated indirect effects model. *Journal of Child and Family Studies* (2016) 25(8), 2405–2414

11. www.ons.gov.uk/peoplepopulationandcommunity/birthsdeathsandmarriages/families/bulletins/familiesandhouseholds/2022 (accessed October 2024)

12. Bohannon EW, The only child in a family. *The Pedagogical Seminary* (1898) 5(4), 475–496

13. Kowal M, Groyecka-Bernard A, Kochan-Wójcik M and Sorokowski P, When and how does the number of children affect marital satisfaction? An international survey. *PLoS One* (2021) 16(4), e0249516

14. Franklin B, Higgs E, Bartelt K and Sandberg N. Firstborn Children and Only Children More Likely to Have Anxiety and Depression Than Later-Born Children. *Epic Research* (2024) https://epicresearch.org/articles/firstborn-children-and-only-children-more-likely-to-have-anxiety-and-depression-than-later-born-children (accessed March 2025)

15. Falbo T, Only children and interpersonal behavior: An experimental and survey study. *Journal of Applied Social Psychology* (1978) 8(3), 244–253

16. Claudy JG, 'The only child as a young adult: Results from Project Talent' in Falbo T (ed) *The Single Child Family* (1984) Guilford Press, New York

CHAPTER 16

1. Kawamichi, H, Sugawara, S, Hamano, Y *et al*. Increased frequency of social interaction is associated with enjoyment enhancement and reward system activation. *Scientific Reports* (2016) 6, 24561

2. Chaudhary N and Swanepoel A, Editorial Perspective: What can we learn from hunter-gatherers about children's mental health? An evolutionary perspective. *Journal of Child Psychology and Psychiatry* (2023) 64(10), 1522–5

3. www.ons.gov.uk/peoplepopulationandcommunity/birthsdeathsandmarriages/families/bulletins/familiesandhouseholds/2022 (accessed January 2024)

4. www.ethnicity-facts-figures.service.gov.uk/workforce-and-business/workforce-diversity/school-teacher-workforce/latest/ (accessed January 2024)

5. Brown KM, Hoye R and Nicholson M, Self-esteem, self-efficacy, and social connectedness as mediators of the relationship between volunteering and well-being. *Journal of Social Service Research* (2012) 38(4), 468–83

6. Pilkington PD, Windsor TD and Crisp DA, Volunteering and subjective wellbeing in midlife and older adults: The role of supportive social networks. *The Journals of Gerontology – Series B Psychological Sciences and Social Sciences* (2012) 67(2), 249–60

7. Prinstein M, *Popular* (2018) Penguin, London
8. Kross E, Berman MG, Mischel W, Smith EE and Wager TD, Social rejection shares somatosensory representations with physical pain. *Proceedings of the National Academy of Sciences USA* (2011) 108(15), 6270–5
9. Prinstein M, *Popular* (2018) Penguin, London
10. McKenzie SK, Collings S, Jenkin G and River J, Masculinity, social connectedness, and mental health: Men's diverse patterns of practice. *American Journal of Men's Health* (2018) 12(5), 1247–1261
11. www.nytimes.com/2022/11/28/well/family/male-friendship-loneliness.html (accessed September 2023)
12. Hankin BL, Stone L and Wright PA. Corumination, interpersonal stress generation, and internalizing symptoms: accumulating effects and transactional influences in a multiwave study of adolescents. *Development and Psychopathology* (2010) Winter; 22(1): 217–35
13. www.thetimes.com/article/you-dont-understand-me-how-to-talk-to-your-teenager-w5jzdvwk7 (accessed September 2023)
14. www.mentalhealth.org.uk/our-work/public-engagement/unlock-loneliness/loneliness-young-people-research-briefing (accessed September 2023)
15. https://news.ucr.edu/articles/2019/09/16/research-suggests-happiest-introverts-may-be-extraverts (accessed September 2023)
16. www.ft.com/content/8b9f34c3-7a41-4038-a1c4-4a9585866632 (accessed September 2023)
17. https://news.uchicago.edu/story/qa-prof-john-cacioppo-examines-profound-power-loneliness (accessed September 2023)
18. Moran C, *What About Men?* (2023) Ebury, London
19. Swerbenski KL, Barnett KC, Devine PG and Shutts K, Making 'fast friends' online in middle childhood and early adolescence. *Social Development* (2024) 33(1), e12708

CHAPTER 17

1. https://www.uclahealth.org/news/release/study-finds-childhood-bullying-linked-distrust-and-mental (accessed March 2025)
2. Olweus DA, Bully/victim problems in school: Facts and intervention. *European Journal of Psychology of Education* (1977) 12(4), 495–510
3. https://youthendowmentfund.org.uk/reports/children-violence-and-vulnerability-2023/ (accessed January 2024)
4. Schoeler T, Choi SW, Dudbridge F et al, Multi-polygenic score approach to identifying individual vulnerabilities associated with the risk of exposure to bullying. *JAMA Psychiatry* (2019) 76(7), 730–738

5. Bayram Özdemir S, Caravita SCS and Thornberg R, Bias-based harassment and bullying: Addressing mechanisms and outcomes for possible interventions. *European Journal of Developmental Psychology* (2024) 21(4), 505–519

6. https://steer.education/wp-content/uploads/2022/02/Young-Peoples-Mental-Health-in-the-UK-STEER-Report-Feb-2022.pdf (accessed January 2024)

7. Logan K and Cuff S, Council on sports medicine and fitness. Organized sports for children, preadolescents, and adolescents. *Pediatrics* (20 May 2019) e20190997

8. www.who.int/europe/news/item/27-03-2024-one-in-six-school-aged-children-experiences-cyberbullying-finds-new-who-europe-study (accessed January 2024)

9. www.pewresearch.org/internet/2022/12/15/teens-and-cyberbullying-2022/ (accessed January 2024)

10. www.spectator.co.uk/article/dr-jean-twenge-gen-z-arent-ok/ (accessed January 2024)

11. Suler J, The online disinhibition effect. *Cyberpsychology and Behavior* (2004) 7(3), 321–6

CHAPTER 18

1. Slattery J, in conversation with Rachel Kelly (2023)

2. Fisher H, Aron A and Brown LL, Romantic love: An fMRI study of a neural mechanism for mate choice. *Journal of Comparative Neurology* (2005) 493(1), 58–62

3. Price M, Hides L, Cockshaw W, Staneva AA and Stoyanov SR, Young love: Romantic concerns and associated mental health issues among adolescent help-seekers. *Behavioral Science* (Basel) (2016) 6(2), 9

4. Fleming CB, White HR, Oesterle S, Haggerty KP and Catalano RF, Romantic relationship status changes and substance use among 18–20-year-olds. *Journal of Studies on Alcohol and Drugs* (2010) 71(6), 847–56

5. https://counseling.northwestern.edu/blog/how-to-help-teen-experiencing-breakup/ (accessed November 2024)

CHAPTER 19

1. Sheats KJ, Irving SM, Mercy JA, Simon TR, Crosby AE, Ford DC, Merrick MT, Annor FB and Morgan RE, Violence-related disparities experienced by black youth and young adults: Opportunities for prevention. *American Journal of Preventative Medicine* (2018) 55(4), 462–469

2. Watson C and Egberongbe R, *No Filters: A Mother and Teenage Daughter Love Story* (2025) Chatto & Windus, London

3. www.tes.com/magazine/archive/two-thirds-parents-say-exam-stress-affects-mental-health (accessed January 2024)

4. https://resolutionfoundation.org/app/uploads/2017/02/IC-intra-gen.pdf (accessed August 2023)

5. www.cambridgeassessment.org.uk/Images/698454-sex-gaps-in-education-in-england.pdf (accessed January 2024)

6. Voyer D and Voyer SD, Gender differences in scholastic achievement: A meta-analysis. *Psychological Bulletin* (2014) 140(4), 1174–204

7. Krist A H, Tong ST, Aycock R A and Longo DR, Engaging patients in decision-making and behavior change to promote prevention. *Studies in Health Technology and Informatics* (2017) 240, 284–302

8. Grant A, *Hidden Potential: The Science of Achieving Greater Things* (2023) Ebury, London

9. Ciciolla L, Curlee A S, Karageorge J et al, When mothers and fathers are seen as disproportionately valuing achievements: Implications for adjustment among upper middle class youth. *Journal of Adolescence* (2017) 46, 1057–1075

10. Lukianoff G and Haidt J, *The Coddling of the American Mind: How Good Intentions and Bad Ideas Are Setting Up a Generation For Failure* (2018) Penguin Books, London

11. www.ons.gov.uk/peoplepopulationandcommunity/crimeandjustice/bulletins/crimeinenglandandwales/yearendingmarch2024 (accessed October 2024)

12. www.reuters.com/world/britains-king-charles-push-global-action-climate-cop28-speech-2023-12-01/ (accessed October 2024)

13. Hickman C, Marks E, Pihkala P, Clayton S, Lewandowski R E, Mayall EE, Wray B, Mellor C and van Susteren L, Climate anxiety in children and young people and their beliefs about government responses to climate change: A global survey. *The Lancet Planetary Health* (2021) 5(12), e863–e873

14. www.childrenssociety.org.uk/sites/default/files/2022-09/GCR-2022-Full-Report.pdf (accessed November 2024)

15. Philippa Perry writing in *The Sunday Times Magazine*, 26 January 2025

CHAPTER 20

1. www.ofcom.org.uk/media-use-and-attitudes/online-habits/top-trends-from-our-latest-look-at-peoples-online-lives/ (accessed August 2023)

2. Vuorre M and Przybylski A K, Estimating the association between Facebook adoption and wellbeing in 72 countries. *Royal Society Open Science* (2023) 10(8), 221451

3. Haidt J, *The Anxious Generation: How the Great Rewiring of Childhood Is Causing an Epidemic of Mental Illness* (2024) Penguin Random House, New York

4. Bozzola E, Spina G, Agostiniani R, Barni S, Russo R, Scarpato E, Di Mauro A, Di Stefano AV, Caruso C, Corsello G and Staiano A, The use of social media in children

and adolescents: Scoping review on the potential risks. *International Journal of Environmental Research and Public Health* (2022) 19(16), 9960

5. www.newstatesman.com/technology/2023/03/jonathan-haidt-social-media-dangerous-teenage-girls-anxiety-depression (accessed August 2023)

6. www.cdc.gov/healthyyouth/data/yrbs/pdf/YRBS_Data-Summary-Trends_Report2023_508.pdf (accessed August 2023)

7. www.statista.com/chart/9157/instagram-monthly-active-users/ (accessed August 2023)

8. Khouja JN, Munafò MR, Tilling K et al, Is screen time associated with anxiety or depression in young people? Results from a UK birth cohort. *BMC Public Health* (2019) 19(1), 82

9. Santos RMS, Mendes CG, Sen Bressani G et al, The associations between screen time and mental health in adolescents: A systematic review. *BMC Psychology* (2023) 11, 127

10. Chao M, Lei J, He R, Jiang Y and Yang H, TikTok use and psychosocial factors among adolescents: Comparisons of non-users, moderate users, and addictive users. *Psychiatry Research* (2023) 325, 115247

11. Maza MT, Fox KA, Kwon S et al, Association of habitual checking behaviors on social media with longitudinal functional brain development. *JAMA Pediatrics* (2023) 177(2), 160–167

12. Neufeld G and Maté G, *Hold On to Your Kids: Why Parents Need to Matter More Than Peers* (2013) Knopf, Toronto

13. Stagg N, *Artless: Stories 2019–2023* (2023) MIT Press, Massachusetts

14. www.iabuk.com/news-article/uk-youngsters-online-7-hours-day (accessed August 2023)

15. www.ofcom.org.uk/media-use-and-attitudes/media-habits-children/children-and-parents-media-use-and-attitudes-report-2023/ (accessed August 2023)

16. Twenge JM, Haidt J, Blake AB, McAllister C, Lemon H and Le Roy A, Worldwide increases in adolescent loneliness. *Journal of Adolescence* (2021) 93, 257–269

17. Hunt MG, Marx R, Lipson C and Young J, No more FOMO: Limiting social media decreases loneliness and depression. *Journal of Social and Clinical Psychology* (2018) 37(10), 751–768

CHAPTER 21

1. www.ons.gov.uk/peoplepopulationandcommunity/healthandsocialcare/drugusealcoholandsmoking/bulletins/opinionsandlifestylesurveyadultdrinkinghabitsingreatbritain/2005to2016 (accessed August 2023)

2. www.who.int/europe/news/item/25-04-2024-alcohol-e-cigarettes-cannabis-concerning-trends-in-adolescent-substance-use-shows-new-who-europe-report (accessed August 2023)

3. www.ons.gov.uk/peoplepopulationandcommunity/crimeandjustice/articles/ drugmisuseinenglandandwales/yearendingmarch2023 (accessed August 2023)

4. www.who.int/europe/news/item/25-04-2024-alcohol-e-cigarettes-cannabis-concerning-trends-in-adolescent-substance-use-shows-new-who-europe-report (accessed August 2023)

5. https://socialmobility.independent-commission.uk/press_releases/young-people-face-troubling-challenges-to-social-mobility-commission-reveals/ (accessed August 2023)

6. www.who.int/europe/news/item/25-04-2024-alcohol-e-cigarettes-cannabis-concerning-trends-in-adolescent-substance-use-shows-new-who-europe-report (accessed August 2023)

7. www.crimeandjustice.org.uk/sites/crimeandjustice.org.uk/files/Estimating%20 drug%20harms.pdf (accessed August 2023)

8. www.drinkaware.co.uk/media/qnbjblqm/drinkaware_impact_report_2012.pdf (accessed August 2023)

9. Wise J, Childhood should be alcohol free, says England's chief medical officer. *British Medical Journal* (2009) 339, b5537

10. Sigman A, Paediatricians can reduce future alcohol-related morbidity and mortality. *Archives of Disease in Childhood* (2023) 108(11), 897–898

11. Hingson RW, Heeren T and Winter MR, Age at drinking onset and alcohol dependence: Age at onset, duration, and severity. *Archives of Pediatrics and Adolescent Medicine* (2006) 160(7), 739–746

12. www.telegraph.co.uk/news/2024/04/25/child-alcohol-consumption-england-record-lockdown/ (accessed November 2024)

13. Rosenthal R and Jacobson L, Pygmalion in the classroom. *The Urban Review* (1968) 3, 16–20

CHAPTER 22

1. https://digital.nhs.uk/data-and-information/publications/statistical/mental-health-of-children-and-young-people-in-england/2022-follow-up-to-the-2017-survey/ introduction (accessed August 2023)

2. Ibid.

3. www.youngminds.org.uk/about-us/media-centre/press-releases/yearly-referrals-to-young-people-s-mental-health-services-have-risen-by-53-since-2019/ (accessed August 2023)

4. Bölte S, Neufeld J, Marschik PB, Williams ZJ, Gallagher L and Lai MC, Sex and gender in neurodevelopmental conditions. *Nature Reviews Neurology* (2023) 19(3), 136–159

5. https://steer.education/wp-content/uploads/2022/02/Young-Peoples-Mental-Health-in-the-UK-STEER-Report-Feb-2022.pdf (accessed August 2023)

6. https://assets.childrenscommissioner.gov.uk/wpuploads/2021/11/occ_the_big_ask_the_big_answer_2021.pdf (accessed August 2023)

7. www.papyrus-uk.org/latest-statistics/#:~:text=Suicide is the main cause,take their lives each day (accessed January 2024)

8. Kessler RC, Berglund P, Demler O, Jin R, Merikangas KR and Walters EE, Lifetime prevalence and age-of-onset distributions of DSM-IV disorders in the national comorbidity survey replication. *Archives of General Psychiatry* (2005) 62(6), 593–602

9. www.centreforsocialjustice.org.uk/wp-content/uploads/2023/12/CSJ-Two_Nations.pdf (accessed January 2024)

10. Lukianoff G and Haidt J, *The Coddling of the American Mind: How Good Intentions and Bad Ideas Are Setting Up a Generation For Failure* (2018) Penguin Books, London

11. https://mayerhillman.wordpress.com/wp-content/uploads/2014/09/cim_final_report_v9_3_final1.pdf (accessed January 2024)

12. www.thehighperformancepodcast.com/podcast/jonny-wilkinson (accessed January 2024)

13. Gimbrone C, Bates LM, Prins SJ and Keyes KM, The politics of depression: Diverging trends in internalizing symptoms among US adolescents by political beliefs. *SSM Mental Health* (2022) 2, 100043

14. Lut I, Woodman J, Armitage A, Ingram E, Harron K and Hardelid P, Health outcomes, healthcare use and development in children born into or growing up in single-parent households: A systematic review study protocol. *BMJ Open* (2021) 11(2), e043361

15. Freeman H, *Good Girls: A Story and Study of Anorexia* (2023) Fourth Estate, London

16. Soneson E, Puntis S, Chapman N, Mansfield KL, Jones PB and Fazel M, Happier during lockdown: A descriptive analysis of self-reported wellbeing in 17,000 UK school students during Covid-19 lockdown. *European Child and Adolescent Psychiatry* (2023) 32(6), 1131–1146

17. Foulkes L and Andrews J, Are mental health awareness efforts contributing to the rise in reported mental health problems? A call to test the prevalence inflation hypothesis. *New Ideas in Psychology* (2023) 69, 101010

18. www.3dadswalking.uk (accessed January 2024)

19. www.dailymail.co.uk/femail/article-12183359/Three-fathers-lost-daughters-demand-action-Rishi-Sunak.html (accessed January 2024)

20. https://media.nhsbsa.nhs.uk/press-releases/5171d616-95ea-4282-959b-15f8bfed6a0f/nhs-releases-2023-24-mental-health-medicines-statistics-for-england (accessed January 2025)

21. www.spectator.co.uk/article/how-real-is-your-adhd/ (accessed January 2025)

22. www.gov.uk/government/statistics/access-arrangements-for-gcse-as-and-a-level-2023-to-2024-academic-year (accessed January 2025)

23. Kustow J, *How to Thrive with Adult ADHD* (2024) Ebury, London

24. O'Nions E et al, Autism in England: Assessing underdiagnosis in a population-based cohort study of prospectively collected primary care data. The Lancet Regional Health – Europe (2023) 29, 100626

25. www.childrenscommissioner.gov.uk/resource/waiting-times-for-assessment-and-support-for-autism-adhd-and-other-neurodevelopmental-conditions (accessed January 2025)

CHAPTER 23

1. www.politicshome.com/thehouse/article/child-adolescent-mental-health-care-crisis (accessed January 2024)

2. Li K, Zhou G, Xiao Y, Gu J, Chen Q, Xie S and Wu J, Risk of suicidal behaviors and antidepressant exposure among children and adolescents: A meta-analysis of observational studies. *Frontiers in Psychology* (2022) 13, 880496

3. https://evidence.nihr.ac.uk/collection/antidepressants-for-children-and-teenagers-what-works-anxiety-depression/ (accessed January 2024)

4. www.bbc.co.uk/programmes/m001n39z; The Antidepressant Story (accessed January 2024)

5. https://tedxsanantonio.com/2010-speakers/alicia-arenas/ (accessed January 2024)

6. Colizzi M, Lasalvia A and Ruggeri M, Prevention and early intervention in youth mental health: Is it time for a multidisciplinary and trans-diagnostic model for care? *International Journal of Mental Health Systems* (2020) 14, 23

7. https://mhfaengland.org/mhfa-centre/research-and-evaluation/mental-health-statistics/ (accessed August 2023)

8. Gibran K, 'On Children' from *The Prophet* (2020) Alma Classics, London

GLOSSARY OF MENTAL HEALTH CONDITIONS

1. Salari N, Ghasemi H, Abdoli N et al, The global prevalence of ADHD in children and adolescents: A systematic review and meta-analysis. *Italian Journal of Pediatrics* (2023) 49, 48

2. https://digital.nhs.uk/data-and-information/publications/statistical/mental-health-of-children-and-young-people-in-england/2023-wave-4-follow-up/part-5-eating-problems-and-disorders (accessed January 2024)
3. Conversation with author, 2024
4. https://www.mentalhealth.org.uk/about-us/news/young-people-most-likely-feel-anxious-according-our-recent-survey (accessed January 2024)
5. www.bma.org.uk/what-we-do/population-health/improving-the-health-of-specific-groups/autism-spectrum-disorder (accessed January 2024)
6. https://assets.publishing.service.gov.uk/government/uploads/system/uploads/attachment_data/file/556596/apms-2014-full-rpt.pdf (accessed January 2024)
7. https://files.digital.nhs.uk/FB/8EA993/MHCYP%202017%20Less%20Common%20Disorders.pdf (accessed November 2023)
8. https://digital.nhs.uk/data-and-information/publications/statistical/mental-health-of-children-and-young-people-in-england/2023-wave-4-follow-up/part-5-eating-problems-and-disorders (accessed January 2024)
9. www.nice.org.uk/guidance/cg158 (accessed January 2024)
10. https://files.digital.nhs.uk/14/0E2282/MHCYP%202017%20Emotional%20Disorders.pdf (accessed November 2023)
11. Feng W, Ramo DE, Chan SR and Bourgeois JA, Internet gaming disorder: Trends in prevalence 1998–2016. *Addictive Behaviors* (2017) 75, 17–24
12. www.ocduk.org/ocd/how-common-is-ocd/ (accessed January 2024)
13. www.nice.org.uk/guidance/cg155/resources/psychosis-and-schizophrenia-in-children-and-young-people-final-scope2 (accessed January 2024)
14. www.rcpsych.ac.uk/mental-health/parents-and-young-people/schizophrenia-information-for-young-people (accessed January 2024)
15. Stallard P, Spears M, Montgomery AA, Phillips R and Sayal K, Self-harm in young adolescents (12–16 years): Onset and short-term continuation in a community sample. *BMC Psychiatry* (2013) 2(13) 328
16. https://papyrus-uk.org/latest-statistics/ (accessed January 2024)

ACKNOWLEDGEMENTS

Most of this book is personal, and written from the perspective of my own development as an older, and I hope wiser, mother. But it also reflects what I have gleaned about the psychological wellbeing of other parents and their children from my work as someone who writes about mental health. I am an ambassador for SANE and Rethink Mental Illness, as well as being an affiliate of King's College London's psychiatry department. I have met and worked with hundreds of parents and their teenagers, running wellbeing workshops in schools for the past five years. As I've told my story about my experience of depression and recovery, I've heard their stories. I've listened to the doubts and fears of parents and teenagers, which have taught me the life lessons that inform this book – ways to turn down the worry dial and to turn up the enjoyment button. My thanks to all of them, many of them quoted here, for trusting me with their stories, largely in confidence. I have especially benefited from a decade-long conversation with Dr Carla Croft, a mother of three and a consultant clinical psychologist who works at one of the UK's largest NHS Trusts. Many of the ideas and indeed phrases in the book reflect her wisdom and insights.

My thanks to the following in particular, a mix of parents, therapists, teachers, friends and experts in the field of adolescent mental health: Julia Bueno, Helena Cox, Caroline Cox-Johnson, Baroness Jenkin, Clare Kelly, Jane Lunnon, Constance Marquis, Luke Montagu, Lottie Moore, Mary Louise Morris, Charlotte Ridings, Dr Hester Riviere, Tara Saglio, Kate Schlesinger, Sir Anthony Seldon, Jimi Slattery, Tanya Steyn, Flora Taylor, Dr Geraldine Thomas and Miranda Thomas. I especially leaned on the expertise of Dr Gordana Milavić, a Consultant Child and Adolescent Psychiatrist at the Maudsley Hospital in London. My daughter Dr Katherine Grigg, a junior doctor, was an endless source of wisdom on medical and psychological matters.

On the editorial front, I am indebted to Asya Likhtman, who helped me with research as well as tracking down references, while Eliza Hoyer Millar remains the best editor I know. My literary agent Elizabeth Sheinkman waited patiently for this book, on hand with support and wise counsel at every stage. My thanks to my publisher Jo Morrell and her team at Hachette, including Leanne Bryan, for having faith in me and this book, and giving it, in Jo's words, 'Everything we've got'.

Last – and never least – my family: Edward, George, the aforementioned Katherine, Charlotte and Arthur were the inspiration for this book, no longer teenagers but always the joy of my life. And to Sebastian, for everything, as always.

INDEX

A

academic pressures 276–85; exams 282–3; high achievers 277–80; underachievers 280–2

acceptance 72, 114, 164–6

ADHD 323–5, 358–9g

adolescence 111–13; *see also* brain: teenage; sex(uality)

adolescents: *see* teenagers

adult role models 230–4

affirmations 45, 58

Akhlaghi, Farbod 124

alcohol use: *see* drinking

altruism 97, 233, 244, 284–5

amygdala 37

Anderson, Erica 213

anger 27–8, 68–9, 148–9, 364

anorexia 321, 331, 359–60g

antidepressants 336

anxiety 7, 286, 318, 360–1g; parents: about safety 51, 285–6; parents: projection of 3–4; reducing 84, 123–5, 311; teenagers: eco-anxiety 287; *see also* mental health; stress

appearance 159–71; conversations about 166–9; fitting in 160–1; parental support 163–9; puberty 161; self-acceptance 164–6; social media 162–4, 292–3; stereotypical ideals 159, 161

approval, seeking 58

arguments 145–6, 154–5; debating 146–8; language used 150–1; lying 153–4; resolving 151–3; rows 148–50; *see also* conflict

attachment styles 23–5

attention-seeking behaviour 137–9

autism 325, 361–2g

automatic thoughts: awareness of 39–41; identifying 41–3

autonomy: *see* independence, encouraging

B

behaviour: attention-seeking 137–9; boundaries 28, 141–4; reinforcing positives 127–8, 149, 151; risk taking 94–5, 106–8, 286, 301–5; *see also* conflict

beliefs: core beliefs 25, 36; negative 41–3; perfectionism 57; self-belief 165, 213, 241, 256

belonging, need to 73, 112, 207, 291, 293, 294, 303–4

Biddulph, Steve 68

bipolar disorder 362g

birth control 189

bisexual teenagers 162, 171–2, 183

blaming others 43, 49

Bliss, Shepherd 190

body image 162, 168–9; and pornography 185; and social media 162–4; teenage girls 202; *see also* appearance boundaries 28, 141–4

Bowlby, John 24

brain 35–6; of children 93; fight, flight, freeze or fawn response 36–7; hippocampus 146–7; hypothalamus 97; of mothers vs fathers 18–19; negativity bias 38; neural pathways 39, 41, 46, 48, 93–4; neuroplasticity 39; prefrontal lobe development 94, 96; right and left hemispheres 68

brain: teenage 93–107, 235–7, 266; abstract thinking 96; and alcohol 308; and drugs 302–3; emotional centres dominate 96; fight, flight, freeze or fawn response 104; heightened empathy 96; and learning 281–2; and negative thinking 283–5; new experiences and learning 95, 106–8; peer pressure 95–6, 106–8; prefrontal lobe development 94, 96, 108, 109, 302; regulating emotions 103–6; and risk taking 94–5, 106–8; and romance 265–6; and sleep 98–100

break-ups 263–70

breathing exercises 75–6, 87

Bueno, Julia 33, 149, 227

bulimia 363g

bullying 249–51, 261; building resilience 255–8; getting help 252–3; online 258–61; parental responses 252–5, 260; see also mental health

C

caffeine 103

calmness, importance of 2, 4

CAMHS (Child and Adolescent Mental Health Services) 332–4

cannabis use 299, 300

Cass Report (2024) 210, 212

catastrophizing 41–2, 43–4

CBT (cognitive behavioural therapy) 41–3, 334, 337–8

childhood memories 25–8

classical conditioning 69

climate crisis 287

clinical nurse specialists 334

clinical psychologists 334

co-parents 15–16; differences of opinion 16, 18–19; different skills of 18–19; relationship with teens 20–1; working together 16–20

cognitive distortions 41–5

communication 131–3, 145–6; about pornography 186–9; about sex/sexuality 173–4, 176–82; attention-seeking behaviour 137–9; boys vs girls 134–5; interest in their technology 133–4; limitations to 139–40; listening skills 116, 125, 126–7, 135–7; mobile phones 133–4; parental needs and boundaries 141–3; SLANT method 116, 131; timing of 136; see also conflict

comparison with others 53

Compassion Focused Therapy 46, 59, 338

competitive culture 53, 175, 221, 276

conduct disorder 364g

conflict: arguments 145–6, 154–5; debating 146–8; dislike of 27–8; between parents 20–1; between siblings 222–5; see also bullying

connecting with teenagers 109–20; importance of parental support 113–15; individuation and peer relationships 110, 111–13; quality of interactions 115–18; redefining the relationship 118–20

consent 180–4, 194

conversation, art of 242–5

core beliefs 25

corrective scripts 29–30

counselling 337–9; CBT (cognitive behavioural therapy) 41–3, 334, 337–8; Compassion Focused Therapy 46, 59, 338
Covid pandemic 95, 101, 229, 277, 289, 321–2
cyberbullying 258–61

D

debating 146–8
depression 327, 365g
dichotomous thinking 42–3
Dick, Danielle 132
diet and nutrition 84–5, 87–8, 100–3, 169–70
digital world 289–91; appeal of 291–3; benefits of 293–4; digital detox 295; and mental health 320–1; parental responses 293–8; smartphones 133–4, 289–91, 320–1; *see also* social media
discounting positives 42
divorce 15, 19–20, 320–1; *see also* single parents
dopamine 104, 105, 302, 303
drinking 299–300, 307–8; parental responses 307–12; responsible drinking 310–12
drug use 299–301; attraction of 302–3; parental responses 303–4

E

eating disorders 101, 290, 321, 331
eco-anxiety 287
economic growth, fixation with 52
education: *see* academic pressures
embarrassment 68–9
emotional differentiation 96
emotional dysregulation 69
emotional intimacy: with own parents 26, 30; with teens 32
emotional reasoning 43

emotional regulation 69–71, 121–5
emotions 67–8; accepting 72; benefits of 73–5; Compassion Focused Therapy 46; definition of 68–9; emotional intensity 96; expressed physically 68–9; and food 84–5; identifying 70; overwhelming 69; parasympathetic nervous system 75–8; provide insight 74–5; regulating 69–71, 75–8, 96–7, 103–6; validating 125–7; and vulnerability 73–4; window of tolerance 37
enmeshment, avoiding 28
Erikson, Erik 112–13
exam pressure 277, 280, 282–5
exercise 82–4, 117–18, 169–70, 242
eye contact 134–5

F

Facebook 290
facial expressions 68–9
failure 62–4, 104–5
family scripts 29–32; corrective scripts 29–30; improvised scripts 30, 31–2; replicative scripts 29, 30
family support workers 335
fathers 15, 17–18, 73
fear 37, 68–9; of rejection 26–9, 236–7, 293
feelings: *see* emotions
fight, flight, freeze or fawn response 36–7, 104
financial independence 130
food 84–5, 100–3
fortune-telling 41
Franklin effect 133–4
Fray, Matthew 125
Freeman, Hadley 53, 321
friendships 238–9; ending 263–5; making 241–5; parents support for 240–2; unsuitable 245–6; *see also* peer relationships

G

gaming 289, 366–8g
gatekeeping 16–17
gay teenagers 162, 171–2, 183
gender dysphoria 200, 203–4, 210–12, 214
gender identity 171–2, 197–9, 214–15;
    connecting with teenagers 206–7;
    definitions 199–200; discussing 208–10,
    213–15; high profile of 201–2; medical
    transition 210–13; and mental health
    203–5, 213–14; parental feelings 205–6;
    professional support 213–14; social
    transition 210; and teenage girls 202–3
gender stereotypes 16–17, 159–60, 183,
    190–4, 204–5, 208–10
Gibran, Khalil 2, 119, 347
Gilbert, Paul 46, 75
good enough parenting 54, 61; learning
    from failure 62–3; redefining mistakes
    62, 64
Grant, Adam 148, 282–3
Gray, Peter 129
grounding 47–8
growth mindset 62–4

H

Haidt, Jonathan 290; *The Anxious
    Generation* 3–4
happiness 97
health: *see* mental health; physical health
helplines 331, 353–5
hippocampus 146–7
household chores 127–8
hypothalamus 97

I

identity 112–13, 291–2; *see also* gender
    identity
iGROK 70
imperfection, benefits of 54–6

improvised scripts 30, 31–2
inability to disconfirm 42
independence, encouraging 121–30;
    decision-making 123–4, 281, 295–7,
    305–6; emotional regulation 121–5;
    financial independence 130; freedom
    outside the home 129; household chores
    127–8; stepping back 122–5; validating
    emotions 125–7
individuation 110, 111–13
influencers 160
influences: of attachment styles 23–5; of
    family scripts 29–31; of upbringing 25–8
inner critic 51; *see also* negative thoughts
insomnia 85–8, 100
Instagram 162–3, 164, 290–1, 298
intimacy 73–4, 139

J

journalling 78
joy 69
judgementalism 59–61, 84–5, 176
Jung, Carl 110
junk food 100–1

K

ketamine 305

L

labelling 43
Larkin, Philip 25
LGBTQIA+ teenagers 162, 183, 212, 286
listening skills 116, 125, 126–7, 135–7,
    244–5
loneliness 240–1, 296
lying 153–4

M

mania 368–9g
mantras 283

Maté, Gabor 113–15, 117, 291
mealtimes 102–3
medication 336–7
melatonin 87–8, 98
men: *see* co-parents; fathers
mental health 345–7; assessments 332–4;
    CAMHS (Child and Adolescent Mental
    Health Services) 332–4; communication
    about 340–3; depression 327;
    diagnoses 322–3, 325–9; eating
    disorders 101, 290; exam pressure
    277; and exercise 82–4; and family
    circumstances 320–1; and gender
    identity 203–5; increased awareness of
    320–1; increased rates of 317, 319–21;
    medication 336–7; neurodevelopment
    disorders 323–5; parental responses
    339–43; parental self-care 343–5;
    of parents 3–4; professional support
    213–14, 328–9, 332–4; professionals
    involved 334–5; and social media
    289–91, 296–7; suicide 323; therapy
    and counselling 337–9; treatment
    336–7; *see also* bullying
mind-body connection 69; and exercise
    82–4; gut health 81; parasympathetic
    nervous system 75–8
mind reading 42
mindfulness 47–8, 75–6
mistakes: allowing 122–5, 143; apologies
    for 64–5, 151; redefining 62, 64
money 30–1, 130
Moran, Caitlin 244–5, 246
mothers 1, 16–17, 73

N
needs: to be understood 73; to belong 73,
    112, 207, 291, 293, 294, 303–4; and
    emotions 70–1
negative filtering 42

negative thoughts 38, 39; awareness of
    39–41; CBT (cognitive behavioural
    therapy) 337–8; challenging 43–5,
    47–8, 49, 63, 166; compassion towards
    45–6; distraction from 47–8, 87; and
    exam pressure 283–5; identifying 41–3;
    thought stopping 47–8
negativity bias 38, 104
Neufeld, Gordon 113–15
neural pathways 39, 41, 46, 48, 93–4
neurodevelopment disorders 323–5
neuroplasticity 39
Non-Violent Communication (NVC) 70
nutrition: and parents 84–5, 87–9; and
    teenagers 100–3

O
OCD (Obsessive Compulsive Disorder)
    369–70g
Orbach, Susie 166
over-generalizing 42

P
parasympathetic nervous system 75–8;
    breathing exercises 75–6; relaxation
    exercises 77–8; and teenagers 104–5;
    vagus nerve 76–7, 118
parenting styles: agreement about 16,
    18–19; increased anxiety 321–2;
    influenced by our attachment style 23–5;
    of own parents 29–31
parents 3–4, 293–4; agreement re rules
    19–20; anxiety of 285–6; attachment
    styles of 23–5; avoiding conflict with
    each other 20–1; changing role of 2–3;
    core beliefs 25; differences of opinion 16,
    18–19; different skills of 18–19; divorced
    19–20; 'good enough' 54, 61; as imperfect
    role models 54–5; mental health problems
    3–4; and other adults 231; pressures on

114–15; projection of experiences onto teens 32–3; projection of worries onto teens 3–4, 28–9; quality of interactions 115–18; relationship care 21; as role models 1–2, 13–14, 16, 18–19, 68, 81, 114, 170; self-care 343–5; stay-at-home 17; stress 1, 3–4, 285–6; support during exams 282–5; support for high achievers 277–80; support for underachievers 280–2; supporting friendships 240–2; supportive role 109–20

peer pressure 95–6; benefits of 96; and gender identity 207; at parties 311; sex(uality) 175, 181–2

peer relationships 113–15, 234–5; friends 238–9; importance of 235–8

Perel, Esther 149

perfectionism 51–4; and being judgemental 59–61; benefits of imperfection 54–6; goals vs processes 56–7, 58, 61; and inner worth 57–9; learning from failure 62–3; and mental health 320; redefining mistakes 62, 64

physical health 81–2; diet and nutrition 84–5, 87–8; exercise 82–4; and sleep 85–8

pituitary gland 97

popularity 237–8

pornography 172, 184–9, 286

positive affirmations 45

positive thoughts 48, 49

power struggles, avoiding 19–21

prefrontal lobe development 94, 96, 108, 109, 302

psychiatrists 334–5

psychologists 334

psychosis 370g

psychotherapists 335

PTSD (Post-Traumatic Stress Disorder) 69

puberty 161

puberty-blocking hormones 201–2

Q

queer community 159–60

R

racism 275

Reeves, Richard 192–3

rejection, fear of 26–9, 236–7, 293

relationships, ending 263–70

relationships: parents with teens 349–51; importance of parental support 113–15; individuation and peer relationships 110, 111–13; quality of interactions 115–18, 295; redefining 2–3, 118–20

relationships: parents with teens' other parent(s) 15–16; avoiding conflict 20–1; working together 16–20

relationships: parents with their parents: attachment styles 23–5; breaking the cycle 31–3; family scripts 29–31; influence of their parents 25–8

relationships: parents with themselves 11; inner worth 57–9; judging ourselves 59–60; self-care 12–14

relationships: teens with other adults 229, 246–7; benefits of 230–3; encouraging 233–4

relationships: teens with peers 110, 111–13, 234–5, 238–9; ending 265–6; importance of 235–8; parental support 267–9

relationships: teens with siblings: *see* siblings

relaxation exercises 77–8, 87

replicative scripts 29, 30, 31

resilience 1–2, 286, 287

risk taking 94–5, 106–8, 286, 301–5

Riviere, Hester 103, 105, 106, 143

role models: other adults as 20; parents as 1–2, 13–14, 16, 18–19

Rosenberg, Marshall 70

Rosenthal effect 309–10
rules 142–3

S

sadness 69
safety, anxiety about 285–6
Saglio, Tara 15, 160
schizophrenia 371g
schooling 276–85
Segal, Julius 14
Seldon, Anthony 136
self-acceptance 164–6
self-awareness 235–6
self-care 257; importance of 12–14; for
   parents 343–5
self-compassion 46, 55
self-consciousness 145, 235–6
self-enhancement bias 53
self-esteem 53–4; and exercise 170; parents
   modelling 13–14; and pornography 185;
   and social media 164–6
self-esteem movement 320
self-harm 334, 371–2g
self-judgement 59–60
self-worth 57–9
senses, focusing on 47–8
sex hormones 97
sexting 175, 179
sex(uality) 171–2, 195; birth control
   189; consent 180–4, 194; discussing
   173–4, 176–82; and gender identity
   171–2; LGBTQIA+ teenagers 162,
   171–2, 183; parents as role models
   181–4; pornography 172, 184–9;
   teen experience today 174–6,
   178–80, 189; timing of first
   sexual experience 178–80; toxic
   masculinity 190–4; underage sex 172,
   179–80
shyness 241–2

siblings 219–20, 227–8; birth order 220–1;
   conflict between 221–2; of mentally
   ill teens 344–5; only children 226–8;
   positive relationships 225–6; treating
   equally 222–5
Siegel, Dan 43, 126
single parents 13, 15, 20, 320–1; see also
   co-parents; divorce
Slattery, Jimi 46
sleep 85–8, 98–100
smartphones 133–4, 289–91, 293–4,
   320–1
smoking 299, 300, 301
social comparison 53, 290, 292, 293
social media: appeal of 291–3; and
   appearance 162–4, 292–3; and bullying
   258–61; collective action 297–8; and
   identity 113, 207, 291; and mental
   health 289–91, 296–7, 320–1; parental
   responses 293–8; and perfectionism
   52–3; and sex(uality) 172
social workers 335
societal attitudes: and academic success
   277–80; and appearance 159–60, 162,
   165–6; competitive culture 53, 221, 276;
   and drinking 309; gender stereotypes
   159–60, 183, 190–4; and goal seeking
   56–7; and perfectionism 51–4;
   sex(uality) 193–4; towards parental roles
   16–17
status 237–8
stress 36–7
stress, parental 1, 3–4, 285–6
substance abuse: see drinking; drug use
suicide 323, 336, 372–3g

T

teenage boys 244; appearance
   159, 162; brain development 94,
   235–7; communication with 134–5; and

education 280–2; ending relationships
266; friendships 238–9; gaming 289;
male role models 183, 192; mental health
317, 320; and pornography 184; puberty
161; risk taking 95; and social media
290; stereotypical ideals 161; toxic
masculinity 190–4
teenage girls: appearance 159, 162, 202;
birth control 189; brain development
94, 235–7; communication with 134–5;
eating disorders 101; and education
280–2; emotional intensity 96; false
accusations of rape 193; friendships
238–9, 245–6; gender confusion 202–3;
mental health 317, 320; and pornography
185; puberty 161; and social media 290;
stereotypical ideals 161
teenagers: diet and nutrition 100–3;
emotions 96–7; and exercise 169–70;
fight, flight, freeze or fawn response in
104; friendships 238–9; individuation
110, 111–13; and sleep 98–100; slower
development to adulthood 110–11,
172; transitional times 269; see also
relationships

thalamus 38
therapy and counselling: see counselling
Thomas, Geraldine 139–40
thoughts: see negative thoughts
TikTok 162, 164, 207, 291
toxic masculinity 190–4
transgender people 201–2, 203, 210–13;
see also gender identity
traumatic events 69
tryptophan 88
Twenge, Jean 110

V
vagus nerve 76–7, 118
validation: seeking externally 58, 59; of
teen's emotions 125–7
vaping 300
violence, fear of 285–6
vulnerability 73–4, 140, 239

W
Welch, Martha 118
window of tolerance 37
Winnicott, Donald 52, 54, 55
women: see mothers; parents

ABOUT THE AUTHOR

Rachel Kelly is a writer and former *Times* journalist who has written five books sharing her experience of depression and evidence-based strategies that have helped her feel better – everything from cooking and poetry to mindfulness and exercise. Her books have been widely translated. She is the mother of three boys and two girls, all now grown up.